Circulating Cultures

Exchanges of Australian Indigenous Music, Dance and Media

Circulating Cultures

Exchanges of Australian Indigenous Music, Dance and Media

Edited by Amanda Harris

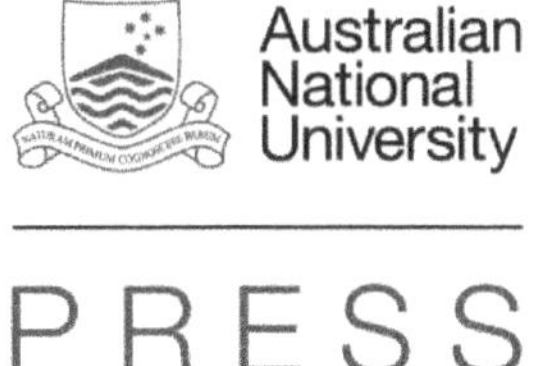

Australian National University

PRESS

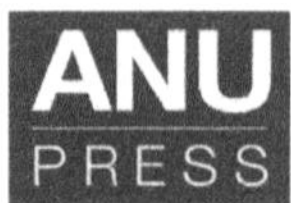

Published by ANU Press
The Australian National University
Canberra ACT 0200, Australia
Email: anupress@anu.edu.au
This title is also available online at http://press.anu.edu.au

National Library of Australia Cataloguing-in-Publication entry

Title: Circulating cultures : exchanges of Australian Indigenous music,
                    dance and media / edited by Amanda Harris.

ISBN: 9781925022193 (paperback) 9781925022216 (ebook)

Subjects: Social change--Australia--Cross-cultural studies.
                    Culture diffusion--Australia.
                    Intercultural communication in art.
                    Music in intercultural communication.
                    Aboriginal Australians--Music--21st century--Cross-cultural
                    studies.
                    Art, Aboriginal Australian--21st century--Cross-cultural studies.

Other Creators/Contributors: Harris, Amanda, 1976- editor.

Dewey Number: 306.4840994

Front cover image: Johnny Divilli and Joanne Nulgit perform *Dudu Mardudu* (the 'circling'
plane dance) at the Mowanjum Festival, 11 July 2013. Photo by Matt Scurfield. Copyright
Mowanjum Art and Culture Centre. Used with permission. *Dudu Marduda* (the 'circling' plane)
is a *balga/junba* dance-song created by Worrorra composer Wati Ngerdu following the extensive
search for a Royal Flying Doctor Service aeroplane that disappeared and crashed after leaving
Tablelands Station in the Kimberley in 1956. The dance was revived in 2013 by the performers
and the Mowanjum Art and Culture Centre for the annual Mowanjum Festival, after their
recovery and circulation of an archival photo of the dance taken in the Mowanjum Community
in the late 1950s. Thanks to Sally Treloyn for sourcing and describing the image.

Back cover image: Recording session at Oenpelli (now Gunbalanya). Larry Marawana, Tommy
Madjalkaidj, Colin Simpson, Raymond Giles and three unidentified individuals around the
Pyrox Wire Recorder, 1948. Photograph by Howell Walker. By permission of the National
Library of Australia. NLA MS5253, Box 99, Bag B.

Cover design and layout by ANU Press

Contents

Part 3: Cultural Journeys in the Top End

Contributors

Reuben Brown is completing his doctoral thesis at the University of Sydney. He spent two years carrying out fieldwork in the communities of Gunbalanya and Warruwi in western Arnhem Land of the Northern Territory. He is enthusiastic about documenting and sustaining the tradition of *kun-borrk* in this region, and has worked with a number of singers and dancers to record and promote their music at festivals, academic conferences, funeral ceremonies and other community events. Reuben has a background in musicology and experience as an actor and singer.

Genevieve Campbell has worked for twenty years as a professional French Horn player. In 2007 she instigated *Ngarukuruwala: We sing songs,* a collaborative music project between a group of Tiwi strong women and jazz musicians from Sydney. Her professional interest in Tiwi music in the context of contemporary performance and the desire to be part of the rediscovery and preservation of old Tiwi songs led her to complete a PhD at the University of Sydney in 2014.

Amanda Harris is Research Associate on the ARC Discovery Project *Intercultural Inquiry in a Trans-National Context: Exploring the legacy of the 1948 American-Australian Scientific Expedition to Arnhem Land,* headed by The Australian National University's Martin Thomas and University of Sydney's Linda Barwick and Allan Marett. In 2011, she organised a research forum at the University of Sydney which brought together the researchers whose work appears in this book. She obtained a PhD from the University of NSW in 2009 with a historical thesis on women composers and feminism in the late nineteenth and early twentieth centuries. Her publications have appeared in *Women & Music, Life Writing, Women's History Review, History and Anthropology,* and *Lilith: A feminist history journal* as well as several book volumes.

Victoria Haskins is an Associate Professor of History at the University of Newcastle in New South Wales, Australia. She publishes widely on gender and Indigenous cross-cultural history, and is the author of two books, *One Bright Spot* (Palgrave Macmillan, 2005), and *Matrons and Maids: Regulating Indian Domestic Service in Tucson, 1914–1934* (University of Arizona Press, 2012). As a curator at the National Museum of Australia in 1999, Victoria first encountered the choreography of Beth Dean's Aboriginal-inspired ballet. In 2006 she held a Council of Australian State Libraries Fellowship to research Dean's archives, held at the Mitchell Library in Sydney. She has published several articles and book chapters on Aboriginal cultural appropriation, including two focusing on Beth Dean's *Corroboree* ('Dancing in the Dust,' in Allen and Dhawan, *Intersections,* 2005; and 'To Touch the Infinity of a Far Horizon,' *Australasian Drama Studies,* 2011).

Anthony Linden Jones is a candidate for a PhD in Musicology at the Sydney Conservatorium of Music. His research area is the representation of Aboriginality in Australian Film Music. He holds a B.Mus (Hons) in Composition from Sydney Conservatorium, as well as a B.Eng (Elec.) from the University of New South Wales. In past lives he has performed in a wide range of musical genres, on violin and electric bass. He is active as a composer of concert and film music, a performer on violin, and directs Chorella—an *a cappella* community choir based in Richmond, NSW. He also teaches music in TAFE, and regularly contributes reviews and articles for Music Forum, the journal of the Music Council of Australia.

John Mansfield researches language and culture at Wadeye in Northern Australia. He recently completed his PhD at The Australian National University, focusing on youth subculture and language change. He is now working on the *Language Acquisition of Murrinhpatha* Project at the University of Melbourne.

Martin Thomas teaches in the School of History at The Australian National University. He has held research fellowships at the University of Technology, Sydney, and at the University of Sydney, where he now holds an adjunct position in the Pacific and Regional Archive for Digital Sources in Endangered Cultures. His current work is in the field of Australian and trans-national cultural history, as revealed through perceptions of place, representations of landscape and narratives of cross-cultural encounter. A book-in-progress takes up the story of the 1948 American-Australian Scientific Expedition to Arnhem Land, led by Charles Mountford. His recent publications include *The Many Worlds of R. H. Mathews: In search of an Australian anthropologist* (Allen & Unwin, 2011) and, as editor, *Expedition into Empire: Exploratory journeys and the making of the modern world* (Routledge, 2014).

Sally Treloyn is a Postdoctoral Research Fellow in the Melbourne Conservatorium of Music at the University of Melbourne, having received her PhD in Ethnomusicology from the University of Sydney in 2007. Her current research is focused on developing strategies to support Indigenous stakeholders and organisations in their efforts to sustain musical practices and associated knowledge systems into the future. She currently leads two Linkage projects funded by the Australian Research Council in partnership with peak Aboriginal organisations in the Kimberley. She is also an Honorary Research Fellow at the University of Sydney (PARADISEC: the Pacific and Regional Archive for Digital Sources in Endangered Cultures) and is Secretary to the Steering Committee of the National Recording Project for Indigenous Performance in Australia: http://www.aboriginalartists.com.au/NRP.htm.

1. Archival Objects and the Circulation of Culture

Amanda Harris

Exchanges of cultural capital facilitated cross-cultural communication in a variety of Australian contexts, both before and after the arrival of Europeans in Australia at the end of the eighteenth century. In the absence of common languages on the colonial frontier, exchanges of music, dance, and painting can become tangible means of communication between people seeking to understand the culture of others. This book explores the circulation of ephemeral, physical and spiritual media across the lines that separate cultures from one another. Objects of cultural capital are transformed across landscapes and media through technology, people and their relationships with each other and with the otherworldly space beyond.

In his exploration of cross-cultural communication in Central and North America, Michael Taussig describes R. O. Marsh's use of the gramophone, as a means of navigating initial hostility between groups of meeting strangers: 'It proved to be an easy way for making an intercultural nexus, a new cultural zone of white and Indian social interaction for discovering strangeness and confirming sameness'.[1] In his 1934 book, Marsh wrote:

> After my experiences in the Darién I would never think of going into a 'wild' Indian territory without a phonograph. Time and time again we were to encounter surly, unfriendly, and even menacing Indians. We would appear to ignore them entirely. We would bring out and start a record while proceeding with our regular task of camp-pitching or what-not. The attention of the Indians would soon be diverted from us to the 'music-box'. Their hostility would cease and be replaced by curiosity. Gradually they would draw closer to the instrument, discussing it among themselves and finally would end up by crowding around it as closely as possible, touching and feeling it. From then on they would often keep us playing it until midnight, and were no longer our enemies though perhaps not yet our friends.[2]

---

1   Michael Taussig, *Mimesis and Alterity: A Particular History of the Senses* (New York: Routledge, 1993), 195.
2   Richard Oglesby Marsh, *White Indians of Darien* (New York: G.P. Putnam's Sons, 1934), quoted in Michael Taussig, *Mimesis and Alterity* (New York: Routledge, 1993), 194.

Lacking the common language of customary behaviour to communicate intentions to the Indigenous peoples he encountered, Marsh combined the tools of cultural exchange and technology to forge a mode of communication that would transcend cultural boundaries.

This nexus of cultural capital and technology as a means to facilitate exchange and communication is a recurrent theme of the chapters in this book. We focus here, not only on non-Indigenous attempts to communicate through cultural capital with Indigenous peoples, but also look at the ways that culturally foreign technologies have been taken up by Indigenous and non-Indigenous communities alike in order to develop new ways of expressing culture. In doing so, our discussion engages not only with themes of cultural exchange but also thinks about modernity and the changing face of cultural practice in light of developing technologies.

The Catalyst: The 1948 American-Australian Scientific Expedition to Arnhem Land

The 1948 American-Australian Scientific Expedition to Arnhem Land, itself a project laden with the symbols of modernity, was the starting point for the collection of chapters that comprise this volume. Following a conference on the expedition in 2009 entitled *Birds, Barks and Billabongs*, Martin Thomas and Margo Neale published a collection that illuminated the expedition's ongoing legacy.[3] That volume focused on the work of individual members of the expedition and the scholarly, artistic and cultural ramifications of the data and artefacts that they collected. The contributors to the current volume were brought together through a common interest in the expedition's project of gathering information about Aboriginal culture, bringing the tools of modernity to bear on study of the 'stone age', and its representation as a pioneering journey into the uncharted and undiscovered realms of Australia's wild north. However, for us, the expedition was a point of departure rather than subject matter in itself. For the contributors to this volume, it is not the context of the expedition which is the topic of their chapters, but rather what can be made of the circulation of cultural objects. These objects include both those collected on the venture into history-making that was the Arnhem Land Expedition, as well as broader materials involved in living, changing cultural practice. The authors journey well beyond the geographical limits of the expedition's camps in Arnhem Land to the west, north and over the seas.

---

3 Martin Thomas and Margo Neale, eds, *Exploring the Legacy of the 1948 Arnhem Land Expedition* (Canberra: ANU E Press, 2011).

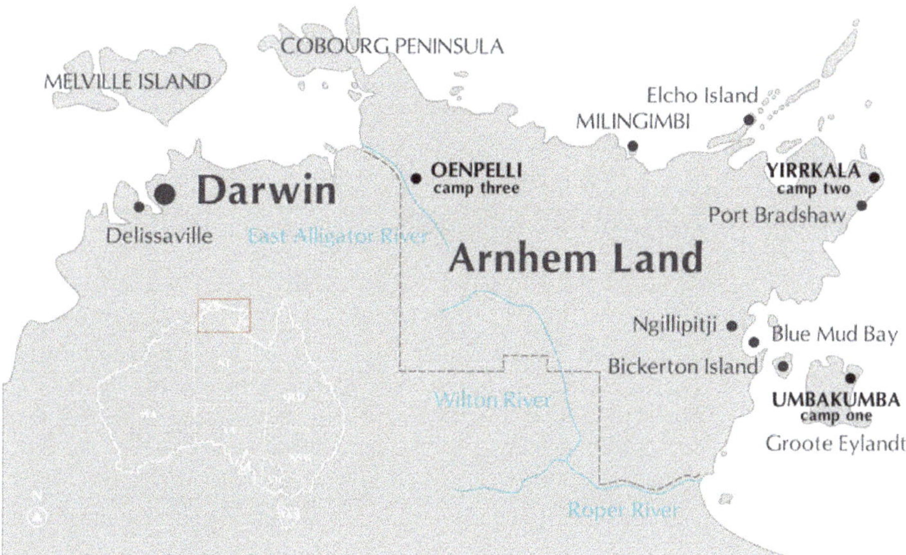

Figure 1: Map showing the main sites visited by the Arnhem Land Expedition.

Source: National Museum of Australia, reproduced with permission.

The 1948 expedition was in many ways an artefact of an earlier style of scientific expeditioning, immersed in notions of Aboriginal culture which were quickly becoming old-fashioned in modern anthropological circles, and representing itself as a pioneering project in spite of protests from anthropologists who had gone before.[4] At the centre of the collection of cultural materials on the expedition was its leader, Charles Pearcy Mountford—amateur ethnographer, photographer, film maker and writer. Mountford's career as a student of Aboriginal culture, writer on Aboriginal art and touring film maker did not begin with the 1948 expedition. Rather, in the 1920s, Mountford had spent several years travelling through central Australia, building a collection of paintings and producing films not only about art but more broadly about Aboriginal culture. His interest in Aboriginal art and culture began while he was an employee of the General Post Office in Adelaide. After observing Aboriginal ceremonies in Darwin when he was transferred there in the early 1920s, he became interested in rock carvings in South Australia and Western New South Wales, and began visiting and making tracings of these, collaborating with the ethnologist Norman B. Tindale at the

---

4   See Sally K. May's discussion of the protests mounted by Ronald and Catherine Berndt and A. P. Elkin who had already worked in the area and who objected to Mountford portraying the area as 'the great unknown'. Sally K. May, *Collecting Cultures: Myth, politics, and collaboration in the 1948 Arnhem Land Expedition* (Lanham: AltaMira Press, 2009), 47–51.

South Australian Museum to report on his findings. Mountford carried out this work with increasing enthusiasm and a growing public profile throughout the 1930s. His mounting expertise on central Australian art led to an appointment to a Commonwealth enquiry into the treatment of Aboriginal mission residents in Hermannsburg, and subsequently to participation in his first anthropological expedition, with the University of Adelaide, to the Warburton Ranges in 1935. This initial expedition was followed by five more through South Australia and the Northern Territory in the late 1930s.[5]

In the mid-1940s, Mountford was given the opportunity to tour the United States of America, showing two films he had made in 1942, *Tjurunga* and *Walkabout*. It was his presentation to the National Geographic Society in February 1945 that prompted the Society to invite Mountford to propose an expedition to Arnhem Land for their consideration.[6] In the process of touring and showing the films throughout Australia and the US, Mountford distributed the products of his collecting far and wide, and came into regular and productive contact with artists and cultural practitioners of all kinds. As contributors to part one of this book elaborate, some of these interactions produced further artworks based on the Indigenous materials collected by Mountford, such as Mirrie and Alfred Hill's film music compositions, Beth Dean's ballet, and Margaret Preston's artworks.[7] The musical recordings, art works and film footage collected by Mountford not only circulated geographically, but were also transformed, reinvented and reanimated by this circulation to create new art and cultural practice. Like much of the circulation of Aboriginal cultural materials in the mid-century, Mountford's publicisation of his collecting both drew attention to Aboriginal culture and stirred up controversy, sometimes causing offence.[8]

The recording of Indigenous culture in modern formats such as film enabled the dissemination of such ephemeral cultural materials as live performances not only throughout Australia, but to far distant places. Scholars of auditory histories have considered both what is lost and what gained by the transmutation of live performance into recorded forms that could be traded and distributed as cultural objects. Lisa Gitelman's discussion of North American blackface minstrelsy focuses on her attempts to hear 'through' the phonograph to the real

---

5   Max Lamshed, *'Monty': The biography of C. P. Mountford* (Adelaide: Rigby, 1972), 28-49; May, *Collecting Cultures*, 38.

6   Sally May, 'The Art of Collecting: Charles Pearcy Mountford', in *The Makers and Making of Indigenous Australian Museum Collections*, eds Nicolas Peterson, Lindy Allen, and Louise Hamby (Carlton: Melbourne University Press, 2008), 450.

7   Nicolas Peterson, Lindy Allen, and Louise Hamby, eds, *The Makers and Making of Indigenous Australian Museum Collections* (Carlton: Melbourne University Press, 2008), 4.

8   For example, Olive Pink condemned Mountford's public showings of sacred material and was prompted by her reaction to this to keep the products of her own research restricted for 50 years, see Julie Marcus, 'The Beauty, Simplicity and Honour of Truth: Olive Pink in the 1940s,' in *First in Their Field: Women and Australian anthropology*, ed. Julie Marcus (Carlton: Melbourne University Press, 1993), 114.

event.[9] In intercultural exchanges through music recordings, Gitelman considers how race is masked and transmuted through the intervention of technology. While the voices and other sounds of the music makers remain in phonograph performances, the performer him or herself is obscured: 'By removing the performer from view, the technology of recorded sound also removed the most keenly felt representation of the performer's race.'[10]

In the sound world of members of the 1948 Arnhem Land Expedition too, the tools of modernity with which they interacted (wireless transmitters, electronic recorders and other radio and sound forms) acted as points of contact between their own proudly modern project and that of the putatively stone-age, endemic, native culture of the Aboriginal people they observed. One of the means through which they sought to bridge the cultural divide was by recording the songs and ceremony of Aboriginal people they encountered in audio and film. In doing so, they converted the strangeness of the sounds heard in the alien surrounds of Arnhem Land into a format comprehensible to their own cultural parameters, a format that they could own, distribute and ultimately manipulate into other forms more readable or audibly intelligible. The Arnhem Land Expedition's participants made a public performance of this contrast of modernity and the stone-age in the popular media, reinforcing perceptions of the gulf between Indigenous and non-Indigenous Australian cultures. As Martin Thomas writes about the expedition's very public staging of their project: 'science must not only be done, but seen to be done by as large an audience as possible'.[11] This performance of science for the Australian public represented one face of the expedition, but was not necessarily reflective of the work being done by all of the expedition's members. Many of the scientists sought to carry out nuanced research which engaged with the cultures of Arnhem Land as rich, complex and culturally sophisticated societies, even while taking part in the public projection of the expedition as a triumph of modernity in contrast with an ancient culture.

The expedition's nutritionist, Margaret McArthur, is a good example of a scientist who sought to produce rigorous research, and politicised her work by speaking out for the Aboriginal people among whom she consulted and against the dehumanising practices of some of the missions she visited.[12] The research McArthur published as a result of her work on the expedition documented the high nutritional value of local foods, and thus the balanced nature of the Indigenous diet, and showed that the diet commonly provided by missionaries

---

9   Lisa Gitelman, 'Recording Sound, Recording Race, Recording Property,' in *Hearing History: A reader*, ed. Mark M. Smith (Athens: University of Georgia Press, 2004), 280.

10   Gitelman, 'Recording Sound', 279.

11   Martin Thomas, 'Expedition as Time Capsule: Introducing the American-Australian Scientific Expedition to Arnhem Land,' in *Exploring the Legacy of the 1948 Arnhem Land Expedition*, eds Martin Thomas and Margo Neale (Canberra: ANU E Press, 2011), 18.

12   Amanda Harris, 'Chaperoned into Arnhem Land: Margaret Mcarthur and the politics of nutrition and fieldwork in 1948', *Lilith: A feminist history journal* 20 (2014): 62–75.

for Aboriginal people was not only deficient but substantially inferior to the missionaries' own diets.[13] A study that she co-authored with anthropologist Fred McCarthy in 1960 was later to become highly influential, and provided the data for Marshall Sahlins' theory of the 'Original Affluent Society', a corrective to evolutionary thinking about hunter-gatherer peoples which portrayed the hunters and gatherers of Arnhem Land as groups who enjoyed abundant leisure time, sufficient food and were not barely subsisting as previous anthropological approaches had suggested.[14] In interviews with Colin Simpson, McArthur also argued that Aboriginal women enjoyed an empowered status in their society, evidenced by the carrying out of their own ceremonies and the fact that they danced and sang separately from the men.[15] And yet, in spite of this attempt at a holistic conceptualisation of Aboriginal culture, McArthur too used the expedition's popular polarisations when publicising her work in the media. In a broadcast for the *Women's Magazine of the Air* in 1949 on group baby-minding in Arnhem Land, McArthur referred to her Aboriginal consultants as 'these stone age people', a term she was never to use in her scientific publications.[16]

The practices of the Arnhem Land Expedition were just one example of the cross-cultural grapplings with modernity occurring in Australia in the mid-to-late twentieth century. The kinds of productive circulation represented by Mountford's wide distribution of cultural capital have led the authors of this book to think about how music, dance and media move and are transformed in other ways in the Australian cultural landscape. The insights of the contributing authors bring ethnographic perspectives to broader international scholarship on objects and their movement across place and culture. In a related study, Maruška Svašek introduces three paradigms for thinking about the way the movement of objects and people interact with each other. Svašek invokes the processes of 'Transit', describing 'the changing social, cultural and spatial environments constituted by objects and individuals before and after coming into contact with each other'; 'Transition', identifying 'transit-related changes in the meaning, value and emotional efficacy of objects and images as opposed simply to changes in their location or ownership'; and 'Transformation', referring to 'transit-related changes in human subjects, specifically in terms of their status, identity formation and emotional subjectivity'.[17] In the first four

---

13 See Margaret McArthur, 'Report on the Nutrition Unit,' in *Records of the American-Australian Scientific Expedition to Arnhem Land*, ed. Charles P. Mountford (Melbourne: Melbourne University Press, 1960), 1–143.

14 Frederick D. McCarthy and Margaret McArthur, 'The Food Quest and the Time Factor in Aboriginal Economic Life,' in *Records of the American-Australian Scientific Expedition to Arnhem Land*, ed. Charles P. Mountford (Melbourne: Melbourne University Press, 1960), 145–94; Marshall Sahlins, *Stone Age Economics* (Chicago: Aldine Atherton, 1972).

15 Colin Simpson, *Adam in Ochre: Inside Aboriginal Australia* (Sydney: Angus & Robertson, 1951), 53.

16 Margaret McArthur, 'Script for Miss M. McArthur. Women's Magazine of the Air' *McArthur, Annie Margaret [1919-2002]*, P205/1/2, University of Sydney Archives, 15 February 1949.

17 Maruska Svašek, ed., *Moving Subjects, Moving Objects: Transnationalism, cultural production and emotions* (New York: Berghahn Books, 2012), 2–5.

chapters, our contributors think about how the long-lasting remnants of the 1948 expedition are still in circulation and *transit* today in various ways, as well as how both positive and negative consequences of the dispersal and *transition* of cultural materials have played out in modern Aboriginal communities. In the final four chapters, the *transformation* of cultural objects from their original context to new and distant ones brings out themes of newly forming identities and emotional subjectivities. These chapters take us well beyond the starting place of the original expedition, and bring the discussion of historical materials and circulation of culture into the present day.

Histories of Collecting and the Context for Cultural Objects

In their book *The Makers and Making of Indigenous Australian Museum Collections*, Nicolas Peterson, Lindy Allen and Louise Hamby define five key periods of collecting anthropological materials in Australian history:

1. From the first contact of Europeans and Aboriginal people to c. 1880—collecting of materials was unsystematic;

2. c. 1880 until c. 1920—collecting was influenced by social evolutionary theory, prompting the search for traditional stone technologies;

3. c. 1920 until 1940—physical anthropologists sought to collect objects 'before it is too late';

4. 1940 to 1980—research adjunct collecting, objects were collected as supporting documentation to the primary research being carried out;

5. 1980 to the present—a period in which the dominance of Aboriginal art is the focus of collections to the exclusion of almost anything else.[18]

Peterson et. al.'s five stages give a broad overview of collecting practices by non-Indigenous Australians (in particular physical anthropologists). While their stages do not fit every historical collecting scenario, they nevertheless provide a useful framework for thinking about the shifts in priorities in what Tom Griffiths has described as the Australian 'antiquarian imagination'.[19] What is not included in these stages is an account of how Indigenous people interacted with the collecting of artefacts embodying their cultural heritage (more on this below).

---

18   Peterson, Allen, and Hamby, eds, *The Makers and Making of Indigenous Australian Museum Collections*, 8–12.
19   Tom Griffiths, *Hunters and Collectors: The antiquarian imagination in Australia* (Cambridge: Cambridge University Press, 1996).

The starting point of most of the investigations in our current book was, like Peterson et. al.'s, also a series of collected things, not necessarily physical objects produced for practical daily purposes, but more ephemeral things, events, songs, ceremonies and performances that were recorded in both audio and visual formats. As I have already suggested, it could be argued that at least the public face of the expedition was trapped in the mores of a much earlier tradition of collection, correlating to stage two in the above list. However, in considering the motives of expedition collectors and the uses to which the objects of their collecting fervour have been put, we may add to Peterson et al.'s categories a sixth period in the collection of materials. This sixth stage, beginning with isolated efforts c. 1970 gained momentum and became widespread by 1990, and has seen collections steadily become the materials for living, ongoing cultural tradition, rather than static, permanent objects for preservation and observation. This shift in the function of collecting and collections has seen the increasing involvement of Aboriginal people in the curation and public representation of collections, as well as the repatriation of copies of collected objects and even the objects themselves to their communities of origin.

Though 1990 was not the first time that materials began to be repatriated to their home communities, and thus made available for reimaginings and renewed uses, the shift in that decade to repatriation not just of the physical ethnographic artefacts, but also of cultural objects such as recordings of music and dance, represents the beginning of a nation-wide (and indeed international) trend. These acts of repatriation followed on from earlier efforts to recognise what might matter to Aboriginal people in the management of Australian museum collections, a movement that began to take hold in the 1970s.[20] Tom Griffiths documents the shift in museum practice in Victoria from the 1970s towards the inclusion of Aboriginal people in the curation of museum collections, and the changing focus on 'present people' instead of only 'past objects'.[21] Similarly, in 1978, the Australian Museum effected a 'major redirection of activities' in the

---

20   This movement is ongoing, and is indeed still in the process of definition. See Sandy O'Sullivan's argument: 'We are still, as Indigenous people, often not included in the most central of questions over policy and engagement, and instead relegated to consultation on isolated moments of representation.' Sandy O'Sullivan, 'Reversing the Gaze: Considering Indigenous perspectives on museums, cultural representation and the equivocal digital remnant', in *Information Technology and Indigenous Communities*, eds Lyndon Ormond-Parker, Aaron Corn, Cressida Fforde, Kazuko Obata, and Sandy O'Sullivan (Canberra: AIATSIS Research Publications, 2013), 147.

21   Griffiths, *Hunters and Collectors*, 95. See also Lancefield's survey of archives across the world (especially in the US), which found that by 1992, a significant number of archives were repatriating materials in their collections, or investigating the possibility of doing so. Robert C. Lancefield, 'Musical Traces' Retraceable Paths: The repatriation of recorded sound', *Journal of Folklore Research* 35:1 (1998): 51; Judith Gray's description of the Federal Cylinder Project's return of digitised early twentieth century wire recordings of Native American music to communities in 1985. Judith Gray, 'Returning Music to the Makers: The Library of Congress, American Indians, and the Federal Cylinder Project', *Cultural Survival Quarterly* 20:4 (1996); and Linda Barwick's return of Elkin recordings and photographs to Belyuen community in the 1990s, described in Linda Barwick, 'Turning It All Upside Down … Imagining a Distributed Digital Audiovisual Archive', *Literary and Linguistic Computing* 19:3 (2004), 257.

management of its Australian Aboriginal collection.[22] In 1975, as Chair of the Aboriginal Arts Board of the Australia Council, Wandjuk Marika had surveyed bark paintings held by the Australian Museum, collected during the 1948 Arnhem Land Expedition (those collected included paintings by Marika and his father), see Figure 2.[23] A few years later, following the participation of the Museum's Director and several staff members in the 1978 UNESCO meeting on 'The Role of Museums in the Preservation of Traditional Cultures', the Australian Museum radically changed its approach to its collections, implementing policies to employ and train Aboriginal people to work in Australian museums, and perhaps more significantly, consulting with Aboriginal people on the retention and disposal of secret/sacred material in their collections. The Museum also began to investigate the return of human remains, following the findings of the UNESCO seminar showing that Aboriginal people strongly wished for greater decision-making power in procedures affecting the representation and revitalisation of their cultural heritage.[24]

The active involvement of Aboriginal people in decisions about national and regional collections has engendered a radical shift in the meanings and purposes with which collected items are imbued. So too, the contributors to the present book discuss a range of ways in which archival things have become animated by their circulation amongst the descendants of their original creators and collectors. As part of their research, the collection of Indigenous materials has taken a collaborative turn where objects are no longer disembodied from their creators and preserved in distant locations, but rather, where cultural materials have come to be fluid, changing objects which circulate in the present, creating practices of the future. Such a shift, from collecting and exhibition as the end product, to collections as a means to further exchange, development and interaction, has been closely tied to advances in technology and mobility, especially to the availability since the 1990s of digital and therefore more portable, accessible and dispersible formats for archival materials. The return of historical and archival materials in digital forms has become central to discussions of technology in Indigenous Australia, as evidenced by the outcomes of recent conferences, the AIATSIS National Indigenous Studies Conference (2009) and the Information Technologies and Indigenous Communities Symposium (2010). In Lyndon Ormond-Parker et. al.'s summary of these discussions, repatriation

---

22 'Australian Museum', in *Annual Report 1978–79*, AMS112_1978-1979, Australian Museum Archives, accessed 15 July 2014, http://australianmuseum.net.au/Uploads/Documents/26912/AMS112_1978-1979_lowres_web.pdf, 13.

23 I am grateful to Martin Thomas for bringing this visit to my attention. 'Australian Museum' in *Annual Report 1974-75*, AMS112_1974-1975, Australian Museum Archives, accessed 15 July 2014, http://australianmuseum.net.au/Uploads/Documents/26908/AMS112_1974-1975_lowres_web.pdf.

24 'Australian Museum', in *Annual Report 1978–79*, AMS112_1978-1979, Australian Museum Archives, accessed 15 July 2014, http://australianmuseum.net.au/Uploads/Documents/26912/AMS112_1978-1979_lowres_web.pdf.

is firmly placed as a priority, the group's findings calling for 'increased support for programs which support the return to community based archives of digitised heritage objects, including photographs, audiovisual recordings and manuscripts from national repositories'.[25]

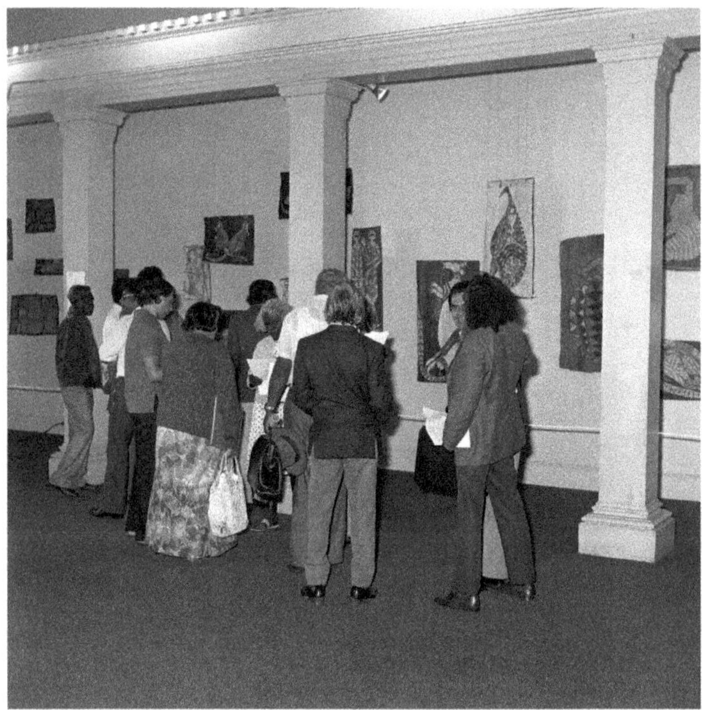

Figure 2: Members of the Aboriginal Arts Board of the Australia Council visited the Australian Museum in April 1975 to inspect the Bark Painting Conservation Project.

Source: Photograph by Gregory Millen, Australian Museum Series (AMS) 391/M606/11, reproduced with permission.

Cross-cultural exchange and the transformation of objects and traditions through cultural interaction has been the subject of several recent scholarly works. The product of postcolonial thinking about cultural materials, recent publications have focused on the way culture changes over time and place, distancing themselves from the anthropological focus on the 'other' and the accompanying search for authentic alien cultures. Studies of recent years have sought to demonstrate the cultural results of interaction and exchange which

---

25 Lyndon Ormond-Parker, Aaron Corn, Cressida Fforde, Kazuko Obata, and Sandy O'Sullivan, eds, *Information Technology and Indigenous Communities* (Canberra: AIATSIS Research Publications, 2013), xiii.

are the product of fluid shifting cultures. Amiria J. M. Henare seeks to 'think through things' rather than through words or abstract ideas. Her *Museums, Anthropology and Imperial Exchange* (2005) documents the history and anthropology of artefacts in Scotland and New Zealand and the way these objects have been exchanged across cultures and places. Nicholas Thomas' *Entangled Objects: Exchange, material culture and colonialism in the Pacific* (1991) presents a history of the reciprocal appropriation of European and Indigenous objects and the transformation of ceremonies. A recent book edited by Fiona Magowan and Karl Neuenfeldt *Landscapes of Indigenous Performance: Music, song and dance of the Torres Strait and Arnhem Land* (2005) explores the metamorphosis of songs and performance traditions across cultures in Australia. And Fiona Richards' edited book *The Soundscapes of Australia: Music, place and spirituality* explores the way both Indigenous and non-Indigenous Australian music is bound to places of different kinds in the landscape.[26] *Circulating Cultures* builds on the foundations of these cross-disciplinary studies, which create a history of colonial and postcolonial interactions through a focus on the creative arts and exchange of culture.

The chapters in this book focus on historical events, tracing the movement of culture through time and place in the last century, as well as current social frameworks and important cultural events occurring as recently as in the last two years. In part one, Victoria Haskins, Anthony Linden Jones and I discuss the fate of recordings of music and dance that began a journey of circulation with the 1948 Arnhem Land Expedition. In a chapter about the choreographer Beth Dean, Haskins places Mountford on the edge of a circle of women in the 1950s negotiating a new kind of transnational cultural circulation. Dean's meetings with Mountford in the United States of America led her on a journey to Australia and into the peculiar position of dancing the role of a male Aboriginal Initiate in a ballet set to signify Australian culture for the visit of Queen Elizabeth II in 1954. Haskins explores the cultural implications of an American woman embodying male Aboriginality on an Australian public stage, and places Dean within a culture of women's post-war transnationalism.

Mountford's recordings from the expedition also landed in the hands of non-Indigenous Australian composers Alfred and Mirrie Hill, and Jones' chapter on the compositions that were subsequently inspired by these recordings explores the circulation of music in film soundtracks in early Australian documentary films. Tracing the melodic and rhythmic themes of the Hills' compositions back

---

26   Amiria J. M. Henare, *Museums, Anthropology and Imperial Exchange* (Cambridge: Cambridge University Press, 2005); Nicholas Thomas, *Entangled Objects: Exchange, material culture, and colonialism in the Pacific* (Cambridge: Harvard University Press, 1991); Fiona Magowan and Karl Neuenfeldt, eds, *Landscapes of Indigenous Performance: Music, song and dance of the Torres Strait and Arnhem Land* (Canberra: Aboriginal Studies Press, 2005); Fiona Richards, ed., *The Soundscapes of Australia: Music, place and spirituality* (Aldershot: Ashgate, 2007).

to songs collected in Arnhem Land in 1948, Jones shows that the soundtracks to Mountford's films represented a brave new world of film scores in the Australian tradition which moved away from the reliance on nineteenth-century European compositional styles.

Mid-twentieth century written descriptions of heard Aboriginal culture forms the subject of my chapter. Taking as my source material a selection of Australian novels, diarised accounts and a musical composition, I demonstrate that non-Indigenous listeners' ability to hear Aboriginal music in the bush was limited by projections of their own culture onto Aboriginal people. I show how themes such as the perceived innate or instinctual nature of Aboriginal musical expression and conflation of Aboriginal people with their surrounds—the land and animals—guided non-Indigenous hearing of the songs, rhythms and didjeridu playing of Aboriginal people in the bush. Incorporating the diaries of members of the Arnhem Land Expedition into my discussion, I show that non-Indigenous travellers' initial impressions of the music they heard were internalised as expressions of alienation and foreignness from the landscape and their surroundings, and that greater familiarity with Aboriginal culture sometimes created a window for listening to Aboriginal music with fresher and more informed ears.

In part two we explore the sixth period of the history of collecting, the repatriation, reanimation and revalidation of archival materials, discussing two instances of transformation of the meanings with which cultural objects are imbued. Part two opens with a chapter discussing the return of song recordings to the Tiwi Islands by Genevieve Campbell. Campbell explores how repatriated recordings have been received by the Tiwi community and have informed contemporary song composition, both as ceremony and entertainment. The music Campbell discusses spans a long period of collection, from Baldwin Spencer's 1912 recordings, through those of Colin Simpson and C. P. Mountford in 1948 and 1954, to recordings as recent as 1981. As Campbell charts the process of reclamation of song materials, she shows that one of the most significant factors in the reception of *Palingarri* (or 'long ago') songs by the Tiwi community has been the cultural owners' pro-active role in repatriating the songs.

In Martin Thomas' chapter, the consequences of removing bones from their resting place in Country and the result of repatriating those people back home, imbues the notion of objects with new meaning. Thomas' chapter documents historical accounts from 1948 of the deliberate theft of bones from their burial place on Injalak hill, outside of Gunbalanya (formally Oenpelli).[27] Thomas contextualises the theft within the wider fervour of museum culture

---

27   The name Oenpelli originated in Paddy Cahill's mishearing of the local name *Unbalanj* as 'Owenpelly' in 1901. See Derek John Mulvaney, *Paddy Cahill of Oenpelli* (Canberra: Aboriginal Studies Press, 2004), 37.

for building large collections of human remains from different cultures in the service of a science which sought to document a kind of evolutionary history of humankind. He explores the way that the assumptions of museum collectors such as Aleš Hrdlička and Frank Setzler acted as scientific validation for the politics of racial differentiation between Anglo-Europeans and the Aboriginal people of Australia. In his description of the ceremony that transported the bones from the Smithsonian Institution in the United States of America back to the Country of the deceased in the north of Australia, Thomas also discovers that for Aboriginal people, bones are anything but objects, rather they are the remaining physical manifestations of the spirits of the people to whom they belonged, spirits who can be communicated with and can communicate to the living in the languages spoken in their lifetimes. Thomas thus explores how theft and repatriation can be thought of as kidnapping and rescue with tangible and poignant meanings for the descendants of the deceased.

Part three offers three current perspectives on cross-cultural circulation and the investment of objects with new and transformed meanings. We remain in the Top End of Australia, beginning in Arnhem Land, but then journey beyond the reaches of the 1948 expedition and its collections, to the Daly region and the Kimberley. Reuben Brown takes as his starting point a funeral ceremony held in 2012 for a leader of the community of Gunbalanya. In interrogating the songs performed at this ceremony, Brown explores the ways in which music can accompany the travels of people's spirits and can move to link people from different places to each other. Locating the different songs used in the ceremony, Brown discovers that music can be understood as communication from the spirit world of one's ancestors. Brown's findings about the way music accompanies the remains of a person bound for burial in Gunbalanya hint at the importance of the burial of people on their own Country in Aboriginal cultures.

Sally Treloyn recounts her surprise at hearing a recording made in 1974 of Kimberley *balga/junba* songs, recorded, not in the Kimberley, but hundreds of kilometres away in Wadeye (formerly Port Keats). On playing the songs to the expert Kimberley *balga* composer Scotty Martin, Treloyn's suspicions of the songs' similarities were confirmed. Treloyn's chapter explores the implications of Martin's assertion that the Wadeye versions of the songs were 'cross and square', not only by exploring the variegation of musical features in the Wadeye and Kimberley songs, but also by mapping onto the region's geography the shapes created by Wurnan trade routes between Wadeye and the Kimberley.

In the final chapter, John Mansfield flips the discussion of repatriation of collected materials on its head and closes the book with an example of how an American and European subculture has been adopted by youth in the remote community of Wadeye. Mansfield shows how groups named after heavy metal bands and represented by their music and reimagined visual symbols have been mapped onto existing kinship systems. His chapter reveals how music heard on television and reaching increasingly wide distribution through recent technology, especially mobile phones, has been taken into circulation as a representation of group and kinship affiliations. The heavy metal music is thus broadcast from phones and home stereos and the symbols of metal culture have come to delineate areas of the community where members of a particular kinship group live.

Conclusion

All together, the chapters in this book present a portrait of new perspectives on circulating materials that have emerged in the twenty-first century. Building on Peterson, Allen and Hamby's classification of five historical periods of ethnographic collecting in the twentieth century, we illuminate a sixth stage of the handling of archival materials. Each chapter in this book contributes a unique perspective on the possibilities for bringing the static materials of the archive back into active circulation. By sharing, interacting with and circulating these objects, they have been imbued with new meanings and we discover some of the living possibilities of historical materials. As objects are returned to the communities from which they came, the descendants of their owners reanimate them with new lives and enliven their histories with new futures. We hope that these discussions make space for further explorations about how objects might be recirculated and may open the way for the revitalisation and reinvention of traditions both historical and continuing.

Acknowledgements

I am grateful for feedback that has helped to refine drafts of this chapter from Martin Thomas and two anonymous reviewers.

References

Barwick, Linda. 'Turning It All Upside Down ... Imagining a Distributed Digital Audiovisual Archive', *Literary and Linguistic Computing* 19:3 (2004): 253–63.

Gitelman, Lisa. 'Recording Sound, Recording Race, Recording Property', in *Hearing History: A reader*, ed. Mark M. Smith (Athens: University of Georgia Press, 2004), 279–94.

Gray, Judith. 'Returning Music to the Makers: The Library of Congress, American Indians, and the Federal Cylinder Project', *Cultural Survival Quarterly* 20:4 (1996), http://www.culturalsurvival.org/ourpublications/csq/article/returning-music-makers-the-library-congress-american-indians-and-federal#sthash.3h2kgO2z.dpuf.

Griffiths, Tom. *Hunters and Collectors: The antiquarian imagination in Australia* (Cambridge: Cambridge University Press, 1996).

Harris, Amanda. 'Chaperoned into Arnhem Land: Margaret McArthur and the politics of nutrition and fieldwork in 1948', *Lilith: A Feminist History Journal* 20 (2014): 62–75.

Henare, Amiria J. M. *Museums, Anthropology and Imperial Exchange* (Cambridge: Cambridge University Press, 2005).

Lamshed, Max. *'Monty': The biography of C. P. Mountford* (Adelaide: Rigby, 1972).

Lancefield, Robert C. 'Musical Traces' Retraceable Paths: The repatriation of recorded sound', *Journal of Folklore Research* 35:1 (1998): 47–68.

Magowan, Fiona, and Karl Neuenfeldt, eds. *Landscapes of Indigenous Performance: Music, song and dance of the Torres Strait and Arnhem Land* (Canberra: Aboriginal Studies Press, 2005).

Marcus, Julie. 'The Beauty, Simplicity and Honour of Truth: Olive Pink in the 1940s', in *First in Their Field: Women and Australian Anthropology*, ed. Julie Marcus (Carlton: Melbourne University Press, 1993), 111–35.

May, Sally. 'The Art of Collecting: Charles Pearcy Mountford', in *The Makers and Making of Indigenous Australian Museum Collections*, eds Nicolas Peterson, Lindy Allen and Louise Hamby (Carlton: Melbourne University Press, 2008), 446–71.

May, Sally K. *Collecting Cultures: Myth, politics, and collaboration in the 1948 Arnhem Land Expedition* (Lanham: AltaMira Press, 2009).

McArthur, Margaret. 'Report on the Nutrition Unit', in *Records of the American-Australian Scientific Expedition to Arnhem Land*, ed. Charles P. Mountford (Melbourne: Melbourne University Press, 1960), 1–143.

McCarthy, Frederick D., and Margaret McArthur. 'The Food Quest and the Time Factor in Aboriginal Economic Life', in *Records of the American-Australian Scientific Expedition to Arnhem Land,* ed. Charles P. Mountford (Melbourne: Melbourne University Press, 1960), 145-94.

Mulvaney, Derek John. *Paddy Cahill of Oenpelli* (Canberra: Aboriginal Studies Press, 2004).

Ormond-Parker, Lyndon, Aaron Corn, Cressida Fforde, Kazuko Obata, and Sandy O'Sullivan, eds. *Information Technology and Indigenous Communities* (Canberra: AIATSIS Research Publications, 2013).

O'Sullivan, Sandy. 'Reversing the Gaze: Considering Indigenous perspectives on museums, cultural representation and the equivocal digital remnant', in *Information Technology and Indigenous Communities*, eds Lyndon Ormond-Parker, Aaron Corn, Cressida Fforde, Kazuko Obata and Sandy O'Sullivan (Canberra: AIATSIS Research Publications, 2013), 139–49.

Peterson, Nicolas, Lindy Allen, and Louise Hamby, eds. *The Makers and Making of Indigenous Australian Museum Collections* (Carlton: Melbourne University Press, 2008).

Richards, Fiona, ed. *The Soundscapes of Australia: Music, place and spirituality* (Aldershot: Ashgate, 2007).

Sahlins, Marshall. *Stone Age Economics* (Chicago: Aldine Atherton, 1972).

Simpson, Colin. *Adam in Ochre: Inside Aboriginal Australia* (Sydney: Angus & Robertson, 1951).

Svašek, Maruska, ed. *Moving Subjects, Moving Objects: Transnationalism, cultural production and emotions* (New York: Berghahn Books, 2012).

Taussig, Michael. *Mimesis and Alterity: A particular history of the senses* (New York: Routledge, 1993).

Thomas, Martin. 'Expedition as Time Capsule: Introducing the American–Australian Scientific Expedition to Arnhem Land', in *Exploring the Legacy of the 1948 Arnhem Land Expedition*, eds Martin Thomas and Margo Neale (Canberra: ANU E Press, 2011), 1–30.

Thomas, Martin, and Margo Neale, eds. *Exploring the Legacy of the 1948 Arnhem Land Expedition* (Canberra: ANU E Press, 2011).

Thomas, Nicholas. *Entangled Objects: Exchange, material culture, and colonialism in the Pacific* (Cambridge: Harvard University Press, 1991).

Part 1: C. P. Mountford and the Circulation of Music, Dance and Film

2. Beth Dean and the Transnational Circulation of Aboriginal Dance Culture: Gender, Authority and C. P. Mountford

Victoria Haskins

One of the highlights of the young Queen Elizabeth II's royal tour to Australia in 1954 was the command performance of an excerpt from the ballet *Corroboree*. Based on Aboriginal dance steps and performed to Australian composer John Antill's 1946 symphonic ballet of the same name, also inspired by Indigenous traditions, the ballet told the story of a young boy's initiation into manhood. The lead role of the boy initiate was played by the choreographer, a dynamic American dancer, Beth Dean, performing in a nylon brown bodystocking and make-up mimicking ochre bodypainting, her hair pulled back in a chignon that suggested the hairstyles of the central desert. A curious spectacle, indeed, as one young English woman watched another young, American woman, play out the initiation to manhood of an Aboriginal youth, as a symbol of Australia's distinctive cultural identity.

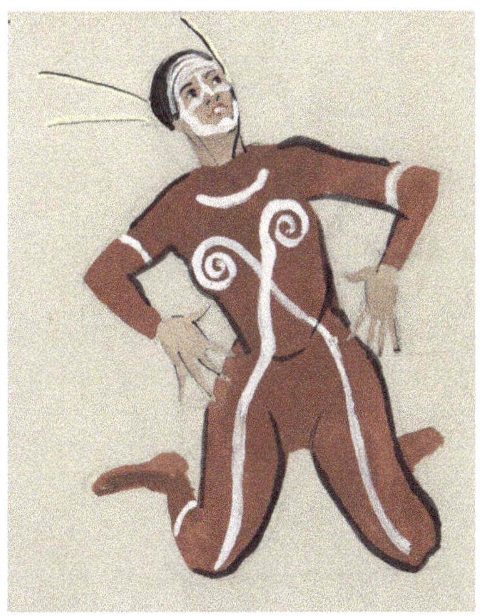

Figure 1: A sketch of Beth Dean in costume for the ballet *Corroboree*, dated 1950. William Constable, 1906 Bendigo, Victoria—1989 Melbourne, Victoria. Drawing, pencil, ink and goache on cream paper, 31.9 cm h x 23.6 cm w.

Source: National Museum of Australia Collection (1997.0047.0060).

Dean's *Corroboree* replaced an earlier version choreographed by the Australian choreographer Rex Reid and performed in 1950, in which a medicine man figure had played the lead role. Despite being popular with audiences, Reid's pageant-like ballet, with its mask-wearing dancers, was seen as an inadequate vehicle for showcasing the best of Australia's national culture. In 1951, journalist and travel writer Colin Simpson pronounced the ballet a 'gaudy, circus-like travesty of corroboree', and complained: 'Through lack of understanding and plain lack of knowledge, the choreographer had completely missed the spirit of the real thing.'[1] Approached by Dorothy Helmrich of the Australian Arts Council to re-choreograph the ballet for the Queen's impending visit two years later, Dean's challenge was to succeed where her predecessor had failed.

And she certainly did so. Crucially, Dean made an eight-month-long and very well publicised research trip around central and northern Australia gathering the material she needed to stage a truly 'authentic' Aboriginal ballet. After showing in Sydney for a few weeks, the ballet was then toured for a period of four months around rural New South Wales, both urban and rural audiences receiving it with enthusiasm. Unlike Reid's version, Dean's ballet was also warmly received by the critics. Rapturous reviews praised the ballet's authenticity and Dean's ability to capture Aboriginality. '[F]or me there's a stone-age antiquity in its atmosphere that makes it supremely Australian. With amazing sensitivity Beth Dean has crept inside the skin of our aborigine: she knows his mind, his spirit, his beliefs, his customs and his art of dancing', wrote Eunice Gardner in the *Columnist*. 'In one grand, sensitive, soul-exposing sweep', the *Daily Examiner* editorialised, 'Beth Dean, an American shows, as even our best writers have not been able to do, what is basically Australian'. Critics felt Dean had 'crept inside the skin of our aborigine', to present something 'supremely Australian'.[2] Indeed, enthused one editor, 'Beth Dean, an American shows, as even our best writers have not been able to do, what is basically Australian'.[3] 'American Beth Dean has with her fine intellect, taken her brush and obliterated the memory of some awful chichi choreography we have had to put up with', wrote another critic. *Corroboree* was 'an Australian masterpiece in which a Yank shares'.[4]

---

1   Colin Simpson, *Adam in Ochre* (Sydney: Angus & Robertson, Sydney, 1951), quoted in Stephanie Burridge, *The Impact of Aboriginal Dance on Twentieth Century Australian Choreography with a Practical and Creative Study* (PhD, London Contemporary Dance School at The Place, University of Kent at Canterbury, 1997), 60.
2   Eunice Gardner, *Daily Telegraph*, 12 February 1954 in 'Reviews cuttings' *Beth Dean and Victor Carell Papers, 1880-1920*, MLMSS 7804/13, Mitchell Library, NSW (hereafter *Dean Papers*). Also transcribed in Margaret Abbie Denton, *Corroboree/Choreography Beth Dean 1954*, MS 9469, National Library of Australia, Canberra, viii–xi.
3   Unattributed, 'Bush Ballet for Britain', *Daily Examiner* (Grafton), 16 March 1954, *Dean Papers* MLMSS 7804/13; and Denton *Corroboree/Choreography Beth Dean 1954*, viii–xi.
4   Transcribed review, Andrea, *Mirror*, 7 February 1954, held in Denton *Corroboree/Choreography Beth Dean 1954*, viii–xi.

Beth Dean's *Corroboree* has garnered attention from numerous scholars over the years, as a particularly iconic moment in the history of the nationalist appropriation of Aboriginal music and dance.[5] Little, however, has been said about the influence of Charles Pearcy Mountford, despite Dean's insistence that the catalyst for the direction her career would take was a chance encounter with the charismatic anthropologist in a New York hotel room. In a previous study of the transnational nature of Dean's performance and of the ballet itself as a transnational production, I touched briefly upon Mountford's role,[6] but an extended examination of the dynamic between the anthropologist and Dean and her ballet allows us to consider the gendered nature of the production of knowledge about Aboriginal culture, through cross-cultural exchange. Through her connection with Mountford, Dean obtained her authority and her credentials as one who could produce an 'authentic' version of Aboriginal culture for reworking in the most Westernised dance form, modern ballet. Dean represented the emancipated modern white woman, yet Mountford's role in Dean's performative appropriation of Aboriginality highlights paradoxically that her transgression of race and gender, embodied in her dancing as an Aboriginal youth becoming a man, was ultimately an appropriation of white male authority.

---

5   Catrina Vignando, 'Corroboree: Aboriginal inspiration in contemporary Australian ballet', *Olive Pink Society Bulletin*, 3:2 (1991): 10–14; Candice Bruce and Anita Callaway, 'Dancing in the Dark: Black corroboree or white spectacle?', *Australian Journal of Art* 9 (1991): 79–104; Lyn A. Riddett, '"Be Aboriginal": Settler women artists inspired by Aboriginal artists', *Northern Perspective* 19:1 (1996): 51–60; Michelle Potter, 'Making Australian Dance: Themes and variations', Voices (1996): 10–20; Amanda Card, 'From "Aboriginal Dance" to Aboriginals Dancing: The appropriation of the "primitive" in Australian dance', in *Speaking of History: Dance scholarship in the '90s: Proceedings of Society of Dance Scholars Nineteenth Annual Conference* (Minnesota: University of Minnesota, 1996), 115–26; Stephanie Burridge, *The Impact of Aboriginal Dance on Twentieth Century Australian Choreography with a Practical and Creative Study* (PhD, London Contemporary Dance School at The Place, University of Kent at Canterbury, 1997); Amanda Card, 'From "Aboriginal Dance" to Aboriginals Dancing: The appropriation of the "primitive" in Australian dance, 1950 to 1963', in *Heritage and Heresy: Green Mill Papers 1997* (Canberra: Australian Dance Council, 1998), 40–6; Jan Kociumbas, 'Performances: Indigenisation and postcolonial culture', in *Cultural History in Australia,* eds Hsu-Ming Teo and Richard White (Sydney: UNSW Press, 2003), 127–41; Amanda Card and Carole Y. Johnson, 'Aboriginal Influences', in *Currency Companion to Music and Dance in Australia,* eds John Whiteoak and Aline Scott-Maxwell (Sydney: Currency House, 2003); 20-3; Anna Haebich, 'Assimilation and Hybrid Art: Reflections on the politics of Aboriginal art', in *The Art of Politics The Politics of Art: The place of contemporary Indigenous art,* ed. Fiona Foley (Southport: Keeaira Press, 2006); Victoria Haskins, 'Dancing in the Dust: A gendered history of indigenising Australian cultural identity', in *Intersections: Gender, race and ethnicity in Australasian studies,* eds Margaret Allen and R K Dhawan (New Delhi: Prestige, 2007), 55–75; Anna Haebich and Jodie Taylor, 'Modern Primitives Leaping and Stomping the Earth: From ballet to bush doofs', *Aboriginal History* 31 (2007): 63–84; Anna Haebich, *Spinning the Dream: Assimilation in Australia 1950–1970* (Fremantle: Fremantle Press, 2008), 320–36; Victoria Haskins, 'To Touch the Infinity of a Far Horizon: A transnational history of transcultural appropriation in Beth Dean's *Corroboree* 1954', *Australasian Drama Studies* 59 (2011): 23–38.

6   Haskins, 'To Touch the Infinity of the Far Horizon', 29.

Meeting Mountford

Following the production of the ballet, Beth Dean and her Australian-born husband and collaborator Victor Carell published an account of their research travels under the title *Dust for the Dancers*. In the book's introduction, they explained that as newly wed performers out of work in New York in 1946, they initially conceived the idea of running a radio program on Australian music. (They had heard an NBC radio program introducing South African folk songs that year.) The couple then sought advice from Charles Buttrose, an Australian journalist working in the newly established Australian News and Information Bureau in New York, on acquiring 'background on aboriginal legends' that might be turned into songs or stories for the planned program, 'Song Stories from Down Under'. Buttrose put them in touch with his friend and fellow South Australian, Mountford:

> … we met a lean, scholarly gentleman who, his eyes lit with enthusiasm, kept us fascinated for three days (in a tiny hotel bedroom) listening to his tales of the Australian aborigines … There, in that crowded New York room, our imaginations were so fired that they were able to leap out over the surrounding skyscrapers … over the vast modern country and the ocean beyond … past Sydney's golden beaches, to light in the centre of a continent where, surrounded by empty silence, an old man, with bearded face and jutting eyebrows, sat chanting. Out of his strange medley of sounds came stories of great spirit heroes wandering through the world when it was young, creating the rivers and making the mountains. The shadows about him were peopled with leaping, virile young men, their dark glistening bodies ochred-daubed and decorated in fantastic designs.
>
> … After Charles Mountford had returned to Australia, the vision he kindled remained with us.[7]

Positioning Mountford in such a place of dominance—the book's opening pages—was clearly a device to assert the credibility and authority of their research from the outset. The book did not come until after the ballet had toured, but even before the ballet opened, Mountford's influence and support had been emphasised in the publicity and promotion. It was, reported *People* magazine in 1953, her meeting with the anthropologist that first brought Dean to the realisation 'that in the hinterland of Australia was a rich and hitherto untapped source of inspiration for the creative artist in dance', and more importantly, it was the inspiration for her to look for an opportunity to come to Australia to learn all about Aboriginal dance, and 'perhaps, later, make ethnic dancing her

---

7   Beth Dean and Victor Carell, *Dust for the Dancers* (Sydney: Ure Smith, 1955), 1–2.

speciality'.[8] *Corroboree* did indeed make Dean's career, transforming her from a little-known musical dancer and choreographer on American entertainment circuits to a renowned international expert on Indigenous dance.[9]

Dean's narrative of her meeting with Mountford, reiterated over the years in various interviews, conforms to an older tradition of women performers' memoirs: a crucial encounter with a powerful man that provided the catalyst for the performer's success being a device which removed agency from the female performer.[10] But what is striking in this construction is the way that it operated to negate not so much Dean's own agency in shaping the direction her career took, but in erasing the broader context in which *Corroboree* was created as a transnational product circulated by women.

White Women and Corroboree

Although Dean never referred to or mentioned any of her predecessors, there was an established, if contested, tradition of white women interpreting or mediating Indigenous dance performance in Australia for white audiences. Public descriptions of corroborees were dominated by white men's voices throughout the colonial period. In that time we find only a few surviving traces of a white female view in the private letters of women allied to the most wealthy and powerful of white men, such as Elizabeth Macarthur,[11] or, at the other end of the colonial century, Queensland pastoralist's wife Jane Bardsley (who boasted that she could 'certainly corroboree as well as any gin').[12] Women's public claims to knowledge were dismissed out of hand. Thus an early colonial

---

8   Unattributed, 'From Primitive to Ballet', *People*, 12 August 1953, 17–20: *Dean Papers* ML MSS 7804/24.

9   She and Carell remained in Australia after the ballet ended, and her next work was a ballet for television, *G'Day Digger*, created around 1956, followed by *Dreaming Time Legends* in 1965, another made for television production which consisted of two ballets based on Aboriginal legends from New South Wales. Dean was invited to participate in Mexico's 1968 Cultural Olympics (where she taught Indigenous dance and arranged for another Aboriginal-themed ballet, *Kukaitcha*, to be performed), but her focus was shifting to the South Pacific. In 1970 she established the Cook Islands National Arts Theatre; she also assisted in the organisation of the first South Pacific Festival of Arts in Suva in 1973, and directed performances for the opening of the Sydney Opera House the same year. Over the years Dean also published numbers of articles and books, some with her husband, about ballet and Indigenous dance. She passed away in 2012 and was the subject of an obituary in the *Sydney Morning Herald*: Unattributed biography, 'Dean, Beth (1918–2012)', *Australia Dancing*, accessed 14 March 2012, http://www.australiadancing.org/subjects/26.html; Don Niles, personal communication to ICTM Oceania Study Group, 22 February 2012, ictm-oceania-l@lists.hawaii.edu; Valerie Lawson, 'Dancer Many Steps Ahead of Her Time: Beth Dean Carell 1918–2012,' *Sydney Morning Herald*, 12 May 2012.

10   See Lena Hammergren, 'Many Sources, Many Voices', in *Rethinking Dance History: A reader,* ed. Alexandra Carter (London: Routledge, 2004), 26

11   Cited in Candice Bruce and Anita Callaway, 'Wild Nights and Savage Festivities: White views of corroborees', *Art and Australia* 27:2 (1989): 275.

12   Letter, Jane Bardsley Atherton, dated October 1898, in *Jane Bardsley's Outback Letterbook, Across the Years 1896–1936*, ed. John Atherton Young (Sydney: Angus & Robertson, 1987), 107–10.

painting of an Aboriginal (male) dance scene by a woman, Sydney merchant's wife Sophia Campbell, bore the blunt notation by her niece's husband: 'NB this Corrobery has no business here as it is never danced in the day-time.' Such was the male conceit of the authoritative eye that the panorama was, until recently, wrongly attributed to this man.[13] The female view was also constrained by the prescriptions of class and gender. As colonial historian of manners Penny Russell has pointed out, the 'colonial lady' demonstrated her moral virtue and rank by 'enactments of social blindness' and 'undisturbed comportment' when confronted by 'savage' male sexuality. While white male accounts could and did freely assert the 'most lewd and disgusting character' of Aboriginal 'corrobbories',[14] white women did not see and certainly did not comment publicly on Aboriginal men or their masculinity.[15]

By the end of the nineteenth century, however, such women—squatters' wives such as Kate Langloh-Parker, or her predecessor, Mary A. Fitzgerald—began to find currency in re-telling 'authentic legends' of Aboriginal people for white readers, referring to Aboriginal men as their sources.[16] In the twentieth century, the Durack sisters, Elizabeth and Mary, daughters of a pastoral dynasty of far-north-western Australia, would achieve recognition for these accounts.[17] Even so they could not always be counted on to bring the writer commercial success— as Mary Grant Bruce discovered in 1922.[18] Rather, the irrepressible spate of Aboriginal legends by white women from the turn of the century reflected an impulse based upon the changing performativity of white womanhood. The production of this cross-cultural knowledge must be seen in the broader context of an emergent feminist movement in which the sanctity of white motherhood was argued,[19] hand-in-hand with the construction of an exemplary white female pioneering past, as embodied in the figure of the mythic 'good fella missus' who cared for Aboriginal people.[20]

---

13   Caroline Jordan, *Picturesque Pursuits: Colonial women artists and the amateur tradition* (Melbourne: Melbourne University Press, Melbourne, 2005), 58–9.

14   Alfred Giles 1887, quoted in C. D. Rowley, *The Destruction of Aboriginal Society* (Ringwood: Penguin, 1986), 214.

15   Penny Russell, 'Cultures of Distinction', in *Cultural History in Australia*, eds Hsu-Ming Teo and Richard White (Sydney: UNSW Press, 2003), 170.

16   K. Langloh Parker, *Australian Legendary Tales* (Middlesex: Tiger Books, 1998); Mary A Fitzgerald, *King Bungaree's Pyalla and Stories Illustrative of Manners and Customs that Prevailed Among Australian Aborigines* (Sydney: William Brooks & Co, 1891), ii.

17   Mary and Elizabeth Durack, *All-About: The story of a black community on Argyle Station, Kimberley* (Sydney: The Bulletin, 1935). See Brenda Niall, *True North: The story of Mary and Elizabeth Durack* (Melbourne: Text Publishing, 2012), 38–9.

18   The research that went into Bruce's *The Stone Axe of Burkamukk* 'cost her more time and effort than any of her [Billabong] novels, but it sold poorly. Evidently her public preferred her to keep to fiction, and had little interest in a sympathetic attempt to study black civilization in Australia.' Brenda Niall, *Seven Little Billabongs: The world of Ethel Turner and Mary Grant Bruce* (Melbourne: Melbourne University Press, 1979), 166.

19   Marilyn Lake, 'Feminist History as National History: Writing the political history of women', *Australian Historical Studies* 27:106 (1996): 158.

20   Madeline E. McGuire, 'The Legend of the Good Fella Missus', *Aboriginal History* 14:2 (1990): 143.

The appearance of female public commentators on Aboriginal culture at this time was a reflection of the same forces. In the newly opened regions of central Australia during the 1920s and 1930s, white women such as the missionary Annie Lock, the anthropologist Olive Pink, and, most famous of all, the journalist-anthropologist Daisy Bates, found opportunities to claim a public voice. These women not only provided firsthand accounts of 'corroborees' but even asserted a directing role in their performance. In 1920, for instance, Bates was asked to arrange an Aboriginal performance for the Prince of Wales on tour in Australia, and shared the dais with him as she explained the significance of the Aboriginal dances.[21] In 1934, she was prevailed upon again, to arrange the performance of 'tribal dances' at Ooldea for the visit of his son, the Duke of Gloucester; Bates described how despite their 'reluctance' to perform their secret initiation ceremonies for outsiders, the 'natives … promised me' they would 'give a little of this amazingly agile dance'. 'Their confidence and trust in me was fully illustrated in their own way when they gave me charge of their young boy novices, whom they took me to see, and touch, and feed', she boasted.

> That journey in itself would have made an interesting camera picture. There were no native women present, only 25 men, all blood relations of the boys, and myself, walking quickly in single file through the tangled bush, and later the ceremony of approach, &c., to the young lads.[22]

This newfound opening for white women generated a certain degree of competition. While Bates was planning her performances, Annie Lock arranged a rival performance for the Duke at Ooldea—declaring that the Prince of Wales had been 'terribly disappointed' by Bates' display in 1920—and she wanted to show his son the Duke 'that they [the Aborigines] are better cared for now the mission has taken them up'.[23] Lock 'had the honor [sic] of setting the corroboree going, and they had conferred upon her some native honours',[24] in a performance notable for the 'attractive' dark blue shorts worn by the dancers.[25]

At the same time Aboriginal people themselves were being prevented from performing corroborees, whether by missionaries or frontier violence in remoter regions, or by an increasingly draconian administration in the 'settled' states. In 1926, the offer of another white woman, Elizabeth McKenzie-Hatton of the Australian Aboriginal Progressive Association (AAPA, an Aboriginal

---

21 Jim Anderson, '"A glorious thing is to live in a tent in the infinite": Daisy Bates', in *Uncommon Ground: White women in Aboriginal history*, eds Anna Cole, Victoria Haskins and Fiona Paisley (Canberra: Aboriginal Studies Press, 2005), 221–2.

22 'Wild Natives to Greet Duke', *The Advertiser*, 8 October 1934.

23 Lock to Sexton, 5 September 1934, *Aborigines Friends Association Correspondence Files*, SRG 139/1/324, State Library of South Australia (SLSA), Adelaide.

24 Report of visit to Ooldea, 25–27 September 1934, Sexton to Hudd (Public Works Commissioner), 4 October 1934, *Aborigines Friends Association Correspondence Files*, SRG 139/1/337, SLSA.

25 'Demonstration by Natives Under Miss Lock', *The Advertiser*, 12 October 1924.

political organisation based in NSW), to organise a performance by the AAPA's 'corroboree group' for the visit of the Duke and Duchess of York was politely but firmly declined.[26] When it came to expressing their opinion of appropriations of corroboree, Aboriginal people were at a great disadvantage, and their voices are few in the record. A rare insight is provided by a 1922 letter to the editor of the *Sydney Morning Herald* from Annie Bowden, an Aboriginal woman at La Perouse, Sydney (and an AAPA member), in response to one of Bates' very early sensational articles. Bowden took issue with many of Bates' statements about Aboriginal culture and her descriptions of initiation ceremonies, challenging Bates' claim to be an authority on this subject in particular:

> As for the awful practices carried out at initiations, just let me say this: If, as Mrs Bates says, they were such cannibals there, and they killed and ate people for the smallest offence, how is it she was allowed to witness so dreadful a scene, without being eaten herself?

'Initiation as I know it was a sacred rite', she continued, 'and no one but a select few were ever allowed to witness it … so how Mrs Bates comes to know so much about initiation I cannot tell.'[27] By the 1930s the surge of white interest in the new 'social anthropology' was seen by Aboriginal activists as a retrograde step away from the equality 'earned' during the First World War, as a way in which white Australians gave themselves 'the pleasure of feeling superior', and diametrically opposed to the demand for equal rights and opportunities.[28]

And yet performing 'corroboree' continued to provide an opportunity for white women to voice authority and knowledge. In 1933, musician and lyricist Varney Monk created a 'corroboree' piece for the musical *Collits Inn* (billed as 'the first Australian historical musical play'),[29] as a way of providing 'the background

---

26   E. McKenzie-Hatton to Governor-General, 5 November 1926; Major-General, Commonwealth Director, to E. McKenzie-Hatton, 3 December 1926, A6680/1 DY25/19, National Archives of Australia (NAA), Canberra. My thanks to John Maynard for bringing my attention to this episode and documentation. See also John Maynard, 'Light in the Darkness: Elizabeth McKenzie-Hatton', in *Uncommon Ground: White women in Aboriginal history*, eds Anna Cole, Victoria Haskins and Fiona Paisley (Canberra: Aboriginal Studies Press, 2005).

27   'Vanishing Aboriginals', Annie Bowden letter to the editor, *Sydney Morning Herald*, 20 May 1922. Thanks to John Maynard for drawing my attention to this source, also.

28   J. T. Patten and W. Ferguson, *Aborigines Claim Citizen Rights!* (Sydney: The Publicist, 1938), 6, 11 (the manifesto of the Australian Aborigines Progressive Association). Similar views were expressed by the leader of the Victorian Aboriginal political group, the Australian Aborigines League. See Cooper to Minister for the Interior (Cmwlth), 15 June 1936, CRS A659, 1940/1/858, NAA: 'The [Australian Aborigines'] League does desire the preservation of the best features of aboriginal culture and feels that the preservation of certain corroboree dances, in the way the old World peoples have retained their folk dances, is in harmony with this … [but] great care should be exercised till such time as the native race is so fully civilised that the outlook on the corroboree is just that of the Old World civilisation on their folk dances.' Cited in Russell McGregor, *Imagined Destinies: Aboriginal Australians and the doomed race theory, 1880–1939*, (Victoria: Melbourne University Press, 1997), 250–1.

29   John Thomson, 'It's Australian – and it's good!' *National Library of Australia News*, 14:3 (2003), accessed 8 June 2014, http://www.australianmusicals.com/article_itsaustralian.htm.

touch of reality of the period'. She claimed she had adapted it from a song she had learned from an Aboriginal 'Queen' Rosie, 'the last full-blooded aborigine of the Illawarra tribe',[30] who had danced and sung for Monk's edification.[31] The inclusion of a 'Corroboree Dance' in the performance probably marks the first known attempt to adapt Aboriginal dance to ballet—'Something for even New York to get excited about', in the words of one reviewer—though we know little about the actual performers, or the choreography.[32] Possibly the first white woman in recorded history to offer a public performance of corroboree herself was the writer Zora Cross, who performed her 'Aboriginal Corroboree' on 5 November 1937, before the Society of Arts and Crafts of New South Wales.[33]

Despite the prominence of women in the cross-cultural re-production of Aboriginal dance and music, it would be a man who would ensure that such an enterprise was taken seriously. In 1946, composer John Antill created the score for which both Reid's and Dean's later ballets would be choreographed, based on his childhood memories of watching tourist corroborees at La Perouse Aboriginal reserve. The score, which he called 'Corroboree', was to be hailed as the first truly Australian piece of contemporary music.[34]

Antill's achievement marked the beginnings of an incorporation of Aboriginal dance into elite culture, hand in hand with the development of modern dance and its interest in 'the primitive' in the wider western world, that would finally register internationally. The following year, Ted Shawn, a leading US exponent of modern dance, came to Australia to learn about Aboriginal dance. Shawn (who co-founded the Denishawn School of Dance with his wife, 'one of America's most famous women dancers, Ruth St Denis') was self-consciously masculinist in his outlook. He had, he wrote in his 1953 account of his travels (published just as Dean and Carell were carrying out their own research in central and northern Australia), begun to feel 'that dancing in western countries had lost some of its vitality through the preponderance of women dancers'.

> This had given the lead to the ballerina, whereas in primitive countries men were the main performers. It was the fact that Australian corroboree was performed almost exclusively by men that made him so anxious to see it.[35]

---

30   Letters (n.d.) from Varney Monk (1892–1967), quoted in J. West, ed. *Collits' Inn: A romantic Australian operetta by T Stuart Gurr with lyrics and music by Varney Monk* (Sydney: Currency Press, 1990), xii.

31   M. H. W., 'Queen Rosie's Requiem,' *Sydney Morning Herald,* 21 June 1932.

32   Robyn Holmes, 'Australian Music Editing and Authenticity: "Would the real Mrs Monk please stand up?"', in *The Editorial Gaze: Mediating texts in literature and the arts,* eds Paul Eggert and Margaret Sankey (Oxon: Routledge, 2013), 221.

33   Glenn R. Cooke, 'Aboriginal Motifs in the Decorative Arts, "an art for Australia from Australians"', in *Motif and Meaning: Aboriginal influences in Australian art 1930–1970,* ed. Claire Baddley (Ballarat: Ballarat Fine Art Gallery, 1999), 15.

34   Vignando, 'Corroboree', 11.

35   John K. Ewers, *With the Sun on My Back* (Sydney: Angus & Robertson, 1953), 26–7.

Meanwhile, Charles Mountford was rising to international prominence. Having established a national profile for his writings on Aboriginal art and culture during the 1930s, he had been sent to New York at the end of 1944 by the Australian government to promote Australia, by conducting a lecture series on Australian and Aboriginal culture.[36] Mountford's popular lectures by and large focused upon Aboriginal men. In New York he had with him a number of ethnographic films and recordings he had produced, including the documentary *Tjurunga* (1946) about his 1942 expedition to the MacDonnell Ranges and the art of sacred objects there; a film about the celebrated artist Albert Namatjira; and a film of circumcision and sub-incision rituals. Like Shawn's determination to study Aboriginal male dancers, the attention to male activities—particularly, we might argue, male rituals around circumcision—reflected a broader phallocentrism within the popular ethnographies of the postwar period. The doings of men were considered of significance and interest to all; Aboriginal women's culture was deemed of interest only to women, and marginalised. As social anthropology became an established discipline, female students and scholars were dissuaded from conducting research on Aboriginal men, although the professors were happy to teach contingents of admiring women about Aboriginal men.[37] Showing his circumcision film to mixed audiences of men and women, Mountford noted that the women 'showed as much interest in the matter as did the men, but did not ask any questions'.[38] Given the anxieties about women's roles in the 1950s, it is somewhat ironic that white women should now assert their interest in 'knowing' Aboriginal men. But after the war, urban, middle-class, mobile and modern white women quickly discovered a new power to flex, both as consumers, and as knowledge-producers in their own right. It was at this point in the trajectory that Beth Dean met Mountford and began to live out her dream to 'tell the world of the Aboriginal culture'.[39]

Mountford in New York

Despite being somewhat estranged from the academic anthropological establishment, Mountford's impact on the transnational circularisation and popularisation of a particular discursive representation of Aboriginality in the 1940s, and particularly the 1950s, was profound. His connections with Dean's ballet might be traced back even to Simpson's much-quoted criticism of her

36   Walter W. Stone, ed., *Charles Pearcy Mountford: An annotated bibliography* (Cremorne: The Stone Copying Company, 1958), 61.

37   See Francesca Merlan, 'Gender in Aboriginal Social Life: A review', in *Social Anthropology and Australian Aboriginal Studies*, eds R. M. Berndt and R. Tonkinson (Canberra: Australian Institute of Aboriginal Studies, 1988), 19–45.

38   C. P. Mountford 'A Journey to America 1945–6', Vol. 4, Mountford-Sheard Collection, PRG 1218/16/4, State Library of South Australia, Adelaide, 6 April 1945.

39   Beth Dean to Mr Green, 27 September 1951, *Dean Papers* MLMSS 7804/3.

predecessor Reid—Simpson had made his scathing remarks in the 1951 book he published based on his association with Mountford's 1948 expedition (the American-Australian Scientific Expedition to Arnhem Land), *Adam in Ochre*, the book which propelled Simpson's own transnational career, 'from journalist to globetrotting writer of travel books'.[40]

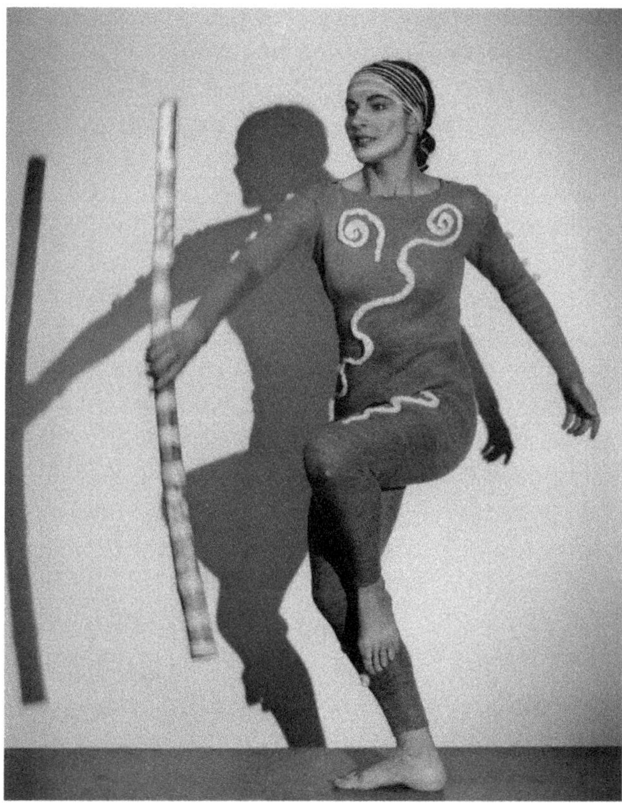

Figure 2: Beth Dean as the Initiate, *Corroboree*, dated 1949.

Source: Photographer unknown. Royce Rees collection, State Library of NSW (PXA 739/1867).

In Dean's own account, it was not until after the couple returned from their first visit to Australia in the early 1950s that she first contemplated creating a balletic 'corroboree' to accompany Antill's 1946 composition. In fact she denied having ever seen Rex Reid's version (rather surprisingly, given that the couple would be in Australia during the entire year of 1950, when Reid's ballet was performed).[41]

---

40   See Martin Thomas, 'A Short History of the 1948 Arnhem Land Expedition,' *Aboriginal History* 34 (2010): 154.

41   Copy, Dean to Peggy van Praagh, 20 April 1962, *Dean Papers* MLMSS 7804/4. It is also curious that both the sketches of her in costume drawn by William Constable and held in the National Museum were dated 1950, and the photograph of her held in the Mitchell Library, in Sydney, was dated 1949, although these dates

Instead she claimed that the idea first came to her when she and her husband heard Antill's symphonic ballet being played on the radio in Canada, where they were holidaying with friends. According to the story, Carell said to Dean at the time, 'You're going to do that ballet someday'. Dean replied, 'Oh, you're teasing, that couldn't be so'. 'No', he said, 'I think that's a good idea'.[42]

Nevertheless it is evident from Mountford's personal papers that Dean and her husband had already thought about developing an Aboriginal-inspired ballet by the time they approached him in New York in March 1945 (not, as they claimed, in 1946). Mountford's diaries record that he had gone to Radio City, an entertainment venue, where he found 'a young chap and his wife' talking to his friend Buttrose about Australian music. As they were 'really after aboriginal music', Buttrose referred them to him; the couple were looking for some recorded music but Buttrose had been able to provide them only with one song, 'rewritten by an Australian, who, although he may have retained the notes certainly had not retained the rhythmic pattern'. So Mountford arranged to meet them the following day at the New York Public Library, to show them a paper on Aboriginal music by Professor E. Harold Davies, an eminent Australian authority on Aboriginal music at that time. When the couple saw this paper, Mountford recorded with satisfaction, 'they realized how far out the other chap was'. The anthropologist then took them to the American Museum of Natural History and played them the recordings they 'badly wanted' to hear, his recordings of Adnyamathanha songs from the Flinders Ranges region of South Australia. After a lunch together, they went to his hotel room, and it was here that Dean and Carell first aired the idea of 'designing the music and choreography for a ballet' based on Aboriginal dance.[43]

Mountford had, somewhat cautiously, supported the idea. 'I personally think it could be done', he mused, 'but the professional ballet dancer would have to unhook his mind from many of the traditional steps and poses'.

> Then, that might not attract the crowd and make money, the be-all and end-all of entertainment. Still, the're [sic] keen, and it won't hurt to talk about it. I feel sure that some of the dances I have seen, ie, the simpler ones, would make wonderful ballets, especially if they were performed by artists that know the background.

---

must be incorrect, as she did not receive the commission to work on the ballet until 1952.

42   Beth Dean, 'Oral History Interview with Hazel De Berg', 4 December 1975, Transcript, in *Hazel de Berg collection*, DebB 902, National Library of Australia, Canberra (hereafter *De Berg Interview*).

43   *Mountford Diaries*, Vol. 3, 22 March 1945, 23 March 1945.

> We had a very happy time, these two young folk and I. They did not leave until 4.30, and that was about 4 hours later than they meant to stay ...[44]

Mountford did not seem to take Dean and Carell particularly seriously. He was encountering all sorts of different women who were interested in learning about Indigenous cultures and had ideas about studying and promoting the same for public audiences. There was, for instance, a Bathie Stewart from New Zealand, who gave lectures on the 'Legends of Maori Land', at the Waldorf Astoria in January 1945.[45] Around the same time that he met the Carells, Mountford promised to visit a Miss Laura Bolton in New York, employed by the Canadian government to record the 'folk music' of that country, 'who had done a great deal of recording of primitive music'. He was a guest at a dinner hosted by the sculptor Malvina Hoffman, who was 'very interested in people, especially primitives'; she told him that in the late 1930s she had organised a 'series of international dances' including those of 'American Indian tribes, Negroes, Haitians, Russians, Polynesians, etc' at Radio City under a program called Dance International, before the whole thing abruptly 'fell to bits' with the onset of the war. 'But they were on the verge of starting something really good, something which Miss Hoffman thought would have lasted', recorded Mountford.[46] He also recorded a conversation he'd had with an American woman, a Mrs Oghtwaite, 'really a delightful person', who told him forthrightly that it was 'the dancer, the artist, the musician', and not the anthropologist, who should be investigating Aboriginal cultural life, and Mountford amiably agreed.[47] Just the month before meeting with the Carells, a leading and influential English ballet critic, Arnold Haskell, had written to Mountford suggesting that if he could do 'an illustrated lecture on aboriginal dancing, [he knew] many ladies that would welcome it', and could 'fix up' some appearances for him in London.[48]

While Mountford capitalised on women's fascination with his subject, such curiosity and interest could quickly turn to competition. His customary equanimity was shaken when he encountered expatriate Australian Winifred Walker (just two weeks after meeting Dean) showing Australian films under the billing 'Lecturer, Photographer, World Traveller'. Walker had, 'by all the bad luck in the world', managed to procure a copy of his film *Tjurunga*, from a 'Yankee' woman who'd bought it in Australia. Walker promised not 'to show it in any place where [he was] likely to appear'. She was, to his relief, 'ever such a

---

44   ibid.

45   Flier, Bathie Stewart, n.d, pasted in *Mountford Diaries*, Vol. 1, 12 January 1945.

46   *Mountford Diaries*, Vol. 3, 9 March 1945; Vol. 4, 11 April 1945, 13 April 1945.

47   *Mountford Diaries*, Vol. 3, 9 March 1945.

48   Letter, Haskell to Mountford, 8 February [1945] enclosed *Mountford Diaries*, Vol. 2.

nice friendly person, a bit of a go-getter, but not to the extent of being greedy'.[49] Dean, for her part, seems to have been cautious not to represent herself as a threat or rival to Mountford.

Dean in Australia

In 1947, the Carells had their opportunity to come to Australia, as part of the cast for the hit musical *Annie Get Your Gun*. The show proved to be as popular in Australia as it was in the US, running for three years, during which time Dean (cast in an undemanding support role) had undertaken to learn all she could about Māori and Aboriginal dance, in order to reinvent herself as an 'ethnic dancer'. (The latter she learned largely from Mountford's films, as well as the published works of T. G. H. Strehlow and A. P. Elkin.) At the conclusion of the *Annie* tour in 1950, Dean gave her first concert performance of Aboriginal dance at the Sydney Conservatorium, then embarked on a tour of country towns in NSW performing Aboriginal and other ethnic dance, under the auspices of the NSW Council of Adult Education.[50] Leaving Australia the following year, the Carells went to England, where Dean's performance of Aboriginal dance in London's Rambert Theatre was reviewed favourably by none other than Arnold Haskell. Dean recorded that his review 'caused quite a lot of publicity and furore because no one had seen Australian Aboriginal dance before'.[51] It is likely that Mountford facilitated this important connection: 'through her we see for the first time the stone age dance of the aboriginal', Haskell had written, 'vouched for in its authenticity by no less an authority than C. P. Mountford, anthropologist and artist'.[52] The couple then returned to New York where Dean ran a program titled 'Dance Around the World', at the Museum of Natural History, based upon the material she had developed for her NSW tours. In an array of costumes she performed a range of exotic characters, a particular highlight being a scene from 'an Australian Aboriginal sacred Inkura ceremony of Initiation'.[53] Performing together—Dean dancing and Carell accompanying her on improvised instruments—they then toured the States, finally ending up in Los Angeles.[54]

From the US now, Dean began to make strenuous efforts to raise funds for a return trip to Australia, to carry out a project researching Aboriginal dance. In the first instance she approached Strehlow for advice and support. Strehlow's

---

49   *Mountford Diaries*, Vol. 4, 6 April 1945; Vol. 3, 21 March 1945.

50   'Fred' to Dean and Carell, 16 May 1950, *Dean Papers* ML MSS 7804/4; and unattributed, 'From Primitive to Ballet', *People*, 12 August 1953, 17–20, *Dean Papers* ML MSS 7804/24.

51   *De Berg Interview*.

52   'Beth Dean: A note by Arnold Haskell', undated transcription, c. 1951, *Dean Papers* ML MSS 7804/22.

53   Program, The Center YMHA, 2 November 1951, *Dean Papers* ML MSS 7804/41.

54   *De Berg Interview*.

work was her source for the 'Inkura' ceremony of male initiation, but it is hard to imagine him approving of her enterprise. The powerful anthropologist was not inclined to endorse white women to the study of Aboriginal customs, as he had shown in his attitude to the anthropologist Olive Pink in the late 1930s. At that time he had advised the authorities to deny Pink a permit to go onto the reserves for her research, on the grounds that she had an inappropriate 'habit of interviewing the old men of the tribe' for information on 'the things that may not be told to a woman'.[55] As Pink had been outspoken on the white sexual abuse of Aboriginal women, Strehlow said she had an 'unhealthy obsession' with sex, and took delight in informing her that her permit to study the Aboriginal people had been denied.[56]

Strehlow's biographer notes that his main motive in blocking Pink was 'territorial'.[57] In Dean's case, however, he seems to have been supportive, advising Dean to approach the head of the Commonwealth Department of Native Affairs, Paul Hasluck, for permission to visit the Aboriginal people of the Northern Territory.[58] She immediately drafted a letter to Hasluck on the back of Strehlow's communication, dropping Strehlow's name as well as those of Mountford and Professor Elkin, and stressing her 'especial interest in collecting women's ceremonies … This aspect of ABO [sic] life has never been tabulated'.[59] Perhaps Strehlow had mellowed since his encounters with Pink, but more likely Dean's care not to challenge his authority in her communications with him made the difference. It is notable that in her correspondence with both Strehlow and Hasluck (although not with Mountford), she used her married name, Ruth Elizabeth Carell, which was unusual for her. Dean was no doubt in full realisation of the power these men wielded. She may well have deliberately downplayed her autonomy as a woman, as well as claiming to be only interested in female dance culture, to avoid any resistance by the authorities to her working too closely with Aboriginal men.

Even so, Dean was unable to secure the permission she needed to visit the reserves, nor was she able to secure funding. Instead the Carells returned to Australia in early 1952 on the strength of another tour of ethnic dance performance, mostly in New Zealand. It was at one performance in Sydney, apparently, when Dorothy Helmrich of the NSW Australian Arts Council invited Dean to choreograph a new version of *Corroboree* for the Queen's visit.[60] This was the break Dean needed. The Carells finally received their official permits from the

---

55   Barry Hill, *Broken Song: T. G. H. Strehlow and Aboriginal Possession* (Sydney: Vintage, 2003), 338.

56   Julie Marcus, 'The Beauty, Simplicity and Honour of Truth: Olive Pink in the 1940s', in *First in their Field: Women and Australian anthropology*, ed. Julie Marcus (Melbourne: Melbourne University Press, 1993), 128–30; Hill, *Broken Song*, 337–9.

57   Hill, *Broken Song*, 338.

58   T. G. H. Strehlow to Mrs Carell, 24 September 1952, *Dean Papers* ML MSS 7804/24.

59   Draft letter, Beth Dean to Paul Hasluck (n.d., c. 24 September 1952), *Dean Papers* ML MSS 7804/24.

60   *De Berg Interview.*

Commonwealth authorities 'to enter and be upon' Aboriginal reserves in July 1953,[61] and set off in a sponsored Holden utility truck soon afterwards.[62] They were in possession of a wire recorder, courtesy of the Wenner-Gren Foundation of New York,[63] and a Kodak 16mm film camera that they would use to make a promotion film of their journeys, *Carrumbo*.[64]

Notwithstanding her plans for the reworking of *Corroboree*, Dean did in fact carry out a great deal of research into Aboriginal women's dance culture. Her focus was not only to mollify the white anthropological establishment, nor satisfy her own curiosity, but was predicated on the limitations placed on her by the Aboriginal people she encountered. Evidence from her research notebooks clearly shows that her husband alone observed and made notes on men-only dances, then described to her the steps performed, with Dean restricted from attending these particular ceremonies. Clearly, she was positioned in the audience herself, by the Aboriginal people, as a woman.

In the published book this fact was something that had to be negotiated carefully. An episode at an initiation ceremony where all the women, Dean included, fled from the ground at the sound of the bullroarer,[65] was reworked with some poetic license so as to have occurred at an earlier part of the ceremony. Here, having implied that she had only joined the women's departure because the panic had alarmed her (rather than because she was obliged to), the incident was used as a device to indicate Dean's difference from Aboriginal women: 'It was obvious that centuries of taboo were too deeply ingrained in the lubra soul for the women ever to disobey the rule not to disturb "blackfellow business".'[66] No mention was made of Dean having covered her eyes during the lead-up (the 'women covered their eyes at specific moments in the ceremony—as I myself did with my notebooks', she had written in her notes), nor of the two boy 'escorts' who held her hands and ensured that she did leave when required.[67]

These young boys played another, inverted role in the book, as pre-initiates from whom she, as the knowledgeable observer, withheld taboo knowledge. As Dean was writing in her notebooks, she found 'Gordon, her shadow, was at her elbow, spelling out words', and 'since so much of her notes was of things taboo to uninitiated boys, she changed into French, which intrigued and mystified

---

61   'Permit to Enter and Be Upon an Aboriginal Reserve', stamped 14 July 1953, *Dean Papers* ML MSS 7804/24.

62   Dean and Carell, *Dust for the Dancers*, 5; Beth Dean and Victor Carell, *Twin Journey: To Sing, To Dance, To Live* (Sydney: Pacific Publications, 1983), 152–3; Victoria Haskins, 'The Smoking Buggy', in *Off the Beaten Track: A journey across the nation*, ed. Allison Russell (Birdwood: National Motor Museum, 2008), 76–7.

63   Mountford to Carells, 2 February 1953, notations by Dean dated April 1999, *Dean Papers* MLMSS 7804/24.

64   Beth Dean, Victor Carell and Roland Litchfield, *Carrumbo; 'to take a long journey'*, motion picture, General Motors-Holden Ltd, n.d., c. 1954. Copy available at Mitchell Library, Sydney.

65   'An experience at an initiation ceremony … Beth Dean', *Dean Papers* ML MSS 7804/34.

66   Dean and Carell, *Dust for the Dancers*, 173–4.

67   An experience at an initiation ceremony … Beth Dean', *Dean Papers* ML MSS 7804/34.

him'. Trying unsuccessfully to keep him and his friend Charlie from catching a 'glimpse of a rough sketch of a tjurunga' (a sacred object owned by an initiated man, not to be seen by non-initiates), she was obliged to close the book altogether: 'Again Beth felt the sense of having no hiding place.'[68] While there are indeed pages written in 'schoolgirl French' (although no accompanying sketch of a tjuringa) amongst Dean's papers, alongside these notes she provided the information that she had as her constant 'companions' two daughters of one of the senior elders, who explained 'what to do at strategic moments' in the ceremonies.[69] In using such a semi-fictional and transgressive anecdote to place herself in a position of knowledge and authority over uninitiated youths in her published account, Dean again sought to distance herself from the gender constraints imposed by her Aboriginal hosts.

She also, significantly, sought to distance herself from the gender constraints upon white women in central and northern Australia. Typically, it was white women who acted as the conduit enabling Dean to meet local Aboriginal women and view their performances. At Mt Doreen station in central Australia, for instance, the owner's wife announced she had a 'surprise' for her guests, following dinner. She led the party around 'the back of the sheds' to find 'all the camp girls' waiting beside their small camp fires to perform a special series of women's dances. Dean reported that the 'dancing women,' painted in black and white designs, demonstrated 'a complete series of secret Yowulyu "women business" dances' for their audience. Dean was convinced that the station-owner's wife, Doreen Braitling, was oblivious to their real meaning:

> The large number of stanzas, sixty-nine in all, told in delicate stylization the full story of lovemaking—gradually evolving it from the first tentative manner of womenkind, to coitus and its resulting languor. All was done symbolically, beautifully, modestly, so much so, that we felt sure that Mrs. Braitling had very little idea of what the girls were telling, with their often gracious, sometimes oddly tense dance movements.

> These dances are so stylistic in arrangement, that the station women everywhere who have seen them are seldom aware of their actual significance and deeply psychological origins. They find them lovely and charming to watch, even as we did.[70]

---

68   Dean and Carell, *Dust for the Dancers*, 168.

69   Red exercise book, 'Strehlow — Ayers Rock Rain Luritja Dance — Raelene', *Dean Papers* ML MSS 7804/33.

70   Dean and Carell, *Dust for the Dancers*, 140–1.

Despite Dean's dependence on women like Doreen Braitling, the portrait presented cemented the difference of 'station women' not only from Aboriginal women but also from the world-travelling dance scholar and ethnologist Beth Dean.

> Mrs Braitling is a charming, capable and sincere woman, who has lived most of her life in this secluded spot with only her husband, her son and the tribe of blacks. Her days are busy, and she works hard at her responsibility of feeding her "family"—for the blacks are dependent on the station homestead for much of their food. Each day she bakes at least sixty large loaves of snowy white bread. All water must be brought to the house in forty-four gallon drums from a small creek a few miles away. With all her busy life, Mrs. Braitling has still found time to be not only interested in but sympathetic toward her aborigines.[71]

As evidence for this, Braitling showed her visitors her personal collection of Aboriginal artefacts, including a tjuringa that her husband had reportedly been given by one of the Aboriginal men. In truth, Dean also depended on her husband to access and display Aboriginal men's culture. But in asserting her understanding of Aboriginal women's sexuality in contrast to her hostess' ignorance, Dean made a powerful, and profoundly gendered, claim for authority.

Were the white men of the party in the audience for these women's dances? As with the other accounts of watching women's dancing in *Dust for the Dancers*, a blurring of masculine and feminine viewpoint made it impossible for the reader to discern when Dean or her husband was the witness. But throughout the book a framing white male gaze was adopted, authority derived from male anthropological knowledge and proven by a frank recognition (and appreciation) of Aboriginal female sexuality. The most powerful statement of the book's perspective resides in the startling voyeuristic images of nubile and naked young girls that appear throughout the book.[72] The message is clear here: the white audience for Aboriginal women was male.

It is possible that Mrs Braitling actually knew more about Aboriginal women and sex than did her guests. Back in 1940, Strehlow had inspected the Braitlings' property, in his capacity as an Aboriginal Patrol Officer, and found that over half of the thirty-three adults tested at the Aboriginal camp had venereal disease (gonorrhoea). There was, Strehlow felt, a very 'low morale of the native community here' in contrast to 'other groups'.[73] Two years later, another patrol officer visiting the station found the children and women there to be 'all naked and in a "deplorable condition"':

---

71 Dean and Carell, *Dust for the Dancers*, 140.
72 Dean and Carell, *Dust for the Dancers*, 56, 101, 127, 128, 179.
73 Hill, *Broken Song*, 339.

The semi-starvation in which they wage their constant battle against a hostile milieu was apparent in their thin limbs and haggard faces. A constant chorus of coughing, spitting and the crying of hungry children arose. My cook worked half the night making johnny cakes from our slender stock, and we did what we could for them.[74]

In light of these two horrific reports, Dean's observations a decade later about Mrs Braitling's 'busy' days baking bread for her Aboriginal 'family' and her inability to recognise the sexuality of the Aboriginal women have a peculiarly macabre ring. White women like Olive Pink were denied the gaze of the colonising white man precisely because of what they might see from that perspective: white male violence against Aboriginal people, sexual and otherwise.[75] But Beth Dean never offered any such challenge to white patriarchal authority. Instead, she allied herself with the white man in her complacent description of Aboriginal women's sexuality: 'sex is as ordinary a part of normal life to the natives as thirst and hunger'.[76]

In some ways, however, Dean's interest in Aboriginal women's dances and the gender divisions in Aboriginal dance culture can be read as a challenge to the very patriarchal attitudes that dominated anthropology, and indeed the wider white Australian society, at the time. She was careful to identify which dances were women's and which were men's dances, her notes scattered with comments such as: 'MATARANKA Buffalo Dance—Women only Dance—Men only may sing—Very strict on this'.[77] She was clearly irritated by the common assumption that Aboriginal women didn't perform 'corroboree',[78] making sure some women's dances were included in the ballet. Like Margaret McArthur, the nutritionist on Mountford's 1948 expedition, Dean seems to have celebrated the existence of women's dances as evidence of Aboriginal women's wellbeing and empowerment.[79]

A review of the ballet sent to her before publication stated, mistakenly, that as women were 'traditionally kept away from significant ceremonies', Dean's female dancers were actually impersonating males. This drew from her the terse

---

74   Quoted in Hill, *Broken Song*, 366–7.

75   Marilyn Lake, 'Frontier Feminism and the Marauding White Man', *Journal of Australian Studies: Australian Frontiers* 49 (1996): 12–20.

76   Dean and Carell, *Dust for the Dancers*, 140–1.

77   'Notes on a Table Listing Different Dances', *Dean Papers* ML MSS 7804/34.

78   Her attempts to refute this belief recur in her book, Beth Dean, *The Many Worlds of Dance* (Sydney: K. G. Murray, 1966), 39, and in her public talks: *Dean Papers* ML MSS 7804/8.

79   See also Harris, this volume.

response: 'note: women do appear. Beth Dean'.[80] After Dean's intervention, the reviewer eventually published an article in which he made more of the taboos she and her husband had been able to evade, instead:

> Some of the secret and sacred dances of the initiation ceremonies, which are strictly taboo for women, were taken down by Mr Carell, whereas Beth Dean was admitted to the exclusive women's dances. As so far most explorers and ethnologists had been men, the existence of many of these dances had not even been suspected. Elated with the result of their work, having gathered fresh material which was "good theatre", the two returned to civilisation.[81]

Of course, the 'taboos' around male performance were those that most titillated the white audiences and would give a particular frisson to Dean's performance as a male initiate.

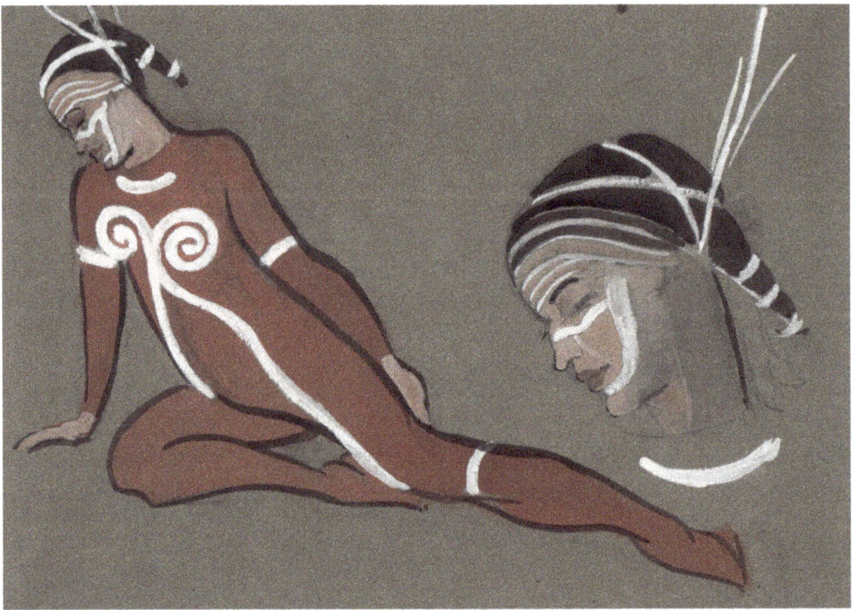

Figure 3: A sketch of Beth Dean in costume for the ballet *Corroboree*, dated 1950. William Constable, 1906 Bendigo, Victoria—1989 Melbourne, Victoria. Drawing, pencil, ink and goache on cream paper, 38.7 cm h x 53 cm w.

Source: National Museum of Australia Collection (1997.0047.0062).

Conclusion

Beth Dean was in a paradoxical position—and not only when she donned the brown tights and pancake make-up to impersonate a male initiate. An emancipated modern woman transcending not only national borders but the boundaries of race and gender, she remained critically dependent upon the support, and indeed endorsement, of the white male expert to achieve her aims. As a representative of a white female audience, Dean vicariously allowed white women to feel that they too could breach the barriers that were 'too deeply ingrained in the lubra soul', and enter into a field of knowledge and power hitherto dominated by white male anthropologists. But whereas the implication was that Dean had transcended these barriers in central Australia, as in the ballet, in fact, she had not.

In the recurrent narrative describing her life's journey Dean chose to allocate a symbolically powerful role to Charles Pearcy Mountford as her inspiration and catalyst. Undoubtedly the meeting between Mountford and the young couple in New York was pivotal for Dean, yet she was just one of many keen and enthusiastic women of her time, seeking benediction for her project. Mountford himself would probably have forgotten her had she not had the determination to persist and to bind his authority to him as tightly as she could. For Dean, Mountford was a kind of elder, conferring the wisdom and status of the white male anthropologist upon her. Dean described her ballet as 'a hymn of praise for Aboriginal traditional life',[82] but the gender and racial transgression she performed in *Corroboree* in many ways represented rather a tribute to the authority of the white male expert, and a quest to replicate his experiences.

And yet at the same time Dean—whether she realised or acknowledged the fact—was part of a longer tradition of white women contesting male authority indirectly through representing and producing cross-cultural knowledges. Her success was in large part due not to the authority that her association with Mountford invested, but to the nature of her times, when efforts by newly privileged white women like herself, to assert their ability to transcend once immutable barriers, met with acclaim and delight. In *Dust for the Dancers*, the initiation ceremonies were described as 'an expression of the utmost feeling and purpose' that would enable 'the boy [to] take his place among the men of the tribe … not going, as before, only with the women. During the ceremonials he would take his place as a man.'[83] So too, we might venture, did Beth Dean take her place.

---

82   'Notes on the ballet CORROBOREE', c. 1954, Letters and notes related to Beth Dean Carell's ballet career, *Beth Dean Carell Collection no. 1*, National Museum of Australia, Canberra.
83   Dean and Carell, *Dust for the Dancers*, 184.

Acknowledgements

The original research for this study was carried out under the auspices of a Council of Australian State Libraries Fellowship in 2006–2007 and supported by an internal grant from the University of Newcastle. I would also like to acknowledge the input and advice of colleagues at the University of Sydney's PARADISEC Sydney Seminar Series in 2011, especially that of Martin Thomas, and the generosity of the William Constable estate, the National Museum of Australia, and the State Library of NSW, in allowing the images herein to be reproduced.

References

Anderson, Jim. '"A glorious thing is to live in a tent in the infinite": Daisy Bates', in *Uncommon Ground: White women in Aboriginal history,* eds Anna Cole, Victoria Haskins and Fiona Paisley (Canberra: Aboriginal Studies Press, 2005), 217–31

Bruce, Candice and Anita Callaway. 'Wild Nights and Savage Festivities: White views of corroborees', *Art and Australia* 27:2 (1989), 269–75.

Bruce, Candice and Anita Callaway. 'Dancing in the Dark: Black corroboree or white spectacle?', *Australian Journal of Art* 9 (1991): 79–104.

Buller-Murphy, Deborah. *An Attempt to Eat the Moon and Other Stories Recounted from the Aborigines* (Melbourne: Georgian House, 1958).

Burridge, Stephanie. *The Impact of Aboriginal Dance on Twentieth Century Australian Choreography with a Practical and Creative Study* (PhD, London Contemporary Dance School at The Place, University of Kent at Canterbury, 1997).

Card, Amanda. 'From "Aboriginal Dance" to Aboriginals Dancing: The appropriation of the "primitive" in Australian dance', in *Speaking of History: Dance scholarship in the '90s: Proceedings of Society of Dance Scholars Nineteenth Annual Conference* (Minnesota: University of Minnesota, 1996), 115–26.

Card, Amanda. 'From "Aboriginal Dance" to Aboriginals Dancing: The appropriation of the "primitive" in Australian Dance, 1950 to 1963', in *Heritage and Heresy: Green Mill Papers 1997* (Canberra: Australian Dance Council, 1998), 40–6.

Card, Amanda and Carole Y. Johnson. 'Aboriginal Influences', in *Currency Companion to Music & Dance in Australia,* eds John Whiteoak and Aline Scott-Maxwell (Sydney: Currency House, 2003), 20–3.

Cooke, Glenn R. 'Aboriginal Motifs in the Decorative Arts, "an art for Australia from Australians"', in *Motif and Meaning: Aboriginal influences in Australian art 1930–1970,* ed. Claire Baddley (Ballarat: Ballarat Fine Art Gallery, 1999), 9–16.

Cubillo, Franchesca. 'I drew very close to these men, sharing their dilemma …: Elizabeth Durack', in *Uncommon Ground: White women in Aboriginal history,* eds Anna Cole, Victoria Haskins and Fiona Paisley (Canberra: Aboriginal Studies Press, 2005), 232–40.

Dean, Beth. *The Many Worlds of Dance* (Sydney: K. G. Murray, 1966).

Dean, Beth and Victor Carell. *Dust for the Dancers* (Sydney: Ure Smith, 1955).

Dean, Beth and Victor Carell. *Twin Journey: To sing, to dance, to live* (Sydney: Pacific Publications, 1983).

Durack, Mary and Elizabeth Durack. *All-About: The story of a black community on Argyle Station, Kimberley* (Sydney: The Bulletin, 1935).

Ewers, John K. *With the Sun on My Back* (Sydney: Angus & Robertson, 1953).

Fitzgerald, Mary A. *King Bungaree's Pyalla and Stories Illustrative of Manners and Customs that Prevailed Among Australian Aborigines* (Sydney: William Brooks & Co, 1891).

Haebich, Anna. 'Assimilation and Hybrid Art: Reflections on the politics of Aboriginal art', in *The Art of Politics The Politics of Art: The place of contemporary Indigenous art,* ed. Fiona Foley (Southport: Keeaira Press, 2006).

Haebich, Anna. *Spinning the Dream: Assimilation in Australia 1950–1970* (Fremantle: Fremantle Press, 2008).

Haebich, Anna and Jodie Taylor. 'Modern Primitives Leaping and Stomping the Earth: From ballet to bush doofs', *Aboriginal History* 31 (2007): 63–84.

Hammergren, Lena. 'Many Sources, Many Voices', in *Rethinking Dance History: A reader,* ed. Alexandra Carter (London: Routledge, 2004), 20–31.

Haskins, Victoria. 'Dancing in the Dust: A gendered history of indigenising Australian cultural identity', in *Intersections: Gender, race and ethnicity in Australasian studies,* eds Margaret Allen and R K Dhawan (New Delhi: Prestige, 2007), 55–75.

Haskins, Victoria. 'The Smoking Buggy', in *Off the Beaten Track: A journey across the nation,* ed. Allison Russell (Birdwood: National Motor Museum, 2008), 72–81.

Haskins, Victoria. 'To Touch the Infinity of a Far Horizon: A transnational history of transcultural appropriation in Beth Dean's *Corroboree 1954*', *Australasian Drama Studies* 59 (2011): 23–38.

Hill, Barry. *Broken Song: T. G. H. Strehlow and Aboriginal possession* (Sydney: Vintage, 2003).

Holmes, Robyn. 'Australian Music Editing and Authenticity: "Would the real Mrs Monk please stand up?"', in *The Editorial Gaze: Mediating texts in literature and the arts,* eds Paul Eggert and Margaret Sankey (Oxon: Routledge, 2013), 209–26.

Jordan, Caroline. *Picturesque Pursuits: Colonial women artists and the amateur tradition* (Melbourne: Melbourne University Press, 2005).

Kociumbas, Jan. 'Performances: Indigenisation and postcolonial culture', in *Cultural History in Australia,* eds Hsu-Ming Teo and Richard White (Sydney: UNSW Press, 2003), 127–41.

Lake, Marilyn. 'Feminist History as National History: Writing the political history of women', *Australian Historical Studies* 27:106 (1996): 154–69.

Lake, Marilyn. 'Frontier Feminism and the Marauding White Man', *Journal of Australian Studies: Australian Frontiers* 49 (1996): 12–20.

Lawson, Valerie. 'Dancer Many Steps Ahead of Her Time: Beth Dean Carell 1918–2012', *Sydney Morning Herald*, 12 May 2012.

Marcus, Julie. 'The Beauty, Simplicity and Honour of Truth: Olive Pink in the 1940s', in *First in their Field: Women and Australian anthropology*, ed. Julie Marcus (Melbourne: Melbourne University Press, 1993), 111–35.

Maynard, John. 'Light in the Darkness: Elizabeth McKenzie-Hatton', in *Uncommon Ground: White women in Aboriginal history,* eds Anna Cole, Victoria Haskins and Fiona Paisley (Canberra: Aboriginal Studies Press, 2005), 3–27.

McGregor, Russell. *Imagined Destinies: Aboriginal Australians and the doomed race theory, 1880–1939* (Melbourne: Melbourne University Press, 1997).

McGuire, Madeline E. 'The Legend of the Good Fella Missus', *Aboriginal History* 14:2 (1990): 135–9.

Merlan, Francesca. 'Gender in Aboriginal Social Life: A review', in *Social Anthropology and Australian Aboriginal Studies,* eds R M Berndt and R Tonkinson (Canberra: Australian Institute of Aboriginal Studies, 1988), 19–45.

Niall, Brenda. *Seven Little Billabongs: The world of Ethel Turner and Mary Grant Bruce* (Melbourne: Melbourne University Press, 1979).

Niall, Brenda. *True North: The story of Mary and Elizabeth Durack* (Melbourne: Text Publishing, 2012).

Parker, K. Langloh. *Australian Legendary Tales* (Middlesex: Tiger Books, 1998).

Pask, Edward H. *Ballet in Australia: The second act 1940–1980* (Melbourne: Oxford University Press, 1982).

Patten, J. T. and W. Ferguson, *Aborigines Claim Citizen Rights!* (Sydney: The Publicist, 1938).

Potter, Michelle. 'Making Australian Dance: Themes and variations', *Voices* (1996): 10–20.

Riddett, Lyn A. '"Be Aboriginal": Settler women artists inspired by Aboriginal artists', *Northern Perspective* 19:1 (1996): 51–60.

Rowley, C. D. *The Destruction of Aboriginal Society* (Ringwood: Penguin, 1986).

Russell, Penny. 'Cultures of Distinction', in *Cultural History in Australia,* eds Hsu-Ming Teo and Richard White (Sydney: UNSW Press, 2003), 158–71

Sayers, Andrew. *Aboriginal Artists of the Nineteenth Century* (Melbourne: Oxford University Press, 1994).

Stone, Walter W., ed. *Charles Pearcy Mountford: An annotated bibliography* (Cremorne: The Stone Copying Company, 1958).

Thomas, Martin. 'A Short History of the 1948 Arnhem Land Expedition', *Aboriginal History* 34 (2010): 143–70.

Thomson, John. 'It's Australian – and it's good!' *National Library of Australia News* 14:3 (2003), http://www.australianmusicals.com/article_itsaustralian.htm.

Unattributed biography. 'Dean, Beth (1918–2012)', *Australia Dancing*, accessed 14 March 2012, http://www.australiadancing.org/subjects/26.html.

Vignando, Catrina. 'Corroboree: Aboriginal inspiration in contemporary Australian ballet,' *Olive Pink Society Bulletin* 3:2 (1991): 10–14.

W., M. H. 'Queen Rosie's Requiem', *Sydney Morning Herald*, 21 June 1932.

West, J., ed. *Collits' Inn: A romantic Australian operetta by T Stuart Gurr with lyrics and music by Varney Monk* (Sydney: Currency Press, 1990).

Young, John Atherton, ed. *Jane Bardsley's Outback Letterbook, Across the Years 1896–1936* (Sydney: Angus & Robertson, 1987).

3. The Circle of Songs: Traditional Song and the Musical Score to C. P. Mountford's Documentary Films

Anthony Linden Jones

This chapter interrogates the process of incorporation of traditional Aboriginal song[1] into the context of musical underscore[2] for two documentary films using Western orchestral instrumentation. I contextualise these practices in the history of ethnographic film-making in Australia and contemporary film scoring practices up to the time of these films and examine the impact of the limitations of recording technology on film composers' interpretation of the songs. By placing the scores in their historical and cultural context and employing a range of analytic tools, I aim to consider how these acts of appropriation of culturally significant artefacts might be understood today.

Why should we concern ourselves with the musical underscore of a film, rather than just with the visual or narrative content? In *Unheard Melodies* (1987), Claudia Gorbman highlights the power of music to influence our engagement with the narrative of a film, made more powerful through its unconscious reception:

> Every moviegoer, every film scholar, tin ear notwithstanding, becomes aware from time to time of the ubiquity and psychological power of music in dramatic films. Such moments of lucidity tend to occur when we take note of how shamelessly emotional or copious a film score has been: what has been blaring in the background the entire time suddenly comes to the foreground of consciousness. Suddenly the story is perceived to inhabit a world strangely replete with musical sound, rhythm, signification … until, a few scenes or measures later, we drop off, become re-invested in the story again. Then the music is "working" once more, masking its own insistence and sawing away in the backfield of consciousness.[3]

---

1   For the purpose of this chapter, 'song' refers to accompanied or unaccompanied singing. In this instance, the traditional songs are captured in field recordings which thus represent a particular instantiation of a song, frozen in time.

2   The term 'underscore' relates to music placed under narration or dialogue in a film. The term is often used synonymously with 'score', but always relates to the music heard rather than the music on paper. Whereas 'score' can mean either the music heard or the music on paper. The melody of songs can be used as an influence in the composition of non-vocal underscore.

3   Claudia Gorbman, *Unheard Melodies: Narrative film music* (Bloomington: Indiana University Press, 1987), 1.

Musical underscore mediates an emotional affiliation between the spectator and the characters and narrative of a film. By deconstructing the underscore, we can uncover an important element of the intended emotional communication of a film. This is especially relevant in the context of documentary film where music is used to unconsciously influence our engagement with real people and cultures.

Travelling with the 1948 American-Australian Expedition to Arnhem Land in the far north of Australia, expedition leader Charles P. Mountford and cameraman Peter Basset-Smith captured audio recordings and shot silent documentary footage of traditional Aboriginal song and ceremony, places, and wildlife. From the footage, three films were compiled with narration, sound effects, composed music and field recordings of traditional song: *Aborigines of the Sea Coast*, *Birds and Billabongs*, and *Arnhem Land*. The US cameraman Howell Walker also travelled with the Arnhem Land Expedition and shot footage for compilation into films to be produced by the National Geographic Society. For this present discussion, I shall consider only the Australian-produced films; 'Arnhem Land Expedition films' in this chapter should be taken here to refer to those films only.

For the composition of the musical underscore for the three sound films, Mountford called on the services of composers Alfred and Mirrie Hill. To inform them of the musical life of the Aboriginal people of Arnhem Land, Mountford organised for Alfred and Mirrie Hill to be supplied with a collection of field recordings of Aboriginal song. Inspired by the idea of incorporating Aboriginal song into the scores for the films, Alfred and Mirrie Hill transcribed a number of the songs. Their transcriptions feature significantly in the scores to two of the Arnhem Land Expedition films: *Aborigines of the Sea Coast*,[4] and *Arnhem Land*.[5]

Before looking at the Arnhem Land Expedition films, I give a brief history of ethnographic filmmaking practice in Australia and the historical events that shaped its path. Included is a discussion of the artistic movement of the Jindyworobaks in literature and in music. After detailing the background to the establishment of the Arnhem Land Expedition, I focus on the use of traditional song as inspiration for the composition of scores to the two Arnhem Land Expedition films.

---

4   The film is named in different archives as either *Aborigines of the Sea Coast*, or *Aborigines of the Seacoast*. Mountford, Charles P. *Aborigines of the Sea Coast*. (Lindfield: Film Australia, 1951). Preservation copies of both the original film of 1950 and an edited version made in 1973 are held in different formats under the same title number at the National Film and Sound Archive of Australia (NFSA). Mountford, C.P., dir. 'Aborigines of the Seacoast', *Film Australia Collection*, title no. 54, NFSA, Canberra, 1950.

5   Also referred to in correspondence as *The Natural History of Arnhem Land*, or *Expedition to Arnhem Land*. This last was also the title for a radio documentary produced by Colin Simpson of the Australian Broadcasting Commission. The film is held in preservation copies: Mountford, C.P., 'Arnhem Land', *Film Australia Collection*, title no. 703, NFSA, Canberra, 1950.

Ethnographic Film and Nationalism in Australia

Soon after the development of moving pictures at the end of the nineteenth century, storytellers and adventurers in Australia quickly recognised the potential of the technology to allow the creation of uniquely Australian stories and capture on film elements of Australian life, beginning with the story films produced by the Limelight Department of the Salvation Army in Melbourne.[6] However, the value of film as a tool for anthropological study took some time to establish. Although some of the earliest ethnographic films had been made in Australia—Alfred Cort Haddon's films of the Mer people of the Torres Strait Islands in 1898, and Baldwin Spencer's central Australian films of 1901 and of Arnhem Land in 1912—there was a reluctance by the academic anthropological community in those early decades to trust in the veracity of film as an ethnographic record.[7] However, a growing awareness of the uniqueness and variety of Aboriginal Australian cultures, generally considered doomed to imminent demise[8] heightened a sense of urgency to capture records of what remained, drawing researchers of the University of Adelaide to make a significant body of films through the 1930s.[9]

Five days after the outbreak of the war in Europe, on 8 September 1939 the Australian federal government formed the Department of Information (DOI) to establish control over the flow of information in a time of international conflict. Soon thereafter, the Film Division was formed as a division of the DOI tasked to commission film production as part of the war effort.[10] The isolation imposed by the remoteness of the continent from Great Britain during the conflict, and Australia's engagement in the conflict in the Pacific, served to foster a sense of independent nationhood.[11] The artistic community in Australia began to look at those elements which marked a differentiation from Europe, making tentative steps towards the celebration of Aboriginal culture.

In April 1945, one month before the surrender of Germany in Europe, the Australian National Film Board was established and tasked to expand, promote and coordinate Australian documentary, educational and instructional films for

---

6   Graham Shirley and Brian Adams, *Australian Cinema, The first eighty years* (Sydney: Currency Press, 1989), 10.

7   Alison Margaret Griffiths, *Origins of Ethnographic Film* (PhD, New York University, 1998), 4.

8   This perception was highlighted by the writings of amateur ethnologist Daisy Bates, among others, as discussed at length in the book: Bob Reece, *Daisy Bates: Grand dame of the desert*, ed. Carol Natsis (Canberra: National Library of Australia, 2007).

9   Ian Dunlop, 'Ethnographic Filmmaking in Australia: The first seventy years (1898–1968)', *Studies in Visual Communication* 9:1 (1983): 12.

10   Graham Shirley, Manager: Access Projects, NFSA, private communication, 26 February 2013; National Archives of Australia. 'Commonwealth Film Unit: Fact sheet 25', (2013), accessed 12 February 2013, http://www.naa.gov.au/collection/fact-sheets/fs25.aspx

11   Geoffrey Blainey, *The Tyranny of Distance: How distance shaped Australia's history* (Sydney: Macmillan, 2001).

exhibition in Australia and abroad. The DOI was the instrument of the Board in production, and was responsible to the Board, while the National Library was its instrument in the acquisition and distribution of films.

In 1950, the Menzies Government dissolved the DOI and control of the Film Division was transferred to the Australian News and Information Bureau (ANIB). In 1973, the Whitlam Government created the Department of Media, to which the Film Division was again transferred, and soon renamed Film Australia. In 2008, Film Australia was absorbed into the government film funding and advocacy body Screen Australia. On 1 July 2011, the Film Australia collection, a collection of over 5,000 films, was transferred from Screen Australia into the holdings of the National Film and Sound Archives of Australia in Canberra.[12]

Although the technology to record synchronised sound for film had first appeared in the late 1920s, the equipment required for sound was bulky and expensive, had significant power requirements and stringent operational limits for temperature and humidity, which was not practical for ethnographic field recording. Until that time, with the exception of big studio films, films would be filmed silent, with sound applied in 'post-production'.[13] It would not be until the development of lightweight tape recording with the capability for synchronisation to film in the 1960s that recording of synchronised sound for film in remote locations would be feasible.

By the time of the production of the Arnhem Land Expedition films, synchronised sound in film had been available for a little over twenty years, yet the conventions of film music had been established and reaffirmed through another earlier forty years of musical accompaniment to silent film. The films made in the Hollywood studio system from the beginning of the twentieth century became the technical and aesthetic standard against which most other national cinema practices were measured. As a result, a number of filmmaking conventions were established as an 'institutional practice for the regulation of nondiegetic music in film',[14] such as the idea that music for a film should fill all the gaps between sound effects and dialogue so as to banish silence, and that the music should use Western orchestral instruments and be usually written in a late-nineteenth century Romantic style.[15] The wider community in Australia had had very little exposure to traditional Aboriginal song and instrumentation, and the perceived 'alien'

---

12 National Archives of Australia. 'Commonwealth Film Unit: Fact sheet 25', (2013), accessed 12 February 2013, http://www.naa.gov.au/collection/fact-sheets/fs25.aspx.

13 James McCarthy, retired Music Officer of Film Australia, personal communication, 17 February 2013.

14 Diegetic music is that which appears to come from within the scene and that the characters on screen can be assumed to hear. Nondiegetic music is therefore music external to the scene, such as musical underscore applied later. Kathryn Kalinak, *Settling the Score: Music and the classical Hollywood film*, (Madison: University of Wisconsin Press, 1992), xiv.

15 A number of complementary explanations have been offered as to why this should be so. See Caryl Flinn, *Strains of Utopia: Gender, nostalgia and Hollywood film music*, (Princeton: Princeton University Press, 1992),

and 'primitive' nature of the music would have made the idea of a Western score based primarily on traditional song almost unthinkable in the context of a film intended for public non-specialist viewing. The documentary films in this study were intended to entertain as much as to inform, and so conventional processes of musical accompaniment were expected without question.

In the late 1930s, an artistic movement had formed in literature, the Jindyworobaks — a term coined by poet Rex Ingamells in a credo he published in 1938, from a Woiwurrung word for 'to join'. The Jindyworobaks took as their inspiration aspects of the language and stories of Aboriginal culture, yet were working in idioms taken from the European culture from which they hoped to distance themselves.[16] In subsequent decades, a number of composers of music became interested in incorporating aspects of traditional Aboriginal culture and language into their composition practice. The practices of these composers have retrospectively been compared to the Jindyworobaks, even though they did not identify themselves as part of a coherent group.[17] Composers usually identified with this approach include Alfred and Mirrie Hill, Clive Douglas, John Antill, Margaret Sutherland, James Penberthy, and Peter Sculthorpe. In addition to composing concert music, most of these composers had an involvement with the composition of music for documentary films as a way of securing an income. With the exception of Peter Sculthorpe in the final decade of his life, these composers appear to have been less concerned to engage with Aboriginal people in the making of music than to create their own filtered view of Aboriginality—seen as a source of influence to colour or exoticise European processes of music making. While for the most part these composers were content to draw only from language and stories in the creation of their 'Aboriginal' works, there were a few who would go further and incorporate elements of Aboriginal traditional song, taking the suggestion from Henry Tate, writing in 1924:

> Aboriginal music is surprisingly interesting. Wild and barbaric as much of it sounds, it is rich in rhythms and themes that, once annotated and fixed, will supply a copious reservoir of melodic gems and rhythmical fragments of the type that composers all over the world are continually seeking.[18]

4; Mark Slobin, 'The Steiner Superculture', in *Global Soundtracks: Worlds of film music*, ed. Mark Slobin (Middleton: Wesleyan University Press, 2008), 12; Anahid Kassabian, *Hearing Film: Tracking identifications in contemporary Hollywood film music* (New York: Routledge, 2001), 58.

16   The movement is detailed in David Symons, 'The Jindyworobak Connection in Australian Music, c. 1940–1960', *Context: Journal of music research* 23 (2002): 35.

17   Symons debates the suitability of this term to composers in Symons, 'The Jindyworobak Connection': 47.

18   Quoted in Christine Mercer, 'Henry Tate: Views on the artistic possibilities of Aboriginal music', in *Encounters: Meetings in Australian music: Essays, images, interviews*, eds Vincent Plush, Huib Schippers and Jocelyn Wolfe (Brisbane: Queensland Conservatorium Research Centre, 2005): 23.

What spurred Alfred and Mirrie Hill on to engaging with Aboriginal song is not certain. Alfred had certainly been interested in Māori culture in New Zealand, although his engagement to write the score to the film *Adventures in Maoriland* was terminated in 1930 because of a disagreement with the Hollywood director Alexander Markey.[19] Alfred and Mirrie Hill were aware of John Antill's ballet *Corroboree*, although Mirrie states that they did not see a performance of the ballet until the Beth Dean production of 1954.[20] John Antill had been a composition student of Alfred's at the NSW Conservatorium of Music, and Alfred and Mirrie were friends of the conductor Eugene Goossens, so it is likely they would have heard a performance of the concert suite of *Corroboree* and may also have seen the score. Their first introduction to genuine Australian Aboriginal music might have been through the act of writing for Mountford's films, and for both composers, the fascination would not be long sustained. Each wrote only a small number of pieces using Aboriginal song over the next couple of years. In the early 1960s, after the death of Alfred, Mirrie Hill did set a number of poems written by Dame Mary Gilmore (a poet associated with the Jindyworobak movement) under the title *Aboriginal Themes*, but in this instance she chose not to use Aboriginal song as source material.

Mountford's Ethnographic Films

Conducting expeditions to central Australia in 1940 and 1942, South Australian amateur ethnologist Charles P. Mountford made the films *Brown Men and Red Sand/Walkabout* and *Brown Men and Blue Mountains/Tjurunga*. In creating an underscore for the films, an assortment of 'production' or 'library' music was used—no music was purpose-written for the film.[21] The production music provides a buffer between phrases of Mountford's own narration but bears little relevance to the images or the narration. A couple of the production music clips used in the film exhibit characteristic musical stereotypes of the kind typically used at that time in Hollywood films to represent North American First

---

19   Peter Limbrick, *Making Settler Cinemas: Film and colonial encounters in the United States, Australia and New Zealand* (New York: Palgrave Macmillan, 2010), 153.

20   Mirrie Hill, 'Mirrie Hill Interviewed by Hazel De Berg' in *Hazel De Berg Collection*, National Library of Australia, Canberra, 10 June 1975, henceforth *De Berg Interview*.

21   Even before the technology for synchronisation of sound and film was developed in the late 1920s, British and US music publishing companies were producing and promoting libraries of printed or recorded music intended for use either with specific films or for general synchronisation in different end-uses. The recorded 'production' or 'library' music would be available on 78 rpm discs for individual purchase or regular subscription by film or radio producers or other potential clients. To use this music, clients would pay a licensing fee dependent on the type of use and the size of the territory to be covered.

Nations peoples—for example, grunting ostinato figures, harmonic intervals of parallel fourths, and pentatonic scales.[22] These musical stereotypes bear little resemblance to any traditional Australian Aboriginal music.

Mountford used these two films as the basis of a successful series of lectures in Australia in 1945. Looking for opportunities to strengthen relationships between Australia and the US, the Australian government sent Mountford to conduct lecture tours there. While in the US, Mountford was able to begin discussions with the National Geographic Society and, through them, the Smithsonian Institution on the possibility of a cooperative expedition to Arnhem Land. These discussions culminated in the formation of the Arnhem Land Expedition, as a partnership between with the Australian government, the National Geographic Society, and the Smithsonian Institution.[23]

On his return in 1946, Mountford acted as an advisor on the Film Division production of the film *Namatjira, the Painter* (1946) directed by Stanley Hawes. The musical underscore for the film is quite indifferent to the subject matter of the film, but was not unusual for documentary music of the time. For this film, the brilliant young nineteen-year-old composer/conductor Charles Mackerras, having just completed a score for the short Film Division documentary *Watch Over Japan* (1946), was commissioned to write a score incorporating a surprisingly large orchestra. Unfortunately, although Mackerras' score is a wonderful piece of music in its own right, his orchestration was too big for the film, and was not written to leave space for the narration. As James McCarthy, the Music Officer of the Film Division/Film Australia describes: 'The commentary always came last, so the composers hadn't a hope of adjusting to it. The Canberra bureaucrats … always wanted the last word, right up to the last minute.'[24] We are left with the unintentionally amusing result that at climactic points in the music, the volume is suddenly reduced to allow the narrator's voice to come through. I have found no evidence that Mackerras had considered making reference to Aboriginal music in the score. The primary influences on the music in his score were post-Romantic European composers.

---

22   See examples in Michael V. Pisani, *Imagining Native America in Music* (New Haven: Yale University Press, 2005).

23   For a précis on the establishment of the Arnhem Land Expedition and its political significance, see Martin Thomas, 'A Short History of the 1948 Arnhem Land Expedition', *Aboriginal History* 34 (2010): 143–73.

24   James McCarthy, personal communication, 21 February 2013.

Film and Audio Recordings from the Arnhem Land Expedition

Martin Thomas describes the Arnhem Land Expedition as 'the last of the big expeditions', representing the end of an era of conquest.[25] An international collaboration between Australia and the United States, the Arnhem Land Expedition party included researchers and support staff from the two countries, specialists in various flora and fauna as well as anthropology, Aboriginal art and cultural practice. DOI cinematographer Peter Bassett-Smith travelled with the Arnhem Land Expedition to document in film the findings of the researchers at three different sites in Arnhem Land in the far north of Australia.

Unsynchronised sound was recorded using a wire recorder and an omni-directional dynamic microphone.[26] These represented a much better quality than direct-to-disc recording, but had their own technical limitations.[27] The wire recorder brought on the Arnhem Land Expedition, supplied by the Film Division, failed at the first camp, near Umbakumba on the coast of Groote Eylandt in east Arnhem Land, but not before Mountford was able to record a number of ceremonial songs. From these recordings, Mountford would publish a set of three 78rpm discs of Groote Eylandt songs (disc serial numbers PRX2712–14), one disc of songs recorded at Port Darwin in the weeks before the Arnhem Land Expedition (PRX2715), and two discs entitled *Oenpelli Aboriginal Songs* (PRX2716–17), although these last recordings were not made by him.[28]

Meeting with the Arnhem Land Expedition at Oenpelli for two weeks, were radio producer Colin Simpson of the Australian Broadcasting Commission (now Australian Broadcasting Corporation, ABC) with technical officer Ray Giles of the Post-Master General's department bearing another wire recorder and omni-directional dynamic microphone. Tasked with producing two radio

---

25   Martin Thomas, 'Expedition as Time Capsule: Introducing the American-Australian Scientific Expedition to Arnhem Land', in *Exploring the Legacy of the 1948 Expedition*, eds Margo Neale and Martin Thomas, (Canberra: ANU E Press, 2011), 2.

26   The dynamic microphone has a much more limited 'reach' than a condenser microphone, but does not require power and is much less susceptible to the effects of humidity. These factors would exclude the use of the much more sensitive condenser microphone from field work until more rugged FET-based condenser microphones were produced in the 1960s.

27   Of particular relevance is the effect of speed variations in the wire recorder and their impact on the reception and recognition of voices, important in repatriation efforts. See Anthony L. Jones, '"The Nostalgia of the Audio Souvenir": Technology limitations in the 1948 Arnhem Land field recordings of Colin Simpson', paper presented at the *11th Symposium on Indigenous Music and Dance*, The Australian National University, Canberra, 2 December 2012.

28   Linda Barwick and Allan Marett, 'Aural Snapshots of Musical Life: The 1948 Recordings', in *Exploring the Legacy of the 1948 Arnhem Land Expedition*, eds Martin Thomas and Margo Neale (Canberra: ANU E Press, 2011), 357.

documentaries for the ABC,[29] Simpson and Giles recorded many traditional songs and ceremonies, the sound of morning birds on the lake at Oenpelli, and a wild buffalo hunt. After leaving the Arnhem Land Expedition, Simpson and Giles continued on to Delissaville (now Belyuen), and then Melville Island off the northern coast of Arnhem Land to make more recordings for the planned radio documentaries. These recordings by Simpson and Giles were published as a twelve-disc set of 78rpm discs under the title *Aboriginal Music from the Northern Territory of Australia, 1948, with Annotations by Professor A. P. Elkin* (disc serial numbers PRX2645–52 and PRX2708–11).[30] A number of the recordings made in Oenpelli from this set were given to Mountford in an abbreviated form, and it was these that Mountford published as *Oenpelli Aboriginal Songs* under his own name.

Because of the failure of Mountford's wire recorder at the first camp on Groote Eylandt, no audio recordings were made at Yirrkala, which was the site of the second camp for the expedition and the subject of one of the documentary films, which would be produced. No field recordings of traditional song were carried out at Yirrkala until those of Richard A. Waterman in 1952.

Before the Arnhem Land Expedition, Mountford had proposed the production of five sound films. At the conclusion of the Arnhem Land Expedition after nine months of field work, with 'several miles of colour film on aboriginal life and natural history' to work with, Mountford proposed a new ambitious plan for nine films to be collated from the Arnhem Land Expedition footage.[31] The Film Division was concerned at the potential cost of production of a series of nine films. They also considered that each of the proposed films would not of themselves hold enough interest for their potential audience. After a screening of rough cuts of the nine films on 29 September 1949, it was decided to reduce the series to three sound films for public exhibition, to be called *Arnhem Land* (incorporating scenes from the three different camps), *Birds and Billabongs* (filmed at Oenpelli), and *Aborigines of the Seacoast* (about the people of Yirrkala), with an additional silent film on the Arawaitja ceremony of Groote Eylandt and other unused source footage for Mountford's use in lecture tours.[32] Since Mountford's death in 1976, these have been held at the Australian Institute for Aboriginal and Torres Strait Islander Studies in Canberra.

---

29   Tony MacGregor, 'Birds on the Wire: Wild, sound, informal speech and the emergence of the radio documentary', in *Exploring the Legacy of the 1948 Arnhem Land Expedition*, eds Martin Thomas and Margo Neale (Canberra: ANU E Press, 2011), 87.

30   Barwick and Marett, 'Aural Snapshots of Musical Life', 358.

31   Charles P. Mountford, *Records of the American-Australian Scientific Expedition to Arnhem Land: Vol. 1 'art, myth and symbolism'*, ed. C. P. Mountford (Melbourne: Melbourne University Press, 1956), xxx.

32   'Memo to file (pencil)', in *FPN160 Arnhem Land*, SP1265/1 Part 2, National Archives of Australia (NAA), Sydney, 15 August 1949.

The three sound films, produced for a general audience, would each include narration, limited sound effects (recorded separately),[33] short fragments of field recordings of traditional song, and musical underscoring. Advice was sought from a number of scientists in the writing of the narration for the films on details of the flora and fauna to correct errors in the narration, yet the editing of the films was principally driven by perceived audience interest rather than striving for absolute accuracy. I now look at the process of scoring the films, and then discuss the influence of field-recorded traditional songs in the composition of the musical underscore.

Scoring the Three Arnhem Land Expedition Documentary Films

To write the musical underscore for the three sound films, Mountford and the DOI sought a composer with experience writing for film. A journalist friend of C. P. Mountford lived in the Sydney suburb of Mosman, next door to composers Alfred and Mirrie Hill. Alfred was at that time highly regarded, with an established international reputation as a composer of concert music and popular song. He had already gained some experience by this time in the writing of music for film, both in New Zealand and Australia,[34] although he openly voiced disdain for the process and its inherent constraints—at the age of nearly eighty, he was not known as a patient man.[35] Mirrie, twenty years his junior, was a well-regarded composer, but at that time lacked the extensive experience or the international renown of her husband.

Mountford arranged a meeting with Alfred Hill with the aim of commissioning him to write the scores for the Arnhem Land Expedition films.[36] Mirrie Hill reported a conversation between the two men in two interviews recorded in 1982 and 1975.

> [Alfred] invited Mr Mountford to come up [to our home] … and Mr Mountford said to Alfred he would like him to write the background music for these three films. Without Alfred even asking me, he said "Well, I'll write two … and she can write the other one!". Of course, you know who "she" was!" Well, I'd never written background music in my life![37]

---

33 These included the ambient recordings of Simpson and Giles of birds on the billabong at Oenpelli, as well as other sounds such as waves lapping, children laughing, and so on.

34 Peter Limbrick, *Making Settler Cinemas*, 153.

35 Hill, Mirrie, 'On Music: Mirrie Hill Interviewed by James Murdoch' (South Melbourne: AFI Distribution Ltd, 1982), henceforth *Murdoch Interview*.

36 The exact date of the first meeting is not known, but was most likely early in August 1949.

37 *Murdoch Interview*.

Alfred was asked to write the music for the films. And Alfred hated writing commissions — he didn't like to have to do a certain thing in a certain time. And I persuaded him to do them.[38]

After that meeting between the Hills and Mountford, matters were discussed amongst the production staff of the Film Division. A handwritten note in the correspondence folder for the film *Arnhem Land* at the National Archives of Australia reads:

Arnhem Land — 15/8/49

Mountford talked to Hill — Alfred Hill — would like him to do music for these films.

Get aboriginal songs on to soft discs for Hill's guidance — will give 20/30 playings — [Mountford?] now in Adelaide with Bishop.

About 10 or 12 records — about 10/- each

Dept going to make hard recordings of all the songs.[39]

The particular custom 'soft discs' cut for the Hills have not yet been found, if indeed they still survive. It is possible that the Film Division did not have these 'soft discs' made up, but instead opted to purchase an existing set. If so, they might have used the twelve-disc set recorded by Simpson and Giles to which I have already referred. It is more likely, however, that Mountford would have seen to it that Mirrie and Alfred were supplied with his own complete six-disc set described above, including the two discs of abbreviated material that had been recorded by Simpson and Giles. In the Mountford-Sheard collection held by the State Library of South Australia, there is notice of receipt of an order for six custom discs (five double-sided and one single-sided) from the EMI company, dated 24th January, 1950—the six-disc set mentioned above.[40] It is not known if this set of six discs was intended for the Hills—this order was placed about four months after their first meeting with Mountford. Some of the songs released as part of this set correspond to those transcriptions included in the Hills' notebooks.

In preparation for the writing of musical underscore for the three films, Mirrie and Alfred Hill both filled several music manuscript books with sketches for music that would go into the scores for the films, transcriptions from the field recordings of traditional song, and ideas for other works such as Mirrie's

---

38   *De Berg Interview.*
39   'Memo to file (pencil)', FPN160 *Arnhem Land*, SP1265/1 Part 2, NAA, Sydney, 15 August 1949.
40   R. V. Southey to C. P. Moutford, *Mountford-Sheard Collection*, PRG 1218/28/8 document 10, State Library of South Australia (SLSA), Adelaide, 24 January 1950.

Symphony in A (Arnhem Land) (1954) (hereafter, the *Symphony*).[41] Also held in the Hill family collection of the State Library of NSW with these manuscript books of Mirrie's, is a set of fully scored sketches for the *Aborigines of the Seacoast* (hereafter, *Seacoast*) music and a shortscore for both *Arnhem Land,* and for *Birds and Billabongs.*[42] The final orchestral manuscripts and instrumental parts used for the recording of the three film scores are held at the National Archives of Australia in their Film Australia music collection.[43] Access to the film *Arnhem Land* is restricted because of its inclusion of a sacred Ubar burial ceremony, featuring the balnooknook drum, and I have thus not been able to view this film. *Birds and Billabongs* is freely available for viewing by the public, but includes no reference to Aboriginal people or culture. As far as I can determine, there is no influence of Aboriginal song in the composition of the underscore for this film. The third film, *Seacoast,* is held in its original form as a preservation copy not available for viewing, but the version widely distributed and available for public viewing is a re-edit of the film created in 1973, for which a new narration was added, the music was rerecorded, and the underscore edited around the new narration.

In an interview, Mirrie Hill describes how she undertook the task of making transcriptions from the field recordings for both her and Alfred Hill's score writing. Mirrie described the process:

> Mr Mountford lent us a lot [of recordings] and gave us some … I've got some here … to get into the mood of their singing. Well, I found out you couldn't take it down in our scale … it was impossible. You could take down the rhythm in time, by turning it on and turning it off. But, what they sang, it wasn't in our scale. But I took some down as well as I could, and certainly got the rhythms, and the idea and the shape of the melodies. And it was from that, that I did my lot and Alfred did his.

In the same interview, Mirrie describes learning the process of scoring for film on the job, working out all the timings for the music in the three films.

> I found that I had to time everything, and sometimes it was only seconds. Well, it's very hard if you have six seconds to write the background music to fit those six seconds of acting. And it was the timing… I think

---

41   Mirrie Hill, 'Symphony in A (Arnhem Land)', *MUS Symphony Australia Collection*, A/C HIL-M 31, National Library of Australia (NLA), Canberra, 1954.

42   A shortscore indicates the harmonic breakdown of the music on two-staff systems to be played on a piano. It might have annotations giving a rough idea of instrumentation, but is not complete. 'II - AH Music manuscripts, IV - AH Music manuscripts collected, VII - MH Music manuscripts & IX - MH Music manuscripts', *Hill Family Collection*, MLMSS 6357, State Library of NSW (SLNSW).

43   Alfred Hill, 'Arnhem Land' [Music score] *Arnhem Land*, FPN160, C4482, NAA, Sydney, 1950; Mirrie Hill, 'Aborigines of the Seacoast' [Music score] *Aborigines of the Seacoast*, FPN26, C4482, NAA, Sydney, 1950; Alfred Hill, 'Birds and Billabongs' [Music score] *Birds and Billabongs*, FPN350, C4482, NAA, Sydney, 1950.

> I borrowed a stopwatch from somebody. I had to work this all out in seconds for Alfred — he wouldn't be bothered. And finally we got to it.[44]

Working out the timings for each individual music cue was carried out at the DOI facility in Burwood, requiring the repeated viewing of the film with a stopwatch. With those timings and discussions with the producers about where music would sit and what kind of moods it might convey (all undocumented), Alfred and Mirrie Hill could then carry out the composition of the scores.[45]

The music for all three films was originally recorded in one mammoth session on Saturday 29 April 1950. To keep within a budget, both composers wrote for the same ensemble of instruments, except that Alfred's scores employed one extra instrument, an oboe. The total forty-five minutes of music for the three films was composed for a moderately large ensemble of flute, oboe, clarinet in A, bassoon, harp, percussion and strings—fourteen players in total. The size of the ensemble and extent of the music was a cause for some internal concern within the Film Division, finally resolved by a memorandum of 30 May 1950 recommending that Alfred Hill's fee be increased to £150 to allow for more players and more music than set out in the initial contract.[46]

The choice of instruments is not especially unusual for a documentary score of the period, with instrumentation normally derived from the symphony orchestra, but the inclusion of harp is particularly notable. In Alfred Hill's scores, the harp is used to add stereotypical flourish and grandeur, whereas Mirrie Hill's uses of the harp, with gentle arpeggios and simple melodies, alludes to a child-like innocence. No Aboriginal instruments are incorporated, but both Alfred and Mirrie use clave to emulate clap-sticks, and imitate the sound of the didjeridu with double bass or bassoon. Both *Seacoast* and *Arnhem Land* incorporate traditional song as source material to influence the composition of the underscore as well as featuring field recordings of songs in the soundtrack for the films.

I will now look at how Mirrie and Alfred Hill treated traditional Aboriginal song as source material in the scores to *Aborigines of the Seacoast*, and *Arnhem Land*.

---

44 *Murdoch Interview.*

45 It is usual practice for the underscore for a film to be written after the film is edited and all other sound elements are complete and it is a reasonable assumption that this is the case for these films because of the presence of traditional song as both an excerpt of field recording in the film soundtrack and as an influence for the writing of the underscore.

46 Stanley Hawes, Producer-in-Chief, Film Division 'Memorandum to Kevin Murphy, Director, ANIB', *Arnhem Land* FPN160, SP1265/1 Part 1, NAA, Sydney, 30 May 1950.

The Score for *Aborigines of the Seacoast*

Mirrie Hill's sketches for the *Seacoast* score do not clearly indicate sources, although it seems most likely that all the traditional song material was derived from the six-disc set published under Mountford's name, as described above. Clues can be surmised from the composer sketchbooks.[47] In any case, because no field recordings had been possible at Yirrkala, the songs included had to have come from another place, most likely from the field recordings at Groote Eylandt, Oenpelli or Port Darwin. None of the traditional music, whether appearing in the film as field recordings or as influence in the composition of the underscore, comes from Yirrkala. As these other songs come from quite different language groups, the use of these songs from out of Country is as incongruous as, say, a Thai song used to represent Vietnamese people.

There are eight identifiable themes that appear in the *Seacoast* music. Some of the themes undergo variation and development, and at a number of points in the music there is a blending of themes as one transforms into another. Of these eight themes, two can be identified as deriving from Aboriginal song. These two themes are given in an abbreviated form in Figures 1 and 2.

The first of these is annotated in a later sketchbook of Aboriginal themes for Mirrie Hill's *Symphony in A (Arnhem Land)* with a reference to a recording identified as 'Cut 1, Song 59, no. 24'.[48] The numbering system appears to relate to an annotated list to accompany the six-disc set, possibly written by Mountford (hereafter, Notes).[49] From these Notes, this song is indicated as 'Song (Unidentified)' on side B of the disc PX.2716. The same melody was also used for a later piano dance piece that Mirrie Hill wrote in 1951 for Beth Dean, as Dance of the Brolgas, and as we shall see the melody is also used by Alfred in his score for *Arnhem Land*.[50] Appearing several times through the underscore of *Seacoast*, the first iteration of the melody features a drone bass to emulate didjeridu, and clave keeping a regular stick pattern. This first appearance, originally playing under the opening titles for the film, is a forceful and fierce statement, done perhaps to give a dramatic opening to the film and denote the importance of the subject matter. Subsequent iterations of the same melody are presented in a much more gentle style without the constant drone. The contour of the melody

---

47   Mirrie Hill, 'Sketchbook "Aborigines of Arnhem Land"', *Hill Family Collection*, MLMSS 6357, VII - MH Music manuscripts, SLNSW, Sydney.

48   Mirrie Hill 'Sketchbook "Particulars of Aboriginal Themes — Arnhem Land Symph"', *Hill Family Collection*, MLMSS 6357, VII - MH Music manuscripts, SLNSW, Sydney.

49   C. P. Moutford, 'National Geographic Society and Australian Government Expedition to Arnhem Land, 1948: Aboriginal songs recorded by Charles P. Mountford', *Mountford-Sheard Collection*, PRG 1218/28/8, SLSA, Adelaide. The Hills may have been given a copy of this list, or the data may have been written on the disc labels.

50   Beth Dean and Victor Carrell, 'Concert Programme', *Manuscript music of Mirrie Hill*, Bib ID. 4934645, NLA, Canberra, 31 August 1950.

is notable for the 'tumbling strain' which Mirrie Hill had identified in many of the field recordings of Aboriginal songs that she was presented with: 'there seems to be a trend to start the songs in a higher way and then come down, but not low to go up'.[51]

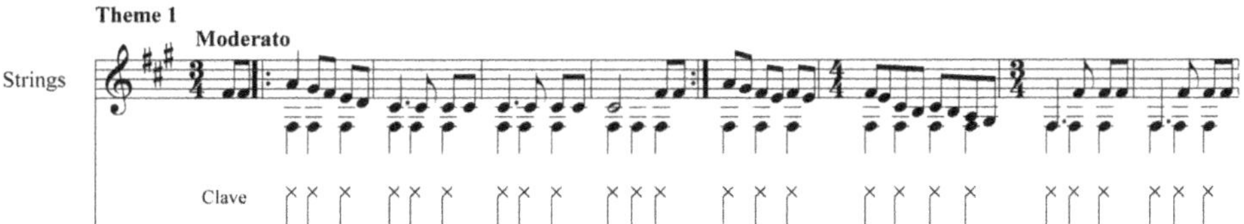

Figure 1: Mirrie Hill, opening theme for *Aborigines of the Seacoast*, derived from an as yet unidentified Aboriginal song.

Source: Author's reduction of the score.

The theme in Figure 2 underscores a group of children playing on the beach, and turtle hunters in a canoe. It can be identified as derived from one of the songs included in the field recordings made by Simpson and Giles and in Mountford's six-disc set in an abbreviated form. The theme also appears in sketches for the *Symphony* annotated as 'No. 53' and as 'Winbalung song'. Barwick and Marett believe this to be a mis-hearing of Gunbalang, a language from the coast to the north-west of Oenpelli, near Maningrida, and is listed in their summary of Simpson's recordings as 'Gunbalang [Kun-barlang] sweetheart song'.[52] The Gunbalang song is featured twice in the 1973 version of the film, at the beginning under the opening titles, and near the end accompanying images of children dancing and playing instruments. In the original version, the song appears only at the end of the film, and the opening titles are underscored by Mirrie Hill's theme given at Figure 1.

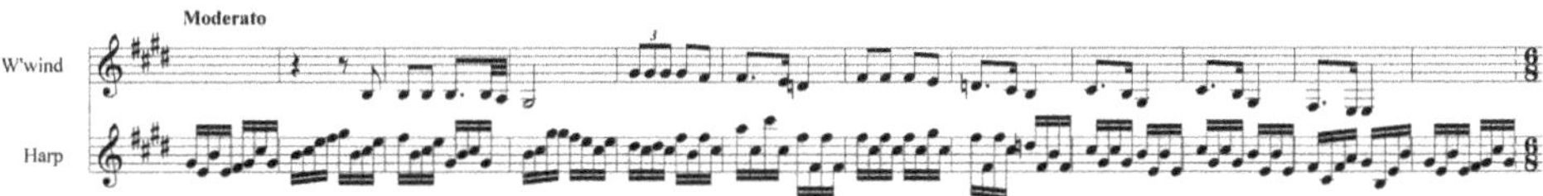

Figure 2: Mirrie Hill, theme for *Aborigines of the Seacoast*, derived from Gunbalang 'Sweetheart'.

Source: Author's reduction of the score.

---

51   *Murdoch Interview.*
52   Barwick and Marett, 'Aural Snapshots of Musical Life', 359.

Technical limitations of the audio recording equipment used in the Arnhem Land Expedition, with the field recordings originally made with the wire recorder then transferred to 78rpm disc, created a speed inconsistency between the recording and the playback. This has two consequences: the pitch is raised for most of the recordings by a variable amount—for this song, approximately two semi-tones—and the formants of the voices are significantly raised, making the adult singers sound more like youths. Towards the end of the film, when we hear the song, it is played underneath images of young children on the beach at Yirrkala playing instruments and dancing.

The song is in a language from Maningrida and was recorded at Oenpelli,[53] both several hundreds of kilometres away from Yirrkala. Additionally, an adult love song is presented as a song performed by children. As this raised-pitch version is the way the song was presented to Mirrie Hill, it is perhaps not surprising that she might have considered it a children's song, and this appears to have affected her choice of instrumentation for the film score as well as the approaches taken in the treatment of the melody in the score.

To compare her melody with the song of the field recording, it might not be immediately apparent that her composition is derived from an Aboriginal song. She has dramatically slowed down the melody, lengthened the gaps between phrases, transposed it into different keys, opted not to use a supporting drone (supplied in the original by didjeridu), and underlaid it with a changing harmonic structure. Additionally, it is her version of the melody which is presented first in the original version of the film and the field recording does not appear until nearly five minutes after Hill's version ends. In a re-edit of the film made in 1973, the version widely available for viewing in Australia, the field recording features under the opening titles, Hill's underscore version commences seven minutes after the field recording fades. The average viewer of the film, with their primary focus on the image rather than the music, is not likely to be aware that this melody, which Hill was evidently so taken with, actually derives from the field recording of an Aboriginal song. Hill passes the melody through a series of variations of texture, harmony and instrumentation, so that this one theme occupies more than one quarter of her entire underscore for the film. As the transcription of the field recording in her sketchbook for the *Symphony* suggests, Hill later reused the melody as the basis of the second movement of the *Symphony*, there played even slower.

By the sound of other themes in the score to *Seacoast*, it is possible that some are influenced by the traditional songs, however, no direct links have been determined. In the theme shown in Figure 3, it appears that Mirrie has conjoined her experience of hearing the field recordings with representations of 'primitive

---

53   Linda Barwick identified the origins of this song, personal communication, 21 February 2013.

people' of the type heard in the music of Hollywood up to that time, as clearly expounded by Mark Slobin in his discussion of the music of Max Steiner.[54] Placed in the film under images of children playing, the theme of Figure 3 has a pulsing tetratonic melody with short repeated melodic cells driven by a constant stick beat, reminiscent of the stereotypical representation of the music of North American First Nations peoples elucidated by both Gorbman and Pisani.[55] Alfred and Mirrie Hill might not have had any experience of Aboriginal music to that time, and it is reasonable therefore to consider that their perception of 'primitive music' might be drawn from the musical representations of Hollywood.

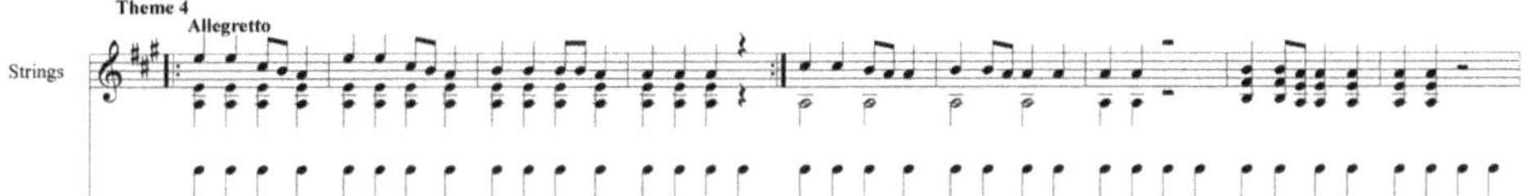

Figure 3: Mirrie Hill, theme for *Aborigines of the Seacoast*, most likely not derived from an Aboriginal song.

Source: Author's reduction of the score.

There are others of the field recordings that Mirrie would later use in her *Symphony* and other works, including the 'Song of the Jungle Fowl', which in her transcription Mirrie indicates as 'not secret'. It is in fact part of what Mountford misnamed the 'Arawaltja' ceremony[56] of Umbakumba on Groote Eylandt and is restricted for audition only by initiated men.[57] The Notes accompanying the recordings do not mention the secret nature of the song.

The Score for *Arnhem Land*

This film is restricted from public access because of the inclusion of an Ubar sacred burial ceremony, and no separate recording of the music has yet been found. Working from the shortscore held in the Hill collection of the State

---

54   Mark Slobin, 'The Steiner Superculture', in *Global Soundtracks: Worlds of film music*, ed. Mark Slobin, (Middleton: Wesleyan University Press, 2008), 3–35.

55   For a full discussion and examples of European renderings of music of First Nations people of North America, see Michael V. Pisani, *Imagining Native America in Music*, 292–329; Claudia Gorbman, 'Drums Along the LA River: Scoring the Indian', in *Cinema and the Sound of Music: Proceedings from the 2nd Cinesonic Conference*, ed. Phillip Brophy (Sydney: Australian Film TV & Radio School, 2000), 97–116.

56   Martin Thomas, 'Unpacking the Testimony of Gerald Blitner: Cross-cultural brokerage and the Arnhem Land Expedition', in *Exploring the Legacy of the 1948 Arnhem Land Expedition,* eds Martin Thomas and Margo Neale (Canberra: ANU E Press, 2011), 398.

57   Alice M. Moyle, *Handlist of Field Collections of Recorded Music in Australia and the Torres Strait: Occasional papers in Aboriginal studies* (Canberra: Australian Institute of Aboriginal Studies, 1966), 28.

Library of NSW, evidence of two Aboriginal songs can be seen.[58] An inscription on the cover of the orchestral score notes 'The Native Tunes used were collected by C. P. Mountford'.[59] The score opens and closes with a strong imperial march in 5/4 time (see Figure 4). A transcription of the original field recording in Alfred's hand is available in another sketchbook, given in Figure 5—described as 'Cut 1 Song 73 Tjarada song Delissaville' recorded by Simpson and Giles at Delissaville.[60] In the Notes, the song is given the number fifty-two and is the second cut on Side B of the disc PRX.2715. The song, with voices accompanied by a four-out-of-five-beat stick pattern, is sung in its original form by both male and female voices. Alfred later adapted his arrangement of the song into the third movement of his *Australia Symphony in B minor* (1951).[61] Alfred's rendering of the melody is grandiose and quite overbearing, distinctly at odds with the sound of the song in the field recording.

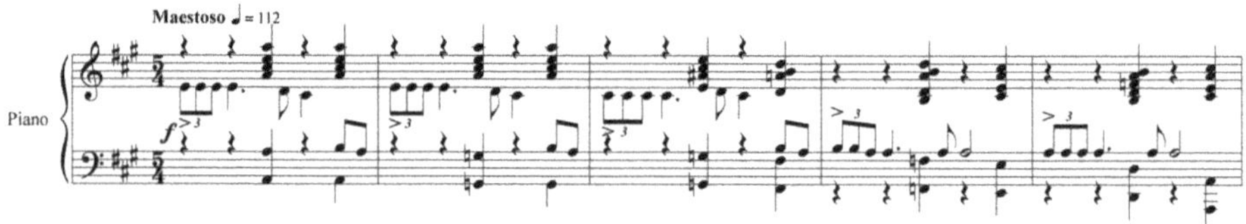

Figure 4: Alfred Hill, opening and closing theme from *Arnhem Land*, derived from a Tjarada song collected at Delissaville.

Source: Author's reduction of the score.

The second Aboriginal song that Alfred used as source material in his score for *Arnhem Land* is one that Mirrie also employed in *Aborigines of the Seacoast*, listed in the six-disc set only as 'Song (Unidentified)', as indicated above. A transcription from the field recording in Alfred's hand is in his sketches for the *Arnhem Land* score. A shortscore reduction of Alfred's rendering of the melody is given in Figure 6. If, as she has suggested, Mirrie Hill did all the transcribing of the songs from record, then Alfred's sketch for this song must be an adaptation from Mirrie's transcription. Compare this with Mirrie Hill's use of the same song in Figure 1. In the film *Arnhem Land*, this music accompanies the entrance of a group of Aboriginal men about to perform the Ubar ceremony. Alfred's setting of the melody is suitably solemn, given the occasion—quite different to Mirrie Hill's multiple settings of the same melody.

---

58 Alfred Hill, 'Arnhem Land' [music shortscore], *Hill Family Collection*, MLMSS 6357, II - AH Music manuscripts and IV - AH Music manuscripts collected, SLNSW, Sydney.

59 Alfred Hill, 'Arnhem Land' [Music score], *Arnhem Land*, FPN160, C4482, NAA, Sydney, 1950.

60 Barwick and Marett, 'Aural Snapshots of Musical Life', 359.

61 Andrew D. McCredie, 'Alfred Hill (1870–1960): Leipzig backgrounds and models and their significance for the later instrumental music (1920–1960)', in *One Hand on the Manuscript: Music in Australian cultural history 1930–1960*, eds Nicholas Brown, Peter Campbell, Robyn Holmes, Peter Read and Larry Sitsky (Canberra: The Humanities Research Centre, Australian National University, 1995), 30.

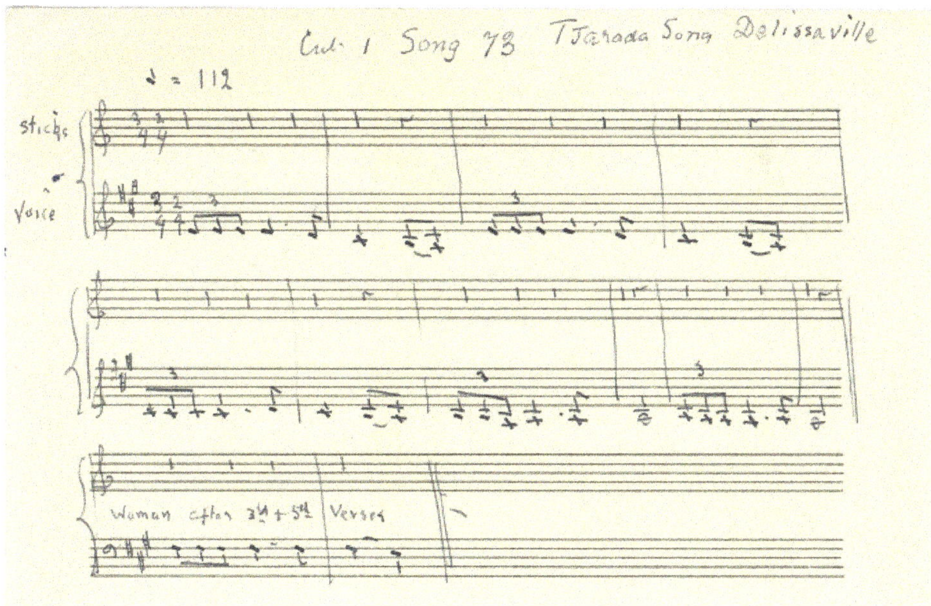

Figure 5: Alfred Hill, transcription of a Tjarada song, used in the score to *Arnhem Land*.

Source: Arnhem Land (sketchbook), in *Hill family - Alfred Hill - music manuscripts and associated papers, 1887–1960*, F. Motion Picture Music, call no. MLMSS 6357/22-23, SLNSW. Used with permission of the Estate of Mirrie Hill.

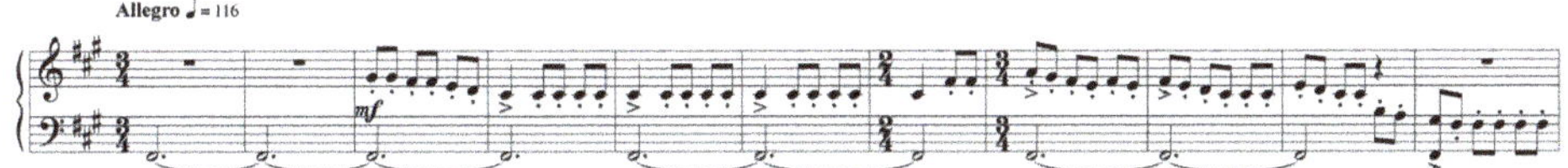

Figure 6: Alfred Hill, shortscore theme for the Ubar ceremony, the same song used by Mirrie Hill, shown in Figure 1.

Source: Author's reduction of the score.

Reconfiguring the DOI Documentaries

In 1950, magnetic tape was not yet available as a recording medium—the standard technology for recording was the optical sound track of film. For documentary films such as these, standard practice was to record the narration, sound effects and music onto separate synchronised film stock, then make a final mix for combination with the visuals. This allowed for replacement of the narration for non-English versions of a film for overseas markets.[62] The quality of optical soundtracks was quite poor, with limited frequency response and dynamic range, and vulnerability to damage from dust and scratches in the process of projection. Because the Arnhem Land Expedition films continued to generate a lot of interest many years after their initial production, an opportunity was sought to upgrade the quality of the soundtrack by using the medium of magnetic tape.

Over the two years from 1973 to 1974, the newly-formed Film Australia made a decision to modify a number of their earlier documentaries in their acquired catalogue to reflect the developing public awareness of and respect for Aboriginal culture.[63] These include the two earlier Mountford films, *Walkabout* (1940) and *Tjurunga* (1942), which were edited into one film under the title of *Walkabout 1974*, removing footage depicting secret/sacred ceremonies but keeping the original narration by C. P. Mountford. The film *Namatjira, the Painter* (1946) was significantly re-edited and a new narration written to show famed artist Albert Namatjira in a much-less paternalistic light than the earlier version of the film had done. The overly-huge Mackerras score was replaced with production music—guitar and harmonica—inoffensive and unobtrusive.[64]

As part of these changes, the scores to two of the Arnhem Land Expedition films were re-recorded by James McCarthy. This new recording, on magnetic tape, was far superior in quality to the original recording. *Aborigines of the Seacoast*, portraying the idyllic and isolated lives of the people on an 'untouched' stretch of east Arnhem Land coast, was reconfigured with a new narration changing the viewpoint of the film to that of a time-capsule of a lost era. Ten years after the Arnhem Land Expedition, the area featured in the film, Yirrkala, would be changed forever by the construction of a bauxite mining and aluminium smelting and shipping facility. In its reconfigured state, the film carries an over-arching sense of melancholy, emotionally intensified (unintentionally) by Mirrie Hill's melodic and very personal composition style. The re-recorded music score was later included on a CD compiled by McCarthy for the Anthology of Australian Music on Disc series produced by the Canberra School of Music.[65] Taking advantage of the opportunity with the ensemble of performers in the studio, McCarthy also re-recorded the score to *Birds and Billabongs*, although the audio for the film has not been redone and the re-recorded music has not been included in other media.

---

62   James McCarthy, personal communication, 17 February 2013.
63   ibid.
64   Efforts are now underway to prepare Mackerras' original score for concert performance as a representation of his early-career composition.
65   James McCarthy is compiling an annotated catalogue of all the music scores to the Film Australia collection.

Why the film *Arnhem Land* was not re-edited with these other early Film Division documentaries is not yet known. Despite the re-recording of the music, the film *Birds and Billabongs,* was also not re-edited, but as the film did not include any reference to Aboriginal people or culture there was no sensitive material to cause offence and the film remains in wide distribution in its original state.

Reflections on the Circulation of Song into New Compositions

In this final section, I employ a number of analytical frameworks to aid the discussion of recontexualising traditional song into the scores for these documentary films. Ownership of the Arnhem Land Expedition field recordings, and through them the songs, is a contested space. Mirrie and Alfred Hill both credited Mountford as a co-composer for each of their film scores, drawing inspiration from the field recordings of traditional Aboriginal song. There was no acknowledgement of the traditional owners/composers of the songs, the originating locations of the songs, or even that some of the field recordings were carried out by Simpson and Giles. It is most probable that Mirrie and Alfred Hill were not aware that the Oenpelli field recordings were not recorded by Mountford. It seems that the secret/sacred nature of some of the material, particularly several of the songs Mountford recorded on Groote Eylandt, was not conveyed to them. In Mirrie's sketches, she has annotated as 'not secret' her transcription of the 'Song of the Jungle Fowl',[66] which became an important theme in her *Symphony*. If the secret/sacred nature of some of the field recordings was discussed, she or Mountford were mistaken in identifying this song as suitable for public use. The Notes do not annotate any songs in the six-disc set as secret, although some songs include 'secret names' for animals, and other songs are listed as 'non-secret'.

Mountford was grateful for Alfred and Mirrie Hill's ongoing support and public acknowledgement of his contribution to their work. A handwritten letter from Mountford to them reads:

Dear Mr & Mrs Hill 13.5.51

I was ever so pleased to get your letter a few weeks ago and to know that you have been able to make use of my recordings … I must thank both

---

66   Found on side two, cut number two of disc PRX-2712, *Groote Eylandt songs.*

of you for the full credit you have given me in every interview. This is valuable because it makes a few people realise that what I have done, in my limited way, in recording Aboriginal songs is of some use.[67]

A letter in the *Arnhem Land* correspondence file from 1956 states:

Further to your inquiry I now find that the records used by Mr Mountford were taken off wire recordings made by Colin Simpson.

I do not know the details of the arrangements made during 1948 between Mr Mountford and Mr Simpson, but the recordings are listed by the A.B.C. as belonging to Colin.

The set, consisting of 12 double sided records, can be ordered from the A.B.C. Sydney at a cost of £6. 0. 0 per set.[68]

What are we to make of Alfred and Mirrie Hill's adaptation of Aboriginal song in the context of newly-composed music as underscore to these films? Commenting on the Jindyworobak poets' use of Aboriginal words and myths in the early twentieth century, David Symons defends their approach:

From today's standpoint this may be seen as a kind of cultural appropriation, as the Jindyworobak preoccupation with things Aboriginal was not primarily for the sake of Aboriginal culture itself, nor was it concerned with that culture's relationship with a white displacing culture. It was rather a means for the white Australian to achieve a similarly deep spiritual link with the unique Australian environment. However, in the Jindyworobak period, the concept of "cultural appropriation" would not have occurred to non-indigenous artists, and certainly not as an ethical issue.[69]

Gregg W. Howard's framework for engagement with recontextualised Aboriginal song may be a useful tool of analysis. Discussing the works of the composer Clive Douglas, Howard identifies three types of engagement:

1. The derived material may be so abstracted from its original form as to lose its recognisable identity.

2. In an attempt to accommodate this fact, the composer may contrive the musical expression to the extent that the derived material is caricature.

---

67   C. P. Mountford. 'Letter to Alfred and Mirrie Hill', *Hill Family Collection*, MLMSS 6357, VI - Mirrie Hill, personal papers, SLNSW, Sydney, 13 May 1951.
68   R. Edwards (for Producer-in-Chief, Stanley Hawes?), 'Letter to (Kevin Murphy?) Director, ANIB', *Arnhem Land*, FPN160, SP1265/1 Part 2, NAA, Sydney, 19 June 1956.
69   Symons, 'Jindyworobak Connection': 34.

3. The material may be allowed to retain its recognisable identity and is 'framed' by rather than integrated into the musical fabric.[70]

For the underscore composition in the two documentary films, the traditional songs are taken from their instrumental, vocal, and extra-musical context. Their purpose and intention is altered, and the music abstracted to the point where it is difficult to identify their origins without recourse to analysis of the written scores and sketchbooks. Identification by ear requires focused attention on the score, not normally afforded in their context accompanying the films.

In *Aborigines of the Seacoast*, Mirrie Hill has incorporated traditional songs, selecting and processing the melodies of the songs in such a way that they become subsumed within her own compositional style. The melody given in Figure 3, which seems not to originate from a field recording in the six-disc set, appears to be Mirrie Hill's interpretation of an Aboriginal style interpolated with the 'primitive music' of Hollywood films, more in the category of a caricature. While her treatment of the 'Winbalung Sweetheart song' is skilful and appealing, accompanying images of children playing on the beach, her composition is far removed from the particulars and application of the original song. It is likely that the pitch alteration in the song and the positioning of the field recording in the film under images of children playing on the beach influenced her use and interpretation of the material. Mirrie Hill's treatment of the other song, annotated as 'Song (untitled)', sits less comfortably in its various settings, and becomes caricature, with the melodic contour constrained to a minor pentatonic scale, imitation of a didjeridu drone and constant click rhythm.

Alfred Hill's composition style was informed by a late-nineteenth century Germanic training, evident in his settings of the songs. The 'Song (untitled)' in his hands becomes slow, sombre and pompous, accompanying images of Aboriginal men walking onto a sacred space to conduct a burial ceremony. His setting of the Tjarada song transforms the song into a stately march in 5/4 with a grandiosity that would seem intended to welcome an imperial procession. The settings of both songs are so removed from the sound and intention of the traditional songs that they acquire the status of caricature. Neither Mirrie's nor Alfred's settings of Aboriginal song could be considered to allow the material to retain its identity as framed in Howard's third kind of engagement above.

A further framework might be pertinent to this consideration of the legacy of composers such as Mirrie and Alfred Hill. Discussing the recording of sounds particular to a place, R. Murray Schafer defined the term *schizophonia* as 'the

---

70   Gregg W. Howard, 'Clive Douglas (1903-1977),' in *Australian Composition in the Twentieth Century*, eds Frank Callaway and David Tunlet (Melbourne: Oxford University Press, 1978), 38, quoted in Symons, 'Jindyworobak Connection': 45.

split between an original sound and its electro-acoustical transmission or reproduction'.[71] Feld expands upon this notion in his discussion of traditional musics taken from their context and used in hybrid commodities created by the commercial music industry in the 'world music' phenomena of the 1980s and 1990s. Feld's voice was one of many questioning the role of the commercial music industry in hybrids such as those of rock artists Paul Simon and Peter Gabriel in the 1980s. Feld's own conundrum comes from his two positions as both an academic and as an active participant in the creation of 'transcultural record productions',[72] with the Kaluli people of Bosavi in Papua New Guinea. While critical of massive international corporations drawing profits from the cultural capital of non-Western cultures through these hybrids, he is very conscious of his own actions in this regard. He highlights the primary argument in defence of these hybrids—that the criticism of these projects is less straightforward when some benefits can be seen to be returned to the source cultures.

In the instance of these film scores, there was no promise of extensive financial gain from the appropriation of traditional song either from the scores or the subsequent concert works, however, the use of the materials gave new impetus to the composing careers of both composers, and Mountford was a beneficiary through continuing association with them, as well as with the choreographer Beth Dean. The Hills' efforts could be considered to be comparable to those of the renowned and highly regarded watercolour artist Albert Namatjira, whose art offered a carefully controlled view of Aboriginal experience of Country through a Western idiom. Mirrie and Alfred Hill took elements of Aboriginal culture and re-presented them in a context palatable to a society for whom Aboriginal culture was quite alien, however, their presentation of elements of Aboriginal culture in a Western idiom is derived from their position outside the culture.

Cycles of culture turn slowly, fitfully. We must consider these efforts in the context of their times and see them as part of a continuum of growing understanding. As was, and still is, common practice in the writing of Western music drawing influence from other sources, both Mirrie and Alfred Hill in their different ways have taken the traditional source materials and integrated them into their own compositional practice, rendering them disconnected from the source materials. Both composers have used songs out of their normal context with little consideration of their place of origin. They have operated within their limited understanding and prejudices of Aboriginal culture. Their lack of understanding is indicative of a broader societal lack of engagement with

---

71   R. Murray Schafer, quoted in Steven Feld, 'From Schizophonia to Schismogenesis: The discourses and practices of world music and world beat', in *The Traffic in Culture: Refiguring art and anthropology*, eds George E. Marcus and Fred R. Myers (Berkeley: University of California Press, 1995), 97.
72   ibid.

Aboriginal culture. Mark Slobin has written: 'every film is ethnographic, and every soundtrack acts like an ethnomusicologist',[73] So it is with these films and these soundtracks—they allow us to take the temperature of the times.

The 'circulation' in the title of this book encourages the notion of a returning, but the processes described in this chapter have resulted in the mining of cultural capital in a unidirectional move into the dominant culture. Repatriation efforts on the traditional songs collected on this and other expeditions begin with the return of historical field recordings, and Brown, Campbell, and Treloyn demonstrate an ongoing engagement with cultures,[74] being the mediators of change.[75] To close the circle, these altered materials could be taken back to the originating communities. In the case of the music composed by Alfred and Mirrie Hill, that is a task which still remains to be done.

There exists still today somewhat of a 'musical tourist' approach to the incorporation of traditional song and instrumentation into contemporary composition[76]—the cultural conversation still flows mostly in one direction. It can be hoped that an awareness of these past attempts can help deepen an understanding of the impacts of misinterpretation and appropriation, and allow for genuine cultural exchange.

Acknowledgements

This research was made possible through the granting of a Scholars and Artists in Residence research fellowship with the National Film and Sound Archive (NFSA) in Canberra in 2011. Thanks especially to the NFSA's Vincent Plush, Jenny Gall, Graham Shirley, Matthew Davies, Christine Eccles, Kylie Doherty, Brenda Gifford and Gerry O'Neill. I am also grateful to the State Library of NSW, in particular Meredith Lawn; Film Australia; the National Archives, especially to Edmund Rutlidge; the National Library of Australia, particularly Robyn Holmes and volunteers; the State Library of South Australia; and the Australian Institute for Aboriginal and Torres Strait Islander studies, especially Grace Koch. Thanks to James McCarthy, Martin Thomas, Linda Barwick and Allan Marett for their time and sharing of knowledge. The chapter has benefitted directly from advice on drafts from Linda Barwick, Amanda Harris and two anonymous reviewers.

---

73   Mark Slobin, 'The Steiner Superculture', in *Global Soundtracks: Worlds of film music*, ed. Mark Slobin, (Middleton: Wesleyan University Press, 2008), 3–4.
74   See the chapters by Brown, Campbell and Treloyn, this volume.
75   See Harris' 'sixth period' in chapter 1 of this volume.
76   James McCarthy, personal communication, 17 February 2013.

References

Barwick, Linda, and Allan Marett. 'Aural Snapshots of Musical Life: The 1948 recordings', in *Exploring the Legacy of the 1948 Arnhem Land Expedition*, eds Martin Thomas and Margo Neale (Canberra: ANU E Press, 2011), 355–76.

Blainey, Geoffrey. *The Tyranny of Distance: How distance shaped Australia's history* (Sydney: Macmillan, 2001).

Chion, Michel. *Audio-Vision: Sound on screen*, trans. Claudia Gorbman (New York: Columbia Unversity Press, 1994).

Chion, Michel. *Film, a Sound Art*, trans. Claudia Gorbman (New York: Columbia University Press, 2009).

Covell, Roger. *Australia's Music: Themes for a new society* (Melbourne: Sun Books, 1967).

Dunlop, Ian. 'Ethnographic Filmmaking in Australia: The first seventy years (1898–1968)', *Studies in Visual Communication* 9:1 (1983): 11–18.

Feld, Steven. 'From Schizophonia to Schismogenesis: The discourses and practices of world music and world beat', in *The Traffic in Culture: Refiguring art and anthropology,* eds George E. Marcus and Fred R. Myers (Berkeley: University of California Press, 1995), 96–126.

Flinn, Caryl. *Strains of Utopia: Gender, nostalgia and Hollywood film music* (Princeton: Princeton University Press, 1992).

Gorbman, Claudia. *Unheard Melodies: Narrative film music* (Bloomington: Indiana University Press, 1987).

Gorbman, Claudia. 'Drums Along the LA River: Scoring the Indian', in *Cinema and the Sound of Music: Proceedings from the 2nd Cinesonic Conference 1999,* ed. Phillip Brophy (Sydney: Australian Film TV and Radio School, 2000), 97–116.

Griffiths, Alison Margaret. *Origins of Ethnographic Film* (PhD, New York University, 1998).

Hill, Mirrie. 'On Music: Mirrie Hill Interviewed by James Murdoch' (South Melbourne: AFI Distribution Ltd, 1982).

Hill, Mirrie. 'Aborigines of the Seacoast', in *Film Music of the 1960s: From the Film Australia collection*, ed. James McCarthy, CSM 36, Anthology of Australian Music on Disc: Series 4 (Canberra: Canberra School of Music, 1999).

Howard, Gregg W. 'Clive Douglas (1903–1977)', in *Australian Composition in the Twentieth Century*, eds Frank Callaway and David Tunley (Melbourne: Oxford University Press, 1978), 37–43.

Jones, Anthony L. '"The Nostalgia of the Audio Souvenir": Technology limitations in the 1948 Arnhem Land field recordings of Colin Simpson', paper presented at the *11th Symposium on Indigenous Music and Dance*, The Australian National University, Canberra, 2 December 2012.

Kalinak, Kathryn. *Settling the Score: Music and the classical Hollywood film* (Madison: University of Wisconsin Press, 1992).

Kassabian, Anahid. *Hearing Film: Tracking identifications in contemporary Hollywood film music* (New York: Routledge, 2001).

Limbrick, Peter. *Making Settler Cinemas: Film and colonial encounters in the United States, Australia and New Zealand* (New York: Palgrave Macmillan, 2010).

MacGregor, Tony. 'Birds on the Wire: Wild, sound, informal speech and the emergence of the radio documentary', in *Exploring the Legacy of the 1948 Arnhem Land Expedition*, eds Martin Thomas and Margo Neale (Canberra: ANU E Press, 2011), 87–111.

McCredie, Andrew D. 'Alfred Hill (1870–1960): Leipzig backgrounds and models and their significance for the later instrumental music (1920–1960)', in *One Hand on the Manuscript: Music in Australian cultural history 1930–1960*, eds Nicholas Brown, Peter Campbell, Robyn Holmes, Peter Read and Larry Sitsky (Canberra: The Humanities Research Centre, The Australian National University, 1995), 18–33.

Mercer, Christine. 'Henry Tate: Views on the artistic possibilities of Aboriginal music', in *Encounters: Meetings in Australian music: Essays, images, interviews*, eds Vincent Plush, Huib Schippers and Jocelyn Wolfe (Brisbane: Queensland Conservatorium Research Centre, 2005).

Mountford, Charles P. *Aborigines of the Sea Coast.* (Lindfield: Film Australia, 1951).

Mountford, Charles P. *Records of the American-Australian Scientific Expedition to Arnhem Land: Vol. 1 'art, myth and symbolism'*, ed. C. P. Mountford (Melbourne: Melbourne University Press, 1956).

Moyle, Alice M. *Handlist of Field Collections of Recorded Music in Australia and the Torres Strait: Occasional papers in Aboriginal studies* (Canberra: Australian Institute of Aboriginal Studies, 1966).

National Archives of Australia. 'Commonwealth Film Unit: Fact sheet 25', (2013), accessed 12 February 2013, http://www.naa.gov.au/collection/fact-sheets/fs25.aspx.

Pisani, Michael V. *Imagining Native America in Music* (New Haven: Yale University Press, 2005).

Reece, Bob. *Daisy Bates: Grand dame of the desert*, ed. Carol Natsis (Canberra: National Library of Australia, 2007).

Shirley, Graham, and Brian Adams. *Australian Cinema: The first eighty years* (Sydney: Currency Press, 1989).

Simpson, Colin. *Adam in Ochre: Inside Aboriginal Australia* (Sydney: Angus & Robertson, 1951).

Slobin, Mark. 'The Steiner Superculture', in *Global Soundtracks: Worlds of film music*, ed. Mark Slobin (Middleton: Wesleyan University Press, 2008), 3–35.

Symons, David. 'The Jindyworobak Connection in Australian Music, c. 1940–1960', *Context: Journal of music research* 23 (2002): 33–47.

Thomas, Martin. 'A Short History of the 1948 Arnhem Land Expedition', *Aboriginal History* 34 (2010): 143–73.

Thomas, Martin. 'Unpacking the Testimony of Gerald Blitner: Cross-cultural brokerage and the Arnhem Land Expedition', in *Exploring the Legacy of the 1948 Arnhem Land Expedition,* eds Martin Thomas and Margo Neale (Canberra: ANU E Press, 2011), 377–401.

Thomas, Martin and Margo Neale, eds. *Exploring the Legacy of the 1948 Expedition.* (Canberra: ANU E Press, 2011).

4. Hearing Aboriginal Music Making in Non-Indigenous Accounts of the Bush from the Mid-Twentieth Century

Amanda Harris

Mid-century non-Indigenous travellers in the Australian bush found themselves confronted with a new auditory world, one in which the sounds of the city were absent, and the sounds of the bush unfamiliar. The reckonings of these travellers with aural encounters of people, place and animals often came to stand for a complex set of reactions to being in the bush. The way they listened to Aboriginal music being sung and played around them crystallised perceptions held about Aboriginal people and how they might be located in the Australian landscape. How non-Indigenous authors heard and performed culturally familiar music also reflected ways that they viewed themselves and was a means of bringing the familiar to alien surroundings. In this chapter, I combine accounts from diaries of the 1948 American-Australian Scientific Expedition to Arnhem Land with depictions from novels written within two decades of the expedition to give examples of the way Aboriginal music was heard by non-Indigenous travellers. In the process I tease out some of the perceptions of a range of commentators on Aboriginal culture that are revealed in these musical encounters. I also consider how this sound world was brought to bear on a musical composition by Peter Sculthorpe from a slightly later period and reflect on how the musical setting of Aboriginal song themes reveals similar preoccupations to these literary descriptions.

Phyllis Weliver's analysis of the nineteenth century novel *The Moonstone* depicts music trumpeting the first British encounters with visitors from India: 'the sound of the Indian drum penetrates the walls of an English country home, announcing the presence of the exotic East to its well-heeled inhabitants … music is heard before the Eastern visitors are seen.'[1] As suggested by this excerpt, Weliver's discussion of Orientalism in British fiction takes as its starting point the auditory space of cross-cultural encounters, in their written manifestations in literature. Weliver's work on aural experiences of the exotic can be seen in the context of recent contributions to historical studies, which have sought not only

---

1   Phyllis Weliver, 'Tom-Toms, Dream-Fugues and Poppy Juice: East meets west in nineteenth-century fiction', in *Music and Orientalism in the British Empire, 1780s–1940s*, eds Martin Clayton and Bennett Zon (Aldershot: Ashgate, 2007), 257. Other studies that have taken up this subject matter include Ian Woodfield, *English Musicians in the Age of Exploration* (Stuyvesant: Pendragon Press, 1995), although Woodfield's book focuses on the role of European musicians in the colonisation and exploration process, rather than the reactions of those musicians to Indigenous musics.

to draw on visual accounts—photographs, artefacts and written descriptions of these—but have also been attentive to auditory historical sources. This relatively new approach responds to history writing in which, as Diane Collins wrote in 2006, '[h]istorians disappoint as listeners'.[2] As one of these new contributors to history drawing on what is heard instead of only what is seen, Martin Thomas has documented the range of recent historical writings which are preoccupied with auditory experience, including the 2004 volume, *Hearing History: A reader*.[3] There is also a growing body of work which seeks to enliven the historical sound world of Australia from pre-colonial to postcolonial times. In this chapter, I contribute a fragment to this greater reconstruction of heard cultures. In describing the sound world of non-Indigenous travellers, I draw on R. Murray Schafer's definition of a 'soundscape' as the 'acoustic environment' of, in this case, the Australian bush as inhabited by both Aboriginal people and more recent arrivals.[4]

I begin with the diaries of a group of American and Australian scientists and support staff who, in 1948, set out on a nine-month journey to east, central and west Arnhem Land in the north of Australia. In the three main camps they established, in Umbakumba on Groote Eylandt, in Yirrkala, and Oenpelli (now Gunbalanya), the travellers focused their attention on different acts of collection: they gathered artworks, archaeological objects, animal and plant specimens, human blood samples and made recordings of music and dance performances. They even stole human bones from burial sites in the vicinity of their camps (some of which have recently been repatriated).[5] In large part, the expeditioners' approach to their surroundings was that of foreign observers to an alien culture. They built only short-term working relationships with the Aboriginal people they encountered, took notes on the phenomena they observed, and used the proceeds of their work to publish four large volumes of *Records* of their expedition in the decade following the trip. Although some of the travellers had visited Aboriginal communities in the past, and some had a working knowledge and acquaintance with Indigenous art forms, such as cave and bark paintings and the construction of tools and implements for daily tasks, for many of the participants (and not just those from the far away US),

---

2   Diane Collins, 'Acoustic Journeys: Exploration and the search for an aural history of Australia', *Australian Historical Studies* 37:128 (2006): 1.

3   Martin Thomas, 'The Rush to Record: Transmitting the sound of Aboriginal culture', *Journal of Australian Studies* 31:90 (2007): 107–202; Mark M. Smith, ed., *Hearing History: A reader* (Athens: University of Georgia Press, 2004); See also Joy Damousi and Desley Deacon, eds., *Talking and Listening in the Age of Modernity: Essays on the history of sound* (Canberra: ANU E Press, 2007).

4   R. Murray Schafer, 'Soundscapes and Earwitnesses,' in *Hearing History: A reader*, ed. Mark M. Smith (Athens: University of Georgia Press, 2004), 6. Schafer's term originates in R. Murray Schafer, *The Tuning of the World* (New York: Knopf, 1977), and has since been employed by other authors working on aural histories. See John M. Picker, *Victorian Soundscapes* (New York: Oxford University Press, 2003); Collins, 'Acoustic Journeys'.

5   See Thomas, this volume.

these were their first encounters with the Indigenous people of Australia in general and the people of different parts of Arnhem Land in particular. One of the ways in which the foreign cultures of the communities of Umbakumba, Yirrkala and Oenpelli were perceived was through auditory experiences of the sounds made by people and the places in which they found themselves. Some of these experiences were recorded in the extensive field diaries that several of the expedition members kept. The auditory experiences recorded fell into three categories: hearing Aboriginal music drifting from nearby camps after dark; on rare occasions, gramophone music or shortwave radio bringing familiar culture from afar; and camp songs that were a spontaneous feature of many an evening's entertainment in the bush.

Novels by authors acquainted with the music of Aboriginal people and those whose knowledge of Indigenous Australians was the result of archival research presented a portrait of Aboriginality that was available for popular consumption. Novels were a medium with a more direct accessibility for the wider Australian public than the research work of ethnologists, whose publications had a narrow and more restricted readership. Where expeditioners' diaries reveal the responses of new travellers to their encounters in the bush, popular novels are indicative of conceptions of Aboriginal people that were placed in circulation in the wider Australian cultural sphere. The novels discussed in this chapter include Katharine Susannah Prichard's *Coonardo*, Mary Durack's *Keep Him My Country*, Xavier Herbert's *Capricornia*, Eleanor Dark's *The Timeless Land*, and Ion L. Idriess' *Drums of Mer*. In order to think more fully about the way music is heard, and in drawing not just on written but auditory sources, I also discuss as a point of comparison, the composer Peter Sculthorpe's *Port Essington*—the first complete work in which he used an Aboriginal melody as his chief melodic material to depict how European colonisers heard their surroundings, and a work held by musicologists as significant in the turn to an Australian compositional style. Before turning to these dramatised accounts of cross-cultural auditory encounters, I begin with the field diaries from 1948.

The Diaries

Several participants in the 1948 American-Australian Scientific Expedition to Arnhem Land kept avidly-written accounts of their experiences in the locations visited by the expedition in the Top End of Australia. These diary accounts take a number of different forms ranging from the scientific field diaries of nutritionist Margaret McArthur to the personal journal of the expedition's cook and logistics officer, John Bray, which contains a record of his feelings of marginalisation as well as amusing commentary on the habits of the expedition scientists.[6] The diaries alternately document their authors' feelings of alienation from their surroundings and excitement at their encounters with new places, people and cultures. Although music is not a dominant theme in any of the diaries in particular, the participants' responses to music and their auditory world provide an interesting lens for their perceptions of strangeness and connections with home. The diaries of four participants in particular—John Bray, Bob Miller, Bessie Mountford, and Fred McCarthy—discuss music with some frequency, and the ways in which they were able to hear the music around them tells us much about their feelings of cross-cultural negotiation during the course of the nine-month expedition.

In expedition cook and logistics manager John Bray's diary, it is possible to observe a movement from alienation to understanding of the foreign cultures with which he interacted in the time he spent in Arnhem Land. In the early days of the expedition, Bray heard the sounds of Aboriginal music not only as foreign and unfamiliar, but also as incomprehensible and monotonous. Of the didjeridu playing that he heard on 19 April, Bray wrote: 'the range of notes is strictly limited and generally is just like a dull booming sound',[7] and on 23 April: 'The corroboree goes on every night. Just a repetition of the first lot'.[8] His measured and unenthusiastic tone in these two descriptions can be contrasted with his experience of listening to the short-wave radio on 4 May. In this description, Bray's experience of the 'soft' and 'glorious music' of Eileen Joyce's piano playing was heightened by the strangeness of his surroundings, 'sitting on the sand in Peter's tent, slapping at mosquitos', and was placed by Bray in stark contrast to the 'Wahs' and 'Hoos' of 'the Nightly Corroboree down at the beach', a description that may relate in particular to the overblown hoots of didjeridu style from north-east Arnhem Land.[9] These early descriptions of how Aboriginal music was heard by Bray correspond with his period of acclimatisation to the new cultural surrounds of Arnhem Land and his attempts to understand the foreign culture of north-east Arnhem Land with which he had only just begun to interact.

Bray's ability to hear subtlety and nuance in the music around him changed in parallel with his growing understanding of the Aboriginal people with whom he worked and studied. His interaction with Aboriginal people continued to be superficial, based mostly around working relationships with assistants employed to help him with the distribution of rations and cooking, until October 1948. In

---

6 See my discussion of John Bray's, Fred McCarthy's, Margaret McArthur's and Bessie Mountford's diary accounts in Amanda Harris, 'Food, Feeding and Consumption (or the Cook, the Wife and the Nutritionist): The politics of gender and class in a 1948 Australian expedition', *History and Anthropology* 24:3 (2013): 1-17.
7 John Bray, 'Arnhem Land Expedition 1948', Private Journal, collection of Andrew Bray, 19 April 1948.
8 ibid., 23 April 1948.
9 ibid., 4 May 1948. I am grateful to Linda Barwick for her insight into the characteristic didjeridu sounds of north-east Arnhem Land style.

that month, he was allocated to a research trip run by the nutritionist, Margaret McArthur, heading out from Oenpelli and camping at a site about twenty kilometres outside of the mission camp for a period of two weeks. Bray travelled with two Aboriginal men, Joshua and Parr-poor-wa (known as Ankor), from the settlement for several days in preparation for the trip, attempting to find a group of people living off the land and wholly independent of rations from the mission. After these days of exploring the surrounding countryside and the two weeks at the designated field site, Fish Creek, or Kunnanj, Bray had developed a more thorough understanding of cultural practice and the lifestyle and habits of the Aboriginal people with whom he was camping, and through this, had come to a deeper relationship with Aboriginal culture. On 30 September he recorded with great interest his experience of encountering a group of people, who were unknown to him and his companions, in the bush and detailed the process they followed of making themselves noticeable to the new group and only slowly approaching them by means of tobacco thrown towards them and shouts to make obvious their presence.[10]

Just as Bray's understanding of cultural practice grew at this time, a shift in his ability to 'hear' Aboriginal music was also evident. Bray's diarised account of the music he heard in this period contrasts significantly with those of April and May of the same year: 'Sat around & listened to the nightly song & dance. They have charming songs with varying rhythms & time & some we heard tonight would make a splendid recording.'[11] Of course, the music he was hearing here, outside of Oenpelli, was rather different in style from the north-east Arnhem Land music he had heard months before. However, Bray's descriptions show not just a preference for this music from a different region, but a higher level of attention to what was going on musically. It suggests that hearing the same kind of detail that he heard in culturally-familiar music was only possible as his understanding of Aboriginal culture developed. This echoes ethnomusicologist John Blacking's assertion that 'perception of sonic order, whether it be innate or learned, or both, must be in the mind before it emerges as music'.[12] Bray needed to learn order in Aboriginal culture before his mind was able to perceive the order in the music that emerged from that culture.

The American ichthyologist, Bob Miller's approach to describing in his diary the Aboriginal music heard was more analytical and descriptive than those accounts of his fellow Australian expeditioners. It was perhaps Miller's distance from preconceptions of Aboriginal culture, and the novelty of the sounds, which meant that, from his first encounters with it, he was able to describe in detail the shape, timbre and playing of the didjeridu, the rhythmic variation

---

10   ibid., 30 September 1948.
11   ibid., 18 October 1948.
12   John Blacking, *How Musical Is Man?* (Seattle: University of Washington Press, 1973), 11.

of the songs heard and the ceremonial context for the music. While Miller also commented on the pleasant evenings by the gramophone in the house of Fred and Marjorie Gray, the group's hosts at Umbakumba on Groote Eylandt, it was not to contrast the familiarity of this music with the foreignness of Aboriginal singing as Bray did. Rather, while the gramophone music was barely described, Miller heard the Aboriginal music of staged corroborees with a keen ear: 'The throbbing rhythms were fascinating + the chanting monotonous but haunting in its repetition.'[13] Miller's ability to appreciate the music he heard as fascinating hints at the fact that he had fewer preconceptions of what was to be heard in Australian Indigenous music.

Other diarists' accounts of Aboriginal music show that they sought to understand its greater social and cultural significance, instead of judging it purely on aesthetic grounds. Some excerpts from Bessie Mountford's diary highlight this approach. From Mountford's discussions with Fred, one of the Bininj men (western Arnhem Land man) resident at Oenpelli and related to some of those she had met at Yirrkala, she learnt that the ongoing performance of corroborees was intimately related to the wellbeing of Aboriginal groups in a particular area, and even with their ongoing empowerment and independence. In response to Mountford's comment that the native residents at Yirrkala were 'pleasant and happy', Fred agreed: '"Yirrkala bin methodis Mission plenty laugh, plenty sing, plenty corroborree". "Oenpelli" he continued, "C.M. Mission no corroborree, people just sullen."' Bessie Mountford agreed, remarking: 'We certainly notice the difference, but one would need greater experience with both sections to say Yes or No to his simple statement.'[14]

In reflecting on this conversation, Mountford touched on an important tenet of Aboriginal cultures across different parts of Australia. As she sought to understand the link between contentment and wellbeing in a particular place, and the practice of singing and dancing or 'corroboree', Mountford grappled with an aspect of culture that non-Indigenous Australians have sought to understand for many years. In her limited contact with Aboriginal people, she had already learned that wellbeing in a particular place was closely linked to the practice of performance traditions linked to that place. Peter Toner's exploration of the link between song and Country confirms the ideas that Mountford was only beginning to understand, not only that songs were intricately linked with particular places, but that singing was intrinsic to the knowledge of Country in its physical, spiritual and historical senses:

---

13   Bob Miller, 'Diary', *Papers of Robert Rush Miller, 1947–51*, MS 10053, National Library of Australia (NLA), Canberra, 28 March 1948.
14   Bessie Mountford, 'Diary', *Mountford, Bessie Ilma, 1890-1996*, PRG487, State Library of South Australia (SLSA), Adelaide, 30 October 1948.

> [P]laces are not only physical landscapes but also countries of the mind. The contemporary socio-historical context is such that songs are not only the expression of pre-existing knowledge about country; it is through songs that many people come to know country in the first place … for those fortunate enough to live on their country, knowledge of songs is a pre-eminent means of learning about the most esoteric aspects of the spiritual connection between places, people, and ancestral beings and events.[15]

As Toner writes, 'the term songline has been widely adopted as a kind of catch-all concept … which attempts to condense the complexity of Aboriginality into an easy-to-digest form'.[16] Mountford's realisation pointed to her growing understanding that a continuous link to the songs of a particular place was one indicator of cultural continuation and the wellbeing of people on Country in Aboriginal Australia.

Margaret McArthur, the expedition's nutritionist, developed a similar understanding of her heard environment when she spent weeks at a time walking in pursuit of food with local women and camping with groups of Aboriginal people gathering food from the landscape. In response to ABC journalist Colin Simpson's questions about 'the allegedly slave-like status of native women', McArthur commented that it was:

> A lot of nonsense. They live their own lives within the tribe … have their own secret lodges where they sing and dance their own secret rituals … go out with them as I did. Listen to them joking and laughing and gossiping as they dig for yams or dive in the lagoon for lily roots. At night watch them dancing, away from the men, their own corroborees, swaying and clapping to the rhythm out there in the fire-glint and the shadows or under the moon. They look, and I think they feel, as little like slaves as I do.[17]

In other words, a chief indicator of the women's wellbeing in McArthur's eyes was women's singing and dancing. Implicit in her refutation of Simpson's claim that Aboriginal women were 'slave-like' was an understanding that to perform corroborees, to maintain one's own musical and dance traditions was to be free or empowered.

It is not difficult to imagine that this understanding of wellbeing associated with music-making was extrapolated from the expedition members' own experiences

---

15   Peter Toner, 'Sing a Country of the Mind: The articulation of place in Dhaḻwangu Song', in *The Soundscapes of Australia: Music, place and spirituality*, ed. Fiona Richards (Aldershot: Ashgate, 2007), 183.
16   Toner, 'Sing a Country of the Mind', 165.
17   Colin Simpson, *Adam in Ochre: Inside Aboriginal Australia* (Sydney: Angus & Robertson, 1951), 53.

in their leisure time over the months of the journey; that this, like many of their observations, was a projection of their own culture onto a foreign one. Fred McCarthy's diaries make perhaps the most commentary on the entertainment provided to the group by the 'singsong' which was a feature of many nights around the camp. In McCarthy's account, members of the group were praised not only for their official expedition role, but also for their ability to contribute songs to the nightly singalong.[18] McCarthy's observations were part of a larger tradition of song-making in the remote Australian bush, as indicated by Bill Harney's account. Harney, a long-term Northern Territory resident, who spent much of his life in the bush, assisted as guide to the expedition, and came to be regarded as an expert communicator with Aboriginal people, also recounted the nightly song and poetry exchange as a crucial feature of life droving cattle and generally camping in the bush, both as a means of entertainment among the campers and a way of calming the dozing cattle.[19]

The Novels

Whether as part of direct first-person observations of the sounds of Aboriginal culture and the bush, or as depictions in literature, the projection of one's own culture onto a foreign one is a recurring theme of mid-twentieth century accounts. In her novel *The Timeless Land*, Eleanor Dark used song-making as a device to indicate the rebelliousness of particular female Aboriginal characters. In Dark's portrayal of a Gadigal woman at the time of British settlement, Bennilong's younger sister, Warreweer, was depicted as transgressing the bounds of cultural expectations of women through the composition of songs:

> [T]hough well past the age when most women found husbands and produced children, [Warreweer] not only remained virgin, but shamelessly and persistently produced songs and tales instead. It was true that her fault was not so glaring as Carangarang's had been, for her songs were not such as a man might make, and her tales were not of battles or feats of strength, or of any matters which were more fittingly immortalised by a man; but there was an element in them, all the same, which some of the more sober-minded women of the tribe deplored ... It was more dignified, they decided to ignore her, to pretend that she was doing no more than most women did — making a lullaby or some such trifle — but in their hearts they could not help knowing that there was more to it than that. Why, they asked each other irritably, should she

---

18   See for example praise for the new cook Reg Hollow who not only makes nice hors d'oeuvres but also contributes songs. Frederick D. McCarthy, 'Diary 5: Yirrkala Diary No. 2 and Oenpelli' *Papers of Frederick David McCarthy*, MS 3513/14/5, AIATSIS, Canberra, 24 August 1948.

19   W. E. Harney, *North of 23°* (Sydney: Australasian Publishing, 1947), 38, 79.

want to make new songs at all? Were there not already innumerable tales for children, hallowed by centuries of use? Were there not lullabies that had been sung to their grandfathers and their great-grandfathers? What other songs should a woman need?[20]

We might reflect on the reasons these female commentators viewed the making of songs as indicative of personal empowerment in Aboriginal women. Just as anthropological history has pointed out the tendency of European colonists to ascribe the vices and traits of their own cultures to the studied other,[21] both Margaret McArthur's diary and Dark's novel transcribed the cultural significance of women writing music in their own culture onto Indigenous contexts. In the 1940s, few women were recognised as significant composers in Australia or in the European tradition from which non-Indigenous Australian musical culture was derived. The depiction of women who composed as transgressive is a persistent theme in Western music history and one which McArthur and Dark mapped on to the Aboriginal cultures about which they were writing.[22]

Katharine Susannah Prichard's 1925 *Coonardoo* is another novel in which the singing and dancing of Aboriginal people was used to evoke nobility and ongoing wellbeing:[23]

> And how Coonardoo sang for the fire corroboree! When Warieda gave the rhythm and air of the song, in a low melodious alto, clicking his kylies and the women began to sing, Coonardoo's voice quivered with her excitement, stretched shriller and higher to the strange magic words, and fell, creaking, whispering when Chitali came from the screen of bushes behind which the men were hiding.[24]

At the same time, this evocation of shrillness and creaking was unsettling to the non-Indigenous characters in the book.

---

20   Eleanor Dark, *The Timeless Land* (Melbourne: Fontana Books, 1980), 41.

21   See Victor Gordon Kiernan, *Imperialism and Its Contradictions* (New York: Routledge, 1995), 159: 'It has been noticed how ready the white man often is to invest the black man with all the worst impulses he is conscious of in himself.' See also Mick Gidley, ed., *Representing Others: White views of Indigenous peoples* (Exeter: University of Exeter Press, 1994). 3; Henrika Kuklick, *The Savage Within: The social history of British anthropology, 1885–1945* (Cambridge: Cambridge University Press, 1991), 1, 279–80; Nicholas Thomas, *Colonialism's Culture: Anthropology, travel and government* (Melbourne: Melbourne University Press, 1994), 6–7.

22   See Amanda Harris, 'The Spectacle of Woman as Creator: Representation of women composers in the French, German and English feminist press 1880–1930', *Women's History Review* 23:1 (2014): 18–42.

23   Prichard also wrote in the preface to her play *Brumby Innes* that the corroboree as a device in the narrative was designed to 'give something of the dignity, beauty and mystery of a primitive people under the condition of a vanquished race'. Quoted in J. J. Healy, *Literature and the Aborigine in Australia* (St Lucia: University of Queensland Press, 1989), 144.

24   Katharine Susannah Prichard, *Coonardoo*, Introduction by Druisilla Modjeska (Sydney: Angus & Robertson, 1994), 20. The use of descriptors such as 'shrill' and 'creaking' is consistent with Diane Collins' observation that Europeans described the music of 'savages' in terms evoking aural primitiveness, linking this to a cultural barbarity that negated any moral claim to the land. Collins, 'Acoustic Journeys': 11.

> On the hottest days of summer, under bare, pale-blue skies, drifts of the men's singing came to her from grey smoke-misted thickets below red bar peaks of the ridge … Whenever she heard those chants, and the murmurous boom of a coolardie, Mrs Bessie knew what was happening. Old men of the tribes away from the camp were preparing youths, by crude rites of circumcision and mutilation, for the standing of men in the camp … She was always restless and irritable while that singing was going on, more particularly if one of her own boys [young Aboriginal men who worked for her] was with the men.[25]

For Mrs Bessie, the agency and power evoked by participation in ceremony and corroboree threatened the control she may be able to exercise over her Aboriginal workers and unsettled her place as head of the station. Prichard's novel opened and closed with the musical theme that acted as a motif for the eponymous character. Prichard set up the book's soundscape from the opening sentence where Coonardoo was depicted singing and clicking two sticks together.

> Over and over again, in a thin reedy voice, away at the back of her head, the melody flowed like water running over smooth pebbles in a dry creek bed. Winding and falling, the words rattled together and flew eerily, as if she were whispering to herself … It was no more than a twitter in the shadow of dark bushes near the veranda; a twitter with the clicking of small sticks.[26]

Coonardoo's song, quoted in these first paragraphs, returns throughout the novel, both in her own voice and in that of her lover and aggressor, Hugh, as he evokes her spirit after assaulting her. Much of the literary analysis of this novel has focused on the equation of Coonardoo with the land, and criticism has revolved around 'the idea that the white man's desire for the Aboriginal woman would, if honoured, place him in a proper spiritual relationship to the land'.[27] This equation is evident in the opening passage in which Coonardoo's singing not only emerges from the sounds of the environment, but is described through evocations of pebbles, creek beds and shadows.

---

25 Prichard, *Coonardoo*, 23–4.

26 Prichard, *Coonardoo*, 1.

27 Susan Sheridan, quoted in Kerryn Goldsworthy, 'Fiction from 1900 to 1970', in *The Cambridge Companion to Australian Literature*, ed. Elizabeth Webby (Cambridge: Cambridge University Press, 2000), 123; see also Drusilla Modjeska's introduction to Prichard, *Coonardoo*, ix. For broader discussions of the conflation of Aboriginal people and land, see Bernard Smith, *The Spectre of Truganini* (Sydney: Australian Broadcasting Commission, 1980), 21; Collins, 'Acoustic Journeys': 12; Ann Curthoys, 'Expulsion, Exodus and Exile in White Australian Historical Mythology', *Journal of Australian Studies* 23:61 (1999): 13; David Symons, 'Words and Music: Clive Douglas and the Jindyworobak Manifesto', in *The Soundscapes of Australia: Music, place and spirituality*, ed. Fiona Richards (Aldershot: Ashgate, 2007), 98; and for the land conflated with woman see Kay Schaffer, *Women and the Bush: Forces of desire in the Australian cultural tradition* (Cambridge: Cambridge University Press, 1988), 62.

Mary Durack's *Keep Him My Country*, published in 1955, also opened and closed with a description of the protagonist Stan Rolt's soundscape. The wafting strains of Aboriginal singing, didjeridu and clapsticks were used to symbolise relationship to, alienation from, and reconciliation with the land and its Indigenous inhabitants. The novel opens with:

> Rolt stood for a moment, listening to the broken phrases of a familiar chant that trailed thinly on the morning air.
>
> It was no more to him now than a song to fade on the wind like the smoke of a dying fire, though once he had believed in its power to hold and to possess.[28]

It ends with:

> Behind them lament for the dead rose on a shivering thread of sound, shattered and broke into a falling cadence of grief, throbbing on through the bush like the pulse beat of her people, desolate, enduring.[29]

As these two excerpts suggest, for Stan Rolt, song drifting through his soundscape symbolised the love he was unable to pursue and the life force of Dalgerie, the Aboriginal woman with whom he had formed a relationship and who was now lost to him. Durack thus established from the outset the role of song in the narrative of Rolt's experience in the bush.

However, music played a more complex role in the novel than the *leitmotif* use for signifying Stan and Dalgerie. Just as John Bray contrasted the calls of Aboriginal singers with sounds of piano playing over the short-wave radio on the Arnhem Land Expedition, Durack used music as a trope for delineating difference between the races depicted in the narrative. The arrival of Stan's Uncle Arthur from the city prompted a shift in Durack's portrayals of music from the Aboriginal camps. Arthur's initial impressions of the music were unsettling, and his account apparently equated the 'lurking horrors' of insects and reptiles with the 'shrill', 'eerie' and 'savage' sounds that reach his ears:

> Arthur retired early, hoping to escape further torture [from mosquitoes] under his net. He tested the unyielding greenhide bunk, played a torch around for lurking horrors and brushed away a goggling toad. A hollow sound like the distant rumble of thunder came from down the river. There was a shrill peal of laughter and a sharp rhythmic tapping of sticks and then the chant began, softly at first, rising to a crescendo like

---

28   Mary Durack, *Keep Him My Country* (Adelaide: Seal Books, 1973), 7.
29   Durack, *Keep Him My Country*, 349.

the hurricane wind of the afternoon until the night was filled with eerie, savage sound, pulsating, deliberate. A fire blazed up on the high bank and black figures, painted like skeletons, stamped, leapt and postured.

"Savages," Arthur murmured, easing himself to a sitting posture on his comfortless bunk. "Surely he's going to tell them to stop? I can't be the only one wants to sleep."

But the revelry continued, uninterrupted and on a rising pitch of frenzy, into the early morning hours.[30]

As the days went on, Arthur began to experience the music not only as eerie and savage but as a collection of sounds directly in conflict with the sounds of his own world, and which created a cacophonous soundscape:

Seated on the exposed verandah he viewed the situation through dark glasses. Never in the heart of the city had he been aware of so much discordant sound. The strident tones of a gramophone mingled crazily with the almost incessant wild rhythm of corroboree. Birds in tens of thousands clustered on the trees, pecked about for insects in the mud, and shrieking like lost souls circled the house in dense clouds. Frogs croaked continuously in every key and thunder rolled like artillery in mountains of massed cloud.[31]

In Arthur's soundscape it was not the contrast of Aboriginal music with the 'strident' familiar music of the gramophone, but the combination of these with the shrieking and war-like noise of birds, frogs and thunder which unsettled him. The corroboree was thus depicted as an implicit and inseparable part of the cacophonous soundscape of the bush in which Aboriginal people as the composers and performers of the music he heard faded into a montage of land and animals.

Arthur's account also reveals the extent to which the industrial noise of the city, through its familiarity, stood for order. Durack's writing represents sentiments reminiscent of early colonial reactions to the organising of industry in Australia and the contrast of these with the uncomprehended and untamed sounds of Aboriginal people and the bush environment. As Diane Collins has shown, many early explorers 'listened with the same economic ear that heard in the industrial cacophony of nineteenth-century England profit's sweet sounds'. Collins notes that it was the sounds of industrious labour that resonated with these early travellers, far from home, not those of the unfamiliar environs of their travels:

---

30   Durack, *Keep Him My Country*, 313.
31   Durack, *Keep Him My Country*, 314.

> When Charles Sturt arrived in Australia the first acoustic he recorded was not the kookaburra but the sound of improvement. With intense satisfaction he heard, on Sydney's hills, that the "lowing of herds had succeeded the wild whoop of the savage; and the stillness of that once desert shore is now broken by the sound of the bugle and the busy hum of commerce".[32]

In Xavier Herbert's 1938 *Capricornia* too, the sound of the landscape was closely linked with Aboriginal music production. Music does not feature heavily as a trope in *Capricornia*, but one significant moment where it is used as a device is the scene in which the protagonist Norman realises his Aboriginality. Having been raised by an uncle to believe that his heritage was Indonesian, Norman's epiphany comes as he finds himself at night in the bush: 'Never before had night found him out of earshot of his kind [the non-Indigenous family who raised him]', and in the form of a song which rose up within him in response to the clicking sound of a golden beetle. As he began to beat in time with the insect's song, his own melody emerged from his chest until he broke the spell with an angry return to consciousness and refusal to identify with what was depicted in the novel as an innate Aboriginality driven by instinct, in spite of his rational self: 'He had to restrain himself from seeking relief in the Song of the Golden Beetle. Then for the first time he realised his Aboriginal heritage.'[33]

The fact that this description of singing and playing was used at a moment so central to the plot of the novel is significant to non-Indigenous conceptions of Aboriginal music. In Norman's experience, the urge to sing and play rhythms was constructed as instinctual and innate, something rising up from a deep indigeneity, revealing Norman's true nature. Here, in Herbert's rendition of Aboriginal instinct, music emerges from the body and ancestry of the people. This stands in contrast to the songs of white travellers which were composed, written and performed as deliberate music-making, and in some cases as attempts to counteract the wild uncontrollable sounds and activities of the land. In this interpretation of Aboriginal music, the agency of individuals who compose and perform is absent, and music-making is understood as native instinct.

The characterisation of Aboriginal music making as involuntary and primal was also a device used in Eleanor Dark's 1941 novel, *The Timeless Land*. In Dark's use of this trope, it functioned as a bridge between cultures for escaped convict, Andrew Prentice, when he distanced himself from his life of suffering as a member of the European underclass and prisoner, and embraced his new life

---

32   Collins, 'Acoustic Journeys': 11.
33   Xavier Herbert, *Capricornia* (Sydney: A & R Classics, 2002), 334–5. See discussion of this passage also in Healy, *Literature and the Aborigine in Australia*, 163.

in the bush and his union with an Aboriginal woman, Cunnembeillee. When Prentice attended an initiation ceremony to which he had been invited by his wife's tribe:

> He found himself beating, as his companions were doing, upon his thighs and buttocks, but he did not stop. He was under some compulsion which he no longer wanted to resist. The glare brightened so that he blinked his dazzled eyes, and the tempo quickened, and his hands beat faster and his pulses with them … the civilisation which had used him so ill fell away like an unfastened garment, and his body taught him what his mind would never grasp.[34]

In this use of Aboriginal music, Dark depicts the surrender of the white body to the compulsions of Indigenous Country and culture.

Adam Shoemaker has argued that considering only those novels still regarded today to be of literary importance does not give a holistic picture of the wider impact of mid-century writing by non-Indigenous authors portraying Aboriginal people. As Shoemaker has pointed out, Ion L. Idriess' fifty-five novels, selling a total of three million copies, offer a different perspective to those of Herbert and Prichard on Aboriginal people.[35] The promotional blurb preceding the title page of Idriess' 1933 novel, *Drums of Mer*, indicates the extent to which his books were marketed as instructive of authentic Aboriginal life:

> A vivid authentic picture of life among the headhunting warriors of the Torres Strait islands. Brought up native-fashion, a white man and two lovely white girls find themselves drawn together by their common desire to escape from primitive savagery to civilized life.[36]

As indicated by this blurb, Idriess' novels not only claimed to portray an authentic version of Aboriginal culture, but explicitly contrasted the 'primitive savagery' of that culture to the far more desirable 'civilized life'. While the caricatured Aboriginal players in Idriess' novels engaged constantly in ceremonial practices which involved brutal killings and unrestrained wildness, their music was not described in any detail, but was portrayed as part of the frenzy of savage behaviour, so incomprehensible to the white refugees from civilisation. Indeed, in *Drums of Mer*, the protagonist, Jakara clearly articulated that lack of comprehension of Indigenous music was a pre-requisite for a proper and correct kind of whiteness. In his interactions with a white woman known as Eyes of the Sea, who had been raised to be part of a neighbouring Indigenous

---

34 Dark, *The Timeless Land*, 437–8.
35 Adam Shoemaker, *Black Words White Page: Aboriginal literature 1929–1988* (St Lucia: University of Queensland Press, 1989), 54.
36 Ion L. Idriess, *Drums of Mer* (Sydney: Pacific Books, 1962).

tribe, Jakara reprimanded her as a 'little white savage' for her appreciation of and absorption in the music of the culture to which she had been raised. Reproaching her for singing, Jakara explained why he disliked her involvement in the music of her tribe:

> A girl of the white people should not sing at the sight of savages bound for murder and things more terrible … can't you realize that you belong to another race? … Don't you understand that we must cling to the ideals of our own people?"[37]

In Idriess' framing of whiteness, an appreciation of Aboriginal music was antithetical to a civilised and proper white life; the ability to comprehend, practice and embrace Indigenous musical culture was an indication of improper behaviour of the white race.

The Music

I began this chapter by suggesting that auditory sources have much to offer history writing, and yet, so far I have discussed only written accounts of auditory encounters. Compositions drawing on recordings of Aboriginal song offer one source of sonic expressions of the understanding and integration of Aboriginal music into non-Indigenous framings of culture. Peter Sculthorpe, perhaps Australia's best-known non-Indigenous composer, has been credited with the cultivation of an Australian national style of Western art music, chiefly through his use of melodies derived from Aboriginal song and the imitation of the sounds of the Australian bush (particularly birds) in his compositions. His earliest work to directly quote an Aboriginal melody was a film score from 1974, later adapted into a free-standing composition for string ensemble, *Port Essington* (1977). Linda Kouvaras describes *Port Essington* as portraying 'the collision between would-be settlers and inhospitable land'.[38] As Kouvaras explains, in order to programmatically depict this collision, Sculthorpe used as his chief melodic material, the *Djilile* (whistling duck) melody derived from a recording made by A. P. Elkin in Arnhem Land in 1949.[39]

---

37 Idriess, *Drums of Mer*, 59.

38 Linda Kouvaras, 'From Port Essington to the Himalayas: Music, place and spirituality in two contemporary Australian compositions', in *The Soundscapes of Australia: Music, place and spirituality*, ed. Fiona Richards (Aldershot: Ashgate, 2007), 230.

39 The melody, part of Maraian ceremonies in central Arnhem Land, was called *djilili* and recorded by Elkin at Mainoru in 1949, although Sculthorpe repeatedly later stated that it was *djilile* recorded in the late 1950s. This spelling is corrected by Michael Hannan who transcribed the melody used by Sculthorpe. Michael Hannan 'Scoring Essington: Composition, comprovisation, collaboration', *Screen Sound* 2 (2011): 51; A. P. Elkin, 'Arnhem Land Music (Part 3)', *Oceania* 25:4 (1955): 331; A. P. Elkin, 'Maraian at Mainoru, 1949: I. Description', *Oceania* 31:4 (1961): 284.

Although Sculthorpe's depiction originates in a period several decades after the Arnhem Land Expedition, the recording which inspired it was made by Elkin just one year after the expedition's conclusion, in an area of central Arnhem Land a couple of hundred kilometres inland from their first stop on Groote Eylandt. Elkin positioned himself in opposition to the work of the expedition, largely because of his disdain for the amateur status of its leader, C. P. Mountford. Martin Thomas has suggested that Elkin's expedition to central Arnhem Land in 1949 was in part an act designed to corner his own segment of the market for ethnographic knowledge about Aboriginal culture, and that this trip was at odds with his usual methods of sustained stays in the communities he studied.[40] Controversy has plagued the modern uses of Elkin's recordings and discussion about issues of ethics and appropriation in Sculthorpe's use of the *Djilile* melody has been, if not extensive, then at least frequently recurring throughout musicological literature and popular discussions of Sculthorpe's compositional methodology. Perhaps the most rigorous of these is given by Stephen Knopoff, who compares Sculthorpe's rendering of the melody with the original recordings made by Elkin and finds that Sculthorpe's *Djilile* melody only approximately resembles the one originally sung by Kandamura, his brother, and a third man in the Djambarrpuyngu language.[41]

Nevertheless, Sculthorpe used his rendering of the melody, transcribed by his research assistant, Michael Hannan, in many forms over his compositional career, each time citing Elkin's recording as the origin of the melody he claimed to quote directly.[42] In *Port Essington*, the transcribed melody is used throughout the work's six movements, though it is transformed in a number of ways. In the sections played by string orchestra, representing the land, the melody is clearly recognisable, while in the string trio, representing European settlement, it is more opaque. In Kouvaras' discussion of this compositional technique, and in Sculthorpe's own framing of the conflict between Europeans and the Australian landscape, Aboriginal music in the form of this single melody, comes to stand for land. This conflation of land and Aboriginal people was a frequent theme of Sculthorpe's discussions of the inspiration drawn from the Australian soundscape. Similarly, David Symons' analysis of other composers, such as Clive Douglas, who drew on Aboriginal music, suggests that they

> see, as an essential vehicle for this Australian identification, the link with the Australian landscape via the evocation of Aboriginal culture. Further, it was not so much Aboriginal human culture which was a focus for either writers or composers, but rather an appreciation of its

---

40   Thomas, this volume; Martin Thomas, 'Expedition as Time Capsule: Introducing the American–Australian Scientific Expedition to Arnhem Land', in *Exploring the Legacy of the 1948 Arnhem Land Expedition*, eds M. Thomas and M. Neale (Canberra: ANU E Press, 2011), 8.

41   Steven Knopoff, 'Cross-Cultural Appropriation: A musicologist's perspective', *Sounds Australian* 67 (2006): 25–6.

42   Hannan, 'Scoring *Essington*', 51.

mystic link with the land and the Dreamtime which was seen as a way of (in Douglas' words) forging a link "which will serve to connect the composer's thought to the land itself".[43]

In Sculthorpe's framing of his work, the bush was represented in music composed in 'my own manner' (or by Kouvaras in 'Sculthorpe's own style').[44] It is not entirely clear what constituted this style, except that the music for string orchestra to which Sculthorpe referred is transparently based on the transcription of the Arnhem Land melody and rhythm, whereas in the string trio this melody is camouflaged in a harmonic style evocative of eighteenth century European string writing. This string trio setting drew its material from the *Djilile* melody as well, and thus Sculthorpe would seem to be commenting on European attempts to civilise the raw material of the Australian bush (conflated here with Aboriginal people and their arts) by altering its essential elements into an unrecognisable form.

As Sculthorpe's introduction to the piece made explicit, the work programmatically depicts the European attempt to create an ongoing settlement at Port Essington, an attempt which failed on two occasions in the course of the nineteenth century.[45] In his description: 'those living there were unable to adapt to the peculiar conditions of the land'.[46] In Sculthorpe's musical rendering of the events, this adaptation also failed, as 'the insistence of the music of the string orchestra [the bush] brings about a withdrawal of the music played by the string trio [the Europeans]'. In musical terms, this withdrawal is characterised in the second movement by the increasingly frequent interjection of dissonant chords from the string orchestra, which unsettle the structured harmonic progressions of the string trio (Figure 1). These interjections become more and more persistent, destabilising the coherence of the string trio's harmony. As Sculthorpe intimates, the failure of the European colony at Port Essington seems to have been mainly due to the difficulty of coping with the tropical environment, in particular with outbreaks of malaria and the unfamiliarity of the climate for the purposes of agriculture. In historical accounts of the settlement from 1838 to 1849, a non-confrontational approach in regard to Aborigines was taken by the Europeans, and the settlement may have been regularly supplied by Aboriginal people with seafood and plant foodstuffs from the surrounding Country.[47] And yet, in his work *Port Essington*, Sculthorpe presents this as an oppositional breakdown with the Europeans, represented by chamber music, versus the bush, represented by an Aboriginal melody.

---

43   Symons, 'Words and Music', 98.

44   Peter Sculthorpe, *Port Essington for Strings* (London: Faber Music, 1980), prologue; Kouvaras, 'From Port Essington', 232.

45   Port Essington was also the endpoint for Ludwig Leichhardt's first exploratory expedition; after being presumed lost, Leichhardt arrived at the settlement in December 1845. Sculthorpe mentions Leichhardt's Expedition in the Prologue to the work. His expeditions were subsequently the inspiration for Patrick White's 1957 novel *Voss*, which contains only very brief descriptions of Aboriginal people singing as the expedition group suffers and struggles through the foreign landscape. Patrick White, *Voss* (Harmondsworth & Ringwood: Penguin, 1960).

46   Sculthorpe, *Port Essington for Strings*, prologue.

47   Jim Allen, *Port Essington: The historical archaeology of a north Australian nineteenth-century military outpost* (Sydney: Sydney University Press, 2008), 128.

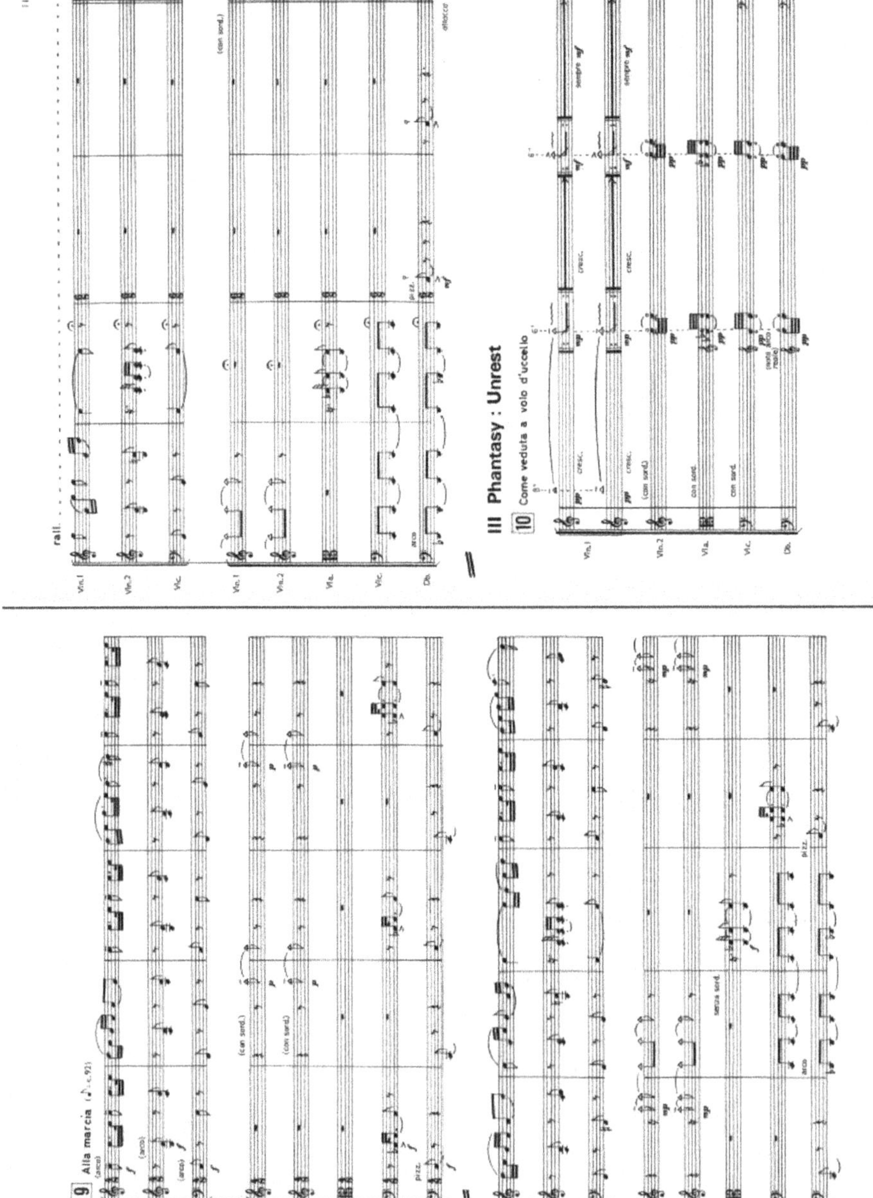

Figure 1: Sculthorpe, *Port Essington*, Second Movement.

Source: Sculthorpe, *Port Essington for Strings*, 10–11. © 1980 by Faber Music Ltd. Reproduced by kind permission of the publishers. All rights reserved.

Following this is a movement for the string orchestra in which all instruments use specialised string techniques to imitate bird sounds from the Australian bush. When the string trio returns, the *Djilile* melody is now transparent, though rhythmically altered, in the cello line throughout the movement, but is again harmonised by diatonic progressions in the remaining two parts of the trio. This harmony is unable to be sustained for the entire movement, and the string orchestra again appears, imposing the *Djilile* melody in its original rhythmic setting and creating bitonal clashes with the consonance of the trio (Figure 2).

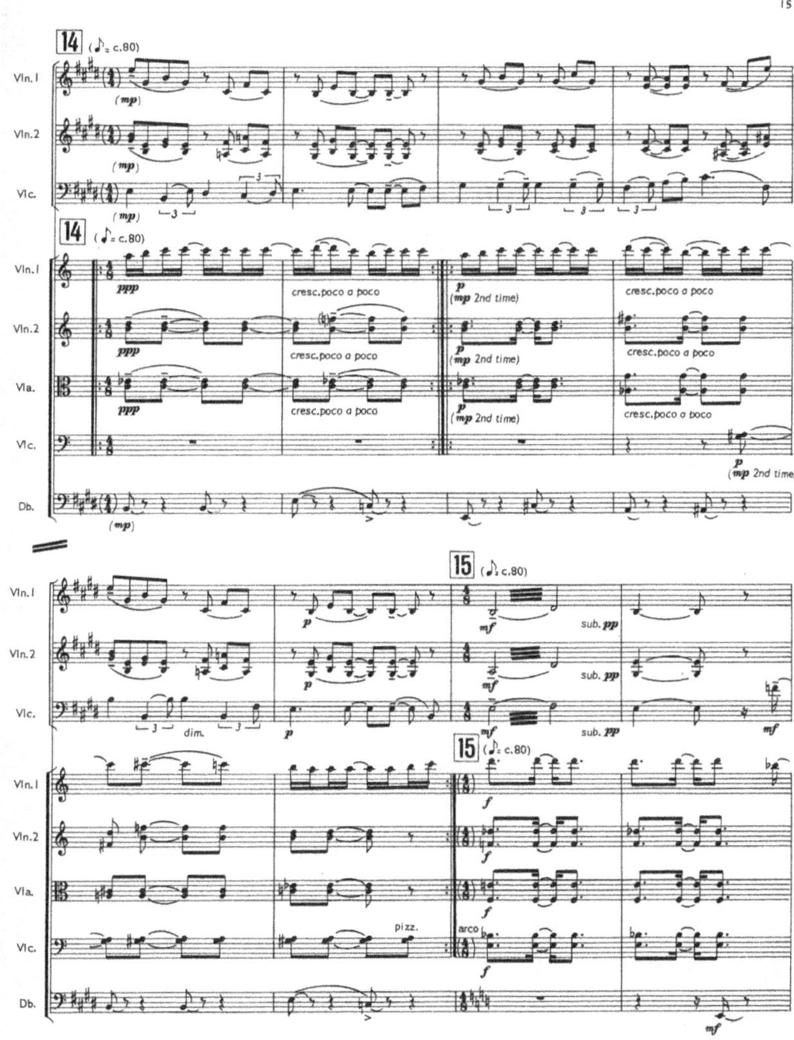

Figure 2: Sculthorpe, *Port Essington*, Fourth Movement.

Sculthorpe described the music of the fifth movement as that of the Europeans withdrawing, following which, 'the music is echoed by the string orchestra, suggesting that some kind of agreement could have been possible'.[48] We can only speculate on how Sculthorpe himself may have conceptualised such an agreement, given that, at this point in the music, the *Djilile* theme has been transformed into such a statement of European classical music as to be barely recognisable as a melody derived from the original transcription (Figure 3). This absorption of the melody implies that the agreement could only have been reached through the assimilation of Arnhem Land into European traditions. This reading of cultural assimilation is justified, I argue, by the very literal programmatic framework in which Sculthorpe inscribes the meaning of the Aboriginal melody in his notes about the piece, published alongside the musical score.

Knopoff suggests that Sculthorpe's positing of an Aboriginal origin to a non-Aboriginal culture raises issues of representation that are quite separate to any discussion of appropriation: 'some critics and listeners have conflated issues of *appropriation* (in this case, taking a melody from one context for use in another) with what are actually issues of *representation* (positing an Aboriginal origin to a melody in a non-Aboriginal composition).' Knopoff implies, but not does not exactly make explicit, the connotations of Sculthorpe's representation of his compositions as based on Aboriginal music.[49] Indeed, it may be possible to conceive of Sculthorpe's frequent reiteration that his works (from *Essington*, through *Djilile*, to *Kakadu*) were based on an authentic Arnhem Land melody, as appropriation of a different kind; that by co-opting the exoticism and prestige derived from drawing on Australian Indigenous culture, Sculthorpe appropriated the rhetorical capital of Aboriginal culture without being attentive to its cultural context, or even without being true to the melodic and rhythmic content of the original musical object. Sculthorpe thereby lay claim to a national style drawing on the materials of the very land of Australia itself, through its Indigenous people.

---

48   Sculthorpe, *Port Essington for Strings*, prologue.

49   Knopoff does state that although works such as *Kakadu* have attracted interest because of their ostensible reference to Aboriginal song, no direct benefit of this success has flowed back to the communities whose music inspired the work. Knopoff, 'Cross-Cultural Appropriation', 26–7.

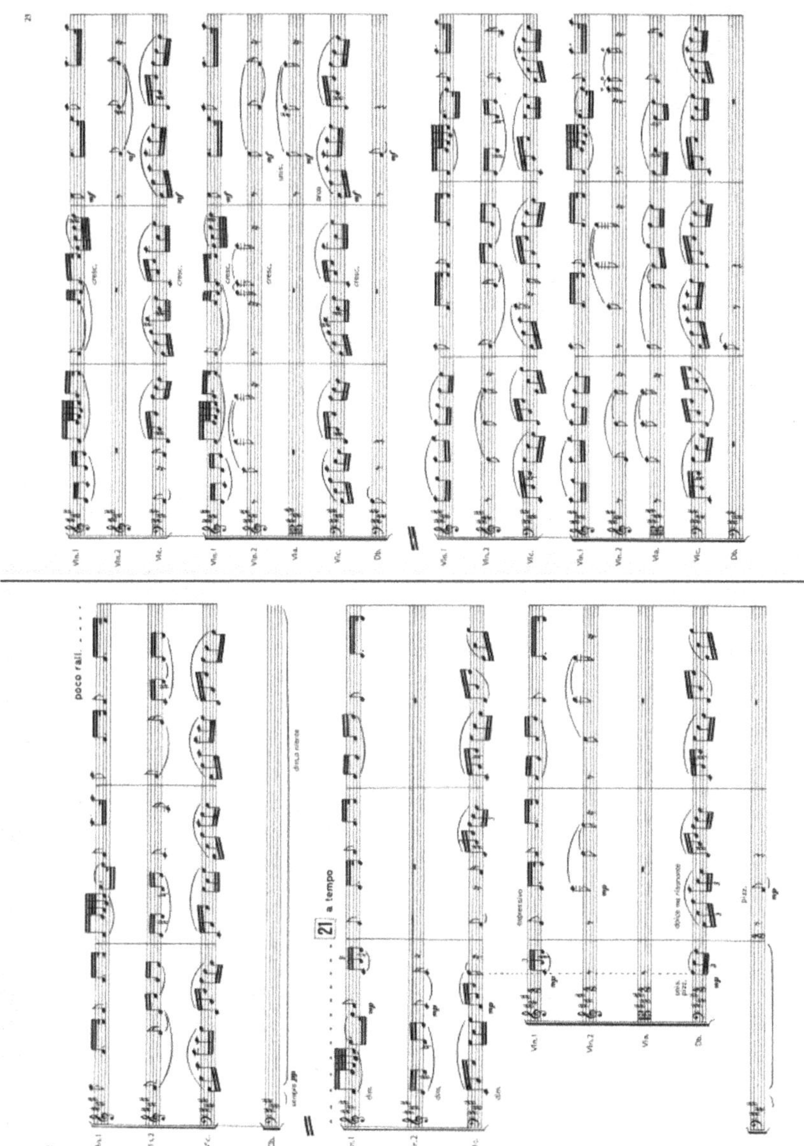

Figure 3: Sculthorpe, *Port Essington*, Sixth Movement.

Source: Sculthorpe, *Port Essington for Strings*, 22–23. © 1980 by Faber Music Ltd. Reproduced by kind permission of the publishers. All rights reserved.

Conclusion

The ways in which Indigenous music has been portrayed by non-Indigenous diarists, novelists and composers reflects broader attitudes towards Indigenous people and culture in the mid-century. As we have seen from diaries, novels and music, limited possibilities were available for Indigenous auditory culture to play a role in non-Indigenous narratives, whether as first-person accounts of heard experience or as fictional portraits of Aboriginal culture. Certain tropes recur with regularity: the contrast of the ordered and familiar sounds of European music with the chaotic, wild and cacophonous sounds of Aboriginal music and the bush soundscape; the conflation of the sounds produced in the musical traditions and practices of Aboriginal people with the organic sounds of animals, weather and the landscape; notions of primal instinct, innateness and compulsion which accompanied ideas about Aboriginal music production; and the association of the practice of music with empowerment and continuation of tradition. There are many parallels here with Ann Curthoys' survey of Australian history-writing in the same period. Curthoys writes about settlement narratives in which Aboriginal people barely appear, or at least not in mutli-dimensional ways:

> The literary critic Peter Otto suggests that the popular narrative of horror in the desert, of the land and landscape as the malignant unknown, is not innocent, or transparent. Rather, it offers a colonial society a way of displacing the conflict between settlers and indigenous peoples onto a more acceptable narrative of a direct conflict between the settler and the land itself. The land and the indigenous people become merged, the former foregrounded, the latter denied a place in history at all.[50]

The narratives I have discussed confined understanding of Aboriginal music to limiting paradigms and always in reference to non-Indigenous culture, rather than seeking to frame Indigenous music within its own cultural references. Indigenous music in these accounts is heard as a projection of the listeners' own cultural experience of the bush or the Australian soundscape, notwithstanding the framing of these experiences in terms of cultural authenticity (in particular by Sculthorpe and Idriess). Most frequently these hearings were projections of the authors' own feelings of isolation, alienation, or exoticised attraction to their surroundings rather than any kind of true representation of an other, or a foreign auditory culture.[51] In this sense, what we can hear through an analysis

---

50 Curthoys, 'Expulsion, Exodus and Exile in White Australian Historical Mythology', 13.
51 See Gidley's discussion (following Edward Said) of non-Indigenous writers being able only to depict elements of themselves in their representation of the other. Gidley, ed., *Representing Others*, 3; and Bernard Smith on the 'guilty colonial hearts that sought to stifle the story of despair, projecting their fear and guilt upon nature itself'. Smith, *The Spectre of Truganini*, 21.

of these written and musical texts is the sound of non-Indigenous Australians grappling with their own dislocation in the country in which they were born, and the heightened awareness of this cultural displacement through hearings of Indigenous music.

Acknowledgements

This chapter has benefitted from comments on an early draft from members of the Musicology Colloquium Series at the Sydney Conservatorium of Music, especially from Linda Barwick, as well as from the insights of two anonymous reviewers.

References

Allen, Jim. *Port Essington: The historical archaeology of a north Australian nineteenth-century military outpost* (Sydney: Sydney University Press, 2008).

Blacking, John. *How Musical Is Man?* (Seattle: University of Washington Press, 1973).

Collins, Diane. 'Acoustic Journeys: Exploration and the search for an aural history of Australia', *Australian Historical Studies* 37:128 (2006): 1–17.

Curthoys, Ann. 'Expulsion, Exodus and Exile in White Australian Historical Mythology', *Journal of Australian Studies* 23:61 (1999): 1–19.

Damousi, Joy, and Desley Deacon, eds. *Talking and Listening in the Age of Modernity: Essays on the history of sound* (Canberra: ANU E Press, 2007).

Dark, Eleanor. *The Timeless Land* (Melbourne: Fontana Books, 1980).

Durack, Mary. *Keep Him My Country* (Adelaide: Seal Books, 1973).

Elkin, A. P. 'Arnhem Land Music (Part 3)', *Oceania* 25:4 (1955): 292–342.

Elkin, A. P. 'Maraian at Mainoru, 1949: I. Description', *Oceania* 31:4 (1961): 259–93.

Gidley, Mick, ed. *Representing Others: White views of Indigenous peoples* (Exeter: University of Exeter Press, 1994).

Goldsworthy, Kerryn. 'Fiction from 1900 to 1970', in *The Cambridge Companion to Australian Literature,* ed. Elizabeth Webby (Cambridge: Cambridge University Press, 2000), 105–33.

Hannan, Michael. 'Scoring Essington: Composition, comprovisation, collaboration', *Screen Sound* 2 (2011): 48–63.

Harney, W. E. *North of 23°* (Sydney: Australasian Publishing, 1947).

Harris, Amanda. 'Food, Feeding and Consumption (or the Cook, the Wife and the Nutritionist): The politics of gender and class in a 1948 Australian expedition', *History and Anthropology* 24:3 (2013): 1–17.

Harris, Amanda. 'The Spectacle of Woman as Creator: Representation of women composers in the French, German and English feminist press 1880–1930', *Women's History Review* 23:1 (2014): 18–42.

Healy, J. J. *Literature and the Aborigine in Australia* (St Lucia: University of Queensland Press, 1989).

Herbert, Xavier. *Capricornia* (Sydney: A & R Classics, 2002).

Idriess, Ion L. *Drums of Mer* (Sydney: Pacific Books, 1962).

Kiernan, Victor Gordon. *Imperialism and Its Contradictions* (New York: Routledge, 1995).

Knopoff, Steven. 'Cross-Cultural Appropriation: A musicologist's perspective', *Sounds Australian* 67 (2006): 2–27.

Kouvaras, Linda. 'From Port Essington to the Himalayas: Music, place and spirituality in two contemporary Australian compositions', in *The Soundscapes of Australia: Music, place and spirituality*, ed. Fiona Richards (Aldershot: Ashgate, 2007), 229–45.

Kuklick, Henrika. *The Savage Within: The social history of British anthropology, 1885–1945* (Cambridge: Cambridge University Press, 1991).

Picker, John M. *Victorian Soundscapes* (New York: Oxford University Press, 2003).

Prichard, Katharine Susannah. *Coonardoo*, Introduction by Drusilla Modjeska (Sydney: Angus & Robertson, 1994).

Schafer, R. Murray. *The Tuning of the World* (New York: Knopf, 1977).

Schafer, R. Murray. 'Soundscapes and Earwitnesses', in *Hearing History: A reader*, ed. Mark M. Smith (Athens: University of Georgia Press, 2004), 3–9.

Schaffer, Kay. *Women and the Bush: Forces of desire in the Australian cultural tradition* (Cambridge: Cambridge University Press, 1988).

Sculthorpe, Peter. *Port Essington for Strings* (London: Faber Music, 1980).

Shoemaker, Adam. *Black Words White Page: Aboriginal literature 1929–1988* (St Lucia: University of Queensland Press, 1989).

Simpson, Colin. *Adam in Ochre: Inside Aboriginal Australia* (Sydney: Angus & Robertson, 1962).

Smith, Bernard. *The Spectre of Truganini* (Sydney: Australian Broadcasting Commission, 1980).

Smith, Mark M., ed. *Hearing History: A reader* (Athens: University of Georgia Press, 2004).

Symons, David. 'Words and Music: Clive Douglas and the Jindyworobak Manifesto', in *The Soundscapes of Australia: Music, place and spirituality*, ed. Fiona Richards (Aldershot: Ashgate, 2007), 93-115.

Thomas, Martin. 'The Rush to Record: Transmitting the sound of Aboriginal culture', *Journal of Australian Studies* 31:90 (2007): 107–202.

Thomas, Martin. 'Expedition as Time Capsule: Introducing the American–Australian Scientific Expedition to Arnhem Land', in *Exploring the Legacy of the 1948 Arnhem Land Expedition*, eds M. Thomas and M. Neale (Canberra: ANU E Press, 2011), 1–30.

Thomas, Nicholas. *Colonialism's Culture: Anthropology, travel and government* (Melbourne: Melbourne University Press, 1994).

Toner, Peter. 'Sing a Country of the Mind: The articulation of place in Dhaḻwangu Song', in *The Soundscapes of Australia: Music, place and spirituality*, ed. Fiona Richards (Aldershot: Ashgate, 2007), 165–83.

Weliver, Phyllis. 'Tom-Toms, Dream-Fugues and Poppy Juice: East meets west in nineteenth-century fiction', in *Music and Orientalism in the British Empire, 1780s–1940s*, eds Martin Clayton and Bennett Zon (Aldershot: Ashgate, 2007), 257–76.

White, Patrick. *Voss* (Harmondsworth & Ringwood: Penguin, 1960).

Woodfield, Ian. *English Musicians in the Age of Exploration* (Stuyvesant: Pendragon Press, 1995).

Part 2: Transformation and Repatriation

5. Song as Artefact: The Reclaiming of Song Recordings Empowering Indigenous Stakeholders—and the Recordings Themselves

Genevieve Campbell

The culture of the Tiwi Islands, northern Australia, has been the subject of much anthropological literature but none focuses on music. Since 2007 I have been working with senior Tiwi song-men and -women and studying contemporary Tiwi song culture in the context of the maintenance of traditions in the development of new music forms. In 2009 I was closely involved in the return to the Tiwi community of a large amount of ethnographic song material housed at the Australian Institute for Aboriginal and Torres Strait Islander Studies (AIATSIS) in Canberra. In this chapter I give an account of the process undertaken by a group of Tiwi people to reclaim[1] that song material, including the emotional, socio-political, legal and ethical issues that my Tiwi colleagues[2] and I encountered, as well as the effect that the material is now having on Tiwi song tradition itself. Documenting the experience of the group of Indigenous owners of the material is essential to an understanding of how their journey to Canberra has informed the reception of the recordings in the context of the four areas listed above. Importantly, the pro-active nature of the Tiwi group's involvement with the repatriation has added an extra level to their understanding of the procedure and therefore resulted in a personal investment and heightened sense of ownership of the recordings.

Repatriation

The repatriation of recordings to Indigenous stakeholders has, over the last two decades, become a central consideration of ethnomusicological research in the

---

1 I use the word 'reclaim' here because that is how the Tiwi people regarded the purpose of the journey to the Institute.

2 Throughout this chapter I refer both to my Tiwi 'colleagues' and 'consultants'. I use both terms to reflect the (small but meaningful) differences in our relationship. As peers working together on professional performance and recording projects we consider ourselves colleagues. In the context of the audition, transcription and documentation of archive recordings our relationship is more one of researcher/informant and in those cases I use the term consultant.

Australian region (and indeed all over the world), with the return of recordings itself becoming an object of research.[3] Reported motivations for repatriation that are relevant to my engagement with the Tiwi recordings include:

- a response to direct request from (Indigenous) people with direct ownership claims;
- the facilitation of analysis and collection of essential accompanying metadata;
- as source material proving ownership in land-rights cases of Country and kinship affiliations;[4]
- the enhancement of cultural maintenance activities within the stakeholders' community and;
- because it is the right thing to do.[5]

The power of repatriated recordings to reinvigorate interest in song practice (which has been the focus of my recent work on the Tiwi Islands) is only one of the benefits. Old recordings hold great social and historical significance, as well as holding ancestral and cultural knowledge of Country[6] and kinship relationships.[7] One of the key themes to emerge is the emotional response of Indigenous owners to the material.

There have been three important and distinct areas of response to the Tiwi recordings that I can report on directly:

---

3   Linda Barwick and Allan Marett, 'Endangered Songs and Endangered Languages', in *Maintaining the Links: Language identity and the land; Seventh Conference of the Foundation for Endangered Languages*, eds Joe Blythe and R. M. Brown (Bath: Foundation for Endangered Languages, 2003); Robert C. Lancefield, 'Musical Traces' Retraceable Paths: The repatriation of recorded sound', *Journal of Folklore Research* 35:1 (1998); Stubington, Jill, 'Collecting Folk Music in Australia: Report of a forum held 4-6 December 1987' (Kensington: University of New South Wales, 1989); Thieberger, Nick, and Simon Musgrave, 'Documentary Linguistics and Ethical Issues', *Documentary and Descriptive Linguistics* 4 (2007); Peter G. Toner, 'History, Memory and Music: The repatriation of digital audio to Yolngu communities, or, memory as metadata', in *Researchers, Communities, Institutions, Sound Recordings*, eds Linda Barwick, Allan Marett, Jane Simpson and Amanda Harris (Sydney: University of Sydney, 2003); Sally Treloyn, Rona Googninda Charles, and Sherika Nulgit, 'Repatriation of Song Materials to Support Intergenerational Transmission of Knowledge About Language in the Kimberley Region of Northwest Australia', in *Endangered Languages Beyond Boundaries: Proceedings of the 17th Foundation for Endangered Languages Conference*, eds Mary Jane Norris, Erik Anonby and Marie-Odile Junker (Bath: Foundation for Endangered Languages, 2013).

4   Amongst the recordings made by Groger-Wurm in 1965 is a segment in which a Tiwi woman lists family names and the Country groups they belong to. It has been used by one of my consultants to contest a current situation in the Tiwi Land Council.

5   Anthony Seeger, 'Do We Need to Remodel Ethnomusicology?', *Ethnomusicology* 31:3 (1987); Sally Treloyn and Andrea Emberly, 'Sustaining Traditions: Ethnomusicological collections, access and sustainability in Australia', *Musicology Australia* 35:2, Special Issue: Sustainability and Ethnomusicology in Australasia (2013).

6   I capitalise 'Country' because this term is used as a proper noun to indicate the area of land with which each Tiwi person identifies as a spiritual and ancestral home.

7   Toner, 'History, Memory and Music'.

Emotional, Personal Responses

Hearing their own voices, those of ancestors, or deceased loved ones has had a powerful effect on some Tiwi people. There have also been strong (positive and negative) sentimental reactions to songs with subject matter pertaining to Tiwi social history. More than with just the recordings themselves, there has been a powerful sense amongst Tiwi listeners that, with their 'trapped'[8] voices being back on the islands, a tangible, almost physical part of the ancestors has been returned home.

Questions of Ownership

a) Differing understandings and opinions have emerged regarding the cultural, physical and intellectual ownership of Tiwi song material. The moral and legal rights of Indigenous 'traditional owners'[9] and non-Tiwi copyright holders, the archive (in this case AIATSIS) and the researcher is an issue that is an ongoing underlying concern for me and my Tiwi colleagues.

b) Questions of ownership have been raised amongst Tiwi people with regard to individual and/or family associations with particular (recorded) songs, ceremonies or singers and therefore the use of those recordings and the documentation, transcription and translation of the songs.

The Effect of the Recordings' Return on the Future of the Song Tradition

Tiwi song culture is primarily based on occasion-specific improvisatory composition. There has been significant (sometimes negative) impact, from an artistic point of view, of hearing old recordings that demonstrate higher quality linguistic and performance values and therefore confirm perceptions of cultural loss. This is a very sensitive issue, especially amongst senior men in the community. In the face of language loss and dwindling numbers of singers with knowledge of composition, the old recordings are becoming a resource of song text to be learned by rote. This has the potential to create, with a library of recorded material, a canon of songs that might eventually take the place of the Tiwi tradition of improvisation.

---

8   Leonie Tipiloura, personal communication, Canberra, 18 November 2009.
9   This is a term widely used in Australia to indicate the Indigenous owners and/or custodians of Aboriginal land and extends to cultural knowledge and heritage.

Gaining Access to the Recordings

The desire (the women's group's and my own) to find the old Tiwi recordings came about largely through the process of workshopping the *Ngarukuruwala* music project, a contemporary performance collaboration between Sydney jazz musicians and Tiwi women singers, founded in 2007. Questions asked by the Sydney musicians about the meanings, melodies and functions of Strong Women's[10] songs sparked conversations about the lineage and associations each song had, as well as notions of how 'old' the songs were. A can of worms of ownership, copyright and intellectual property was opened when we decided to produce a CD, which also necessitated a deeper inquiry into songs than simply their subject matter and melodic structure. I became aware of a large amount of Tiwi song material housed at AIATSIS and, after discussions with the Tiwi women and members of the Tiwi Land Council I requested the material listed in Figure 1.

Collector	Year
Baldwin Spencer	1912
Charles William Hart	1928
Colin Simpson	1948
Charles Mountford	1954
ABC Radio (collection of Alice Moyle)	1955
Helen Groger-Wurm	1965
Sandra Holmes*	1966
Jack Doolan**	1967
Michael Sims***	1972
Alice Moyle	1976
Charles Osborne	1975
Andrée Grau	1981

Figure 1: Ethnographic Tiwi song material housed at AIATSIS.

* At the time of writing permission has not been secured for release of the Holmes material.

** Jack Doolan was superintendent with the Department of Aboriginal Affairs and living at Milikapiti when he made these recordings.

*** Father Michael Sims was a priest at Nguiu at the time he made these recordings.

---

10   The term 'Strong Woman' is a designation given to elder women who hold a particular degree of cultural knowledge.

The recordings housed at AIATSIS (and problems arranging their repatriation)[11] became the focus of my activities with the Tiwi women during 2008 and 2009. It was from this point on that the idea of reclaiming recordings began to generate talk around the Tiwi community about ownership, stakeholders' rights, why they had been 'taken away' in the first place, and that elders felt a sense of duty to arrange for their return.[12] In April 2009 I was advised that the only way to have the material digitised and processed for release was to have Tiwi elders audition it to assess potential cultural restrictions.[13] The material was not in line for digitisation because it had not had cultural restriction appraisal (which could only happen if the elders listened to it). This posed somewhat of a 'Catch 22' problem. The elders could not listen to it unless it was digitised and sent to the islands (in effect, released). With time stretching on, and potentially running out for older Tiwi people with direct interest in and knowledge of this material, it became imperative to the Tiwi elders that they take affirmative action.

Songs as Artefact

In November 2009 I accompanied seven Tiwi women and four men to Canberra to visit AIATSIS (see Figure 2). The group was made up of men and women representative of different Country and family groups in order to have as broad a spread of cultural authority as possible. The aim was to spend two days auditioning the material in order for elders to give authorised permission for its release. In all, we spent one week in Canberra, also visiting the Tiwi collections at the National Museum of Australia and the National Film and Sound Archive. While not pertaining to song material, I include here an account of these adjunct visits because they had a direct impact on the attitudes the group had during their time at AIATSIS.

---

11 While it is not the aim of institutions to make access difficult for Indigenous stakeholders there is evidence that it is by no means a smooth and easy process, and the experience I had reclaiming recordings on behalf of my Tiwi colleagues is not an isolated one, with recent reports indicating that this is not unique to Australia. See Samuel Kahunde, 'Repatriating Archival Sound Recordings to Revive Traditions: The role of the Klaus Wachsmann recordings in the revival of the royal music of Bunyoro-Kitara, Uganda', *Ethnomusicology Forum* 21:2, Special Issue: Ethnomusicology, Archives and Communities: Methodologies for an Equitable Discipline (2012); Don Niles, 'The National Repatriation of Papua New Guinea Recordings: Experiences straddling World War II', *Ethnomusicology Forum* 21:2 (2012); Don Niles and Vincent Palie, 'Challenges in the Repatriation of Historic Recordings to Papua New Guinea', in *Researchers, Communities, Institutions, Sound Recordings*, eds Linda Barwick, Allan Marett, Jane Simpson and Amanda Harris (Sydney: University of Sydney, 2003).

12 A repeating theme of discussions I witnessed was to wonder why these recordings were in the collection without the elders and/or the Land Council having been officially informed already.

13 Although Tiwi songs are not affected by secrecy or gender-restrictions, none of the metadata accompanying the material specifically noted this and so AIATSIS, rightly, was unwilling to release the material without Tiwi approval.

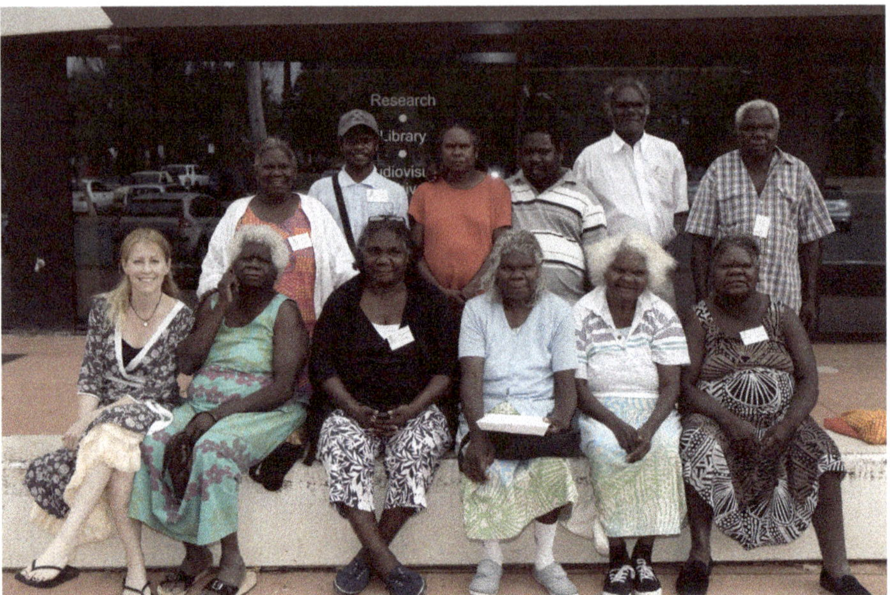

Figure 2: Tiwi delegation to AIATSIS, Canberra, November 2009. L to R (standing): Regina Kantilla, Francis Orsto, Agnes Kerinaiua, Walter Kerinaiua jnr (Wally), Stephen-Paul Kantilla, Eustace Tipiloura (seated), Genevieve Campbell, Mary Elizabeth Moreen, Teresita Puruntatameri, Jacinta Tipungwuti, Leonie Tipiloura, Sheba Fernando.

Source: Photograph by Terrilee Amatto, used with permission.

The equivalency of songs with paintings and artefacts as items of cultural and artistic heritage and as physical 'ownable' objects became clear to my Tiwi colleagues over the course of the week, and I am certain that this has had an ongoing effect on the way the *palingarri*[14] recordings are regarded amongst the Tiwi community.

At the National Museum of Australia the group was shown a large collection of Tiwi artefacts, including ceremonial spears, woven pandanus arm- and head-bands, message sticks, sculptures and paintings on bark, both on public display and in the Museum storage building. To the surprise and dismay of the group, none of the items[15] was marked with the name of the (Tiwi) person who made it, but each was labelled with the (European) collector's name. The painted designs, specific to particular skin groups and Country groups, helped identify

---

14 *Palingarri* translates as 'the deep past', 'forever' or 'long ago'. The repatriated recordings have come to be called the *palingarri* recordings.

15 Apart from a collection of carved poles on public display which did include the names of the artists.

the artist in a number of cases (knowing the year in which they were made and who would have been the senior artist then) and this information was added to the Museum's metadata.

The group was shown photographs of four *Turtuni*[16] *Pukumani*[17] poles collected by Herbert Basedow in 1911. Basedow's notes say these poles were from a *Pukumani Yiloti* (Final) ceremony held for a baby some years before he was there and that the body was exhumed, but was deemed to be in too poor condition to collect.[18] Basedow had these poles repainted (by Tiwi men) and then removed from the site and shipped to Adelaide, where they were eventually housed at the South Australian Museum in 1934. This caused great sadness and some anger amongst the group. There was much discussion as to how the Tiwi locals must have been coerced in some way—either through payment (cigarettes or food perhaps) or a perceived position of power held by the stranger/white man—because no-one would normally ever remove *Turtuni* poles, or even suggest it. They agreed the Tiwi men must have had little understanding of the reality of these poles leaving the Island and being displayed elsewhere.[19] Teresita Puruntatameri said, 'I can't believe they pulled them out of the ground. That is bad for the spirit of the child. It breaks the spirit of the place. They should never be moved.'[20]

At the National Film and Sound Archive a large collection of film material was made available (for viewing on the day and for repatriation). This again was a moving experience for the group. All saw family members, either at a time before they themselves were born or when they were young men and women. Leonie Tipiloura saw herself as a four-year-old, in news footage about the evacuation of mission children from Bathurst Island during the Second World War in 1942. She did not recognise herself because she had never seen an image of herself as a young child. Those in the group agreed with Leonie's feeling that it was an uncomfortable experience to see her 'twice at the same time'.[21] This correlates with consultants' reaction to song recordings when they speak of the singer in the present tense and say that they are present when their voice is heard. As well as the emotions of sentimental reminiscing and curiosity in images from their past, people reported that it was unsettling to have the past overlapping

---

16   Most commonly referred to as *Pukumani* poles.

17   *Pukumani* is a term that refers to mourning restrictions and rites connected with mortuary rituals.

18   Herbert Basedow, 'Notes on the Natives of Bathurst Island, North Australia,' *Journal of the Royal Anthropological Institute* 43 (1913).

19   The men resolved to return to the place and perform Ceremony to attempt to heal the situation.

20   A collection of Tiwi *Turtuni* poles on display in the New South Art Gallery, Sydney were, in 1958, the Gallery's first Indigenous Australian objects to be commissioned as works of art rather than acquired as artefact. Since then so called *Pukumani* poles are painted as artworks to be sold, and they are not associated with Ceremony.

21   Personal communication, Canberra, 18 November 2009.

with the present in this way. Accompanying these experiences was a growing consternation as to why this very significant material was in Canberra, owned by collectors and not available in the Tiwi community.

The issue of ownership came to a head with a holiday movie taken by (Anglo-Australian) tourists in Milikapiti, Melville Island, in 1965. It contains images of men making preparations for Ceremony (painting up) and a dance and song performance. Mary Elizabeth Moreen Mungatopi's father, Allie Miller, is the song-man featured. This footage of her father in 1965 was particularly significant to her, as an active member of the Strong Women's group and a central protagonist in the trip to Canberra. We were not able to give Mary Elizabeth a copy of the footage because the copyright holder, whose parents (now deceased) were the tourists who took the footage, would not agree to its release without substantial payment.[22]

It was within this context of discussions about the collection and ownership of Indigenous cultural property and heritage, as well as a heightened sense of pride and purpose,[23] that the group arrived at AIATSIS ready to reclaim their song material. The older members of the group found it particularly powerful to hear familiar voices amongst the recordings. They expressed their concern at the songs (and the singers' voices) being trapped in recordings and removed from the community in just the same way as some of the objects had been, and their sense of duty to return them to the islands was strong. Amongst the younger members of the group there was the opinion that they were also the rightful owners of the recordings themselves and that there should be no impediment to their being given compact discs to return home. These discs became objects emblematic of the artefact in the other institutions and 'holding on to them'[24] became just as important as listening to them.

Although most of the requested material had been cleared by the copyright holders, digitised and was ready to be auditioned, only the Hart material was on a CD ready for repatriation (pending the elders' approval). Holmes had not given permission for the release of her recordings[25] and the Mountford, Sims and Osborne material was in stasis because the copyright holders could not be traced.

---

22   The National Film and Sound Archive has approached him since, with no success. When I contacted the copyright holder directly he was very unhelpful.

23   They also met with the then Federal Minister for the Arts, Peter Garrett, at Parliament House, and were praised for their pro-active role as community leaders and negotiating directly with the national institutions.

24   Sheba Fernando, personal communication, Canberra, 19 November 2009.

25   In 1966, Mary Elizabeth Moreen Mungatopi was the twelve-year-old daughter of Polly and Allie Miller, Holmes' primary consultants. Holmes' recordings were very moving for Mary as they contained the voice of her father (as lead singer) and of her mother and her sister Eleanor as informants. It was with understandable confusion and sadness that Mary learned that Holmes had not given permission for the recordings to be released to the community.

There was an expectation amongst the group, the Tiwi community, and the Tiwi Land Council (which had given significant financial support) that the group would return with some song material.[26] With the copyright issue the only impediment, the elders signed the required request forms and cultural authority forms[27] so it was hoped that the process of release would, from this point on, be relatively smooth. Unfortunately, at the end of our time in Canberra only one disc, the 1928 Hart material,[28] was ready for the group to take home and there was a clear frustration amongst the group that they were not being given what they deemed rightly theirs. Overall, though the experience had been invigorating and powerful, as each member of the group had had at least one deeply personal discovery amongst the recordings and all felt that going in person had been the right thing to do. After some discussion, the Acting Director gave discretionary permission for release of the Holmes,[29] Osborne and Sims material and these were posted to the group eight months later.

Engagement with the Recordings

The recorded Tiwi song material that I have been working with falls into four broad categories (labelled as they are referred to on the islands). I have seen a clear difference in the way Tiwi listeners relate to these four types of recordings, depending upon their provenance, perceived ownership and archival significance. I will briefly outline them here in order to place the repatriated AIATSIS recordings amongst those already on the islands.

1: The *palingarri* (old) songs recorded by researchers as part of wider anthropological study and housed at AIATSIS, Canberra.

The material repatriated from AIATSIS has an aura of specialness about it and people approach the auditioning of it with a heightened level of interest and concentration. The material that pre-dates living singers (the 1912, 1928, 1948, 1954 and 1955 recordings) and involves song texts in 'hard language'[30] is listened to with reverence for the culturally significant heirloom that it has become. Older people who recall having researchers around in the 1950s, 1960s

---

26 Considering it had been eighteen months since I first requested Tiwi song material, and for four months AIATSIS knew of our planned visit (partially funded by AIATSIS itself) it was disappointing that only the Hart material had been made available for repatriation.

27 Some of these had already been signed and posted in 2008.

28 The Hart material is out of copyright and so was a simpler process. The quality of this recording is very poor and much of it is inaudible.

29 In late 2011 I was advised by AIATSIS that the Holmes material had been released to the Tiwi individuals for personal use only and I was not authorised to use it for research. This issue has not yet been resolved.

30 The language used in songs is referred to as 'hard language' because it is a form that is no longer spoken or understood by anyone but a few elders.

and 1970s did not know there were resultant recordings kept in Canberra.[31] Elders' engagement with the material is therefore not as peers, nor as students, but as descendants discovering an old relic, such as an old family photo album or piece of estate jewellery.

2: 'My Recordings' are those made by me. This category falls into two areas.

> a: the recordings I have made at the request of elder singers with the conscious motivation of preserving their songs for future generations. They want to add their own contributions to what they now understand as being a long-term archive that will become more and more significant and revered as time passes.[32]

> b: the recordings I have made of the Strong Women's group for immediate dispersal and entertainment amongst (mostly) the women themselves. On a number of occasions I have recorded their song in 'draft' form, so that the following day they can listen back to it, or play it for women who have just arrived to be part of the process of composing and rehearsing in preparation for its performance at a funeral or community event.

3: The 'Ngarukuruwala recordings' are commercial or publicity audio and/or video recordings made of Ngarukuruwala performances, small pieces made about the group for television and radio and the two CD recordings we have produced together. The few television and radio pieces that have been made about the project have been transmitted around the community via DVD and I have helped the women create a website on which we can post photos, music tracks and YouTube clips of their new arrangements and compositions. We have used our recent recordings to reclaim ownership of some old material, by sampling it into newly produced tracks.

4: The recordings at 'Literacy' are cassette tapes kept at the *Nginingawila* (story collecting) Literature Production Centre in Nguiu/Wurrumiyanga (Bathurst Island). They were made by Tiwi people and by nuns, teachers or other non-Tiwi people living locally. This material has never left the islands and so is regarded quite differently from that repatriated from Canberra. Older people seek out the recording of a ceremony led by the senior man in their family (for example) to listen to his voice and reminisce about him, not generally as a source of study into the songs themselves or the linguistic or musical techniques therein. These recordings are (at the moment at least) largely ignored with their

---

31   Osborne made recordings in 1975 of senior songman Justin Puruntatameri. I played these to Justin in 2012. He was by then aged 87 years and had never heard them before. To hear his own voice, strong and much younger, was, he told me, a marvellous but also upsetting experience.

32   A group of elders wanted me to record Justin Puruntatameri, for example, because he was the oldest man left with the 'proper' singing skills. Mr Puruntatameri did not want to sing for the recorder, however, because he felt his voice was no longer good enough. He passed away in 2012.

existence in the Literacy Centre taken for granted. It is only in the last five years that the need to digitise this material in order to preserve it has become an issue for discussion.[33]

It is definitely the first category, the *palingarri* recordings repatriated as a result of the visit to Canberra, that holds the most value, as much for its significant cultural and historical content as for its story of having been 'reclaimed'.

Uses for the *Palingarri* Repatriated Recordings

The fact that the AIATSIS recordings' return was a result of pro-active engagement on the part of the Tiwi people themselves has informed the way they have been received. Rather than being lodged (by a non-Tiwi visitor) in a library, school or council office, the CDs went directly into people's homes. The physical CDs were, at first, the property of the people to whom they were posted, who then decided which family or individual should be given particular material—a renegotiation of the ownership of the recordings and of the songs on them. Certain people, for example, were given CDs (which contained the voice of their direct ancestor) even though they had no way of playing them, but because it was decided amongst the group that they should be the 'custodian' of that particular material. A Tiwi song is owned by its composer, and then by whoever he/she has taught it to (if it has been passed down). The vast majority are, however, unique to the point at which they were first performed and so today's listener delegates ownership to his/her direct family. Usually people felt that the (long deceased) singer owned the song, but that his/her family now owns the recording. Amongst several hours of material are numerous singers with different Country and kinship affiliations, so sections of the recordings belong to different people. I have been asked to create 'playlists' of sections of different collections that relate to a particular family, or hold particular interest for an individual.

Discs are played at informal gatherings and, especially when children are present, the material often becomes the subject of talk ranging from family to language to hunting to geography. They are played in vehicles' CD players and in people's houses. At the towns' social clubs, where the music is usually firmly in the realm of rock and roll hits from the 1970s and 1980s, a few times I have been present when someone has put on a *palingarri* CD.

---

33   With the approximately twenty-year break in engagement with these recordings it is likely that when they are digitised and installed in a publicly accessible database they will be the object of a 'rediscovery' much as the AIATSIS recordings have been.

The women's group has used the material as a starting point for new song projects, incorporating old recordings into arrangements by playing them through the sound system either as introductions to songs or with live performance accompanying the recording. Although it has proved difficult and time-consuming to organise permission to play the recordings at public performances it is a matter of principle to the group that they be able to use their own cultural material. The fact that they have had to ask permission from AIATSIS to use segments of the reclaimed recordings in our performances and new recordings has been perplexing for my Tiwi colleagues. From the point of view of the Indigenous stakeholders, the songs belong to them as items of cultural heritage, but from the point of view of an archive (such as AIATSIS) it is more complicated than that. There are many other considerations for an archive charged with the protection of intellectual property of the collector, of usage (commercial or otherwise) and of protecting the Indigenous community in terms of respect for the voices, images and names of the deceased, all of which make this an area of ongoing debate.[34] One outcome of this is that, in applying for permission to use a section of an old recording for a music project in 2011, the same Tiwi elder signed both the request form and the authorisation form for AIATSIS. This adds an extra element to the story of the recordings, with issues of ownership, legalities and cultural property never far from people's minds.

Recordings as Archive and as a Teaching Resource

The recordings are important as an archive for preservation, as a focus for active engagement in the continuation of song traditions, and as a primary resource for learning language, song poetry and vocal technique. From a musical point of view, the recorded songs represent an important piece of cultural heritage. Individual creativity is highly regarded in Tiwi song culture, so, ideally,[35] it is not so much a matter of learning from these recordings by rote, but learning words, phrases and the required poetic devices to be able to create one's own song. A result of the current, topical and context-specific nature of most Tiwi

---

34   Jane Anderson, 'Access and Control of Indigenous Knowledge in Libraries and Archives: Ownership and future use', *American Library Association and The MacArthur Foundation*, 5–7 May (2005); Linda Barwick and Nick Thieberger, 'Cybraries in Paradise: New technologies and ethnographic repositories', in *Libr@ries: Changing information space and practice*, eds C. Kapitzke and B. C. Bruce (Mahwah: Lawrence Erlbaum, 2006); Michael F. Brown, J. A. Barnes, David A. Cleveland, Rosemary J. Coombe, Phiilippe Descola, L. R. Hiatt, Jean Jackson, B. G. Karlsson, Darrell Addison Posey, Willow Roberts Powers, Lawrence Rosen, Fernando Santos Granero, Carlo Severi, David J. Stephenson, Jr., Marilyn Strathern, and Donald Tuzin. 'Can Culture Be Copyrighted? [and Comments and Reply]', *Current Anthropology* 39:2 (1998); Kahunde 'Repatriating Archival Sound Recordings'; Niles 'The National Repatriation'; Martin Thomas 'Taking Them Back: Archival media in Arnhem Land today', *Cultural Studies Review* 13:2 (2007).
35   In the opinion of older singers.

song, we find amongst the old recordings a wealth of social, ancestral and ritual information embedded in song texts. They are also an invaluable resource for a new method of teaching song composition skills.

From the mid 1970s, the marked changes to the spoken Tiwi language and the shrinking attendance at (and involvement in) *Kulama,* an annual ceremony centred on the attainment of cultural knowledge, language and song composition skills,[36] fewer singers were able to compose. This saw people beginning to use cassette recorders to capture the songs of a highly regarded singer, not with long-term preservation in mind, but as a means of entertainment. Venbrux noted that 'relatively few people were able to "copy" (re-enact) these [songs] themselves'.[37] Grau noted (speaking of the changes in instruction in *Kulama* singing):

> [F]rom what I saw it seems that modern technology in the form of cassette recorders has helped a great deal … Every Kulama is taped by a number of people and these tapes are played over and over during the following weeks … Few people state [learning] as the reason for listening to the tapes, and usually say they just enjoy listening to them.[38]

Listening to *Kulama* songs on tape was also a modern means of dispersing the messages within the songs themselves as it became more difficult for people to attend ceremonies. The songs composed for the first day of the *Kulama* ceremony that celebrate deceased kin, for example, remain important as a way of remembering and respecting lost loved ones. Listening to recorded performances of these has become a soothing, healing and almost spiritual experience, for some, replacing the actual ceremony. The thought of archiving these recordings was, however, not on the agenda. One wouldn't want to hear the voice of a recently departed loved one. Venbrux mentions a cassette-tape being destroyed after the man leading the singing had died, making his voice *Pukumani.*[39] Venbrux and Grau also report men in the 1970s and 1980s learning songs via cassette tapes and many of the older men with whom I have spoken (who are the leading singers today) say that they mostly learned this way too. This might have been the beginning of a shift away from what was traditionally an oral and heuristic learning process. Coupled with the almost complete loss of a spoken command of the language in which these songs were composed, there has been a demonstrable change from unique, performance specific composition, to rote-

---

36   See Genevieve Campbell, 'Sustaining Tiwi Song Practice through Kulama', *Musicology Australia* 35:2, Special Issue: Sustainability and Ethnomusicology in Australasia (2013).

37   Eric Venbrux, *A Death in the Tiwi Islands: Conflict, ritual and social life in an Australian Aboriginal Community* (Cambridge: Cambridge University Press, 1995), 122.

38   Andrée Grau, *Dreaming, Dancing, Kinship: The Study of Yoi, the dance of the Tiwi of Melville and Bathurst Islands, North Australia* (PhD, The Queen's University of Belfast, 1983).

39   Venbrux, *A Death in the Tiwi Islands.*

learning from stock phrases.[40] The atrophying of the text resource material is the result of men learning from recordings, from finite performances, rather than learning the skills to create their own word patterns.

At Figure 3 I present the translation of part of a song composed by Joe Puruntatameri in February 1981 in honour of Long Stephen Tipuamantimeri, a well-respected singer, culture man and leader of ceremony.[41]

They all say "that man from Irumakulumi he is a good singer".

People from Nguiu send tapes to him saying "sing for us so we can hear your voice and your words and know what is right."

They all make tapes of him singing

He has got to sing in this tape *imerikungwamili*, *imerikianuwa* and ajipa [first, second and third night of *Kulama*]

We will have every word in the tape and everybody will listen

People will listen the meaning of the right words

They all say "he had *ilantjini* [special necklace worn by the initiates, thus he went through all the initiation grades] it is why he is a good singer, we know about him".

All the government, really old men and ladies come to listen to his songs.

Figure 3: Joe Puruntatameri's song about Long Stephen Tipuamantimeri.

Source: Grau, *Dreaming, Dancing, Kinship*.

The song text says something of how conscious people were of the role of recordings as a teaching tool and as a means of preserving knowledge held in song. It also suggests that there was a sense of what was being lost, even thirty years ago. Just as in 1981, today there is a sense of reverence towards those few left who can sing and a desire to learn from them, using recording as a means of preserving their knowledge. The senior men, on whom the responsibility of performing at funerals falls, have described to me their anxiety at the thought of not being able to sing the required Country, ancestral or Dreaming songs at funerals.[42] Some songmen are turning to the archival recordings as source

---

40   A fuller discussion of this can be found in Campbell, 'Sustaining Tiwi Song Practice through Kulama'.
41   I do not have a recording or the Tiwi text of this song, but the English summary is interesting and sufficient for the purpose of making this point. Grau, *Dreaming, Dancing, Kinship*.
42   Some Tiwi songs include reference to all three of these within one text, but many songs are specifically about Country, tell ancestral stories or refer to Dreaming animals.

material for their own compositions. As I mentioned above, creating a digital archive from this collection of locally made recordings is now on the agenda with the Indigenous Knowledge Centres in Pirlangimpi and Milikapiti (managed by the Northern Territory Library) and the Literacy Centre at Wurrumiyanga (managed by the Catholic School Board) the likely venues.

At this stage there is no evidence that recordings are replacing live performance in Ceremony. Apart from the handful of songs (no more than about a dozen) that can be successfully repeated because of their direct function as Dreaming *Yoi* songs,[43] the vast majority of songs are of the moment, and not ever intended to be repeated. There are a number of dances through which a member of a certain Dreaming will embody the animal or entity (Turtle, Shark, Crocodile, Rainbow for example) that is that Dreaming. As one dances Crocodile (for example) one becomes the ancestral crocodile and sings/speaks as that totemic being. Perhaps due to the individual and 'one-off' nature of Tiwi song, the idea of learning a particular song from the recordings by rote for repetition is outside of current thinking. The current, topical nature of their text and the over-riding culture of the individualism of composition and artistic ownership make most Tiwi songs unsuitable for long-term repetition.

There are some songs that, while they are not repeated exactly, are relatively stable. These are the songs that mark kinship and the songs that accompany the Dreaming dances. Both of these are essential for the mortuary-associated *Yoi* events performed at *Pukumani* ceremonies and at funerals. In the face of dwindling numbers of singers who can compose these songs (as would traditionally have been the case) there is talk of 'setting' a list of the required songs that would be taught to young people, enabling the ceremonies to continue to be held in the proper way.[44] It is in this context that the repatriated recordings have the potential to change the entire basis of Tiwi song practice, from one that was primarily about extemporisation, to one that is based on the rote learning of a finite set of songs. Deciding which songs these will be is something that has already begun to cause some concerns amongst elders. The 'privileging' and reification of particular songs over others due to their inclusion in recordings is a problem that people are just starting to think about.[45] Preserving an orally transmitted tradition by making it finite brings with it complications of ownership of the songs themselves and of the associated connection through esoteric knowledge that is passed on through oral transmission.

---

43   *Yoi* songs, and their corresponding dances, refer to specific Dreaming groups and are owned and passed down through those Dreaming groups. See Grau, *Dreaming, Dancing, Kinship*; Campbell, 'Sustaining Tiwi Song Practice through Kulama'.

44   I was present at a meeting at the Literacy Centre in late 2012 where this was discussed.

45   Barbara Kirschenblatt-Gimblett, *Destination Culture: Tourism, museums and heritage* (Berkeley: University of California Press, 2006); Treloyn, Charles and Nulgit, 'Repatriation of Song Materials'.

Mary Elizabeth's Song

While the overall and community-wide results of the repatriation of recordings are broadly the subject of this chapter, I now discuss one woman's personal experience of the return of some of the material. Many of the songs sung at *Kulama,* a now almost defunct annual ceremony, were a record of current events, including announcements of births and the naming of babies, thus creating an aural historical record. There have been many instances of oral history current to the time of their performance (as well as record of people's actions or opinions that were previously unknown) being reflected in the recordings.

Mary Elizabeth Moreen Mungatopi is a member of the Strong Women's Group. As a young woman she was sent away from her parents (in Milikapiti) to board at the mission school on Bathurst Island. She returned to Milikapiti as a seventeen-year–old wanting to learn the language and culture she had been removed from.[46] Mary Elizabeth was among the group that travelled to Canberra with me in November 2009 to make the initial audition of the recordings at AIATSIS. Amongst the recordings made by Mountford in 1954 was one song that had a profound effect on those in the room. People had always known anecdotally that Mary Elizabeth (full Tiwi name: Kuwiyini Mirri Ilityipiti) had been named after the Queen.[47] Mary's father, Allie Miller Mungatopi, travelled to Brisbane in March 1954 as part of a group that performed for the Royal visit.[48] He had taken the opportunity to embed the name in his *Kulama* song, in effect naming her in honour of the experience.[49] Now, all those years later, in what was a very moving moment for all present, Mary heard her father singing the announcement of her birth. The text (shown at Figure 4) alludes to the telling of an important piece of news (symbolised by the radio). It also records the current event that was the Queen's visit to Australia (with the Queen literally being heard on the radio). The third layer of meaning is the naming of his daughter in honour of the event.

---

46   While at the mission school, the children were not allowed to attend ceremonies and the girls were full-time boarders (the boys were allowed home at weekends). Many of my elderly female consultants report on feeling disconnected from their culture and their parents and not being able to speak their language when they returned to their families as young adults.

47   Queen Elizabeth II of England.

48   The Queen was in Brisbane 9–18 March 1954. Cardo Kerinaiua, Allie Miller Mungatopi and Aloysius Puantilura were among a larger group of Aboriginal men performing at this event.

49   This is a *Jipuwakirimi* song (see Campbell, 'Sustaining Tiwi Song Practice through Kulama') that Mountford says was performed at the *Yilaniya* stage of the *Pukumani* Ceremony.

Gloss of text:

Kuwiyini mirr- ilityipiti ritiya wu- ni- wati- pa- wa- ningi- yangirri

Queen Mary Elizabeth radio np- to- morn – vol- talk – send- push*

Free translation: Queen Mary Elizabeth sends a message on the radio

np: non-past
morn: morning time prefix
vol: volitional

Figure 4: Queen Mary Elizabeth's song.

Source: Allie Miller, 1954, C01-2916-37, AIATSIS, Canberra.

* Charles Roland Osborne, 'Tiwi Chanted Verse' (Ann Arbor, MI: University Microform International, 1989), 842.

The discovery of this song is emblematic of the significant personal effect the recordings have had on many people.[50] It has become a tangible piece of Mary Elizabeth's family history, documented evidence of what had always been anecdotal. Mary Elizabeth has played the recording to her children and grandchildren and it has become at once an item of sentiment, a family heirloom and a piece of Tiwi social history. As well as the value of Allie's words and the story gained from the text, his voice is a powerful conduit between Mary Elizabeth and her father.

Responses to the Recordings from the Point of View of Current Singers

Respect for Singers of the Past

Amongst the recordings repatriated from AIATSIS are performances showing a high level of vocal talent. The strength of tone, length of phrasing and quality of diction and pitch of some recorded performances can objectively be regarded as being at a technically more difficult level than is found today. Over the years, through the process of oral transmission, song-men have made their own variations to vocal techniques and rhythmic and melodic ornamentation.

---

50 There are numerous other instances where individual personal connections have been found in the recordings.

It is only by hearing the 'old men' again after sixty years or more[51] that these incremental changes become apparent. The singer who had attained the skills of composition through *Kulama* was a highly respected person in the community. There is a sense of performance as a means of impressing those around. In a recording made by Jack Doolan of a *Kulama* ceremony in 1967[52] we hear singer Karla's[53] performance inspiring enthusiastic response from the 'audience'. While not a performance in the sense of him being on the stage, Karla's singing was of a particularly impressive quality both in terms of words and in the vocal strength, tone and length of phrases. I have played this file to a number of Tiwi colleagues and they have often given the same spontaneous response (like bravo) at the end of his songs. In this case, the recording itself has become a performance by Karla, because, although he is not physically present, his recorded voice manifests his presence and (Tiwi) listeners respond to that presence as a tangible experience of the man himself. Well-respected senior singers are anecdotally remembered for particular performances and for the Ceremonies they have led. Hearing them in recordings confirms this collective memory and, for younger listeners, adds their voices to the lineage of songmen.

Elders recall being present (as children) at Ceremony when these men sang. Current song leaders at Wurrumiyanga[54] have been very interested to hear the stylistic differences between their way of performing particular parts of Ceremony and that of the men on the old recordings. While novelty and change are inherent in Tiwi song practice, it was a difficult experience for the men to hear so clearly the degree of quantifiable loss that has occurred. The numbers of people singing, the 'strength'[55] of people's voices, the length of phrases, the linguistic complexity and the number of songs in each event are all elements that my consultants had to admit to themselves have been diminished in the last fifty years. This is a difficult thing to accept, especially for those elder men and women who feel the responsibility of sustaining the traditions.[56]

Rediscovering Song Traditions

The reverse can also occur, and rediscovering an element of song practice can be exhilarating and empowering for the song leaders. One such instance occurred

---

51   The 1912, 1948, 1954 and 1955 recordings have had the biggest impact in this regard.

52   DOOLAN_J02-000628A 05:32, AIATSIS, Canberra.

53   Karla (Tractor Joe) was also known as Prijina Lokemup. He is remembered as a particularly talented singer and the older men are listening to his recorded performances with the aim of emulating him.

54   Stephen-Paul Kantilla, Eustace Tipiloura, Roger Tipungwuti, Robert Biscuit Tipungwuti and Walter Kerinaiua snr. Mr Walter Kerinaiua and Robert Tipungwuti are recently deceased but I have permission to use their names here.

55   The strength and dynamic of the lead voices is a feature of the old recordings that a number of consultants have remarked upon, comparing their 'short wind' when singing today.

56   My role in analysing the songs has necessitated sensitivity in this area and respect for senior singers. I therefore note only those examples of loss of quality that my consultants discussed openly.

during our visit to the National Film and Sound Archive in Canberra when the group was shown a collection of film footage with Tiwi content. Amongst this was film of a *Tepuwaturinga* (Wallaby) *Yoi* dance (filmed by Spencer in 1912) that has not been performed for many years. Wallaby had been 'forgotten',[57] having fallen out of practice because the men who would have danced Wallaby had stopped leading Ceremony. Wallaby is not amongst Spencer's audio recordings, but the visual footage had a great impact regardless. Basedow (1913) describes the Kangaroo[58] dance but there is no further mention of it in the literature until Grau, who writes that she never witnessed it and was told that 'at Pularumpi only one old man, Mickey Geranium Warlapini, knew the dance but that he was too old to perform it, the series of jumps requiring a lot of stamina'.[59]

We know from the recording made by Alice Moyle in 1976 at the Pacific Festival at Rotorua that Aloysious Puantilura, Leo Tungutalum and Max Kerinaiua performed Wallaby, but without video it is difficult to make a comparison with 1912.

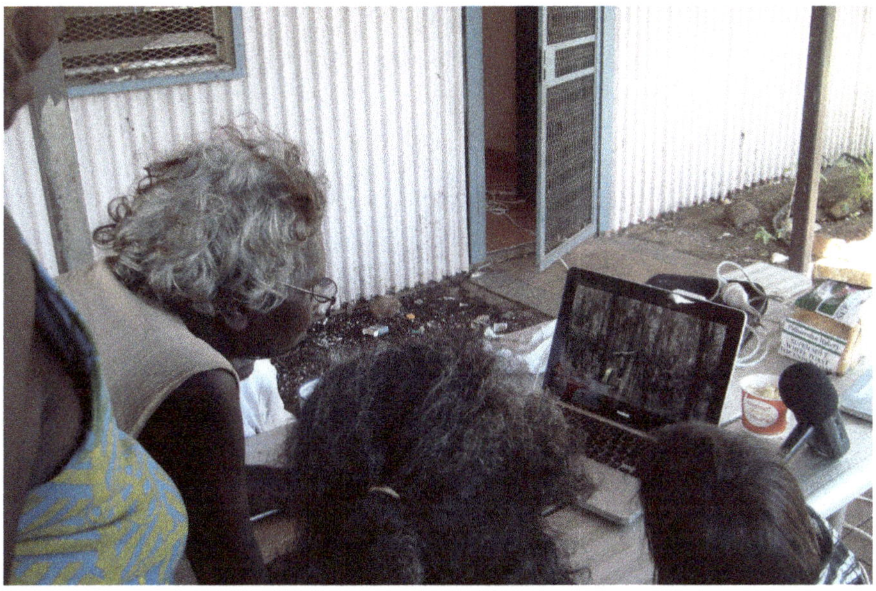

Figure 5: Watching the 1912 (Spencer) footage of Wallaby *Yoi*, Nguiu March 2010.

Source: Author's collection.

---

57   Walter Kerinaiua jnr, personal communication, 18 October 2009.

58   Among the native fauna of the Tiwi Islands are wallabies (not kangaroos). It seems to have been a matter of using the generalised term that has meant that at times in the Tiwi literature we read about kangaroos. Basedow 'Notes on the Natives'; *The Tiwi of North Australia*, 3rd edition (New York: Holt, Rhinehart and Winston, 1988).

59   Grau, *Dreaming, Dancing, Kinship*.

The group was invited to give a performance in the outdoor courtyard at the National Film and Sound Archive. This was a free lunchtime concert that was very well attended, with about 100 people in the audience. The men and women performed *Kulama* songs and *Yoi* songs and dances and Walter spontaneously performed Wallaby. It was a marvellous moment, one that the audience would not have been aware of, but one in which the other Tiwi performers suddenly found themselves also amongst the audience. Walter had brought this *Yoi* to life again. Walter Kerinaiua (jnr) has been watching the 1912 footage to learn the dance. He intends to bring it back to Ceremony when he next has the chance. The Spencer footage has been viewed around the Tiwi community since then (see Figure 5), with Walter's performance in Canberra now part of its accompanying story.

Embedding the Songs Back into the Continuum of Tradition

While the vast majority of recorded Tiwi songs are unique, there is a strong degree of continuity of text elements and melody, especially along hereditary lines (of singers) and this has had an important effect on those directly connected with them. It seems likely that each few generations have a horizon of living memory of knowledge; one's father learned from his father, who learned from his father—that being about as far as it goes back. By the time the current grandfather is passing on his knowledge, he has defined and perhaps refined the knowledge he was taught and now owns it in order to pass it down. So we find in Tiwi songs a clear correlation and some exact stability of text and melody, but with a large degree of individual imprint and expression and a moving away from the old to create the new. This movement is so imperceptible that the elders themselves only realised it when they heard the old recordings. The *Nyingawi* song gives us one such example of the transmission of a song text through nearly seventy years. In March 2010, old lady Stephanie Tipuamantimeri (shown wearing headphones in Figure 6) listened to the *Nyingawi* recordings made in 1928, 1954 and 1975. She then spontaneously sang her *Nyingawi* song, saying that she remembered the words from the old days.[60] Stephanie sang three lines that compare very closely to the old recordings and one that she created. Although she only sang four lines (whereas the old recordings had up to seven lines), she told me she was singing it 'the old way'.

---

60   This was an informal meeting on 5 March 2010 and I did not record Stephanie. She died a few months later.

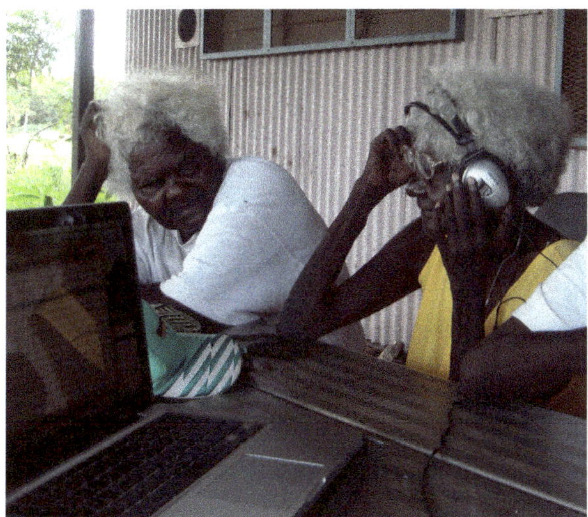

Figure 6: Stephanie Tipuamantimeri listening to the *Nyingawi* recordings (with Leonie Tipiloura) 2010.

Source: Author's collection.

When Casmira Munkara had recorded her *Nyingawi* for our CD in 2008 she told me she was singing it in 'the old way'. Although it contains some text that is identical to the old recorded songs, Casmira's performance is noticeably different, rhythmically, from the 'old way'. People's perception, however, (not having heard the recordings) is that she sings it how it always has been sung, continuing the transmission of this song through her family line. It has become a point of pride for Casmira that she sang it at exactly the same pitch as her predecessors even though she had not heard the old recordings when she made her recording. This connection, through a recording, directly to the voices of her ancestors is another powerful and tangible outcome of the recordings' return.

The Effect of Recording on Performance

A repeated point of discussion during listening sessions has been whether the singers were aware they were being recorded and how that might have had an effect on performance style and song choice. When basing analysis on recorded examples, one must take into consideration the fact that a performance will most likely be affected by the relationship between the singer and the researcher. The reason for the performance is necessarily altered, as are the social, functional and performative contexts. The venue (indoors or outdoors) has a marked effect on both the quality of the sound and the way the singer will relate physically to the microphone. Sitting in a room across the table from the microphone will result in a very different performance from one recorded sitting outside on the ground with birds, dogs, children, cars and passers-by distracting the singer and adding to the sound that is captured.

The audience aspect is perhaps the element that most affects the performance. I have had occasions, during a recording session, when a palpable sense of respect and import is felt by the group, witnessing an elderly woman recording her song, or a group of three senior singers correcting each other's performances as they sing. The desire to be correct, preserving the song (and the performance) for posterity that the singer might (or might not) have been experiencing can be heard amongst the repatriated recordings. Amongst Osborne's recordings, for example, we hear some singers correct themselves as they sing, reiterating a line of text with the syllabic count corrected. This is how it would be done in a 'real' performance context and this suggests that the singer is approaching his task of recording a song in much the same way as he would a performance in Ceremony. My experience is somewhat different. Perhaps it is the result of hearing their antecedents make mistakes that has meant some of my consultants ask me to delete a recording if they make a mistake, or they ask me not to record until they have practised a few times. There might well have been similar re-takes during recording sessions in the past, but it is certainly a feature of my consultants' recording sessions that they are aiming at a correct performance to be recorded for posterity. Perhaps this is due to a heightened sense of creating an archive in the light of the repatriation of the *palingarri* recordings.

Amongst songs recorded by Mountford as part of a *Kulama* ceremony held on Melville Island in May 1954 is an interesting example of the self-awareness of the research subject with the singer using the performance to comment, in song, on the process he is going through at the time. It is most likely Ray Giles, the ABC radio recordist who worked with Mountford, to whom the singer, Allie Miller, is referring. The text is at Figure 7 (translation given by Eustace Tipiloura).

<table>
<tr><td>Ngilaghama karirijiyo waliji miningu merreke wanga pinguwangamini</td></tr>
<tr><td>I am the radio talking</td></tr>
<tr><td>Ngiyawungarri karra apuji yintawayalangimi</td></tr>
<tr><td>I am putting it in the radio</td></tr>
<tr><td>Kalipulijimani rijio yinuwalumurri</td></tr>
<tr><td>He is talking on the radio</td></tr>
</table>

Figure 7: Radio song.

Source: Allie Miller, 1954, C01-002917-38, AIATSIS, Canberra.

Listening to the recording, Eustace Tipiloura told me, 'he's telling people about something new. That's the main part of the ceremony, around about 3pm. He must be talking about the white bloke being there with his recorder I think.'[61]

There will inevitably be questions as to the motivation of both researcher and performer in anthropological research, especially in the context of perceived cultural loss. While Tiwi people filmed and/or recorded by Spencer and Hart may well have had very little understanding of the long-term implications of their participation, the fact remains that they were being asked to sing for a visitor and this must have had some effect on their motivations and resulting performance.[62] Singing into a machine that could play sound back immediately, the singer would have been aware that their voice was being reproduced and stored in some way. The experience of hearing their own singing replayed would have changed the nature of performance as a one-off. As any musician will perform in a slightly heightened state in front of an audience or at a recording session, so too Tiwi people may have altered their performance when they were being recorded or filmed. The sense of presenting the culture in the best possible way for the cameras (or recorder) might arguably result in a performance that is not entirely natural. It is very difficult to decide whether this is a problem or not. If being recorded (or having a non-Tiwi audience) inspires a more elaborate version or a more enthusiastic dance or more rehearsal then that is a valid part of the notion of performance.

Amongst my consultants there have been widely differing opinions as to the ethics of the collection of some of the recorded material, especially the recordings of mourning songs in the *Pukumani* (mortuary-associated) ceremony. Some (Tiwi) people listened with interest to the melodic and linguistic artistry of a performance, some recognised the voice of a deceased loved one with sentimental joy, and some heard personal grief and pain and thought it inappropriate for anyone other than close family to listen. I have witnessed a number of heated discussions about the difference between singing for family and singing for visitors/researchers (in the context of a ceremony), with many people concerned that singers might not always have been aware of the intrusion of the recorder, or of the long term ramifications of being recorded. In the following quotation, Holmes makes the distinction between a ceremony and performance. The *Pukumani* ceremony for Polly and Allie Miller's young son was held in May 1966 at the then Bagot Aboriginal Reserve in Darwin.[63] The segment below indicates that the occasion was seen by the government Welfare Department as a good opportunity to give (white) people a new cultural experience. The Tiwi people do not seem to have been given much of a choice in the matter. Allie is

---

61   Eustace Tipiloura Wurrumiyanga/Nguiu, personal communication, 18 March 2010.
62   Venbrux, *A Death in the Tiwi Islands*.
63   The ceremony was held in Darwin because the child had died in Darwin en route to hospital.

quoted as having been upset at the lack of understanding and respect for his son's Ceremony: 'Too many white people come … we never ask them to come, only Welfare man can say.'[64]

> The Welfare Branch had declared an Open Day for tourists and locals … Polly sang softly to the ghost of her dead son and signalled for me to record it … Crowds of white visitors jostled each other for photo opportunities, staring expectantly up the hill to where the Tiwi mourners were assembled in full ceremonial regalia.[65]

By Holmes' account, the ceremony was just as it would have been (in terms of structure and ritual) without any non-Tiwi onlookers. Clearly though they were being watched as spectacle. Holmes goes on to report:

> At this point a senior welfare officer stood up and made a speech to thank the public for attending the ceremony and the Tiwi people for the performance. By prior arrangement the sculptures and grave posts would be sold to various dealers and other outlets.[66]

The distinction between 'ceremony' and 'performance' in the welfare officer's words (or in Holmes' reporting of his words) implies there was a difference in perception between the audience's and the mourners' experience of the event. It should really have been the other way around; the white audience was watching a performance (although with the extra exoticism of knowing it was a ceremony), while the mourners were attempting to have Ceremony, knowing they were being watched and photographed. Yes, the mourners knew they were being recorded, but it is arguable whether they were aware of the legal and moral ramifications of that recording's journey to Canberra and eventual return to the community.

Conclusion

This example brings us back to the notion of a performance, and a song (owned by its performer) becoming an item, trapped in a recording which then becomes an artefact (owned by its collector). In the moment it is recorded the song's ownership shifts and it is only the process of repatriation that enables that ownership to be shifted back. I have explained how the 'discovery' of the recorded song material in the AIATSIS catalogue, the process of going to Canberra to reclaim it, and the ongoing associated negotiations regarding

---

64 Sandra Holmes, *The Goddess and the Moon Man: The sacred art of the Tiwi Aborigines* (Roseville East: Craftsman House, 1995), 31.
65 ibid., 22.
66 ibid., 29.

usage rights have created a story around the repatriated recordings. The fact that they have been 'reclaimed' gives them a presence in the Tiwi community as highly valued and important cultural property that has been returned. The repatriated recordings have been the focus of close study, from the point of view of their historical, cultural, social and artistic significance and their return has had substantial positive and empowering outcomes for elders as they share the knowledge in the songs with young Tiwi people. While some feel that many of these recordings should perhaps not have been taken in the first place, others believe that with the tenuous state of Tiwi song, language and ceremony they are now of great value to the community for the preservation of culture as well as being a meaningful resource for the continuation of existing and new forms of Tiwi music making. Whatever the differing opinions as to the ethics of such recordings being made and collected, it is evident that the process of their return, even with (and perhaps due to) the difficulties and lengthy bureaucratic processes, has imbued these old recordings with an extra significance. It has also opened a new chapter of engagement between Indigenous knowledge holders and researchers in the recording and documentation of song.

Acknowledgements

Thanks go to my Tiwi colleagues for sharing their opinions and experiences and to the Australian Institute of Aboriginal and Torres Strait Islander Studies, the National Museum of Australia, the National Film and Sound Archive, the Northern Territory Government through Arts NT, and the Tiwi Land Council for co-funding the visit to Canberra.

References

Anderson, Jane. 'Access and Control of Indigenous Knowledge in Libraries and Archives: Ownership and future use', *American Library Association and The MacArthur Foundation*, May 5–7 (2005), http://ccnmtl.columbia.edu/projects/alaconf2005/paper_anderson.pdf.

Barwick, Linda, and Allan Marett. 'Endangered Songs and Endangered Languages', in *Maintaining the Links: Language identity and the land; Seventh Conference of the Foundation for Endangered Languages*, eds Joe Blythe and R. M. Brown (Bath: Foundation for Endangered Languages, 2003), 144–51.

Barwick, Linda, and Nick Thieberger. 'Cybraries in Paradise: New technologies and ethnographic repositories', in *Libr@ries: Changing information space and practice*, eds C. Kapitzke and B. C. Bruce (Mahwah: Lawrence Erlbaum, 2006), 133–49.

Basedow, Herbert. 'Notes on the Natives of Bathurst Island, North Australia', *Journal of the Royal Anthropological Institute* 43 (1913): 291–323.

Brown, Michael F., J. A. Barnes, David A. Cleveland, Rosemary J. Coombe, Phiilippe Descola, L. R. Hiatt, Jean Jackson, B. G. Karlsson, Darrell Addison Posey, Willow Roberts Powers, Lawrence Rosen, Fernando Santos Granero, Carlo Severi, David J. Stephenson, Jr., Marilyn Strathern, and Donald Tuzin. 'Can Culture Be Copyrighted? [and Comments and Reply]', *Current Anthropology* 39:2 (1998): 193–222.

Campbell, Genevieve. 'Sustaining Tiwi Song Practice through Kulama', *Musicology Australia* 35:2, Special Issue: Sustainability and Ethnomusicology in Australasia (2013): 237–52.

Grau, Andrée. *Dreaming, Dancing, Kinship: The Study of Yoi, the dance of the Tiwi of Melville and Bathurst Islands, North Australia* (PhD, The Queen's University of Belfast, 1983).

Hart, C. W. M. *The Tiwi of North Australia*, 3rd edition (New York: Holt, Rhinehart and Winston, 1988).

Holmes, Sandra. *The Goddess and the Moon Man: The sacred art of the Tiwi Aborigines* (Roseville East: Craftsman House, 1995).

Kahunde, Samuel. 'Repatriating Archival Sound Recordings to Revive Traditions: The role of the Klaus Wachsmann recordings in the revival of the royal music of Bunyoro-Kitara, Uganda', *Ethnomusicology Forum* 212, Special Issue: Ethnomusicology, Archives and Communities: Methodologies for an Equitable Discipline (2012): 197–219.

Kirschenblatt-Gimblett, Barbara. *Destination Culture: Tourism, museums and heritage* (Berkley: University of California Press, 2006).

Lancefield, Robert C. 'Musical Traces' Retraceable Paths: The repatriation of recorded sound', *Journal of Folklore Research* 35:1 (1998), 47–68.

Mountford, C. P. *The Tiwi: Their art, myth and ceremony* (London: Phoenix House, 1958).

Niles, Don. 'The National Repatriation of Papua New Guinea Recordings: Experiences straddling World War II', *Ethnomusicology Forum* 21:2 (2012): 141–59.

Niles, Don, and Vincent Palie. 'Challenges in the Repatriation of Historic Recordings to Papua New Guinea', in *Researchers, Communities, Institutions, Sound Recordings*, eds Linda Barwick, Allan Marett, Jane Simpson and Amanda Harris (Sydney: University of Sydney, 2003).

Osborne, Charles Roland. *Tiwi Chanted Verse* (Ann Arbor: University Microform International, 1989).

Seeger, Anthony. 'Do We Need to Remodel Ethnomusicology?', *Ethnomusicology* 31:3 (1987): 491–95.

Stubington, Jill. 'Collecting Folk Music in Australia: Report of a forum held 4-6 December 1987' (Kensington, University of New South Wales, 1989).

Thieberger, Nick, and Simon Musgrave. 'Documentary Linguistics and Ethical Issues', *Documentary and Descriptive Linguistics* 4 (2007): 26–37.

Thomas, Martin. 'Taking Them Back: Archival media in Arnhem Land today', *Cultural Studies Review* 13:2 (2007): 20–37.

Toner, Peter G. 'History, Memory and Music: The repatriation of digital audio to Yolngu communities, or, memory as metadata', in *Researchers, Communities, Institutions, Sound Recordings*, eds Linda Barwick, Allan Marett, Jane Simpson and Amanda Harris (Sydney: University of Sydney, 2003).

Treloyn, Sally, and Andrea Emberly. 'Sustaining Traditions: Ethnomusicological collections, access and sustainability in Australia', *Musicology Australia* 35:2, Special Issue: Sustainability and Ethnomusicology in Australasia (2013): 159–77.

Treloyn, Sally, Rona Googninda Charles, and Sherika Nulgit. 'Repatriation of Song Materials to Support Intergenerational Transmission of Knowledge About Language in the Kimberley Region of Northwest Australia', in *Endangered Languages Beyond Boundaries: Proceedings of the 17th Foundation for Endangered Languages Conference*, eds Mary Jane Norris, Erik Anonby and Marie-Odile Junker (Bath: Foundation for Endangered Languages, 2013), 18–24.

Venbrux, Eric. *A Death in the Tiwi Islands: Conflict, ritual and social life in an Australian Aboriginal Community* (Cambridge: Cambridge University Press, 1995).

6. Turning Subjects into Objects and Objects into Subjects: Collecting Human Remains on the 1948 Arnhem Land Expedition

Martin Thomas

The Archaeologist Removes the Bones

He's taking the bones now, taking the bones. He reaches into the hollow of a crevice; the rear of his trousers, protruding towards the camera, is stained with channels of sweat. Turning to face us, he unwraps a mandible from a blackened shred of rag. Bespectacled, and with lips pursed beneath a trim moustache, his officer's deportment is upset by a slash of blue headband that gives him a piratical craziness. He adds the jaw to a wooden crate already full of arm and leg bones, butted up against a skull. The guts of this narrative—if 'guts' is quite the word when we are dealing with bodies so fleshless—hinge on this and other kindred events.

At the time of writing, it is more than sixty-five years since the bones were extracted from their not-quite-final resting place. Much is forgotten in so long a period of time, and yet the story of the stolen bones from Arnhem Land is far from buried (although it did end with an interment). Captured on celluloid, projected onto the surface that is the present, the theft is possessed of a luminous immortality. As raw spectacle, the bone taking is irksome and yet compelling; a trait accentuated by the conversion of the footage to digital format, bringing as it does a brave new world of accessibility and convenience.[1] I can stop, start and magnify the image while I write; pull it apart like some anatomist of the screen. It was always intended that the act of seizure would transcend the fleetingness of the event itself. The archaeologist's diary makes it clear, as might be supposed, that the presence of the cameraman was anything but accidental.[2] Between them, the archaeologist and the cameraman made of the

---

1 Howell Walker (cine-photographer), *Aboriginal Australia* (lecture film), 1950, National Geographic Society, Washington DC. For further detail of the film see Joshua Harris, 'Hidden for Sixty Years: The motion pictures of the American-Australian Scientific Expedition to Arnhem Land', in *Exploring the Legacy of the 1948 Arnhem Land Expedition*, eds Martin Thomas and Margo Neale (Canberra: ANU E Press, 2011).
2 'Diaries 1948' *Frank Maryl Setzler Papers 1927-1960*, Box 14, National Anthropological Archives, Suitland MD, 28 October 1948 (henceforth *Frank Maryl Setzler Papers 1927–1960*).

theft a pedagogical performance, perhaps in an effort to give it scientific import. We see the archaeologist lifting and handling the skull, pointing out distinctive features, before slotting the jaw in place and presenting to the camera its largely toothless grin. The final seconds of the sequence show a glimpse of scenery from the hilltop where the event occurred: a body of water, a yellowed strip of land, a few scant dwellings. The archaeologist and another white man (of whom more will be said later) cross the frame as they clamber downhill. Manhandling the crate—lidded now, and destined for America—they disappear from the picture.

The pillaging of a mortuary site and the decision to film it are sufficient to unsettle many a viewer. For Aboriginal people with whom I have watched the footage, the close physical handling—the intimate contact of the living flesh of the intruder with the remains of the interred—is particularly unnatural and disturbing. In processing my own response, I have come to realise that there are technical aspects to the footage that accentuate the violence and uncanniness of the actions portrayed. The content of the film is unashamedly atavistic—it stinks of the nineteenth century—yet it is shot in colour. Colour film usually has a soundtrack, but this is silent. His mute presence and the absence of an ambient acoustic give a ghostliness to the archaeologist and the scene he inhabits. While his actions involve dislocation, a wealth of evidence concerning his activities means that the events depicted can be precisely located in space and time. The film was shot on 28 October 1948 near the top of Injalak, a hill just outside the perimeter of what was then known as Oenpelli Mission in the Northern Territory of Australia.[3] Oenpelli, which lies to the east of Kakadu National Park, is now a township, more often known by its Kunwinjku name, Gunbalanya. The archaeologist, who was employed as Head Curator of Anthropology at the Smithsonian Institution in Washington DC, was visiting this western region of the great Arnhem Land Aboriginal Reserve as a member of the American-Australian Scientific Expedition to Arnhem Land (otherwise known as the Arnhem Land Expedition).

The man who documented the seizure of bones from Gunbalanya was the photographer Howell Walker, official representative of the National Geographic Society (NGS) on the Arnhem Land Expedition (see Figure 1). As a staff writer/ photographer who spent much time in Australia, Walker was responsible for many of the stories on the Pacific that appeared in National Geographic Magazine in the mid-twentieth century.[4] On the Arnhem Land Expedition he had with him a large supply of colour film stock, still scarce in Australia in 1948. His 16 mm camera, a lightweight machine powered by a windup mechanism,

---

3 ibid., 28 October 1948.
4 See Mark Collins Jenkins, 'A Robinson Crusoe in Arnhem Land: Howell Walker, *National Geographic* and the Arnhem Land Expedition of 1948', in *Exploring the Legacy of the 1948 Arnhem Land Expedition*, eds Martin Thomas and Margo Neale (Canberra: ANU E Press, 2011), 73-85.

shot vision only. By that time it was common for documentary filmmakers to edit their silent footage into a coherent narrative and add a studio-generated soundtrack that might include music, commentary and 'canned' sound effects.[5] But no soundtrack was ever created for the Arnhem Land film shot by Walker. Instead, as was common practice at the NGS—ever devout to the cult of the roving adventurer—the footage was edited into a silent presentation to which a lecturer (in this case the archaeologist) spoke, slideshow style.[6] The longevity of this type of film presentation was due in part to the caution with which the Society responded to the rising medium of television. Not until 1958 did the NGS allow one of its productions to grace the small screen.[7] In the immediate post-war era, the Society's documentary films, usually conceived as spinoffs to *National Geographic* articles, were shown exclusively to live audiences and thereby treated as inseparable from the travelling lecturer: a flesh-and-blood talisman of the events and geography depicted therein.

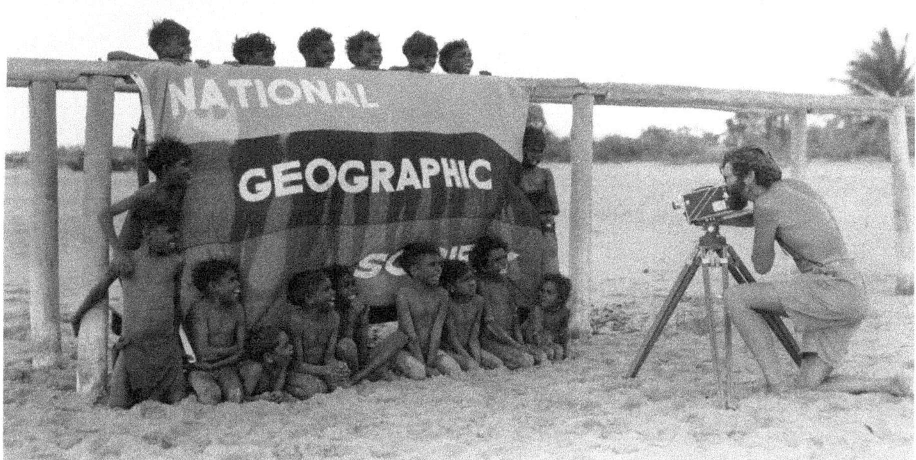

Figure 1: Howell Walker from the National Geographic Society photographing at Umbakumba, 1948. Photograph by Charles P. Mountford.

Source: By permission of the State Library of South Australia. PRG 487/1/2/209/1.

While the theft and its documentation by the filmmaker constitute the originary performance that I will investigate and contextualise in this chapter, it cannot be separated from a sequence of subsequent performances that should be recognised as short- and long-term reverberations of the primary event. Having performed

---

5   For more on audio for film in this period, see Jones, this volume.
6   Walker, *Aboriginal Australia*.
7   Robert M. Poole, *Explorer's House: National Geographic and the world it made* (New York: Penguin, 2004), 226.

the theft for the camera, the archaeologist, when he had returned home to the US, took the lecture film on the road and performed to his earlier performance of taking the bones, morphing from museum curator into showman. The words he used when he performed to the Arnhem Land film are recoverable, for a typescript of his narration, carefully composed and synchronised, still survives in a ring binder among his papers. As the footage of him handling the skull was projected, he would declare:

> These specimens are most important to the science of physical anthropology. Note the pathological condition above the right orbit, the large mastoid process of the male, and these bony ridges for the attachment of the neck muscles. This skull will not only be well preserved in the Smithsonian but will contribute much to the study of these primitive aborigines. Even though we could not obtain all the skeletal material I had located, that which I did bring back constitutes one of the largest collection [sic] of Australian material in this country.[8]

The pronouncement that the haul of human remains would be subject to scientific study was erroneous. There is no evidence that even a single scientific paper analysing the Arnhem Land bones was ever published. Although much of what he said in the film lecture is deeply suspect, the archaeologist's prediction that the bones would be 'well preserved' was shown to be correct when, sixty-two years later, in a latterday reverberation of the bone theft, I was on the outskirts of Washington with cinema-photographer Adis Hondo, where we were doing some filmmaking of our own. The bones collected by the archaeologist had by this time reached the end of their long tenure in the US. After ten years of delay and disagreement, the Department of Anthropology in the Smithsonian Institution's National Museum of Natural History had consented to a request from the Australian government that the bones be returned to their places of origin. Now they were packed in cartons, ready to travel to their home Country. These flimsy boxes—coffins of cardboard—were stacked on a flat-base trolley and wheeled outside into bright sunlight, each draped in an Aboriginal flag. The three colours of the flag—red for land, black for people, yellow for sun—had never seemed more vibrant or poignant. A handful of smouldering gum leaves were waved around the boxes by Joe Neparrnga Gumbula, an elder from Elcho Island and one of three men who had come from different parts of Arnhem Land to receive the remains of their ancestors and accompany them home. Clap sticks beat as Gumbula sang. With a whiff of Australian bushfire in the Washington air, Howell Walker's footage of the theft, long internalised, played in my mind. And I thought of the archaeologist, deceased for many a year, whose archives—which betray so much about the taking of the bones—lay in storage in a building a hundred metres away.

---

8   'Film Lecture', Box 20, *Frank Maryl Setzler Papers 1927–1960*.

The theft of the bones in 1948, their removal to Washington, their recovery and repatriation in the early twenty-first century, and the eventual interment of some of them in ancestral territory marks an orbit—wide in breadth and profound in impact—that I wish not only to describe and analyse, but to subject to a type of archaeological investigation; one that is attuned to a postcolonial, rather than a colonial, paradigm. The presence of human remains in museum collections has been the subject of organised contestation by Indigenous groups from many parts of the world at least since the 1970s. One of the few points of agreement in the large and ever-growing literature on this subject is the diversity of institutional responses to the repatriation phenomenon. Some organisations have embraced it and come to celebrate the improved relations with Indigenous communities that have developed as a consequence. Others have resisted it, while a number, especially in the US, have had it forced upon them through legislation.

Arguments between supporters and opponents of repatriation invariably involve a clash of values and knowledge systems. Consider, as an example, some remarks by the British archaeologist Don Brothwell, lamenting the trend towards repatriation in the journal *Antiquity*. In a 2004 article he argued that rationalism must prevail and scientists be allowed to pursue their analysis of these remains, which is of universal benefit: 'We are surely now living in a world, when all understand geological and astronomical time, and there is no sense in denying it in order to prop up old cultural mythologies.'[9] In just the sort of argument that Brothwell was hoping to dispel, Joe Gumbula explained his thinking about the ceremony that ushered the Arnhem Land bones out of the Smithsonian Institution. Gumbula explained that the choice of funeral songs that he would perform was determined by the needs of the people in the cardboard boxes who required the guidance of familiar languages to steer them homeward.

> These people will be listening to us too. They know. It's not us doing the show, or doing this business just today, for the eyes of the public or the eyes of the living people here now. They are listening to us.[10]

Gumbula's view on the relationship between the living and the dead which, though subject to regional variation, is broadly shared by those Aboriginal people from various parts of Arnhem Land with whom I have discussed this issue. A person's spirit remains indelibly associated with the bones of the deceased. Living people have responsibilities towards the spirit, as much as they do to each other.

Brothwell and Gumbula have very different beliefs about the world, although both of them attach value to the dead. It's just that they do so in such divergent

---

9   Don Brothwell, 'Bring out Your Dead: People, pots and politics', *Antiquity* 78:300 (2004): 415.
10   Joe Neparrnga Gumbula in interview with the author, 30 June 2010.

ways. For Brothwell, it is a morally defensible position that human remains are collectable. They can be subject to handling and analysis by persons who have no cultural or familial association with them because the expiration of their life force has rendered them biological remnants. No longer human subjects, they can be treated as objects and stored in an institution where researchers might use them to advance their knowledge of the greater human story. For Gumbula, in contradistinction, death has not altered their subject status. As was the case when they were living and breathing, they can still expect to connect with, and reside within, their ancestral Country. Gumbula's obligations to the deceased are in no way affected by scientific theories about the origins of humanity.

In investigating this case study of a bone theft, and in plumbing the life stories and intellectual genealogies of its chief perpetrator, it is this subject/object dichotomy that I want to expose and analyse. How and in what situations do we objectify? What is the relationship between objectification and power? Those questions—which go to the heart of both colonial and postcolonial relations—are the fulcrum of my inquiry here. In exploring them, the transformation of human subjects into museum objects can be seen as part of a much larger history, being part of an array of social and cultural practices that are as much to do with relations between living persons as they are between the living and the dead.

Trans-National Journeys

What to say of the Arnhem Land Expedition, the vehicle for the theft of the Arnhem Land remains, which ran for much of 1948? Firstly, to locate it temporally, it was conceived in the last year of the Second World War—a moment of liminality, for the end of hostilities was by then discernible, although the geopolitics of the post-war age had yet to be hammered out. For Australia, the strategic and historical connections with the United Kingdom had been battered by the wartime experience, while the future relationship with the US seemed uncertain.[11] This was the moment when Australia's Department of Information, of which the America-friendly Arthur Calwell was minister, sent the Adelaide photographer-cum-ethnologist Charles P. Mountford (1890–1976) on a mission to raise awareness of the island-continent by giving lectures and exhibiting films throughout the US. Mountford's documentaries, depicting Aboriginal life in central Australia, were shot during extensive journeys by camel around Uluru (known to him as Ayers Rock) and Kata Tjuta (the Olgas), at that time seldom seen by anyone but their traditional owners (see Figure 2).

---

11 See Kim Beazley, 'Nation Building or Cold War: Political settings for the Arnhem Land Expedition', in *Exploring the Legacy of the 1948 Arnhem Land Expedition*, eds Martin Thomas and Margo Neale (Canberra: ANU E Press, 2011), 55–71.

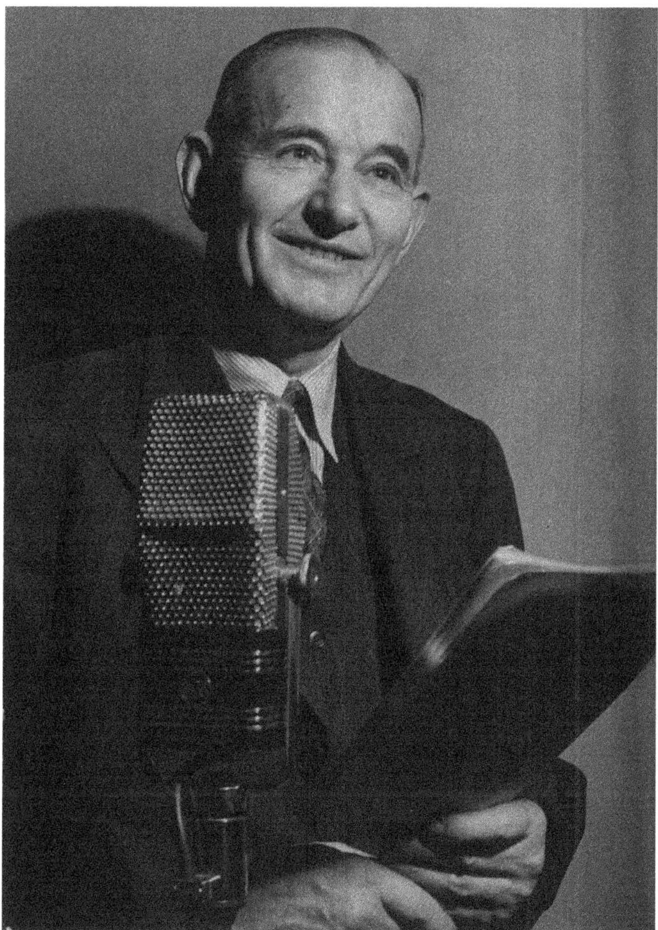

Figure 2: Charles P. Mountford during his lecture tour of the United States, 1945.

Source: By permission of the State Library of South Australia. PRG 1218/16/2.

The pedigree of the 1948 bone theft has many branches. All of them, including Mountford's dissemination of Australian film in the US, involved the dislocation of cultural materials and their circulation in contexts where they were utterly foreign. Mountford's film tour, a key example of this pattern of dislocation and circulation, was a finely tuned exercise in the cultivation of the exotic.[12] His time abroad reveals conflicts and contradictions that would resurface in the expedition he led three years later.

---

12   See Haskins, this volume.

Although his reputation has waned in the years since his death in 1976, for much of the mid-twentieth century, Mountford was a highly visible figure in Australian cultural life. In his home state he enjoyed special prominence as a local boy made good; the press would write of him as 'among the greatest' of South Australians. Mountford's improbable rise from working-class obscurity as a telephone mechanic to globetrotting authority on Australian Aborigines was enabled in the first instance by his proficiency as a photographer. As a camera club enthusiast in Adelaide, he was encouraged by officials at the South Australian Museum to document rock art. This kindled an interest that led him to participate in museum-backed expeditions to Aboriginal settlements where he took photos and studied mythology, which he documented by distributing paper and crayons and encouraging local artists to draw their legends.[13] In the field of Aboriginal studies, Mountford is best remembered as a writer and collector, but it is worth remembering that he began his career as a visual communicator. Interest in the visual arts lay at the heart of his preoccupation with Aboriginal culture. This explains his passion as a collector and promoter of Aboriginal art, which he did much to popularise on the international stage.[14] Deeply humanist in its vision, Mountford's oeuvre is distinguished by intimate portraiture of Aboriginal people in their homeland settings, as is evident in his photographs of Mawalan Marika and his son Wandjuk, who worked extensively with the 1948 expedition when it was stationed at Yirrkala in north-east Arnhem Land (see Figures 3 and 4). Mountford always argued that the dignity, creativity and morality of the people whom he studied must be recognised. In his visits to Aboriginal communities, he photographed everyone from babies to octogenarians, producing images that were attractive and highly efficacious in portraying the individuality and subjectivity of a people who had been endlessly typecast, degraded and objectified. The universalism of Mountford's approach to his Aboriginal subjects resonates strongly with other humanist deployments of photography in the mid-twentieth century, most notably the famed *The Family of Man* exhibition, curated by Edward Steichen for the Museum of Modern Art (MOMA) in New York in 1955 which, when it went on tour, became an international sensation.

---

13   Philip Jones, 'Inside Mountford's Tent: Paint, politics and paperwork', in *Exploring the Legacy of the 1948 Arnhem Land Expedition*, eds Martin Thomas and Margo Neale (Canberra: ANU E Press, 2011), 33–54.

14   See Philip Jones, 'Perceptions of Aboriginal Art: A history', in *Dreamings: The art of Aboriginal Australia*, ed. Peter Sutton (Ringwood: Viking, 1988), 143–79.

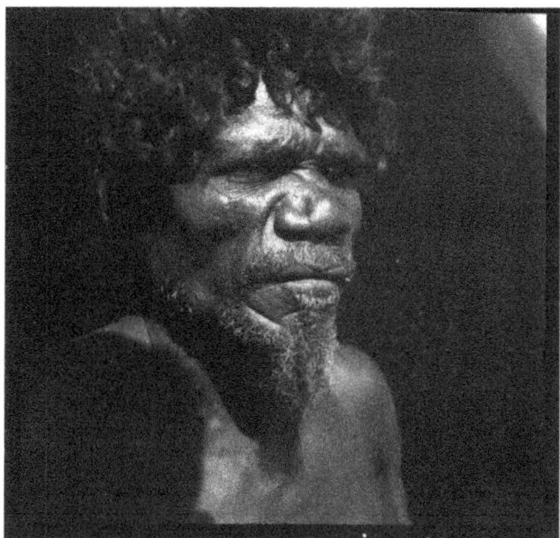

Figure 3: Portrait of Mawalan Marika, 1948. Photograph by Charles P. Mountford.

Source: By permission of the State Library of South Australia. PRG 1218/17/26.

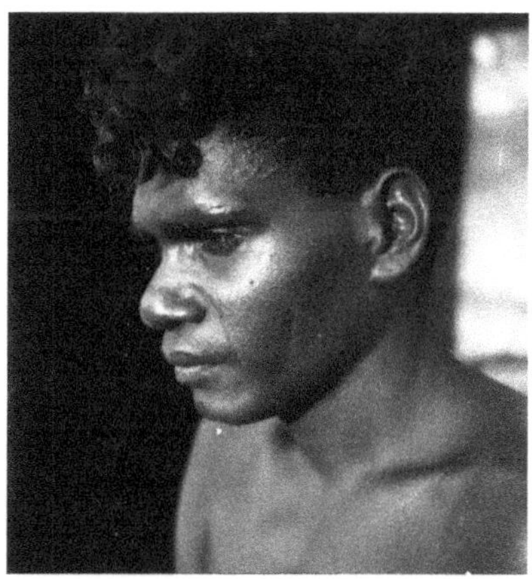

Figure 4: Portrait of Wandjuk Marika, 1948. Photograph by Charles P. Mountford.

Source: By permission of the State Library of South Australia. PRG 1218/17/26.

Like *The Family of Man*, the humanist doctrine espoused by Mountford was in various ways conflicted. His personal cachet as a humanitarian was due to his preparedness to work among people whom he regularly described as the most primitive in the human family. The extent and limits of his empathy are suggested in his public pronouncements, as we see in an interview, published in an Indiana newspaper in 1945, in which he claimed to have made eight or ten expeditions to central Australia where he studied 'the earth's most primitive people', the Pitjantjatjara. With some astonishment, the journalist reported that these people were so simple that they had

> less than five tools, and not more than ten personal possessions. They wear no clothing, not even a g-string and build no houses. They wander about their country, living off the land, killing kangaroos … Interesting people, no doubt, but what has our civilization to learn from theirs?
>
> Mr Mountford thinks it has plenty.
>
> "They are a fundamental society," he says, "and if we can get a complete study of them, how they live, what tools they use, what beliefs and philosophies they have, how they can live without warfare, how they can balance their laws so well, — if we can learn that, perhaps we can apply some of what we learn to our own problems.
>
> "Here is a human society that works simply and well, while our complex society is working badly … I am consecrating the rest of my life to the task of helping to make these people understood by our people. I believe if I do that, I shall have made a small contribution to human betterment."[15]

Some intimation of the power of Mountford's presentations can be found in responses from those who saw them. Mountford always kept his fan mail, preserving it in a detailed diary-cum-scrapbook that he maintained throughout his American tour. One writer was John P. Harrington, an official at the Smithsonian Institution's Bureau of Ethnology, whose encounter with Mountford's films of primordial Australia came close to a religious experience.

> The introductory background talk was enlightening and the colored motion pictures showed a country beautiful in coloration in addition to containing the most primitive humans in the entire world … We have nothing in America equal to the primitiveness of these Australian people. I thank God for the privilege of having been able to witness what is really worth while.[16]

Ever confident of his altruistic motives, Mountford enjoyed a remarkable ascendancy by riding the surge of interest in 'traditional' or 'primitive' arts that was taking hold in metropolitan centres, especially in the US. Throughout its

---

15   Maurice Frink, 'Home Town Slants: Man From Australia', *Daily Truth* (Elkhart, Indiana), undated press cutting in C. P. Mountford, 'A Journey to America 1944–5', Vol. 9, PRG 1218/16/9, *Mountford-Sheard Collection*, State Library of South Australia (SLSA), Adelaide, 766.
16   Harrington to Mountford, 10 March 1945, Mountford 'A Journey to America 1944–5,' Vol. 9, PRG 1218/16/9, *Mountford-Sheard Collection*, SLSA, 1080.

history, modernism has exhibited an interest in, and orchestrated an impressive array of dalliances with cultures and societies categorised as 'primitive'. While the roots of this fascination extend back to the nineteenth century and beyond, the Second World War brought a new and rather different attitude towards so-called traditional societies—a development we might associate with reactions to Nazism and the use it made of scientific racism. Other factors were at work here, most notably the move towards decolonisation, inflected as it was by the prominence of Africa, Asia and the Pacific as theatres of war where all sorts of collaboration between servicemen and native populations had occurred. Certainly, new attitudes towards formerly colonised people were gaining acceptance, and the very notion of racial difference was being disputed. In 1950, UNESCO issued its landmark declaration that '[f]or all practical social purposes "race" is not so much a biological phenomenon as a social myth'.[17]

While Mountford himself was not a collector of human anatomy, and considered himself a great friend to 'the Aborigine', he was nonetheless at home with the pre-war certitudes of a racially categorised humanity. At a film screening in Chicago, he complained about audience members who 'start up with describing the aborigines as low, mentally and physically, whereas my talk shows them to be the opposite'.[18] In Chicago's Field Museum of Natural History he looked with fascination through the Hall of the Races of Mankind, with its ninety-plus sculptures by Malvina Hoffman representing the human species in its multitudinous forms. Here too, Mountford would criticise the detail, but not the underlying principle.[19] The sculptures of Aborigines were not done from life, he complained; the depiction of Aboriginal women was 'definitely libellous'. He noted that if Hoffman had 'seen the Abo as I have, her statue of him would be very different'.[20] Yet Mountford was sufficiently intrigued by this woman sculptor, a former student of Rodin who had attained so prominent a position in the art and museum world, that he sought to meet her. She invited him to her studio where they had a productive conversation.[21]

Mountford's mission of providing a corrective within a racialised, developmental paradigm provided him with extraordinary opportunities to develop his career in the US. Between lecture engagements, he spent time knocking on doors and

---

17   UNESCO, 'The Race Question', 18 July 1950, accessed 1 July 2014, http://unesdoc.unesco.org/images/0012/001282/128291eo.pdf.

18   Mountford 'A Journey to America 1944–5,' Vol. 4, PRG 1218/16/4, *Mountford-Sheard Collection*, SLSA, 1473.

19   The historian Michelle Brattain has described Hoffman's anthropological sculptures as typical of a pre-war mentality that presents '"race" in the form of literally static bronze figures depicting idealised racial "types"'. Michelle Brattain, 'Race, Racism, and Antiracism: UNESCO and the politics of presenting science to the postwar public', *American Historical Review* 112:5 (2007): 1407.

20   Mountford 'A Journey to America 1944–5,' Vol. 4, PRG 1218/16/4, *Mountford-Sheard Collection*, SLSA, 1461.

21   ibid., 1570.

canvassing support for various projects. He consistently gained access to key officials in leading institutions. In New York he was called upon to advise René d'Harnoncourt, a curator at (and future director of) MOMA, on the Australian Aboriginal content for *Arts of the South Seas* (1946), a book and blockbuster exhibition of Oceanic art.[22] Mountford at that stage had never been to Arnhem Land, but he had written about its culture of bark paintings, as represented in the collections of the South Australian Museum.[23] D'Harnoncourt invited him to help negotiate the loan of these paintings and other objects for the MOMA exhibition.[24] The MOMA show presented a carefully arranged smorgasbord of Pacific cultures in which the Aboriginal material had special status. Mountford noted in his diary: 'The opening court of the show is to be Australian, the most primitive … It should be an excellent show and bring Australia well to the fore.'[25]

Mountford won a great many friends and admirers when touring the US. Among them were executives at the NGS who raised the prospect of awarding him a research grant for an Australian project. This was the point at which the idea of an expedition to Arnhem Land began to coalesce. When NGS funds were promised, the Smithsonian Institution became interested to the extent that it offered to provide scientific personnel, four of whom were eventually assigned to the expedition. Minister Calwell, delighted at this coming together of flagship US institutions on Australian soil, arranged for the Commonwealth Government to become an official partner. The American-Australian Scientific Expedition to Arnhem Land, as it became known, was an all-round anthropological, natural history, photographic and filmmaking adventure—a seven-month odyssey intended as an overt display of bilateral friendliness. Needless to say, the inhabitants of Arnhem Land were never consulted about the visitation of this scientific and propagandist extravaganza.[26]

The 1948 expedition was spawned by Mountford's films of central Australia, and it provided the occasion for another—and much larger—set of cultural objects and records to be thrown into circulation. With museum curators on its payroll, all eager to expand the collections of their own institutions, the expedition was a wholesale exercise in the collection of data and objects. Its

---

22   Mountford's role in the exhibition is documented in his US diaries, cited above, and in Ralph Linton, Paul S. Wingert and Rene D'Harnoncourt, *Arts of the South Seas* (New York: Museum of Modern Art, 1946), 6, 190–5.

23   Charles P. Mountford, 'Aboriginal Decorative Art from Arnhem Land, Northern Territory of Australia', *Transactions of the Royal Society of South Australia* 63:2 (1939), 365–71.

24   D'Harnoncourt to Mountford, 19 April 1945, Mountford, 'A Journey to America 1944–5', Vol. 4, PRG 1218/16/4, *Mountford-Sheard Collection*, SLSA.

25   ibid., 10 April 1945, 1503–5.

26   This summation of the expedition is drawn largely from Martin Thomas, 'A Short History of the 1948 Arnhem Land Expedition', *Aboriginal History* 34 (2010); and Martin Thomas and Margo Neale, eds, *Exploring the Legacy of the 1948 Arnhem Land Expedition* (Canberra: ANU E Press, 2011). See also Sally K. May, *Collecting Cultures: Myth, politics, and collaboration in the 1948 Arnhem Land Expedition* (Lanham: AltaMira Press, 2010).

gatherings included scientific and anthropological reports, popular publications, ethnological collections (including a great many examples of Aboriginal art), sound recordings and numerous examples of still and moving photography. The removal of human remains fell within this broader project of collection.

The Archaeologist and his Context

In my opening description of the bone theft and its documentation on film, I deliberately left the archaeologist nameless. Tempting as it is to continue in this vein, and thereby detach him from his social fabric and identifiers, as he did the men, women and children who became 'specimens' in his collection, I will not do so. To replicate his logic is to submit to its limitations (and these are considerable). Much more can be said of his actions and their consequences if his individuality is recognised.

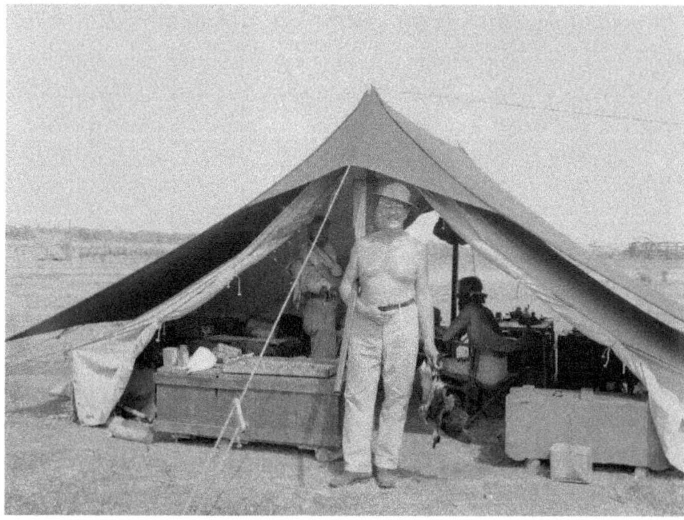

Figure 5: Frank Setzler at Gunbalanya (Oenpelli Mission) during the American Australian Scientific Expedition to Arnhem Land, 1948. Photographer unknown.

Source: By permission of the National Anthropological Archives, Smithsonian Institution. Photo Lot 36 Oenpelli_128.

The name of the bone taker was Frank Maryl Setzler (1902–1975) (see Figure 5). By 1948, when he went to Australia, he was something of an old hand at the Smithsonian, having joined the institution's US National Museum (now the National Museum of Natural History) in 1930. As the most senior of the four Smithsonian scientists who went to Arnhem Land in 1948, he served as deputy leader of the expedition. Setzler did his undergraduate study at the State University of Ohio and then moved to Chicago where he received an all-round training in social and physical anthropology, graduating as a Bachelor of Philosophy (PhB) in 1928. For the next two years he remained at Chicago as a graduate student. While often, perhaps mostly, known as 'Dr Setzler' (he was invariably referred to as such in the Australian press), he had no doctoral qualification.[27] The PhB was sufficient to win him the job at the US National Museum, which seems to have perfectly matched his interests and ambitions. Setzler's sympathies were with the museum side of anthropological study, where the analysis of material culture took precedence over the social and kinship study that preoccupied so many academic anthropologists in this period, and where opportunities for excavation and collection building abounded. His previous work experience had included curatorship at the state museum in Ohio, where he grew up.[28] He worked as the state archaeologist in Indiana before winning the Smithsonian appointment. By 1930, the Smithsonian was already a gargantuan museum and research organisation, centred in Washington DC and named after its benefactor, the English chemist James Smithson (c. 1765–1829). Although a single 'institution', administered by a Secretary and governed by a Board of Regents, it is in reality an unwieldy conglomeration that includes national museums, zoological gardens, art galleries, herbaria, research stations and libraries. In number of staff and size of collections, it is the leviathan of the museum world.

Setzler's obituary in the *Washington Post* included a photograph of him surrounded by bark paintings collected in Australia. Although he is said to have 'achieved particular note' with the expedition to 'primitive Arnhem Land', a more sober assessment would recognise that his time in Australia was something of a deviation in a career otherwise dedicated to North American anthropology and archaeology.[29] His work on Hopewell Mounds, the earthworks indigenous to the Midwest and south-east United States, was his major contribution to the discipline, according to the *International Dictionary of Anthropologists*.[30] In Australia, Setzler's work is not well known, although his reports on his 1948 excavations, co-authored with F. D. McCarthy (who represented the Australian Museum on the Arnhem Land Expedition), should be recognised as something of a milestone in the development of professional archaeology in Australia. Recent historical interest in intercultural research has kindled some renewed

---

27   Academic record of Frank Maryl Setzler, Office of the Recorder, University of Chicago. A search of other university records reveals that Setzler was awarded an Honorary Doctorate of Science by Indiana University in 1971.
28   'Frank Setzler, Biographical File' RU 7098, Smithsonian Institution Archives, Smithsonian Institution, Washington DC.
29   'Anthropologist Frank M. Setzler Dies', *Washington Post*, 20 February 1975.
30   James R. Glenn, 'Frank M. Setzler', in *International Dictionary of Anthropologists*, ed. Christopher Winters (New York: Garland Publishing, 1991), 633.

interest in Setzler's non-American investigations. Michael Davis pays detailed attention to Setzler and his collaborators in his 2007 study of the depiction of Indigenous heritage in European-Australian writings and my own work has addressed the motivations for his appointment to the expedition and the long-term impact of his osteological collecting.[31]

By the end of 1948, there was little love lost between Setzler and Mountford. Arguments about the carve-up of collections between institutions—especially the bark paintings that Mountford valued so highly—had taken a heavy toll on their relationship. Setzler's sense of professional superiority over the self-taught Mountford further contributed to the differences between them. Yet in spite of their contrasting experiences in terms of education and employment, there are interesting parallels in the careers of the expedition leader and his deputy. Setzler's engagement with Aboriginal Australia, including his circulation in the US of photography and artefacts acquired in Arnhem Land, won him a degree of celebrity that he had never previously enjoyed. The vehicle for this was the Arnhem Land lecture film, officially titled *Aboriginal Australia*, which had its first major screening in 1950 when it was shown to 3,800 members of the NGS in Washington's Constitution Hall.[32] Word of the film spread and Setzler engaged an agent who for several years secured him bookings on the US lecture circuit, providing a tidy supplement to his Smithsonian salary. Having fallen into the hands of publicists, the lecture film's benign if unexciting title, *Aboriginal Australia*, was supplanted by more florid descriptors. When it became part of the 'World Adventure Series', hosted by the Detroit Institute of the Arts, the show was dubbed 'Australia's Stone Age Tribesmen'. As was the case with Mountford's films, the thrill of the primeval was the principal point of interest in a market already cluttered with exploration and adventure. Key aspects of Setzler's presentation, highlighted in a promotional brochure, included: 'Clay-smeared primitive natives'; 'The Blood Feud ceremony'; 'Eating insects'; 'Shooting big crocodiles'; 'The Stone Age native at home'; and 'Weird rites'.[33]

When Setzler first joined the Smithsonian he fell under the influence of Aleš Hrdlička, the founder and veteran Curator of Physical Anthropology at the US National Museum. A prolific writer, lecturer and racial theorist, Hrdlička was internationally recognised in the field of physical anthropology.

---

31   Michael Davis, *Writing Heritage: The depiction of Indigenous heritage in European-Australian writings* (North Melbourne: Australian Scholarly Publishing and the National Museum of Australia Press, 2007), 182–212; Martin Thomas, 'Expedition as Time Capsule: Introducing the American-Australian Scientific Expedition to Arnhem Land', in *Exploring the Legacy of the 1948 Arnhem Land Expedition*, eds Martin Thomas and Margo Neale (Canberra: ANU E Press, 2011), 1–30; and Martin Thomas, 'Because It's Your Country: Death and its meanings in west Arnhem Land', *Life Writing*, (2013), http://www.tandfonline.com/doi/abs/10.1080/.VA54Cg4Z4g.
32   Lectures on 'Aboriginal Australia', Lectures National Geographic Soc, Box 20, *Frank Maryl Setzler Papers 1927–1960*.
33   Brochure in Setzler, Lectures 1951, Box 20, *Frank Maryl Setzler Papers 1927–1960*.

A man thoroughly steeped in the eugenic theory that held such sway in the early twentieth century, he is widely regarded as the patriarch of physical anthropology in North America. When Hrdlička died of a heart attack in 1943, Setzler was sufficiently close to him to serve at his funeral as a pallbearer.[34] Hrdlička is relevant to this discussion for a number of reasons. Firstly and generally, his preoccupation with the origins of humanity, which inspired his interest in collecting and analysing the bones of various peoples from around the world, emphasises the embedded trans-nationalism of the quest to understand the origins of humanity and its development. Secondly, but just as important, is the personal and professional influence of Hrdlička upon his younger colleague. Hrdlička was the 'founding father' of the collection into which the bones from Arnhem Land were accessioned. So some understanding of his career gives significant context to Setzler's activities in Australia (where Hrdlička himself did research in the 1920s).

Born in Bohemia, Hrdlička migrated with his family to New York when he was thirteen. He qualified in medicine and served his internship at the State Homeopathic Hospital for the Insane in Middletown, New York. It was there, working daily with psychiatric patients, that he began his investigations in physical anthropology. Dealing in his medical practice with the 'abnormality' of the insane, he embarked on a sustained quest to establish baseline 'normal' human physiology. This he identified in the skeletal structure of what he dubbed the 'Old Americans': whites of European descent whose ancestors had resided in the US for at least two generations.[35] Much of his work concerned the physiology of contemporary humans and its relationship to earlier forms of hominid physiology, as determinable from archaeological evidence. When recruited to the Smithsonian in 1903, he made it his mission to dramatically expand his department's collection of human remains, which then consisted of some 2,200 skulls. During Hrdlička's tenure, transfers from other anatomy collections were negotiated and he led expeditions of his own, collecting with gusto. In his forty years at the Smithsonian, he grew a collection that has been described as 'a great scientific assemblage'.[36] By the time of his retirement it contained bones and soft tissue from more than 10,000 individuals. As detailed below, Setzler himself contributed to the collection through the excavation of Native American burial sites.

Hrdlička's short visit to Australia in mid-1925 was part of an international study tour that involved excavation and collection-based research, as well as a

---

34   'Dr. Hrdlicka Funeral Rites To Be Today', *Washington Post*, 8 September 1943.

35   Linda Magaña, *Mr. America's Creator: The race science of Dr. Ales Hrdlicka, 1896–1943* (Undergraduate Thesis, Columbia University, 2011), 45.

36   Stephen Loring and Miroslav Prokopec, 'A Most Peculiar Man: The life and times of Aleš Hrdlička', in *Reckoning with the Dead: The Larsen Bay repatriation and the Smithsonian Institution*, eds Tamara L. Bray and Thomas W. Killion (Washington and London: Smithsonian Institution Press, 1994), 27.

good deal of spruiking for his discipline. At Jersey and Broome in north-west Australia he visited Aboriginal communities where he measured people and made observations on physique, skin tone and hair colour. In the United States, where his presence as a fieldworker has been closely scrutinised, Hrdlička is said to have had a 'gruff and belligerent manner of dealing with native people', especially when—as happened on occasion—they confronted him about his excavation of mortuary sites.[37] His relationships with Aboriginal Australians seem to have been no less cursory. Of his encounter with some Aboriginal South Australians, he remarked that they 'beg with no more shame than so many monkeys'.[38] Although he did argue that Australia should 'set aside regions in which the natives could be kept from contamination by the whites', he did so only to prevent 'this most interesting race' being 'lost to science and to the world, in the course of a few years'.[39]

Gregory Smithers, a historian of race and racism, has argued that Hrdlička's thoughts on the Indigenous peoples of both North America and Australia are emblematic of a paradox deeply inscribed in the racial thinking of his era. Hrdlička positioned himself as an enemy of racial discrimination, but claimed that the key to abolishing it was the elimination of racial difference by the breeding out of colour.[40] While in Australia, he made detailed examination of osteological collections, both public and private, ever determined to chart the distribution of racial difference and theorise its origins in terms of evolutionary history. Hrdlička's temperament, as described by the *New York Times*, was 'intense, leonine and picturesque'; his platform manner was 'both disarming and impressive'.[41] Australian pressmen were similarly in awe of the visiting American, who made numerous public appearances. It was reported that he measured 1,000 Aboriginal crania in the course of his visit. During his Australian tour he negotiated the acquisition of some human remains for the Smithsonian collection. Records in Washington establish that at Hrdlička's behest, the Public Library, Museum and Art Gallery of Western Australia sent to the Smithsonian Institution some seventy items of ethnological interest, including '[b]ones of two incomplete skeletons from a tree burial' originating from near Derby in the Kimberley. The Western Australian curator hoped that in exchange the Smithsonian would supply his collection with samples of South American ceramics and a series of North and South American scorpions.[42]

---

37   William W. Fitzhugh, 'Foreword', in *Reckoning with the Dead: The Larsen Bay repatriation and the Smithsonian Institution*, eds Tamara L. Bray and Thomas W. Killion (Washington DC and London: Smithsonian Institution Press, 1994), viii.

38   Cited in Gregory D. Smithers, 'The Dark Side of Anti-Racism: "Half-breeds" and the anthropology of Aleš Hrdlička', *Transnational Subjects: History, science and culture* 1:1 (2011): 74.

39   Hrdlička quoted in 'Ancient Man', *Mercury* (Hobart, Tas.), 9 January 1926.

40   Smithers, 'The Dark Side of Anti-Racism'.

41   'Dr. Ales Hrdlicka, Anthropologist, 74', *New York Times*, 6 September 1943.

42   'United States National Museum Accession Memorandum, Department of Anthropology, Division of Physical Anthropology', RU 305, Accession File 94717, Office of the Registrar, Smithsonian Institution

Hrdlička visited a range of Australian institutions. At the South Australian Museum more than 600 skulls and other skeletal material were made available for him to examine. He promulgated the view that the Australian and Tasmanian Aborigines were a 'fundamental race' that represented 'a paleolithic stage of stone culture'. In championing his line of research, he explained that the cardinal objective of physical anthropology was to understand the origins of 'ancient man and fossil apes'. In discussions with journalists, he gave detailed accounts of famed excavations of the period, all of which yielded osteological evidence of the human form in earlier stages of development.[43]

The claim that his research might answer the great questions of human origin, and the imputation, in his dealings with the public, that the bones of interest to archaeologists were those of great antiquity, was for Hrdlička a standard rhetorical gambit—one that is indicative of a considerable disjunction between theory and practice. If it really had been true that physical anthropology was only interested in the earliest examples of humans and their antecedents, and confined the scope of its collecting accordingly, then it is likely that the great animus towards his collections, felt especially strongly by Native Americans, would be less intense. But physical anthropology did not—and arguably could not—confine itself to cherry picking from the archaeological record the ancient skulls that became celebrity objects in the history of paleontology. Such a collection, bereft of recent examples of human physiology, would have been of little practical use to Hrdlička and his peers. Being a comparative discipline, physical anthropology required a range of specimens from across the spectrum of human history. That much was essential if an evolutionary sequence was to be established. For that reason it was necessary for Hrdlička to pursue strategies of collection building that threw his own personal ambitions—inseparable as they were from the collective ambition of scientific advancement—into direct conflict with the localised knowledge systems of those allegedly primitive societies, the great majority of which continued to suffer an extraordinary level of disempowerment as a result of their colonial past.

In her study of human dissection in Britain and Australia, historian Helen MacDonald draws connections between nineteenth-century medical research, the collecting of bodies and body parts, and notions of criminality. While cadavers of condemned felons were made available to surgeons for the purpose of study and teaching, the relative scarcity of executions in Britain notoriously resulted in the blackest of black markets: an illicit trade in corpses, acquired from unscrupulous undertakers or stolen from fresh graves.[44] In the clash

---

Archives, Washington DC. This record contains an internal memorandum from Hrdlička dated 3 November 1926 stating: 'This is an exchange with the Perth Museum which I have arranged during my visit to Australia.'
43   'Australian Blacks' Origin', *The Mail* (Adelaide, SA), 6 November 1926.
44   Helen MacDonald, *Human Remains: Episodes in human dissection* (Carlton: Melbourne University Press, 2005).

between indigenes and colonisers, there was frequent conflation of the primitive and the criminal. Those who killed in defence of their territory were described as 'murderous' and it is hardly incidental that the heads of many warriors who died for their cause became specimens in museums or private collections. The process of 'desubjectification' that occurred here was of course dependent upon political and cultural processes that targeted particular social or ethnic groups for objectification. Any pretence that science was objectively removed from these processes is of course an absurdity. It both benefited from, and contributed to, this history. Hrdlička, for example, drew personal profit from his oft-made claim that certain branches of humanity were Paleolithic survivals in which science had a special interest. Such arguments from such a source gave scientific validation to the differential treatment of these peoples on the part of those who governed them.

Indigenous societies in twentieth-century Australia, like those in so many parts of the world, existed within the strictures of an elaborate web of ordinances, threats and strategies of containment, collectively intended to manage, administer and curtail their livelihoods, and to legitimise the exploitation of their ancestral Country. At the time of Hrdlička's visit to Australia, Aboriginal people were not counted in the national census and were prevented from enrolling as voters. These were among a suite of measures that for the most part excluded them from the citizenry. When, as had been happening intermittently since the nineteenth century, outsiders arrived to ransack cemeteries or other mortuary sites, the affected communities had little recourse, legal or otherwise. In some jurisdictions in the years when bone taking was particularly rife, Aboriginal burials *were* covered by laws for the protection of graves—although prosecution of thieves was rare or non-existent.[45] In South Australia, the state's sense of proprietorship over Aboriginal land and culture extended to the bodies of the deceased. Hrdlička approvingly told a journalist that the osteological collection in Adelaide had grown rapidly as the result of 'a beneficial law, which obliges all police officials of the State to forward to the Museum any aboriginal skeleton remains that may be found'.[46]

In contradistinction to his public pronouncements, the archaeological culture fostered by Hrdlička encouraged the exhumation of a great many burials that were historically recent. His fieldbooks from Alaska reveal horrific incidents.

---

45 Paul Turnbull, 'Indigenous Australians and Native Title', in *The Dead and Their Possessions*, eds Cressida Fforde, Jane Hubert and Paul Turnbull (New York: Routledge, 2004), 83.

46 'Australian Blacks' Origin', *The Mail* (Adelaide, SA), 6 November 1926. The 'beneficial law' mentioned probably refers to a memorandum from the South Australian Commissioner of Crown Lands to the Chief Secretary: 'The recent discovery of the remains of aboriginal natives at the River Murray has brought to my mind the fact that all such remains on Crown lands belong to this department. I shall be obliged if the Hon. Minister will give instructions to any field officers in his department that should they at any time discover human remains, or any articles that have been in use by aboriginals, or any other article of use on Crown lands, they will at once take possession of the discovery, and telegraph your office for instructions as to its disposal.' *South Australian Police Gazette*, no. 18, 3 May 1911. Thanks to Paul Turnbull for sharing this information.

On one occasion he was forced to abandon an exhumation because the body was 'too fresh'. In 1926 on the Yukon River he was nearly intercepted by mourners of the person whose skeleton he had loaded into a boat. As he and his assistant fled the scene, an 'old Indian and his crone' stood watching. 'They know already', he recorded.[47] Frank Setzler began working alongside Hrdlička a few years after this incident occurred, and he too began to contribute to the osteological collection. Writing from Comstock, Texas, in 1933, he described an extensive excavation performed in a large cave containing substantial evidence of Native American occupation. The site yielded 'nearly 500 recorded specimens and over a dozen burials'. The survival in good condition of fibre matting in the cave and a fur robe draped over one of the bodies suggests that they were not of great antiquity.[48] The same can be said of the burials that he disturbed in Arnhem Land, as the film footage, in which he is seen unwrapping a jawbone from a cloth surround, makes clear.

Setzler and the Theft

It was six years after the expedition that the first of the four volumes of *Records of the American-Australian Scientific Expedition to Arnhem Land* was published. Volume 1, titled *Art, Myth and Symbolism* (1956) and written solely by Mountford, began with an essay titled 'The Story of the Expedition'. He summarised their collective achievement as follows:

> The results of the expedition could hardly have been richer, both from the standpoint of human companionship and scientific results … The gross results of the collections, too, were impressive: 13,500 plant specimens, 30,000 fish, 850 birds, 460 animals, several thousand aboriginal implements and weapons, together with photographs and drawings of a large number of cave paintings … There was also a collection of several hundred aboriginal bark paintings and two hundred string figures. In addition to the physical collections of natural history and ethnological specimens, each scientist had written extensive field notes as a basis for his scientific papers. There were also many hundreds of monochrome and coloured photographs as well as several miles of colour film on aboriginal life and natural history.[49]

---

47 Cited in Gordon L. Pullar, 'The Qikertarmiut and the Scientist: Fifty years of clashing world views', in *Reckoning with the Dead: The Larsen Bay repatriation and the Smithsonian Institution*, eds Tamara L. Bray and Thomas W. Killion (Washington DC and London: Smithsonian Institution Press, 1994), 21–2.

48 Setzler to Wetmore, 28 April 1933, *Alexander Wetmore Papers*, c. 1848–1979, RU 7006, Box 60, Smithsonian Institution Archives, Smithsonian Institution, Washington DC.

49 Charles P. Mountford, *Records of the American-Australian Scientific Expedition to Arnhem Land: Vol. 1: Art, myth and symbolism* (Melbourne: Melbourne University Press, 1956), xxx.

This list is revealing—for its exclusions as much as its inclusions. Not until 1960, when Volume 2 of the Records appeared, was the collection of human remains officially acknowledged in Australia. McCarthy and Setzler's jointly authored contribution to that volume, titled 'The Archaeology of Arnhem Land', did discuss the bone taking, but it was well after the event. This is a substantial, eighty-page paper that provides detailed evidence of the archaeological work performed by the expedition including descriptions of most sites from which human remains were collected.[50] Further detail is contained in Setzler's fieldbooks, held by the Smithsonian's National Anthropological Archives, and in a list of physical anthropology specimens, prepared in Washington when they were accessioned into the US National Museum.[51] These records establish that the bones originated from three sites on Groote and nearby islands; one site on the Gove Peninsula in north-east Arnhem Land; one site from the island of Milingimbi (although the bones are said to have been transported there from mainland Arnhem Land); and three sites in the vicinity of Gunbalanya. Notably, not all the bones collected were of people indigenous to Arnhem Land. Graves of three mariners from South Sulawesi, who had died while harvesting trepang, were excavated from Groote Eylandt. Another two males who were reputedly murdered by Aborigines in 1916—one of mixed European-Aboriginal ancestry and the other Asian—were excavated and collected at Port Bradshaw on the Gove Peninsula.[52] Of the Aboriginal remains, some 170 bones were inventoried as individual items. Others were registered as bundles of bones or as packets of fragments. They included pieces of skull from at least three people; bones of at least five children (including two babies) that were wrapped in paperbark bundles; and assorted 'skeletal parts' of at least one other person. The number of bones collected from such a range of sites makes it plain that for Setzler, and to a lesser extent McCarthy, the collection of human remains was a major part of the work conducted in Arnhem Land. Other members of the expedition came to regard it as Setzler's signature activity — to the extent that it was caricatured in doggerel songs that were performed in evening singalongs.[53] In lyrics set to the melody of *Ain't Gonna Grieve My Lord No More*, expedition members sang of their deputy leader:

---

50   Frederick D. McCarthy and Frank M. Setzler, 'The Archaeology of Arnhem Land', in *Records of the American-Australian Scientific Expedition to Arnhem Land: Vol. 2: Anthropology and nutrition*, ed. Charles P. Mountford (Melbourne: Melbourne University Press, 1960), 215–95.

51   'List of Specimens Collected by F. M. Setzler, Australia, 1948', Arnhem Land Expedition, RU 305, Accession File 178294, Smithsonian Institution Archives, Smithsonian Institution, Washington DC.

52   Patrol officer and writer William E. Harney (official guide on the 1948 expedition) was the source of information about the death of these men. See 'Notes on the human skeletal material recovered in Arnhem Land, northern Australia, in 1948, by F. M. Setzler', Arnhem Land Expedition, RU 305, Accession File 178294, Smithsonian Institution Archives, Smithsonian Institution, Washington DC.

53   See Harris, this volume.

There's no room in Heaven
For a man like Frank,
To exhuming skulls
Is what he sank.[54]

This is not the only occasion where bone theft was treated as an object of mirth. A photograph of Setzler 'discovering' a crevice containing a human skull and other bones was reproduced in a *National Geographic* article with a caption that begins: 'Alas, Poor Yorick! Alas, Poor Setzler!'[55] Published in 1949 and titled 'Exploring Stone Age Arnhem Land', this was the most extensive of several articles published in the magazine as a result of the expedition. Mountford wrote the text, but as was customary at the *Geographic*, the selection of photographs and drafting of the captions or 'legends' were done in-house. National Geographic Society records establish that Howell Walker wrote all the legends and, with input from Setzler, also played a major role in editing the article.[56] Mountford's leadership had been the cause of great acrimony during the expedition, to the extent that the Department of Information attempted (unsuccessfully) to depose him as leader when they were stationed at Yirrkala, their second base.[57] Walker and Setzler both had ill feelings about his leadership and they gleefully embraced the opportunity to edit his work. Walker told Setzler that his editor had given them 'carte blanche to butcher, build, destroy or do anything to improve' Mountford's 'unmasterpiece'.[58]

The fault-lines of the expedition—resulting as they did from an array of national, cultural, disciplinary and interpersonal differences—are manifest in that *National Geographic* article, which deceptively presents as the initiative of a single author, though it is really a composite creation, as the behind-the-scenes wrangling makes clear. In any case, the visual component of the article—long recognised at the *Geographic* as having much more impact than the printed word—was the work of Walker, aided and abetted by Setzler and the editorial executives who played a major role in selecting images for publication from the thousands shot in Arnhem Land. The depiction of Setzler in his glory as the discoverer of bones is one of various tensions between the written and visual narratives. Like 'The Story of the Expedition', the written text of 'Exploring Stone Age Arnhem Land' omits mention of bone taking, even when it summarises Setzler's archaeological work at Injalak. Mountford would

---

54   'I ain't gunna [sic] grieve' (unattributed lyrics), Frank M. Setzler, Arnhem Land Exped. Corresp. 1948–9, Folder 2, Box 7, *Frank Maryl Setzler Papers 1927–1960*.

55   Charles P. Mountford, 'Exploring Stone Age Arnhem Land', *National Geographic Magazine* 96:6 (1949): 778.

56   'Memorandum from J. R. Hildebrand', 12 September 1949, Manuscripts Accepted, Exploring Stone Age Arnhem Land, Mountford, Charles P., Microfiche Archive #510-1.3249, Archives and Records Library, National Geographic Society (NGS), Washington DC.

57   See Jones, 'Inside Mountford's Tent', and Thomas, 'A Short History of the 1948 Arnhem Land Expedition'.

58   Walker to Setzler, 9 September 1949, 'National Geographic Society Correspondence 1948–49', Box 32, *Frank Maryl Setzler Papers 1927–1960*.

have his reader believe that the yield of those excavations was confined to 'a complete series of projectile points, adze stones and quartzite scraper'.[59] I quote here from the manuscript of his first draft, for the passage cited was entirely eliminated from the published version. The closest he came to the subject of burial was an account of a night in a cave where he slept near the scattered bones of a skeleton. This passage *did* make it to publication and it appeared under a subheading, 'Slept Next to Human Skeleton'.[60] Mountford's reticence on this matter is apparent in many other documents, including his final report on the expedition to the Department of Information.[61] 'Discovery' was of course a key trope in the many cables and press releases that he issued during the expedition to advertise their accomplishments, but the discussion of human remains was usually suppressed or, on rare occasions, acknowledged in heavily coded language. Specific mention of the *removal* of bones was assiduously avoided, as can be seen in a press release where Setzler is said to have 'unearthed several strange types of burial, and discovered many human skeletons in the clefts of the rocks'.[62]

While Mountford himself seems not to have participated in the plunder of mortuary sites, he made no effort to prevent it happening. As the leader he had the power to do so and as someone with long experience of Aboriginal society, he would—or should—have known that it would cause deep and lasting offence. Some explanation for Mountford's position on this matter can be found in the aforementioned fault lines, which became manifest in a series of disputes between him and others in the expedition, especially Setzler and McCarthy. While personality differences and condescension towards Mountford's supposed amateurism were certainly at work here, the principal point of contention, often mentioned in the expedition diaries, concerned the division of the ethnographic collections that were being amassed. Mountford, who hoarded bark paintings with something close to fetishism, resented the claims of his colleagues upon those collections. The friction generated was considerable, for as curators doing extended fieldwork on full salary, Setzler and McCarthy were expected to return to their home museums with substantial riches in terms of collections. Mountford, who had no interest in physical anthropology, was prepared to let

59   C. P. Mountford, 'The Arnhem Land Expedition' (draft), Manuscripts Accepted, Exploring Stone Age Arnhem Land, Mountford, Charles P., Microfiche Archive #510-1.3249, Archives and Records Library, NGS, 36.
60   Mountford, 'Exploring Stone Age Arnhem Land': 779.
61   Mountford, 'The Report of the Origin, Objects Activities and Results of the … Expedition to Arnhem Land', Reports of Staff, PRG 1218/17/17, *Mountford-Sheard Papers*, American Australian Scientific Expedition to Arnhem Land 1948, SLSA.
62   Press release signed by Mountford and received by the Northern Territory Administrator on 25 October 1948, 'Scientific Expedition to Arnhem Land & Northern Territory — C. P. Mountford', *Correspondence files, Northern Territory*, F1, Item 1945/151, National Archives of Australia (NAA), Darwin.

Setzler collect bones, hopeful that the acquisition of these trophies would lessen his requirement for the types of object—particularly the bark paintings—that Mountford so coveted.

There is nothing to suggest that Mountford's covering up of the bone taking was due to regret at its happening. More likely it was because Setzler was planning to take his prizes abroad. Mountford had made many enemies in the course of his career and his antennae were habitually attuned to those who could do him harm. Few white people at that time thought to challenge the pillaging of burial sites for the offence it gave to Aboriginal people, but the export, if it became known, could be queried on nationalistic grounds—the argument being that objects significant to Australia's heritage should go to an Australian museum. Moreover, Mountford had brokered an agreement that all type specimens collected on the expedition would remain the property of Australian institutions, while the 'ethnological material' would be divided between Setzler, McCarthy and himself.[63] Concerning the skeletal collections, it was eventually decided at the Australian end (long after the export to the US) that two-thirds of them should be housed in Australian collections.[64] Correspondence dating from the period when the expedition was wrapping up reveals sensitivity about the export of collections. Walker reported that there was anxiety among expedition members about whether cases of specimens, intended for the Smithsonian, would, on inspection, be blocked from leaving Australia by local authorities.[65] An indication that they were eager to get the bones out of the country as discreetly as possible is reflected in documentation pertaining to the freight of cases bound for the US. The bones were part of this consignment, but the contents are ambiguously described as 'Natural History Specimens'.[66]

Setzler, as we know, was anything but coy about the bone taking once he returned home and began his film lectures, but it is possible that Mountford put pressure on him to keep quiet about the business while on Australian soil. Setzler's own final report on his research, intended for Australian authorities,

---

63   Mountford put this proposal to Alexander Wetmore, Secretary of the Smithsonian, in a letter dated 3 February 1948. Wetmore confirmed agreement on 9 February 1948. Correspondence in RU 305, Accession File 178294, Smithsonian Institution Archives, Smithsonian Institution, Washington DC..

64   May, *Collecting Cultures*, 191.

65   Howell Walker, who assumed responsibility for overseeing shipping arrangements, reported to his superiors in Washington of the 'possibility that Australian Department of Internal Affairs might examine all cases of specimens with view to holding in Australia any specimen not in duplicate. But the Department of Information is trying to iron this business out with the Department of Internal Affairs, pointing out that an earlier decision not to examine the cases had been reached. McRae will keep us advised.' Walker to Melvin M. Payne, 2 April 1949, Setzler, 'National Geographic Society Correspondence 1948-49', Box 32, *Frank Maryl Setzler Papers 1927–1960*.

66   Northern Territory Administration to Department of Information, 19 January 1949, 'Arnhem Land Expedition: C. P. Mountford', *General correspondence files, two number series, Department of Information*, CP815/1, Item 005.87 Part 3, NAA, Canberra.

does acknowledge that human remains were encountered, but refers to their collection only implicitly—as his description of excavating at Injalak makes plain.

> Ten distinct sites were selected … These produced hundreds of quartzite scrapers, hematite stones with rubbed faces as a result of use for obtaining their red ochre used in making the cave paintings, uniface and biface chipped projectile points, human burials, glass beads, pieces of iron, etc.[67]

The language used here is fascinating. The burials are themselves buried in the mass of other data; their unburying is attributed not to the writer but to the sites themselves that are said to have 'produced' the archaeological haul. Nowhere in this report does Setzler admit to disturbing the deceased. He preferred a passive voice for these sections of his report: 'Here before us, overlooking the sea, were many skulls and skeletons'; or, more actively, though not confessing to the act of removal: 'We were most fortunate in finding the well preserved skeletons, extended full length'. This is otherwise atypical of Setzler's reporting, where his own agency is strongly emphasised.

> [M]y program called for various anthropological approaches. These included the taking of palm and finger prints, testing their taste buds, collecting hair samples, photographing their heads, the making of facial casts and anthropological measurements, studying their material culture … and archaeological investigations.[68]

When he returned to Washington DC, Setzler wavered in his choice of euphemism for describing the thefts. 'Collecting' was probably the most common, though in the film lecture he spoke of the bones being 'preserved' in his museum. Even more intriguingly, he would claim that the bones had been 'recovered' when he removed them from the rock or ground.[69] The displacement of the theft became a restitution; a return to their rightful place.

Am I being too harsh in describing the bone collector as a thief? Should I recognise that according to his own way of thinking, he was not stealing but 'recovering' perishable evidence in the service of a beneficent science? I say *no* to this question because I am convinced that Setzler knew perfectly well that he was stealing. So detailed are his fieldbooks that they allow his moral workings, such as they are, to be at least partially *recovered*. On 7 October 1948, he made an initial visit to Gallery Hill, as he called Injalak, to survey sites for the

---

67 Memorandum from Setzler to Mountford, 4 November 1948, Reports of Staff, American Australian Scientific Expedition to Arnhem Land 1948, PRG 1218/17/17, *Mountford-Sheard Papers*, SLSA.
68 ibid.
69 'Arnhem Land Ethno Objects', Box 23, *Frank Maryl Setzler Papers 1927–1960*.

excavations that would dominate the weeks to come. He was accompanied by two young men employed as assistants. Aged in their teens, they resided at the cultural melting pot that was Oenpelli Mission, already occupied by Aboriginal people from a myriad of clans and language groups. One of the assistants was identified only as Micky, a name likely to have been bestowed by missionaries. The other can be firmly identified as Jimmy Bungaroo, who later in his life would become a well-known personality in Maningrida, a large settlement east of Oenpelli (see Figure 6).

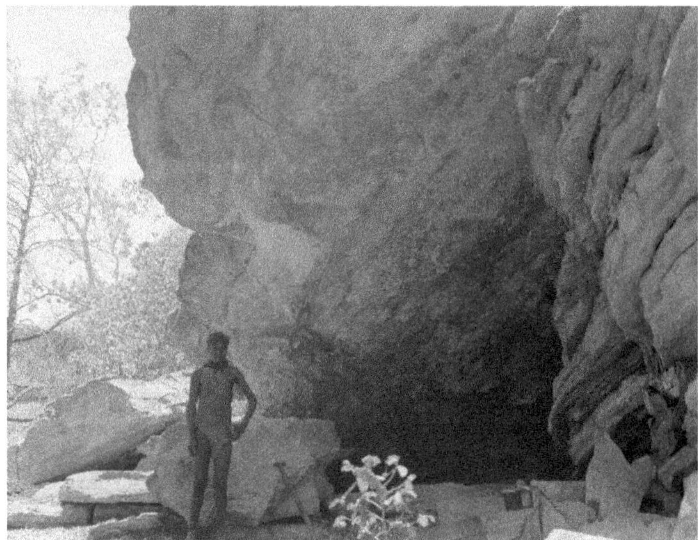

Figure 6: Jimmy Bungaroo at Injalak on the outskirts of Gunbalanya (Oenpelli Mission) during the American–Australian Scientific Expedition to Arnhem Land, 1948. Photograph by Frank Setzler.

Source: By permission of the National Anthropological Archives, Smithsonian Institution. Photo Lot 36 Oenpelli_053.

Composed of heavily weathered sandstone, the boulderous rise that is Injalak is defined by its many gaps, cracks, fissures, overhangs and deeper passages leading into caves. The latter are often referred to as galleries—rightly so, for they are full of art. Said to have been created by a fish, the Long Tom, when he leapt from the billabong at its base, Injalak is a natural dwelling place, traditionally occupied in the wet season when the movement of Bininj (as the local Aboriginal people call themselves) was greatly curtailed by the swelling of the rivers and the inundation of the flood plains. A rich sequence of rock paintings, created over centuries, can still be seen. The debris of habitation provided material that Setzler would excavate and sieve as part of his research program. The former residents of these caves were evidently at home living in close proximity to the mortal remains of their ancestors. As is the case throughout the plateau country of Kakadu National Park and west Arnhem Land, the crevice-ridden sandstone of Injalak served as a natural ossuary. Funerary rites in this region required sequences of ceremony, sometimes lasting several years, of which the Lorrkon or 'hollow log rite' is best known.[70] Each stage of memorialisation involved caring for the remains of the deceased in a particular way. At the conclusion of the rites, the bones—by this time coloured with a solution of red ochre and wrapped in sheets of the pliant paperbark that grows abundantly in this region—were placed in perpetuity in caves or crevices. With the deterioration of the bark over time, the bones would spill from their wrappings, serving as a visible reminder of the enduring presence of ancestor spirits.

Setzler was in the company of one of his Aboriginal assistants when he made the initial survey of Injalak. He entered a large cave that is readily identifiable and where *some* human remains can still be seen. There were many more bones when Setzler first went there. He described in his notebook how '[o]ne skull and accompanying long bones have a dark red pigment well preserved over them. I paid no attention to these bones as long as the native was with me'.[71]

Setzler's own record of his archaeological work around Injalak and the nearby hill, Argaluk (an important ceremonial site), establishes that he consistently avoided the scrutiny of his assistants or of any other Aboriginal people when he collected human remains. Of bones stolen on 28 October (the same day he filmed with Walker, although this appears to have been a separate incident), he writes of Bungaroo and Micky:

> During the lunch period, while the two native boys were asleep, I gathered the two skeletons which had been placed in crevices outside the caves. These were disarticulated … and only skull and long bones. One had been painted with red ochre. These I carried down to the camp in burlap sacks and later packed in ammunition boxes.[72]

Setzler's surreptitiousness leaves little doubt of his awareness that this was theft. He waited for Jimmy and Micky, who had been labouring since dawn in the heat, to take their siesta before doing the deed. Similarly, no Aboriginal people are present in the film of him taking the bones. The timing of the event—late October—is itself notable, for it was just days before the expedition shipped out. By delaying the act until the final possible moment, Setzler reduced his

---

70   See Ronald M. Berndt and Catherine H. Berndt, *Man, Land and Myth in North Australia: The Gunwinggu people* (Sydney: Ure Smith, 1970), 133–5.

71   Mountford 'Diaries 1948', Box 14, *Frank Maryl Setzler Papers 1927–1960*, 7 October 1948.

72   Mountford 'Diaries 1948', Box 14, *Frank Maryl Setzler Papers 1927–1960*, 28 October 1948.

chances of being challenged by the traditional owners of the site. The stealth continued as the bones were sealed in boxes, shipped to Darwin then Sydney, and spirited out of the country.

Setzler was the most assiduous body snatcher on the Arnhem Land Expedition, but he was not the only one. As noted, McCarthy assisted him in excavating and collecting human skeletons. By the end of the expedition, bone collecting had become normalised—a mere extension of the natural history collecting that continued throughout. The expedition included a botanist, a mammalogist, an ichthyologist, and an ornithologist. Between them, these men amassed tens of thousands of specimens. John Bray, a farmer and former serviceman, was an employee of the expedition. Recruited as the cook, he became the transport officer when that position fell vacant.[73] An interest in insects inspired him to start collecting, to the extent that he was recognised in the expedition *Records* as 'honorary entomologist'.[74] His diary records how he worked with McCarthy in excavating what seemed to be a woman's skeleton, lodged in a cave near Kunnanj or Fish Creek, a site beyond Oenpelli where he and other expedition members were stationed.[75]

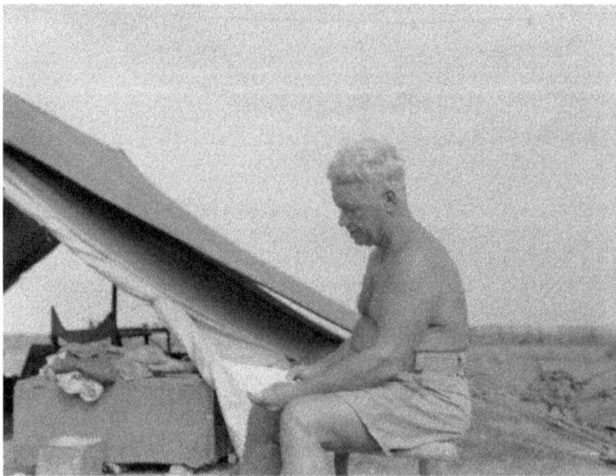

Figure 7: W. E. Harney at Gunbalanya (Oenpelli Mission) during the American Australian Scientific Expedition to Arnhem Land, 1948. Photograph by Frank Setzler.

Source: By permission of the National Anthropological Archives, Smithsonian Institution. Photo Lot 36 Oenpelli_143.

73   See Amanda Harris, 'Food, Feeding and Consumption (or the Cook, the Wife and the Nutritionist): The politics of gender and class in a 1948 Australian expedition', *History and Anthropology* 124:3 (2013): 363–79.
74   Mountford, *Records of the American-Australian Scientific Expedition to Arnhem Land*, xi.
75   John Bray, 'Arnhem Land Expedition 1948', Private Journal, collection of Andrew Bray, Canberra, 19 October 1948. See Harris, this volume.

A further skull was collected by W. E. 'Bill' Harney, the expedition's official guide (see Figure 7). Harney is the second white man visible in the film footage, described at the beginning of this chapter. He is seen near the top of Injalak, assisting Setzler as they transport a wooden crate of remains. Harney was a well known character in the Northern Territory: a renowned bushman who had recently retired as Commonwealth patrol officer, a position that required travel among, and extensive liaison with, a wide variety of Aboriginal groups. Fluent in Kriol, he was regarded as the go-to person for access to all things Aboriginal. Since 1943, when he published his first work of non-fiction, *Taboo*, Harney's renown beyond the Territory had grown. A string of other books, mostly combining memoir and observation on Aboriginal life, followed throughout the years until his death in 1962. Journalists, filmmakers, anthropologists and administrators all made use of him as a cultural intermediary, and it is not surprising that in the early planning stages of the 1948 expedition, Mountford was keen to have him involved. Harney joined the expedition in July 1948.

Harney has been portrayed as a significant ally of Mountford in his long conflict with Professor A. P. Elkin and Elkin's beloved protégés, Ronald and Catherine Berndt.[76] Occupying the Chair of Anthropology at the University of Sydney, Elkin looked down on Mountford as an amateur interloper. He viewed the whole Arnhem Land Expedition with distrust and distaste. Although Harney was keen to participate in Mountford's expedition, his loyalties lay chiefly with the professor, whom he once lauded in an unpublished poem titled 'To You My Friend'.[77] The pair had corresponded since 1937 and Elkin was seminal in kick-starting Harney's literary career. He liaised with publishers, collected royalties, wrote prefaces, and effectively acted as the bushman's agent in the city.[78] Harney's references to Mountford were invariably disparaging, to the extent that when he told Elkin he would participate in the expedition as a guide, he said of Mountford that he would 'show him little'.[79] When Harney joined the expedition at Yirrkala, its second base, Elkin wrote to ask if he could obtain for him 'a good Aboriginal skull with jaw-bone'.[80] In November, once the expedition was over, Harney advised Elkin that 'I have the Aborigine skull you required a good one & will send it down in a week or so'.[81] The origin of the

---

76 Jones, 'Inside Mountford's Tent', 49.

77 'To You My Friend', Correspondence Files, P. 130, Series 8, File 1/8/2, *A. P. Elkin Papers*, University of Sydney Archives.

78 Correspondence between Elkin and the Commonwealth Literary Fund reveals how Elkin assisted in the publication of Harney's first book, *Taboo* (1943). See H. S. Temby (Secretary of Commonwealth Literary Fund) to Elkin, 29 April 1943, ibid. Series 8 of Elkin's papers at the University of Sydney provides extensive evidence of how he advised and acted for Harney. They co-authored *Songs of the Songmen* (1949), although Elkin's contribution involved editing and rewriting Harney's manuscript.

79 Harney to Elkin, 4 January 1948, Correspondence Files, P. 130, Series 8, File 1/8/3, *A. P. Elkin Papers*, University of Sydney Archives.

80 Elkin to Harney, 6 July 1948, ibid.

81 Harney to Elkin, 17 November 1948, ibid.

skull is not mentioned in the correspondence, but the great abundance of bones around Injalak, and the fact that Harney was helping Setzler collect them, make Oenpelli the likely source.

So noticeable in all these episodes of twentieth-century bone collecting is the great disjunction between the lightness with which it was done and the gravity with which it is regarded in the Aboriginal world. Human matter was a tradeable asset. It could be itemised in a ledger that put it on par with dead scorpions or antique pots. Its acquisition could be laughed at in song, or trivialised in crass literary allusion. In the case of Elkin, there is suggestion that he was after a trophy, seized from under the nose of an expedition leader he clearly despised. The actors in this drama had diverse attitudes to Aboriginal society. Their familiarity with Indigenous people varied enormously. Hrdlička looked down on them from an evolutionary height; Setzler treated them largely as a resource to be mined; Harney positioned himself the 'blackfellow's friend'; Elkin wrote a famous book, *The Australian Aborigines: How to understand them* (1938). Despite their diversity of experiences and intellectual positions, all saw it as absolutely normal and acceptable that the bones of Aboriginal people were available for the service of their own scientific, pedagogic, or political agenda. The extremity of this objectification—a common thread between all these individuals—becomes utterly clear. So it is the matter of 'subjectification' to which we will now turn.

The View from Gunbalanya

Beliefs about reincarnation and the origin of spirits among the Gagudju-speaking people of Gunbalanya were described by Baldwin Spencer in *Native Tribes of the Northern Territory of Australia* (1914), a monograph based on fieldwork in 1912. As he explained it, the Gagadu (spelled 'Kakadu' by Spencer) people of the present are reincarnations of the first people who inhabited the Country. The spirit, known as the Yalmaru, has a cyclical existence, treading back and forth between the worlds of the living and the dead. When a person dies and the mourning ceremonies take place, the Yalmaru watches over the bones in a role of guardianship. With the passage of time, the Yalmaru divides in two. One half remains the original Yalmaru; the other is a discrete though inextricably connected entity, named Iwaiyu. 'The two are distinct and have somewhat the same relationship to one another as a man and his shadow, which, in the native mind, are very intimately associated.'[82] After a long period of watching over the bones, the time to reincarnate arrives. Iwaiyu assumes the form of a frog who,

---

82   Baldwin Spencer, *Native Tribes of the Northern Territory of Australia* (London: Macmillan, 1914), 270.

with Yalmaru's aid, finds a woman suitably placed in the kinship system and enters her. Iwaiyu develops into a baby and in this way the spirit returns to the domain of the living while retaining a presence in the world of the dead.[83]

Arnhem Land (a designation created by Europeans for what became a vast Aboriginal reserve) is a mosaic of different cultures, languages and kinship systems. Yet the potency of the spiritual realm and the significance of the human body in beliefs pertaining to the afterlife are common throughout. Like Spencer, the anthropologist Howard Morphy, whose ethnographic research with the Yolngu of north-east Arnhem Land began in the 1970s, describes a belief in 'the existence of two souls or perhaps two dimensions of soul: mokuy and birrimbirr'. After death, 'the mokuy soul goes to part of the clan's territory where mokuy spirits live, and exists there as a ghost'. The mokuy is to do with place, whereas birrimbirr can be thought of as 'the animating spirit effective in a person's conception'.[84] Like the west Arnhem Landers, Yolngu believe that spirits, especially the mokuy part of them, can be harmful to the living. As Reuben Brown notes in this volume, one of the primary functions of funeral rites relates to the journey that a deceased person's spirit takes after death. Mortuary rites serve the living as an expression of respect and an outlet for grief. But more importantly, they guide the spirit through the local topography and allow it to integrate harmoniously with the world from whence it came.

Contemporary beliefs in Gunbalanya, insofar as they have been explained to me, do not exactly equate with Spencer's account. Of course, much has changed in the past century. Gunbalanya was a cattle station and buffalo camp when Spencer visited. In 1925 it was taken over by the Church Missionary Society who developed it into Oenpelli Mission.[85] The distribution of food from the mission, and changes forced by military presence in the region during the Second World War, encouraged settlement by disparate clan groups from a wide catchment. Today, only a few residents claim lineage with the Gagudju, whose ancestral estates lie to the west of the town, with some falling within the boundaries of what is now Kakadu National Park. Numerically at least, the settlement has long been dominated by speakers of Kunwinjku, a dialect of the language known among linguists as Bininj Gunwok, which until the mid-twentieth century was spoken chiefly around the Liverpool River (near the present site of Maningrida). Christian influence has certainly affected Gunbalanya, but in these syncretic cultures the Bible tends to be regarded as a belief system that sits alongside, rather than overriding, the Aboriginal traditions. So despite the many changes of the twentieth century, there are significant areas of continuity between the

---

83   Spencer, *Native Tribes of the Northern Territory of Australia*, 271–2.

84   Howard Morphy, *Journey to the Crocodile's Nest: An accompanying monograph to the film* Madarrpa funeral at Gurka'wuy (Canberra: Australian Institute of Aboriginal Studies, 1984), 40.

85   Ronald M. Berndt and Catherine H. Berndt, *Arnhem Land: Its history and its people* (Melbourne: Cheshire, 1954), 191.

beliefs articulated by Spencer and those of today. The situation at Gunbalanya resonates with Morphy's observation of the Yolngu that while new ceremonies, some with a Christian origin, have substituted old ones, the contemporary ritual contains significant allusions to past practices. For example, a painted hollow log, once used as a container for bones of the deceased, is still used as a symbolic object in certain mortuary rites, although its function as a coffin has ended. The fusion of old and new custom was fully apparent at Gunbalanya in 2011 when the bones taken by Setzler, after their repatriation in two instalments in 2009–2010, were interred in the ground. Traditional dance occurred in tandem with the Last Rites of the Christian faith.[86]

Despite significant cultural overlaps, the ethnographies point to notable divergences between west and north-east Arnhem Land in relation to beliefs about the attachment of spirits to bones. Environmental differences have played a role in shaping the regional cultures, for west Arnhem Land is plateau and escarpment country where eroded sandstone is a dominant feature of the landscape. In contrast to the beach, swamp and forest of the Yolngu lands, the Bininj estates contain thousands of caves and rock shelters where the bones of the dead can be housed once the mortuary rituals have ended. Morphy says of Yolngu that the effect of funeral rites upon a corpse involve

> a series of transformations from a live and potentially dangerous state to a dead and relatively inert state. The body begins as flesh and bones contained within skin, becomes bones within a bark skin, and ends up reconstituted in a dead or inert form, as the bones inside the hollow log coffin. In the meantime, the spiritual components of the dead person have been separated out, the mokuy spirit has dispersed with the flesh, and the birrimbirr spirit has returned to the ancestral domain. The bones have ceased to be the bones of the person and have, to use a Yolngu metaphor, become part of "the bones [*ngaraka*] of the clan".[87]

For the Bininj—and for many cultures within Aboriginal Australia—the association between bones and spirit is far more enduring than what Morphy describes. What has been communicated to me in talking about these issues, and in being taken to sites where remains were stolen, is that the dead never become objects or object-like. This is a fundamental contrast to the Judeo-Christian tradition where death marks a rupture between flesh and spirit; where the soul goes elsewhere.

---

86 For a description of this ceremony see Martin Thomas, 'Bones as a Bridge between Worlds: Repatriation and reconciliation between Australia and the United States', in *Conciliation on Colonial Frontiers: Conflict, performance, and commemoration in Australia and the Pacific Rim*, eds Kate Darian-Smith and Penelope Edmonds (New York and London: Routledge, 2015 forthcoming). See also Brown, this volume.

87 Howard Morphy, *Ancestral Connections: Art and an Aboriginal system of knowledge* (Chicago: Chicago University Press, 1991), 110.

In west Arnhem Land, spirits live in proximity to bones, though they are not embodied within them. Spirits and bones are intimately related. One is immaterial; the other is material. But neither will perish. In this culture, both the living and the dead exist in relation to one another. Being cohabitants in this place-based cosmology, it is only natural that a person's bones should be laid to rest in their ancestral estates. For Bininj, the actions of Frank Setzler were a brazen theft, and it is not really surprising that when the stolen bones were buried on the edge of Gunbalanya in 2011, the chief or 'boss man' who presided over the public mortuary ceremony lectured severely in English: 'Stealing people's bones for study is no bloody good.' But to confine the transgression to the act of theft is to understate the gravity and complexity of the problem. Theft is a crime against property, whereas this was a crime against people. The removal of bones is closer to kidnap from this standpoint. Taking the bones presented Bininj and Aboriginal people from other parts of Arnhem Land with the terrifying possibility that spirits had been wrenched from their Country and taken abroad. Now they must deal with the bewilderment and possible anger of the spirits with their return to Australia.

Hence the role of song and smoke in Washington on the occasion in 2010 when the bones were *truly* recovered. As clap sticks beat, the contents of the cardboard coffins ended their tenure as museum objects. Recognised again as subjects, they commenced their homeward journey. Song and language guided them again when, a year later, the boxes were opened at Gunbalanya. A group of senior men and women massaged the bones with a solution of ochre. It was a form of 'dressing' as the boss man described it, seated in his wheelchair. Swaddled in sheets of paperbark, the remains were tied into compact bundles. All the while, the boss man spoke to the spirits, assuaging and comforting them. He spoke Kunwinjku, Gagadju, Urningangk, Erre and Mengerrdji—languages that they might have known in life. He introduced himself and he told them where they were. So the process of re-orientation continued as the sound of song and didjeridu led them to the grave. Anger at the theft had not disappeared, but through the labour of caring for the dead, it seemed to have abated.

I do not use the name of the boss man, for he died in the first days of 2012, a terrible though not unexpected loss for all of us who knew him, but especially for his community in Gunbalanya where the young die too often and the elders die too young.[88] Cultural restrictions on the naming of those who have recently died mean that I can call him only by his 'death name', Nakodjok Nayinggul. I understand that he had cancer and other illnesses, and in the last year of his

---

88   Reuben Brown provides a description and analysis of his funeral in this volume.

life, when I saw him fairly often, I could tell that the pain was insufferable. We were all aware, though no one was so indelicate to admit, that dealing with the bones returned from the Smithsonian Institution would be his last great work.[89]

Not until the mourning period is over can his name be uttered or his likeness in film or photograph be shown again. In the last year of his life, he and I spoke often to the camera or recorder about the importance of the placement of human remains. His English, acquired from missionaries, was impeccable; he spoke quizzically, and always with measured deliberation.

> They would get all bones, they would paint them in either yellow or red ochre, and then they would take them up onto the hill and put them in cave and they would say to them … in language: "I'll leave you here," and talk to them, and then they would tell them, "Look I'm following you, I'm coming too, so wait for me." And they would put them to sleep then in their own country, in their own territory. Doing all that first, putting someone in the cave, doing that, that was the main traditional owner in there, or elderly person, who was the last one, and then next one took over, maybe his son, and then it went on … [We do it] not because we love you and we leave you here but because it's your country, we'll come back to you and we'll call out for help if you can help us …
>
> Having the bones here it means that you've got the man still staying in his own territory … I can call to him any time because I know he's here. No other questions … I know he's here, I go to that cave and call out for help. Like somebody might be in danger. That's when you really need someone. So the traditional owner would help and in spirit they would still help.[90]

As these words make plain, the removal of bones fundamentally disrupts the relationship between the dead and those who knew them, whether as living people or as skeletons in a cave. The Bininj, who were known and whose lives were honoured in the rituals that led them to a particular place in their own Country, become a racial type—as posited in someone else's classificatory system. Except in certain enclaves, where physical anthropology collections are jealously guarded and claims for repatriation deflected, bone stealing is no longer seen as such an acceptable sport. Yet the branches of knowledge that took root from these collections, from that transformation of people into objects—including the mighty narrative of human evolution—remain very much in vogue.

---

89   See Thomas, 'Because It's Your Country'.
90   Nagodjok Nayinggul in interview with the author, 9 July 2010.

Acknowledgements

Thanks to members of the Gunbalanya community who supported this research and to Margo Daly for research assistance. I am indebted to the two peer reviewers for their close readings and suggestions. My archival research in the US was supported by a Smithsonian Fellowship. Subsequent research was supported by the Australian Research Council (DP1096897 and FT0992291).

References

Beazley, Kim. 'Nation Building or Cold War: Political settings for the Arnhem Land Expedition', in *Exploring the Legacy of the 1948 Arnhem Land Expedition*, eds Martin Thomas and Margo Neale (Canberra: ANU E Press, 2011), 55–71.

Berndt, Ronald M., and Catherine H. Berndt. *Arnhem Land: Its history and its people* (Melbourne: Cheshire, 1954).

Berndt, Ronald M., and Catherine H. Berndt. *Man, Land and Myth in North Australia: The Gunwinggu people* (Sydney: Ure Smith, 1970).

Brattain, Michelle. 'Race, Racism, and Antiracism: UNESCO and the politics of presenting science to the postwar public', *American Historical Review* 112:5 (2007): 1386–413.

Brothwell, Don. 'Bring out Your Dead: People, pots and politics', *Antiquity* 78:300 (2004): 414–18.

Davis, Michael. *Writing Heritage: The depiction of Indigenous heritage in European-Australian writings* (North Melbourne: Australian Scholarly Publishing and the National Museum of Australia Press, 2007).

Fitzhugh, William W. 'Foreword', in *Reckoning with the Dead: The Larsen Bay repatriation and the Smithsonian Institution*, eds Tamara L. Bray and Thomas W. Killion (Washington DC and London: Smithsonian Institution Press, 1994), vii-x.

Glenn, James R. 'Frank M. Setzler', in *International Dictionary of Anthropologists*, ed. Christopher Winters (New York: Garland Publishing, 1991), 633–4.

Harris, Amanda. 'Food, Feeding and Consumption (or the Cook, the Wife and the Nutritionist): The politics of gender and class in a 1948 Australian expedition', *History and Anthropology* 124:3 (2013): 363–79.

Harris, Joshua. 'Hidden for Sixty Years: The motion pictures of the American-Australian Scientific Expedition to Arnhem Land', in *Exploring the Legacy of the 1948 Arnhem Land Expedition*, eds Martin Thomas and Margo Neale (Canberra: ANU E Press, 2011), 239–51.

Jenkins, Mark Collins. 'A Robinson Crusoe in Arnhem Land: Howell Walker, *National Geographic* and the Arnhem Land Expedition of 1948', in *Exploring the Legacy of the 1948 Arnhem Land Expedition*, eds Martin Thomas and Margo Neale (Canberra: ANU E Press, 2011), 73–85.

Jones, Philip. 'Perceptions of Aboriginal Art: A history', in *Dreamings: The art of Aboriginal Australia*, ed. Peter Sutton (Ringwood: Viking, 1988), 143–79.

Jones, Philip. 'Inside Mountford's Tent: Paint, politics and paperwork', in *Exploring the Legacy of the 1948 Arnhem Land Expedition*, eds Martin Thomas and Margo Neale (Canberra: ANU E Press, 2011), 33-54.

Linton, Ralph, Paul S. Wingert, and Rene D'Harnoncourt. *Arts of the South Seas* (New York: Museum of Modern Art, 1946).

Loring, Stephen, and Miroslav Prokopec. 'A Most Peculiar Man: The life and times of Aleš Hrdlička', in *Reckoning with the Dead: The Larsen Bay repatriation and the Smithsonian Institution*, eds Tamara L. Bray and Thomas W. Killion (Washington and London: Smithsonian Institution Press, 1994), 26–40.

MacDonald, Helen. *Human Remains: Episodes in human dissection* (Carlton: Melbourne University Press, 2005).

Magaña, Linda. *Mr. America's Creator: The race science of Dr. Ales Hrdlicka, 1896–1943* (Undergraduate Thesis, Columbia University, 2011).

May, Sally K. *Collecting Cultures: Myth, politics, and collaboration in the 1948 Arnhem Land Expedition* (Lanham: AltaMira Press, 2010).

McCarthy, Frederick D., and Frank M. Setzler. 'The Archaeology of Arnhem Land', in *Records of the American-Australian Scientific Expedition to Arnhem Land: Vol. 2: Anthropology and nutrition*, ed. Charles P. Mountford (Melbourne: Melbourne University Press, 1960), 215–95.

Mountford, Charles P. 'Aboriginal Decorative Art from Arnhem Land, Northern Territory of Australia', *Transactions of the Royal Society of South Australia* 63:2 (1939): 365–71.

Mountford, Charles P. 'Exploring Stone Age Arnhem Land', *National Geographic Magazine* 96:6 (1949): 745–82.

Mountford, Charles P. *Records of the American-Australian Scientific Expedition to Arnhem Land: Vol. 1: Art, myth and symbolism* (Melbourne: Melbourne University Press, 1956).

Morphy, Howard. *Journey to the Crocodile's Nest: An accompanying monograph to the film* Madarrpa funeral at Gurka'wuy (Canberra: Australian Institute of Aboriginal Studies, 1984).

Morphy, Howard. *Ancestral Connections: Art and an Aboriginal system of knowledge* (Chicago: Chicago University Press, 1991).

Poole, Robert M. *Explorer's House: National Geographic and the world it made* (New York: Penguin, 2004).

Pullar, Gordon L. 'The Qikertarmiut and the Scientist: Fifty years of clashing world views', in *Reckoning with the Dead: The Larsen Bay repatriation and the Smithsonian Institution*, eds Tamara L. Bray and Thomas W. Killion (Washington DC and London: Smithsonian Institution Press, 1994), 15–25.

Smithers, Gregory D. 'The Dark Side of Anti-Racism: "Half-breeds" and the anthropology of Aleš Hrdlička', *Transnational Subjects: History, science and culture* 1:1 (2011): 65–88.

Spencer, Baldwin. *Native Tribes of the Northern Territory of Australia*. London: Macmillan, 1914.

Thomas, Martin. 'A Short History of the 1948 Arnhem Land Expedition.' *Aboriginal History* 34 (2010): 143–69.

Thomas, Martin. 'Expedition as Time Capsule: Introducing the American–Australian Scientific Expedition to Arnhem Land', in *Exploring the Legacy of the 1948 Arnhem Land Expedition*, eds Martin Thomas and Margo Neale (Canberra: ANU E Press, 2011), 1–30.

Thomas, Martin. 'Because It's Your Country: Death and its meanings in west Arnhem Land', *Life Writing*, (2013): 1–21, http://www.tandfonline.com/doi/abs/10.1080/.VA5-4Cg4Z4g.

Thomas, Martin. 'Bones as a Bridge between Worlds: Repatriation and reconciliation between Australia and the United States', in *Conciliation on Colonial Frontiers: Conflict, performance, and commemoration in Australia and the Pacific Rim*, eds Kate Darian-Smith and Penelope Edmonds (New York and London: Routledge, 2015 forthcoming).

Thomas, Martin, and Margo Neale, eds, *Exploring the Legacy of the 1948 Arnhem Land Expedition* (Canberra: ANU E Press, 2011).

Turnbull, Paul. 'Indigenous Australians and Native Title', in *The Dead and Their Possessions*, eds Cressida Fforde, Jane Hubert and Paul Turnbull (New York: Routledge, 2004), 63–86.

Part 3: Cultural Journeys in the Top End

7. The Role of Songs in Connecting the Living and the Dead: A Funeral Ceremony for Nakodjok in Western Arnhem Land

Reuben Brown

Prologue: Nakodjok returns

The family had waited a long time for this. Their father had passed away some six months earlier, in the middle of the wet season in the Top End of the Northern Territory, and his body had been held in a morgue in Katherine all this time. Now that the dry season had begun and the water levels along the rivers and flood plains had receded, some of the remote dirt roads through Arnhem Land were once again open. The family's outstation on their ancestral Country at Mikkinj Valley was now accessible via a road that ran east from the Aboriginal community of Gunbalanya (also known as Oenpelli),[1] and then west around the other side of the Arnhem Land escarpment, and preparations to bury their father on his Country could begin in earnest. The burial had been planned for August, but with more deaths in the community of Gunbalanya creating a backlog of funerals and limiting space in the local morgue, the date was brought forward. In late June, the body of Nakodjok Nayinggul (or Nakodjok Namanilakarr,[2] as he was referred to post-mortem) was finally returned to the family in a charter plane from Katherine to Gunbalanya.

---

1 Gunbalanya is the Kunwinjku name for the Aboriginal community formerly known (and still referred to by some) as Oenpelli. Oenpelli was first established as a buffalo-skinning camp in the early 1900s before it became a government cattle station and then a mission in 1925. Opportunities for work and rations drew various clans from the region to Oenpelli, reflected in the multilingual makeup of the population today.

2 *Nakodjok* means a male (Kunwinjku noun class prefix *na-*) belonging to the *kodjok* subsection (in the kinship system of western Arnhem Land), while *Namanilakarr* means a male of the *Manilakarr* clan group. Throughout this chapter, significant words that form part of the lexicon of western Arnhem Land songs in the Aboriginal languages of Kunwinjku (K) and Mawng (M) are indicated in italics (except proper nouns such as names of people and songs). English translations are glossed in brackets the first time the word appears in the text. I adopt standard orthographies for both Kunwinjku and Mawng. See Nicholas Evans, *Bininj Gunwok: A pan-dialectal grammar of Mayali, Kunwinjku and Kune*. 2 volumes (Canberra: Pacific Linguistics, 2003); Ruth Singer, *Agreement in Mawng: Productive and lexicalised uses of agreement in an Australian language* (PhD, Department of Linguistics and Applied Linguistics, University of Melbourne, 2006).

Under instructions from the family, all work in the community finished for the day at 2:30 pm. Bininj and Balanda[3] gathered outside the house where Nakodjok had lived during the last part of his life, waiting in the sweat-inducing afternoon sun. There in the front yard, Nakodjok used to sit in his wheelchair, smoking a cigarette, waiting to greet the next researcher to show them his Country, the next council worker to accompany him to a community meeting, or a family member who would wheel him over to the 'club' in the evening. Now the yard was occupied by his extended family, who sat with their children in the shade of tents. A tub of *delek* (K: white ochre mixed with water to form clay) was passed around for those who wished to paint their arms, legs, face and hair—a ritual that accompanies ceremonial song and dance in Bininj culture. At one end of the yard, further away from the tents, a visiting group from Ramingining sat under a tree singing, in part to keep their hosts—the family of Nakodjok— company. I saw my chance to go inside and pay my respects to the family, and asked one of Nakodjok's grandchildren, 'Kamak bu ngam-re-ngimen?' ('Is it OK if I go inside?'). He gave me the sort of slightly quizzical look that I was now accustomed to receiving from younger Bininj who were not used to a Balanda addressing them in Kunwinjku.[4] Then he replied, 'Mah, kamak' ('OK, that's fine'). He led me through the house into a dark bedroom, where I found Nakodjok's daughters sitting around the coffin, with their heads lowered and hands resting on the polished wood that encased their father.

One of Nakodjok's daughters, Connie Nayinggul, acknowledged me with a nod as I came in. Like many of Nakodjok's children, Connie took a leading role in the community, particularly around cultural matters. Like her father, she was generous about sharing Bininj knowledge with outsiders, and sought to bring the various elements of the Gunbalanya community together by including them in cultural practices, such as gathering, preparing and cooking food in the traditional way. Now she was covered in *delek*, and her hair had been teased into a frizz. Her voice was hoarse from an earlier display of public grief at the airstrip in Gunbalanya upon the return of Nakodjok's body. She spoke quietly and determinedly, informing me of the funeral arrangements, and asking if I could pass on the invitation to some other Balanda researchers who had worked with Nakodjok in recent times. She pointed out Nakodjok's black cowboy hat hanging proudly on the wall. Once a symbol of his affiliation with stockmen,[5] it

---

3 'Bininj' means Aboriginal person, while the Macassan loan word 'Balanda' (from 'Hollander') refers to a non-Aboriginal person or European. The second meaning of *bininj* (italicised, no capitals) is 'male', as opposed to *daluk* (female).

4 Kunwinjku is one of six dialects in western Arnhem Land referred to collectively as Bininj Gun-wok ('Aboriginal people's language'). It is the main language spoken at Gunbalanya and is also spoken in other communities of western Arnhem Land. Evans, *Bininj Gun-wok*, 6.

5 Nakodjok's family and other traditional owners of Gunbalanya helped establish a locally owned meatworks where the cattle that graze on the floodplains of Gunbalanya are slaughtered, processed and packaged for delivery all around the region.

had now become a sort of cult fashion item among the grandchildren, who wore their own hats as a sign of respect for Nakodjok. Connie then pointed out a gold plate at the head of the coffin, etched with Nakodjok's name. To an outsider, this detail, along with the large framed photograph of Nakodjok wearing his iconic hat that was later displayed during the funeral service at Gunbalanya church, seemed to sit awkwardly with the Bininj practice of avoiding the name, image or other aspects of the deceased during the period of mourning. Yet it also indicated the incorporation of Judaeo-Christian traditions by Bininj, ever since they had moved from the bush to live among the missionaries in the early twentieth century, the era into which Nakodjok was born.[6]

I said *bobo* (K: goodbye) to the daughters and stepped back outside into the blinding sun. Soon the *bininj* (K: men) went inside the house to collect the coffin. This was when the local group of singers started to perform their Karrbarda (K: long yam) songs, starting as all western Arnhem Land songs do, with the blowing of the *mako* (K: didjeridu). Then came the fast beating of the clapsticks, providing the tempo for the didjeridu and a cue for the men to begin dancing. The 'dance captain'[7] of the group, Joey Nganjmirra, took off his shirt and wrapped it around each fist, pulling it tight in the middle. The men came together for the opening dance call, a shouting 'oh, argh', slapping their thighs twice before pointing their fingers to the sky and calling 'yi!' At the end of the verse they danced toward the body and began the 'stamping phrase', lifting their knees high in the air and kicking up the sand with their feet to the beat of the clapstick, and pausing with the suspension of the beat.[8] Accompanying each stamp, they gave a different dance call that sounded like a hiss, while Nganjmirra held the taut shirt out in front of him and rotated it at different angles to articulate the movement. Then the sound of the singing, didjeridu and clapsticks, and the flicking of sand was joined with a loud banging against the thin metal walls of the house, as the coffin was hoisted above the heads of the young men and taken out of the house away from the grieving daughters. Outside, other *daluk* (K: women) joined in the wailing and crying, and onlookers shouted directions at the coffin-bearers, helping to steer the coffin from the narrow entrance of the house towards the back of the 'troopy'[9] that waited

---

6   The practice of displaying a photo of the deceased at the funeral service is also common among Yolngu of east Arnhem Land. See Jennifer Deger, 'Imprinting on the Heart: Photography and contemporary Yolngu mournings', *Visual Anthropology* 21 (2008): 292-309.

7   English term used by Eric Mardday to describe the leader of the male dancers for the Karrbarda song-set. Eric Mardday, interview with the author, September 2013.

8   The description of the 'stamping phrase'—one of the conventions of western Arnhem Land dance—is based on similar descriptions of *wangga* dance provided by Marett. Allan Marett, *Songs, Dreamings, and Ghosts: The wangga of north Australia*, (Middletown: Wesleyan University Press, 2005).

9   The Toyota Land Cruiser is a four-wheel-drive vehicle that can seat many passengers, ubiquitous throughout remote Aboriginal Australia, and commonly referred to as a 'troop carrier' or 'troopy'. In western Arnhem Land these *mutika* (vehicles) are used frequently for the transportation of deceased, after which they are ceremonially smoked and streaked with red ochre.

in the yard. Some *daluk* held rocks above their heads, threatening to strike themselves in a gesture of their uncontrollable grief, before *bininj* intervened and restrained them. As the sounds of grief grew to a crescendo, I reflected how the emotion was at once real and well rehearsed, the actions both spontaneous and semi-staged.

Rising above the sounds of the bereaved, the Karrbarda singers slowed down the tempo of their clapstick beating and began singing a sweet melody, the notes of which were more elongated than before. Leading songman Eric Marddary kept singing, repeating another verse until the coffin had been securely placed inside the troopy and the rear doors swung shut. At this point, the wailing turned to sobbing, and the song came to a close. With emergency lights flashing, the vehicle slowly made its way out of the yard, around the corner and down the street to a small room at the back of the Gunbalanya health clinic known as the 'morgue house'. The family stayed close to the troopy while the rest of us followed behind in quiet reflection. Once more the Ramingining mob took over, singing Nakodjok's coffin out of the troopy and into the morgue. Connie then addressed everyone, thanking them for coming and confirming plans for a memorial service in Gunbalanya, followed by a burial ceremony out at Mikkinj Valley outstation in three weeks' time. 'Mah, bonj' she said ('Ok, that's it'). It was decided.

Introduction

This description of the movement of the deceased from his family home to the local morgue—reconstructed from field notes I took in Gunbalanya in western Arnhem Land in 2012—relates to just one of the many stages of the burial of Nakodjok involving song and dance. Each of these stages marked an aspect of the deceased's transition, both in terms of the body and the spirit. In this chapter I show how song and dance express and mediate relationships between Aboriginal people, both living and deceased. Taking as a case study Nakodjok's funeral ceremony, which began in the community of Gunbalanya and ended at his outstation at Mikkinj Valley, I trace the diverse range of songs that were performed at various stages of transition. By attending the funeral ceremony and performing songs for the families of the deceased, Bininj and other Aboriginal people from around the region show their respect for and their personal connection to the deceased, framing their performance as an acknowledgement of particular kinship and marriage ties.

A number of scholars have remarked on the important role that song and dance plays as part of mortuary rites both in this region and throughout Aboriginal society.[10] Music not only interacts with and directs the ritual action of the bereaved—as in the passage above where the Karrbarda songs cue the departure of the coffin and the outpouring of grief—it also influences and interacts with the spirit world. Analysing the performance of *wangga* at rag-burning (mortuary) ceremonies in the Daly region, Allan Marett describes how elements of the music and the dance reference both the ghostly and human worlds. By overlapping these elements in the performance, the living are brought into a liminal space with the spirits, enabling the spirit of the deceased to exit the world of the living and enter the world of the ancestors who reside in the Country.[11] Following Marett's analysis, I argue that the performance of *kun-borrk*—the Bininj Gunwok name for western Arnhem Land public dance-accompanied songs (also referred to as *manyardi* in Mawng language)[12]—at funeral ceremonies facilitates a kind of creative exchange between the living and the dead. In this exchange, songmen construct their performance partly for the benefit of spirits, while the spirits give them new songs in their dreams to perform for the occasion, and take part in—even influence—their ceremonial performance. This circulation of songs between the living and the dead is ultimately productive in sustaining the song tradition: as long as songs that were handed down continue to be performed in ceremony, the possibility of new compositions in the future—via spirit intervention in dreams—remains.[13]

The first section of this chapter provides an overview of the role of funerals in Aboriginal society, and the influence of Christianity on contemporary funeral rites in western Arnhem Land. I discuss Aboriginal spiritual beliefs about the cycle of life and death and the important place of dream-conceived spirit-language songs in fulfilling this cycle. In western Arnhem Land, the language of the songs is fundamental to this ongoing connection between the living and the dead, because of the way it communicates with the spirit world. The ancestors

---

10 Some earlier studies include Ronald Berndt's overview of mortuary rituals in northern Australia: Ronald M. Berndt, *Australian Aboriginal Religion* (Leiden: E. J. Brill, 1974), 23–31. See also Spencer's description of mortuary ceremonies of Gaagadju at Oenpelli: Baldwin Spencer, *Native Tribes of the Northern Territory of Australia* (London: Macmillan, 1914). Morphy, Reid, and Warner give accounts of Yolngu funeral ceremonies in east Arnhem Land: Howard Morphy, *Journey to the Crocodile's Nest: An accompanying monograph to the film* Madarrpa funeral at Gurka'wuy (Canberra: Australian Institute of Aboriginal Studies, 1984); Janice Reid, 'A Time to Live, a Time to Grieve: Patterns and processes of mourning among the Yolngu of Australia', *Culture, Medicine and Psychiatry* 3:4 (1979); Lloyd W. Warner, *A Black Civilization: A social study of an Australian tribe* (Gloucester: P. Smith, 1969). More recent perspectives on contemporary attitudes to death in Aboriginal Australia are discussed in Katie Glaskin, Myrna Tonkinson, Yasmine Musharbash, and Victoria Burbank, eds. *Mortality, Mourning and Mortuary Practices in Indigenous Australia* (Surrey: Ashgate, 2008).

11 Allan Marett, 'Ghostly Voices: Some observations on song-creation, ceremony and being in north western Australia', *Oceania* 71:1 (2000): 24–5.

12 For the purposes of this chapter, I adopt the Bininj Gunwok term, unless differentiating between songs of the two language groups.

13 Funeral ceremonies are the primary occasions in which *kun-borrk* is performed, however other occasions include circumcision ceremonies, gift exchange ceremonies, official community events such as the opening of a building or cultural festivals, and informal settings such as around the campfire.

who first performed the songs (and handed them down to successive male relatives) understand the song text (even if the living do not), and the songs that current songmen receive from them contain the same words.

The second section discusses the diverse network of sociality represented in the funeral ceremony for Nakodjok, which brought together Aboriginal people from the Tiwi Islands, east Arnhem Land and western Arnhem Land. I outline the different song traditions that were represented, the sequence in which they were performed during the ceremony, and discuss how the music reflected the western Arnhem Land singers' relationship with the deceased. Finally, I examine a performance of a *kun-borrk* song repertory called Mirrijpu (M: seagull), on the penultimate evening of the funeral ceremony for Nakodjok before his burial at Mikkinj Valley. Based on insights provided by the Mirrijpu songmen—whom I accompanied to the burial—about the choices they made in ordering the songs, as well as my own analysis of changes in tempo and clapstick beating, I discuss how the performance was constructed with an awareness of both the funeral mourners *and* the spirits of the deceased.

Background to the Event

Nakodjok Nayinggul was an important ceremony man and senior traditional owner of Country surrounding Gunbalanya and parts of Kakadu National Park. He was well known and respected by both Bininj and Balanda. I met him in 2011 during fieldwork which involved repatriating digital recordings of song and other documentation of Bininj cultural activities, produced during the 1948 American-Australian Expedition to Arnhem Land, with the aim of understanding these recordings from a Bininj perspective. Not long after I arrived at Gunbalanya, a ceremony was held to conduct a repatriation of a different kind, which was once again connected to the Arnhem Land Expedition: the return of physical remains to Oenpelli, taken at different stages in the twentieth century, including by archaeologist Frank Setzler in 1948. A re-burial ceremony was carried out by traditional owners of Gunbalanya, led by Nakodjok, with members of government, museums, local organisations, and researchers giving assistance.[14] As with Nakodjok's funeral ceremony one year later, I took part by helping out where it was needed—with transport, logistics (organising the hire of an amplification system for outdoor speeches and operating music played over the speakers) and catering. During the reburial ceremony, I was introduced to *kun-borrk* singers resident at Gunbalanya, including Mirrijpu (M: seagull), Inyjalarrku (M: mermaid) and Karrbarda (K: long yam) singers and dancers. Solomon Nangamu, lead singer for Mirrijpu, invited me to record

---

14   See Thomas, this volume.

the songs performed for this reburial ceremony, and later to accompany him to other ceremonial occasions that he attended during my time in western Arnhem Land. My project involving repatriation of digital records therefore led to a documentation project of a living song tradition in western Arnhem Land, focusing on Nangamu's performances with other western Arnhem Land songmen that we met along the way. By showing me how *kun-borrk* continued to operate in contemporary life, Nangamu and other songmen were able to shed light on the older *kun-borrk* recordings made by Simpson.[15]

Mortuary Rites in Aboriginal Society

Contemporary Funerals in Western Arnhem Land

Funerals are an important feature of Aboriginal life in Australia. Aboriginal societies are kinship-based; in western Arnhem Land as in other areas of Australia, Bininj are born into a particular skin group or subsection that gives everyone a relationship with one another, ensuring that no one is a complete stranger.[16] When someone passes away, close kin come together at the funeral ceremony to play their part in assisting the bereaved and to express their own feelings of loss for the deceased.[17] In east Arnhem Land and parts of western Arnhem Land, ritual managers of the deceased and of the Country where the ceremony takes place—referred to as *djungkay* (K)—help to coordinate the various stages of the funeral ceremony. In the dry season when the roads are open—making it easier to travel to and from towns and outstations in Arnhem Land—funerals may occur on a weekly basis. Before my arrival at Gunbalanya, I had only ever attended two funerals. In my second year in western Arnhem Land, I attended five, and was aware of another half dozen that took place during my stay.

Funeral ceremonies are also a significant part of Aboriginal cultural and spiritual expression. Aboriginal people anticipate death; those who are elderly and are dying generally become the focus of community interest rather than being shut

---

15   Simpson's recordings at Gunbalanya are also discussed by Anthony Linden Jones (this volume). I analyse Bininj responses to Simpson's recordings at Oenpelli in my thesis. Reuben Brown, *Performance as Exchange: The role of western Arnhem Land song traditions in contemporary society* (PhD, Sydney Conservatorium of Music, The University of Sydney, 2014 forthcoming).

16   For an overview of systems of kinship in Aboriginal Australia, see Ian Keen, *Aboriginal Economy and Society: Australia at the threshold of colonisation* (South Melbourne: Oxford University Press, 2004), 174–209. For western Arnhem Land kinship names, see Khaki Marrala, *Kindi Ngamin Nuwung? What Do I Call You?* 'Ma!'. Vol. 1, (Jabiru: Iwaidja Inyman, 2008).

17   See Myrna Tonkinson, 'Solidarity in Shared Loss: Death-related observances among the Martu of the Western Desert', in *Mortality, Mourning and Mortuary Practices in Indigenous Australia*, eds Katie Glaskin et al. (Surrey: Ashgate, 2008).

away, and mourning rituals take place over a long period of time—sometimes years.[18] As Morphy and Morphy suggest, the way that Aboriginal cultures deal with death is for many people a marker of their Aboriginality:

> All over Australia, it seems, and in very different colonial settings, the rituals surrounding death have become a constant theatre of life, where, in a relatively autonomous space indigenous values are affirmed and asserted, with greater or lesser degrees of consciousness, in contrast to those of the encapsulating society.[19]

Throughout Arnhem Land an elaborate secondary burial ceremony called the *lorrkkon* traditionally took place some years after the initial burial, in which the bones of the deceased would be excavated, rubbed in red ochre and placed in a log hollowed out by termites and decorated with clan emblems (the *lorrkkon*).[20] This ceremony represented the final departure of the spirit of the deceased from the world of the living. Over time, Aboriginal people of Arnhem Land have adapted their funeral ceremonies to various advances in technology, as well as a number of social changes, including the influence of missionaries who brought Christian beliefs and rituals. The *lorrkkon* ceremony met with the disapproval of missionaries, who believed that bodies buried on 'consecrated' ground should not be disturbed.[21] As a consequence, along with other factors including the passing of senior elders who held important knowledge about how to conduct *lorrkkon*, the ceremony has been replaced with a single, final burial.[22]

Contemporary funeral ceremonies usually incorporate a Christian service into the ceremony. This may involve a sermon and hymns as part of an earlier memorial service for the community in the church (if the deceased was well-known) and a separate sermon for the burial, as was the case for Nakodjok Nayinggul. In Spencer's account of Bininj ceremonial life at Gunbalanya (then referred to as Oenpelli) in 1912, initial burials were held the day after someone passed away, and were not as prolonged as they can be today.[23] In western Arnhem Land, the deceased may be flown to a central morgue in Darwin or Katherine and kept there for some months while the family wait for relatives from other areas of Arnhem Land to come and attend the funeral ceremony. In the earlier part

---

18   Morphy, *Journey to the Crocodile's Nest*, 37.
19   Howard Morphy and Frances Morphy, 'Afterword: Demography and destiny', in *Mortality, Mourning and Mortuary Practices in Indigenous Australia*, eds Katie Glaskin, Myrna Tonkinson, Yasmine Musharbash and Victoria Burbank (Surrey: Ashgate, 2008), 210–11.
20   Margaret Clunies Ross and Stephen A. Wild, 'Formal Performance: The relations of music, text and dance in Arnhem Land clan songs', *Ethnomusicology* 28:2 (1984): 210. The ceremony is depicted in the film *Waiting for Harry* for a funeral that takes place east of Maningrida. Kim McKenzie, *Waiting for Harry* (Canberra: Australian Institute of Aboriginal Studies, 1980).
21   See Morphy, *Journey to the Crocodile's Nest*, 44–5.
22   Reid observes that *lorrkkon* is no longer widely practiced in north-east Arnhem Land. Reid, 'A Time to Live, a Time to Grieve', 328.
23   Spencer, *Native tribes of the Northern Territory*, 240.

of the twentieth century when missionaries established themselves in Arnhem Land, funerals were more frequently held at missions, settlements or towns, whereas today, due to the availability of charter planes, the ceremony can be held at outstations and the deceased can be buried on their Country.[24] This often means that the ceremony requires significant pooling of money and resources to organise and can last weeks, while the family waits for an important person to attend.

The Role of Song in Effecting the 'Life Cycle' of the Spirit

Although mortuary rites vary across northern Australia, they have in common a purpose beyond allowing for a process of grieving: to ensure that the spirit of the deceased no longer dwells among the living (potentially causing them trouble or danger), and is satisfied to leave, joining the ancestral dead and returning to its Country. Underpinning this journey is the belief in what some have referred to as the 'life cycle'[25] or 'existence cycle'[26] of the spirit. In some areas of northern Australia, a person's spirit is believed to emerge from a specific totemic Dreaming site that is associated with fertility, while in others, such as the Daly region, it emerges from 'fairly broadly defined stretches of country'.[27] The spirit then enters the mother's womb and takes up residence in the human body. When a person dies they become a spirit again, initially dwelling near the place where they lived.[28] In western Arnhem Land, after someone dies, Bininj immediately take branches from the ironbark tree, place them in a metal drum and set them alight, spreading the smoke through the houses where the deceased lived, as well as other places where that person spent significant time (the medical clinic or the local art centre, for example). Vehicles are also ceremonially smoked and in some cases when a songman dies, his songs are performed and simultaneously smoked, before a period of dormancy where they are not performed.[29]

Songs play a vital role in the deceased spirit's transition from the living world. North-east Arnhem Land mortuary rites involve the performance of ritual episodes or individual 'song series' according to a conceptual movement

---

24 For further discussion about the significance of burial on Country, see Deborah B. Rose, *Dingo Makes Us Human: Life and land in an Australian Aboriginal culture* (Cambridge: Cambridge University Press, 2009), 73.

25 Berndt, *Australian Aboriginal Religion*, 25; Morphy, *Journey to the Crocodile's Nest*, 32.

26 Marett, 'Ghostly Voices': 24.

27 ibid.

28 See Thomas, this volume.

29 The period of time that songs remain dormant after death varies widely, and depends on the individual who inherits the songs. In this sense, as Barwick and Garde have suggested, *kun-borrk* songs in western Arnhem Land are more like 'personal property', as opposed to *manikay* from north-east and central Arnhem Land songs which belong to one's father's clan. Linda Barwick and Murray Garde, personal communication, 14 January 2013. See also Ross and Wild, 'Formal Performance': 209.

through the landscape, which takes the deceased spirit on a particular route to its ancestral Country.[30] At Wadeye and Belyuen in the Daly region, *burnim-rag* ceremonies involve driving the spirit away through the ritual burning of 'rags' belonging to the deceased (clothes, bedding, cooking and hunting utensils and other prized possessions) in which the deceased spirit may have taken refuge.[31] As Marett explains, the performance of song and dance brings together the living with the Walakandha (ghosts) of the spirit world:

> By joining with their Walakandha ancestors, through singing their songs, playing didjeridu, dancing their dances, painting the masks of Walakandha [ancestral spirits] on their bodies, and witnessing the production of their ceremonial forms, the living participants draw close to and interpenetrate with the dead. It is within this context that the spirits of the deceased are released from their attachments to the living and are freed to join the ancestral dead.[32]

While individual beliefs about what happens to the spirit of the deceased vary in western Arnhem Land, the function of music and dance is generally understood as it is in the Daly region: to coax the deceased spirit to return once more to its ancestral Country, where other ancestral spirits live. Re-absorbed in the landscape, the spirit is 'able to hear human voices, smell human presences, respond to human footprints', and may enter the womb of another Bininj where it will start the life-cycle once more.[33]

Songs at funeral ceremonies in western Arnhem Land do not follow a broader narrative or specific journey as they do in north-east Arnhem Land. However, similar principles relating to how the deceased spirit is oriented back to its Country affect the presentation of different songs, depending on the origin of those songs. *Kun-borrk* song repertories—referred to here as song-sets[34]— are generally thought of as belonging to one of two subcategories: *wardde-ken* (K: 'of the stone country')—referring to the Arnhem Land plateau area—and *kurrula* (M: sea; saltwater country) along the north-western coast of Arnhem

---

30   See Fiona Magowan, *Melodies of Mourning: Music and emotion in northern Australia*, (Crawley: University of Western Australia Press, 2007); P. G. Toner, 'Tropes of Longing and Belonging: Nostalgia and musical instruments in northeast Arnhem Land', *Yearbook for Traditional Music* 37 (2005): 4.
31   Marett, 'Ghostly Voices': 25–6.
32   Marett, *Songs, Dreamings, and Ghosts*, 31.
33   Marett, 'Ghostly Voices': 24–5.
34   Ronald and Catherine Berndt refer to *kun-borrk* repertories as 'song cycles'. Ronald M. Berndt, *Love Songs of Arnhem Land* (Melbourne: T. Nelson, 1976). However, following recent scholars such as Barwick et al., O'Keeffe and Garde, I use the term 'song-sets', since this does not imply a complete corpus of ordered songs. See Linda Barwick, Bruce Birch, and Nicholas Evans, 'Iwaidja Jurtbirrk Songs: Bringing language and music together', *Australian Aboriginal Studies* 2 (2007); Isabel O'Keeffe, 'Sung and Spoken: An analysis of two different versions of a Kun-Barlang love song', *Australian Aboriginal Studies* 2 (2007); Garde, 'The Language of *Kun-borrk* in Western Arnhem Land', *Musicology Australia* 28 (2006).

Land, including the Coburg Peninsula and Goulburn and Croker Islands.[35] If the deceased was from *wardde-ken* country for example, *wardde-ken* songs would be performed last, at the moment of burial. This was the case during the reburial ceremony in 2011 for the repatriated remains of people taken in 1948 whose traditional Country was Gunbalanya (*wardde-ken*). In the following passage, Mirrijpu songman Solomon Nangamu explains how the journey that the spirits of the remains had taken from Washington to Gunbalanya was metaphorically enacted through the performance of *kun-borrk*. Specifically, he discusses the choice first to perform his *kurrula* songs as the mourners made their way from the north of the town where the bones had been stored and prepared for burial, before reaching the burial ground facing the Arnhem Land plateau, where the *wardde-ken* singers took over the singing:

> I'm from the saltwater country, I was born there. So when the bones [from Washington] arrived here [in Australia], I came and collected the bones and I took it and gave it to all the stone [country] mob, from this country [Gunbalanya]. I passed it on to them, them mob now, them take it and bury it.[36]

Neither Nangamu nor the Karrbarda group physically handled the bones at any stage. Nangamu's explanation shows how the act of singing songs from a particular Country is understood to carry the spirit through that Country—in his case, collecting the spirits from the north coast of Arnhem Land after they had crossed the Pacific Ocean from the US, and bringing them to the *wardde-ken* people of Gunbalanya.

Kun-borrk song-sets consist of a number of individual song items, which are collectively named after animals, plants, and spirit beings specific to the region—(seagull, long yam, mermaid, etc.). The dances and body paint designs that accompany the performance of these songs-sets often relate to the name given to the songs. For example, when women dance Karrbarda, their arm movements imitate digging the yam and carrying it above their heads with their dilly bags (see Figure 1). Each song-set contains one or two songs referred to as *nigi* in Mawng, meaning 'mother'.[37] These songs are recognisable by the fact that they have the slowest tempo of all of the songs, and are considered the essence of the song-set (the other songs, which have similar melodies and words, are its children). In western Arnhem Land funerals, the *nigi* is always performed last, to finish off the performance of the song-set and carry the deceased home. During the *nigi* song, the singers and didjeridu player will often stand up and

---

35   For further discussion, see Barwick et al., 'Iwaidja Jurtbirrk songs', 9.
36   Solomon Nangamu, interview with the author, August 2011.
37   In Kunwinjku, the 'mother' song is referred to as *ngalbadjan*.

walk over to the grave (sometimes the leading songman may dance himself), while the women line up in the direction of the deceased's Country, and dance them into the grave.

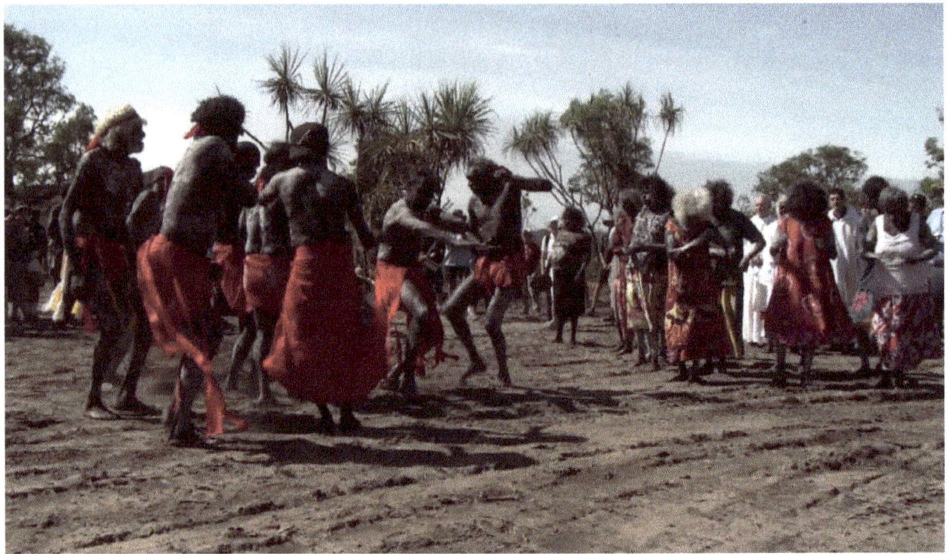

Figure 1: *Bininj* (left) and *daluk* (right) dance Karrbarda at Gunbalanya, 2011, as part of a reburial ceremony for bones taken during the Arnhem Land Expedition. Photograph by Addis Hondo.

Source: By permission of photographer.

Funeral ceremonies are important occasions for the presentation of newly composed songs, which arise when deceased spirits intervene in a songman's dreams and inspire new musical material for him to sing as part of his inherited song-set. Dreams act as a kind of portal through which certain songmen gain access to the spirit world, and the presence of spirits may be heightened during the period after death and leading up to the funeral. The significance of dream-composed songs has been discussed elsewhere by Marett with regard to *wangga* of the Daly region,[38] and by Treloyn with regard to Scotty Martin's *junba* of the Kimberley region.[39] Barwick, Birch and Evans have observed that in western Arnhem Land, songs that come from dreams are given the status of 'true' songs, as opposed to songs that come to the singer 'spontaneously' without spirit intervention.[40] As Murray Garde notes, *kun-borrk* songmen establish authority

---

38   Marett, *Songs, Dreamings, and Ghosts*, 36–45.

39   Sally Treloyn, 'Scotty Martin's *Jadmi Junba*: A song series from the Kimberley region of northwest Australia', *Oceania* 73:3 (2003).

40   Barwick et al., 'Iwaidja Jurtbirrk songs', 9.

over their song repertories through the way that they access 'new' songs through the supernatural, interpret these songs given by spirits, and continue to perform the songs in ceremony.[41]

The language of *kun-borrk* songs are an important component linking people to ancestral spirits of the Country. Each *kun-borrk* song-set is associated with one or more of the languages of western Arnhem Land (see Figure 2). Many song-sets are associated with languages that are no longer spoken (the Mirrijpu song-set associated with Manangkardi, for example) or are highly endangered (the Karrbarda song-set associated with Kunbarlang, for example);[42] therefore songs are a powerful means of communicating with ancestors who spoke these languages. Song texts can be in one or more 'ordinary' languages (reflecting the multilingual environment of Bininj in western Arnhem Land),[43] as well as what has been referred to by various scholars in the literature on north Australian songs as 'spirit language'.[44] Spirit languages are regarded as belonging to song–giving spirits who live in the landscape. As Mirrijpu songman Russell Agalara explains, 'it's not any language that we speak now, that's a different language from back then, passed on from generation to generation'.[45] In Mawng the term for these song words is *wurrgal ngaralk,* which translates as 'dream words'.[46] These untranslatable spirit language words are 'fixed' in song; unlike improvised vocables (as in jazz scat singing), they vary little from one performance to the next.[47] As Meiki Apted found with regard to the Inyjalarrku song-set, spirit language words are distinct from but also sound similar to the 'ordinary' language of the singers (in this case, Mawng).[48] They are particularly potent in the context of funeral ceremonies because they 'speak' exclusively to ancestral

---

41   Garde, 'The language of *Kun-borrk*', 86.

42   The Karrbarda song-set, predominantly in spirit language, also incorporates Bob Balir-Balir's 'everyday' language songs in Kun-barlang (after which the song-set is also known). See O'Keeffe, 'Sung and Spoken', 48.

43   Most Bininj speak three or four Aboriginal languages and it is not uncommon for a song text to switch between languages within the song. See Isabel O'Keeffe, 'Kaddikkaddik Ka-Wokdjanganj "Kaddikkaddik Spoke": Language and music of the Kun-barlang *Kaddikkaddik* songs from western Arnhem Land', *Australian Journal of Linguistics* 30:1 (2010).

44   See Meiki Elizabeth Apted, 'Songs from the Inyjalarrku: The use of a non-translatable spirit language in a song set from north-west Arnhem Land, Australia', *Australian Journal of Linguistics* 30:1 (2010): 94; Garde, 'The Language of *Kun-borrk*': 78–81; O'Keeffe, 'Sung and Spoken': 46. Marett also discusses spirit language in various texts of wangga songs of the Daly region. Marett, *Songs, Dreamings, and Ghosts.*

45   Russell Agalara, Reuben Brown, and Solomon Nangamu, 'That Spirit Changed My Voice: The performance of *kun-borrk* at a funeral ceremony in Mikkinj Valley, western Arnhem Land', Paper presented at the *Musicological Society of Australia Annual Conference*, The Australian National University, Canberra, 3–5 December 2012.

46   Rosemary Urabadi, personal communication, 6 November 2012.

47   Apted, 'Songs from the Inyjalarrku': 93–4. See also Garde, 'The Language of *Kun-borrk*': 81. From my observations of the Mirrijpu song-set, the current singer may realise the spirit language words in song slightly differently from the singer that passed on the songs, as part of their own interpretation of the music.

48   Apted, 'Songs from the Inyjalarrku': 98–100.

spirits who understand them. As Apted observes, by singing spirit language songs, 'spiritual faith and connection to country is asserted in a way that may not be possible with an ordinary spoken language'.[49]

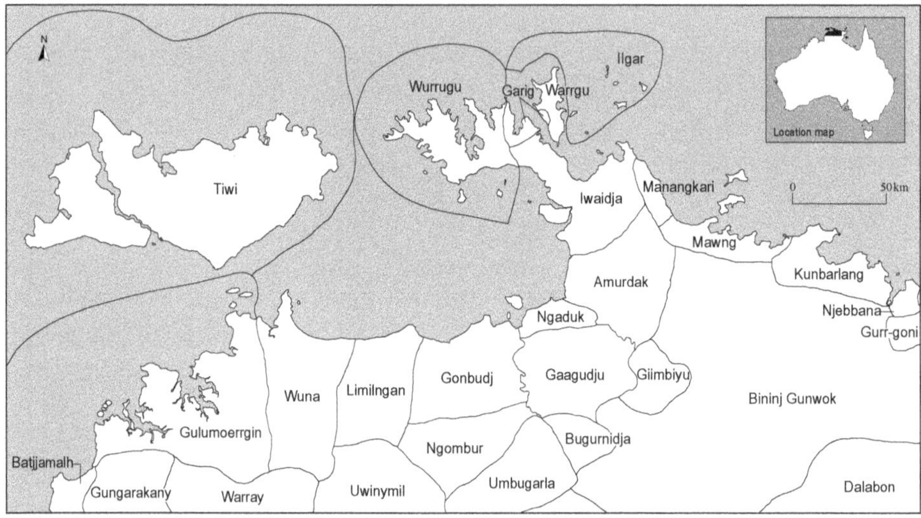

Figure 2: The languages of western Arnhem Land and surrounds.

Source: Aidan Wilson, *Tiwi Revisited: A reanalysis of traditional Tiwi verb morphology* (Masters, University of Melbourne, 2013), xii. Reproduced by permission of Aidan Wilson.

The Funeral Ceremony for Nakodjok

Song Repertories Performed and their Sequence in the Ceremony

Whilst it is not unusual to find a number of different song genres and repertories performed at funerals or indeed any ceremonial occasions in western Arnhem Land,[50] the funeral ceremony for Nakodjok Nayinggul was particularly unique, in that it brought together such a diverse range of song traditions from all over the broader region of the Top End. All together, seven different Aboriginal song

---

49   Apted, 'Songs from the Inyjalarrku': 101.

50   Funeral ceremonies that I attended in and around Gunbalanya during my fieldwork commonly featured two or three song-sets by singers both residing in the region of the deceased or visiting from outside the region, usually from central Arnhem Land or the Daly region. Barwick and Marett's findings about the origins of Colin Simpson's recordings at Oenpelli/Gunbalanya in 1948 similarly reveal an assortment of songs from all over the region (three *kun-borrk* 'love songs', two *kun-borrk wardde-ken* songs, two *manyardi kurrula* songs and one *wangga* song). See Linda Barwick and Allan Marrett, 'Snapshots of Musical Life: The 1948 recordings', in *Exploring the Legacy of the 1948 Arnhem Land Expedition*, eds Martin Thomas and Margo Neale (Canberra: ANU E Press, 2011), 364.

groups performed at various stages of the ceremony (see Figure 3). Of equal significance was the music not representative of Aboriginal Australian genres that featured in the ceremony, including Christian hymns in Kunwinjku led by the local Reverend and sung by the congregation, as well as various country and western songs that were played through speakers on an mp3 player at Nakodjok's memorial service. The high participation from a diversity of singers in the ceremony reflected not only Nakodjok's importance as a leader in his immediate community of Gunbalanya and western Arnhem Land, but also showed how Bininj like Nakodjok have kinship ties right across Arnhem Land and the Top End region.

Song-set	Genre	Singer	Singer's residence	Language
Inyjalarrku (mermaid)	western Arnhem Land *manyardi*	David and Rupert Manmurulu	Warruwi (Goulburn Island)	Spirit language associated with Mawng
Inyjalarrku/ Marrawiwi (salmon)	western Arnhem Land *manyardi*	Tommy Madjalkaidj	Maningrida (born Warruwi)	Spirit language associated with Mawng
Mirrijpu (seagull)	western Arnhem Land *manyardi*	Solomon Nangamu and Russell Agalara	Gunbalanya (born Warruwi)	Spirit language associated with Manangkardi
Karrbarda (long yam)	western Arnhem Land *kun-borrk*	Eric Mardday	Gunbalanya	Spirit language, Kun-barlang, Mawng and Kunwinjku mixed
Ramingining singers (unknown clan)	central Arnhem Land *bunggurl*	Stanley Djalarra	Ramingining	Rembarrnga
Galpu clan	north-east Arnhem Land *manikay*	Gurruwiwi family (and Johnny Burarrwanga)	Warruwi (born Gove)	Yolngu Matha
Buffalo dance	Tiwi *kulama* songs	Wesley Kerunauia (and Solomon Nangamu)	Bathurst Island	Tiwi
Christian hymns	Anglican church music	Congregation led by Rev. Lois Nadjamerrek	Gunbalanya	Kunwinjku and English
Various artists	country and western	Troy Cassar-Daley Slim Dusty Charley Pride	Australia America	English

Figure 3: Songs performed or played at the funeral ceremony for Nakodjok.

Unsurprisingly, the majority of the singers who performed at Nakodjok's ceremony were from western Arnhem Land, the region in which Nakodjok was born and where he spent most of his life. Many of the song repertories performed were *manyardi* song-sets originating from Goulburn Island. This is owing to the fact that numerous Mawng songmen who were born on Goulburn

Island today reside not only in the community of Warruwi (Goulburn Island)—arguably the centre of the western Arnhem Land song tradition today—but also in other neighbouring communities, where they continue to perform the songs and receive new songs. The Inyjalarrku song-set is a good example of the way *manyardi* has spread throughout western Arnhem Land on account of the Goulburn Island 'diaspora'; the songs have been inherited by a number of singers including David Manmurulu, his brother James Gulamuwu, and Tommy Madjalkaidj,[51] who today live in Warruwi, Gunbalanya and Maningrida respectively.[52] Only one song-set performed at the funeral—Karrbarda—originated from *wardde-ken* (the stone country) where Nakodjok's Country is situated.[53] This song-set, (also performed by inheriting singers living on Croker Island, Maningrida and Gunbalanya), plays a central role in many funeral ceremonies held in Gunbalanya.

Perhaps more unusually, a number of songs from outside western Arnhem Land were represented, including patrilineal clan 'song series' from central and north-east Arnhem Land, referred to as *bunggurl* and *manikay* respectively. Each clan performs a number of song subjects in a series that relate to different aspects of their ancestral stories.[54] Although I was unable to establish the clan affiliation of the group from Ramingining, the most prominent subject of their songs was the Waak (K: crow), which was accompanied by a dance that imitates the bird's movement and sound. (The dancers circled and hopped as they moved toward the gravesite, calling out 'waak, waak!'). Crows are associated with death in this region, and Waak *manikay* are often performed during the final stages of burial.[55] Galpu *manikay* was also performed by the Gurruwiwi family and accompanied by Gumatj clan singer Johnny Burarrwanga, who was born in east Arnhem Land and married a Galpu clan woman. Burarrwanga lives with other Galpu and Gumatj people who have long been resident at Warruwi, but who still maintain their *manikay* performance traditions by performing in western Arnhem Land.

Not only are these song series from central and north-east Arnhem Land different from those from western Arnhem Land in the way that they are inherited (through one's clan as opposed to individually), they also sound different in a number of ways. Unlike western Arnhem Land songs, north-east Arnhem Land

---

51   The fathers of these songmen were part of the same family and shared the songs.

52   Solomon Nangamu—singer of the third *manyardi* Mirrijpu song-set of North Goulburn Island—was also born in Warruwi, and now resides in the larger community of Gunbalanya where he lives with his Kunwinjku fiancée.

53   Another *wardde-ken* song-set called Kurri (K: blue tongue lizard) is also more closely associated with Nakodjok's Country and is well remembered by his family. However, as far as I have observed, this song-set is no longer performed.

54   Ross and Wild, 'Formal Performance': 9; Toner, 'Tropes of Longing and Belonging': 4.

55   Clunies Ross and Wild, 'Formal Performance': 213. Also depicted in the final scenes of the *lorrkkon* ceremony in McKenzie, *Waiting for Harry*.

melodies do not necessarily take their pitch from the didjeridu, and both north-east and central Arnhem Land songs feature didjeridu overtones that are absent from western Arnhem Land *mako* accompaniment. There are subtle differences in layering of the musical texture too: whereas *kun-borrk/manyardi* begins with didjeridu accompaniment, followed by the beat of the clapstick and then the vocal line, and ends with solitary beating of the clapsticks, *manikay/bunggurl* songs often begin with clapstick accompaniment and finish with unaccompanied singing. These aural characteristics make the geographic identity of the songs instantly recognisable to mourners in larger funeral ceremonies such as Nakodjok's, where different groups performed simultaneously, both in the daytime and in the evening.[56]

The last genre of Aboriginal songs from outside Arnhem Land was Tiwi songs associated with the *kulama* (yam) ceremony. These songs were performed unaccompanied (without clapsticks or didjeridu) led by Wesley Kerunauia, with Dean Rioli and Solomon Nangamu joining the dancing (Nangamu lived in Tiwi for a number of years and was invited to join as he was familiar with the songs). The dance they performed—referred to as the 'buffalo'—took place next to the grave, after the coffin was put in the ground.[57] The melody of the song had a limited range, resembling something closer to speech. Each song culminated in a percussive slap of the body, followed by the distinctive dance call: 'ah-eh-yah'.

Of the Western musical genres performed, Reverend Lois Nadjamerrek and a small congregation of Bininj sang unaccompanied Christian biblical hymns during the memorial service in the church at Gunbalanya, and as part of an open-air sermon by the gravesite at Mikkinj Valley, as the grave was being filled (see Figure 4). Nadjamerrek led the service in both Kunwinjku and English, and composed one of the hymns in Kunwinjku. In addition, the family of Nakodjok requested three particular songs to be played at the end of the memorial service, as the mourners said goodbye to the coffin. The first song—'Gunbalanya' by Troy Cassar-Daley—pays homage to Nakodjok's Country, with references to fishing for saratoga at Red Lily billabong near the East Alligator River. Cassar-Daley is an Indigenous country and western singer from New South Wales who travelled to Gunbalanya and met Nakodjok, later dedicating the song to him.

---

56   See Linda Barwick, 'Musical Form and Style in Murriny Patha Djanba Songs at Wadeye (Northern Territory, Australia)', in *Analytical and Cross-Cultural Studies in World Music*, eds Michael Tenzer and John Roeder (Oxford Scholarship Online: Oxford University Press, 2011), 349; Allan Marett, Linda Barwick, and Lysbeth Ford, *For the Sake of a Song: Wangga songmen and their repertories: The Indigenous music of Australia*, Book 2 (Sydney: Sydney University Press, 2013), 63.

57   Similar dances were photographed and described by Baldwin Spencer when he travelled to Melville Island in 1911. Spencer, *Native tribes of the Northern Territory*, 237.

6 June 2012 Gunbalanya: Transition to local morgue	28 June 2012 Gunbalanya: Memorial service	29 June 2012 Mikkinj Valley: Pre-interment	30 June 2012 Mikkinj valley: Interment and post-interment
Ramingining singers sing outside Nakodjok's home while family stays with coffin inside. **Karrbarda** dance coffin out of house and accompany procession of mourners to Gunbalanya morgue. **Ramingining** singers then take over and sing Nakodjok inside.	**Galpu** *manikay* singers accompany procession from morgue to church. Upon arrival at church, **Mirrijpu** singers lead coffin and procession of mourners into church. Reverend Lois Nadjamerrek leads **Christian hymns in English** during service. **country and western** songs played over PA as local mourners farewell Nakodjok. **Inyjalarrku** is performed as the coffin is taken from church to airport and placed on plane to Mikkinj Valley, where **Karrbarda** greets it.	**Mirrijpu, Raminging** singers and **Karrbarda** share singing after sundown while families cook dinner in separate camps. **Karrbarda** perform later in the evening, with children joining in dancing. **Mirrijpu** take over and continue to sing until early the next morning.	**Mirrijpu, Inyjalarrku and Karrbarda** lead groups of mourners into bough shelter to farewell Nakodjok. **Ramingining** mob join them and all groups dance outside bough shelter. **Karrbarda** 'mother' song leads Nakodjok into grave. **Tiwi Island Buffalo dance** performed beside the grave, followed by **Christian hymns in Kunwinjku**. After interment, **Ramingining** and **Tiwi Island** group remain for *kun-woning* (cleansing/ washing ceremony) followed by smoking ceremony of Nakodjok's belongings and home at Mikkinj Valley.

Figure 4: The main stages of the funeral ceremony for Nakodjok involving ritual song and dance.

The second song, 'We've Done us Proud' by Slim Dusty is a nationalistic song about the progress of the Australian nation. Slim Dusty's music is well known in many Aboriginal communities in the Top End where he toured and performed throughout his career.[58] The song resonates with the history of this area, in particular the Bininj-owned cattle station at Gunbalanya ('I built the fences to hold the cattle/I worked the land'). Sentiments about uniting people together for a common good ('side by side, hand in hand') also resonate with Nakodjok's achievements as a key negotiator between Balanda and Bininj during his work for the Northern Land Council and as a board member of the joint-managed Kakadu National Park.

The third song—'Blue Ridge Mountains' by African American singer Charley Pride—was, according to Nakodjok's son Alfred Nayinggul, a favourite of Nakodjok's because it reminded him of the landscape of his Country. Nayinggul recalled his father sitting outside at Mikkinj Valley outstation, listening to the song on the record player while taking in the surrounding escarpment. These

---

58 Jon Fitzgerald and Philip Hayward, 'At the Confluence: Slim Dusty and Australian country music', in *Outback and Urban: Australian country music*, ed. Philip Hayward (Gympie: AICM Press, 2003), 43.

three songs indicate how country and western music in particular has come to be emblematic of Aboriginal experience and identification with the land,[59] and how popular music genres have been incorporated into the Bininj world view, taking on meanings that are locally-specific (see also Mansfield, this volume).

The sequence in which the song repertories were performed (outlined in Figure 4) was partly determined by practical factors (such as who could attend the ceremonies at Gunbalanya and Mikkinj Valley), and partly negotiated by the parties involved so that certain song repertories could be emphasised at certain stages of the ceremony (see below for further discussion). Many Balanda and Bininj mourners who were unable to attend the burial at Mikkinj—including the *manikay* and *manyardi* singers resident at Warruwi—were given the opportunity to farewell the deceased after the memorial service at Gunbalanya. A number of people from the community and local organisations were asked by the family to speak about Nakodjok at the service.[60] To the extent that it included Christian prayers and readings from the Bible conducted largely in English, a eulogy, hymns, and country and western songs, the Balanda-oriented memorial service complemented the ceremony at Mikkinj Valley, with its focus on Bininj rituals. This seemed fitting, given the bi-cultural world that Nakodjok had occupied.

Those groups who did not go on to Mikkinj accompanied Nakodjok from the morgue to the church for the service, including the Galpu clan, who performed *manikay* without didjeridu accompaniment, as well as David and Rupert Manmurulu who performed Inyjalarrku as Nakodjok's coffin was taken from the church and placed into a troopy, before it was transported by plane to Mikkinj Valley. Rupert Manmurulu led the singing of the Inyjalarrku 'mother' song, before David Manmurulu performed a dance that he had learnt from his father George Winungudj which is reserved for the end of such ceremonial occasions, when the dancers and singers say *bobo* (K/M: goodbye) to the spirit of the deceased. Unusually, the dance is performed at a moderate tempo normally reserved for women's dancing (see discussion of rhythmic modes below). Manmurulu took on the character of a *yumparrparr* (M: giant spirit), standing in a semi-crouched position and swaying his arms as he walked to the beat of the clapstick, creating a sense of gravity through the movement. As the coffin was carried away, he extended both arms out to it and pulled them in to his chest, as if reaching out to make a connection, then held one arm out, rotating his hand as if waving 'goodbye' to the spirit of the deceased.[61]

---

59 See Clinton Walker, *Buried Country: The story of Aboriginal country music* (Sydney: Pluto Press, 2000).
60 For a Kunwinjku and English transcription of the eulogy given on behalf of Nakodjok's family, see Murray Garde, 'Nakodjok Namanilakarr,' *Bininj Gunwok* (blog), 27 June 2012, http://bininjgunwok.org.au/blog/page/3/.
61 This interpretation was informed by discussions with David Manmurulu, interview with the author, 3 November 2012.

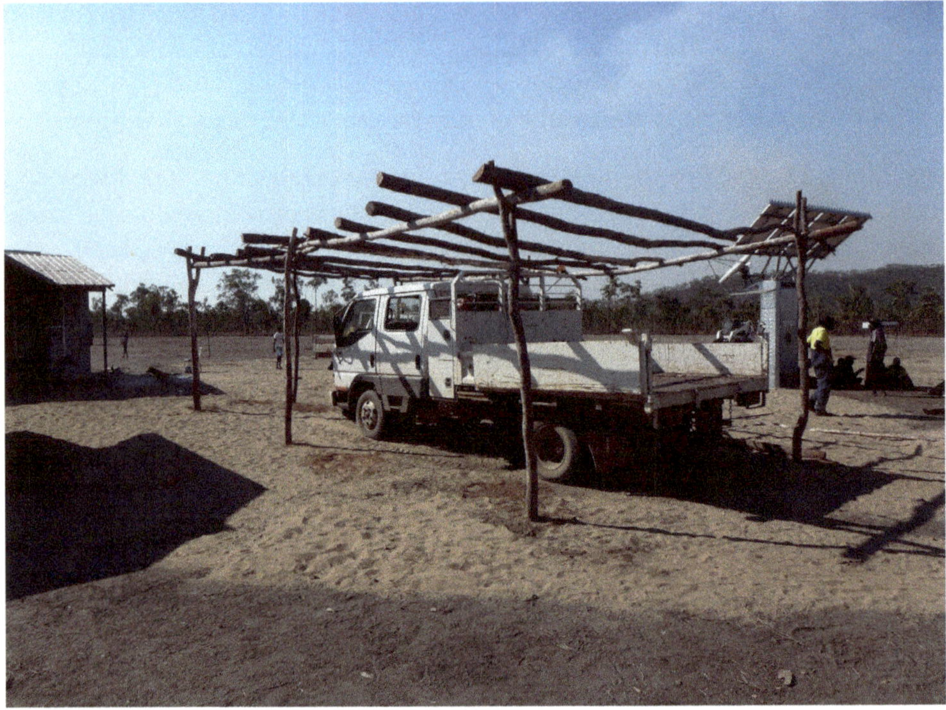

Figure 5: The construction of the bough shelter or 'shade' for the body of Nakodjok at Mikkinj Valley outstation.

Source: Photo by the author.

The Karrbarda and Ramingining singers stayed with the family of the deceased, many of whom did not attend the memorial service at Gunbalanya but awaited Nakodjok at Mikkinj Valley inside the bough shelter constructed for his coffin. Bough shelters are usually made of stringybark branches and leaves, providing shade for the mourners (see Figure 5). The shelter where the coffin is kept is an enclosed structure, sometimes covered in red or yellow cloth, representing the moiety of the deceased (Nakodjok's duwa moiety was represented with red cloth). The *daluk* members of the family stay inside the shelter beside the coffin until the burial. In the evening at Mikkinj Valley, the Karrbarda, Ramingining and Mirrijpu singers performed next to the shelter in order to keep the family company through the night. On the morning of the interment, Inyjalarrku singer Tommy Madjalkaidj joined them, performing 'old' Inyjalarrku songs as well 'new' dream-composed songs named Marrawiwi (M: salmon). Some of these newly conceived songs were performed for the first time in honour of the spirit of the deceased. Together, the four song groups took turns accompanying groups of mourners, including their own kin, into the bough shelter to visit Nakodjok one final time. Significantly, the Karrbarda group—representing *wardde-ken* people and their ancestors—performed the 'mother' song as the body was interred in order to carry Nakodjok's spirit away at the final moment. As the grave was being filled in, the opportunity arose for any other groups to pay their respects to the deceased, and the Tiwi group obliged, performing their Buffalo dance for Nakodjok. A Christian sermon and Kunwinjku hymns followed, concluding with a ritual in which the mourners throw a handful of dirt into the grave as a final goodbye.

Relationships Expressed Through Song

A number of significant connections between the living and deceased were enacted and highlighted through these performances at Nakodjok's funeral ceremony. As Peter Toner suggests, the choice to perform, as well as the sequence of the performance—which is decided not only among the singers but also other senior members of different patrifilial groups—are highly social and political acts in Arnhem Land ceremonies:

> Yolngu musical performances are events in which complex social identities are expressed, negotiated, constructed, and re-constructed; they are occasions during which a great deal of the work of Yolngu sociality gets done at a number of different levels.[62]

Even the performance of Kunwinjku hymns, framed by a sermon delivered by Reverend Lois Nadjamerrek, in which she mentioned Nakodjok's baptism and first marriage that had taken place at the Gunbalanya church,[63] emphasised his relationship to the local congregation and to God. Underpinning many of the social connections between the mourners and the deceased are cultural practices of clan exogamy (marriage outside one's own clan)[64] and marriage agreements. The large representation of *kurrula* song-sets at Nakodjok's funeral reflected not only the prevalence of *manyardi* in western Arnhem Land, but also Nakodjok's connection to Mawng-speaking families through his mother, Priscilla, who was *kurrula* (from the saltwater). Nakodjok's father was *wardde-ken* (from the stone country) and helped resolve a dispute between the Gunbalanya and Goulburn Island communities. As thanks he was promised a Mawng woman (Priscilla) for marriage.[65] This connection (between *wardde-ken* and *kurrula* people) was maintained when Priscilla made a pre-birth marriage agreement with the uncle of Tommy Madjalkaidj, that Nakodjok would marry Tommy (if he were a woman) or his sisters. Although the marriage didn't eventuate because Nakodjok was too young when the potential spouses were of the right age, Madjalkaidj and

---

62   Toner, 'Tropes of Longing and Belonging': 5–6.

63   See 'Book of Births, Deaths and Marriages' NTRS 864, Box 6, Location 75/5/4, Northern Territory Archives, Darwin.

64   See Barwick and Marett, 'Snapshots of Musical Life': 364–5.

65   Alfred Nayinggul, personal communication, 16 November 2012.

Nakodjok recognised the fact that they were in an affinal relationship, and would refer to each other as brother-in-law. Madjalkaidj continued to recognise this relationship (marked by a degree of physical avoidance) during his performance at the ceremony, accompanying the mourners to the edge of the bough shelter with his Marrawiwi songs, but remaining outside while they went in. The Tiwi performance was given by family groups who were connected through two members of Nakodjok's family who shared ownership of his Country at Mikkinj Valley, but were taken away as children and sent first to Channel Island and then to Bathurst Island, where they had grown up. (Government policies affecting generations of stolen Aboriginal children have created a situation where family ties are spread far and wide.)

At the same time that performances highlight or emphasise connections between the mourners and the deceased, they also reinforce connections among the living, in particular through the rituals that are performed for the family of the deceased to guide them through the grieving process. On the evening before Nakodjok's burial, Mirrijpu singers Solomon Nangamu and Russell Agalara came together with didjeridu player Alfred Gawaraidji, and Karrbarda singers led by Eric Mardday, to take it in turns singing throughout the evening and into the next morning. Positioning themselves close to the family of the deceased inside the main bough shelter, they performed a mixture of moderate and fast-tempo songs (see Figure 6), encouraging the children to get up and join in the dance. The mood was high and the atmosphere jovial. The boisterous children kept themselves entertained through their own attempts to dance, and by watching the adults, including Madjalkaidj, dancing to the songs. As Agalara explained, part of the purpose of their singing and dancing at funerals is to keep the emotions of the bereaved in check so that they can not only mourn but also feel supported and happy. Explaining why they sing and dance, and its effect on the mourners, Agalara used the idiomatic Mawng expression *arnamawu kumpil*, which translates roughly as, 'they get a strong feeling in their chests':[66]

> [By singing], we respect and we connect with their families among them
> … being close to them[67] [we] lift their feelings a bit … they have sadness
> in their emotions and we … *arnamawu kumpil* means we have to be
> there for them to express their emotions and balance it.[68]

Again on the morning of the burial, all of the song groups present performed fast songs, with Joey Nganjmirra and Russell Agalara taking turns playing the role of 'dance captain', helping the children to put on their *nagas* (dance-cloths)

---

66 This translation was assisted by Ruth Singer, who observes that the phrase is similar to an expression such as 'break (someone's) heart' in English. In this example, a transitive prefix is missing which would provide a clearer meaning of the expression. Ruth Singer, personal communication, 25 February 2013.
67 By singing next to the bough shelter.
68 Agalara, Brown, and Nangamu, 'That Spirit Changed My Voice'.

and cover themselves in *delek*, and instructing those who were unfamiliar with *kun-borrk* how to dance to the various clapstick patterns. By bringing these different groups together to perform their song traditions and articulate their language/clan identities in the process, funeral events provide a much desired setting for the intergenerational transmission of song and dance traditions.

#	Song item	Song text association	Rhythmic mode	Clapstick(bpm)
1	MP01	*Kiwken* (M: boss song)	Fast even	124
2	MP02	*Bobo: bininj* (K: farewell song—men's dancing)	Fast even	122
3	MP03	*Bobo: daluk* (K: farewell song—women's dancing)	Moderate	116
4	MP03 (R)	*Bobo: daluk* (K: farewell song—women)	Moderate	117
5	MP03 (R)	*Bobo: daluk* (K: farewell song—women)	Moderate	116
6	MP04	*Man-me* (K: food; tucker)	Fast–doubled	250
7	MP04 (R)	*Man-me* (K: food; tucker)	Fast–doubled	244
8	MP05	*Ngaya* (M: 'daughter')	Moderate	117
9	MP05 (R)	*Ngaya* (M: 'daughter')	Moderate	118
10	MP06	*Warramumpik* (M: love song)	Fast even	122
11	MP06 (R)	*Warramumpik* (M: love song)	Fast even	120
12	MP06 (R)	*Warramumpik nulatparlangkat* (M: love song, fast rhythmic mode)	Fast–doubled	264
13	MP04	*Man-me* (K: food; tucker)	Fast–doubled	260
14	MP07	*Ngapawurru* (M: respect)	Moderate	119
15	MP01	*Kiwken* (M: boss song)	Fast even	123
16	MP08/ MP09	'Going down'	Fast even	122
17	MP08	'Going down'	Fast even	124
18	MP08 (R)	'Going down'	Fast even	122
19	MP08 (R)	'Going down'	Fast even	123
20	MP09	*Bobo* (K: farewell song)	Moderate	118
21	MP09 (R)	*Bobo* (K: farewell song)	Moderate	119
22	MP10	Gift song	Fast even	123
23	MP10 (R)	Gift song	Fast even	120
24	MP10 (R)	Gift song	Fast even	120
25	MP11	Bobo (K: farewell song)	Slow	95
26	MP12	'Going down'	Fast–doubled	200
27	MP12 (R)	'Going down'	Fast–doubled	198
28	MP13	*Man-me* (K: tucker)	Fast even	121
29	MP01	*Kiwken* (M: boss song)	Fast even	121
30	MP01 (R)	*Kiwken* (M: boss song)	Fast even	121

Figure 6: Mirrijpu songs in performed order by Solomon Nangamu and Russell Agalara at Mikkinj Valley.

Note: MP indicates a Mirrijpu song item, (R) indicates a repeated song item and 'bpm' indicates 'beats per minute'. Recently conceived songs performed for the occasion are shaded grey.

Song Order and Spirit Intervention in Solomon Nangamu and Russell Agalara's Performance of Mirrijpu Songs

The extent to which performances in funeral ceremonies are constructed in order to reflect these connections between the living and the deceased was revealed to me in discussions with Mirrijpu songmen Nangamu and Agalara about how they ordered the songs during the performance they gave the evening before the burial (see Figure 4). Generally speaking, there is no strict order to the performance of western Arnhem Land songs; song order varies from one performance to the next, depending on the occasion. Nevertheless, songmen make particular choices according to ceremonial precedents established by their ancestors, and according to the action taking place in their immediate environment. The effect is to produce a sequence of songs that is desirable both to their living audience (the mourners and dancers) and to their deceased audience (ancestral spirits listening in).[69]

In determining how a performance is put together, western Arnhem Land songmen consider the familiarity of a particular song for both the living and the deceased. Often, they use the English terms 'old' and 'new' to make the distinction between songs that have been passed down from *korroko* (K: before; a long time ago), and recent dream-conceived songs. Of course, the use of these terms can set up a false dichotomy since, from a Bininj perspective, all songs come from the same ancestral source, and 'new' songs are often attributed to the same relative who taught them the 'old' songs while they were alive. (This explains why songmen sometimes describe recently conceived songs as 'new, but old' or 'still the same one [as others in the song-set]'). On a musical level, 'new' songs usually share the same sung syllables (or song text), the same rhythmic modes and the same melodic units[70] as 'old' songs, but slightly re-arranged and varied, to give the impression of 'new, but old'.[71] One of Nangamu's reasons for attending the ceremony was out of respect for the important role that Nakodjok had played as a ceremony leader. Before the ceremony, he told me that he intended to perform three songs for the first time, including two songs (song items MP04 and MP10 in Figure 6) that had been given to him by the spirit of Nakodjok not long after the 'old man' had passed away. On a social level, the debut of these new songs on such an important occasion would have generated interest among Bininj who were already familiar with Mirrijpu songs, listening to the 'new' songs for the first time. On a political

---

69   This is consistent with Treloyn's observation of Kimberley performance, where the pairing of slow/fast songs which share subject matter and lexical content in Scotty Martin's *junba* repertory 'has the overall effect of foregrounding the relationship between the living performers, and the spirits ... that they enact on the dance ground'. Sally Treloyn, '"When Everybody There Together ... Then I Call That One": Song order in the Kimberley', *Context* 32 (2007): 110. See also Barwick's discussion of the pairing of slow and fast songs that are thematically linked in Marri Ngarr *lirrga* songs. Linda Barwick, 'Marri Ngarr *Lirrga* Songs: A musicological analysis of song pairs in performance', *Musicology Australia* 28 (2005): 13; Linda Barwick, 'Tempo Bands, Metre and Rhythmic Mode in Marri Ngarr "Church *Lirrga*" Songs', *Australasian Music Research* 7 (2002): 82.
70   See Treloyn, this volume.
71   For similar discussion in relation to north-east Arnhem Land song traditions, see Steven Knopoff, 'Yuta Manikay: Juxtaposition of ancestral and contemporary elements in the performance of Yolngu clan songs', *Yearbook for Traditional Music* 24 (1992): 138–53.

level, as mentioned earlier, it would have further demonstrated the singer's affiliation with the song-set and the Country connected to it. Given this, one might expect Nangamu to have begun with one of these songs. Instead, following the precedents set down by his own Manangkardi ancestors, and in order to pay respect to the songmen before him, he performed first a number of old songs in the set, building up to the new material that he intended to sing for both his immediate audience and for Nakodjok himself (see Figure 6). Towards the end of the session, he returned once more to the songs from *korroko*, which would be more familiar to his ancestors.

A second consideration songmen make in ordering the songs is the 'rhythmic mode' in which the song is performed. Rhythmic modes—defined as 'the intersection of tempo bands and clapstick-beating patterns'[72]—correspond to different dance styles across song repertories all over northern Australia.[73] For example, many of the Mirrijpu songs performed that evening were in fast tempo band (120–125 beats per minute), named *nulatparlangkat* in Mawng. *Nulatparlangkat* songs feature men's dancing, and are performed in this instance either with 'even' beating of the clapsticks on the beat ('fast even' rhythmic mode) or 'doubled' beating ('fast–doubled' rhythmic mode, 240–260 beats per minute). Moderate (110–119 beats per minute) and slow (95–110 beats per minute) tempo bands—called *nulatparlilil* in Mawng—typically feature women's dancing.[74] During 'instrumental sections' of the song (in between verses where the song text is sung), the clapstick beating usually changes to a gapped pattern—for example, MP06 has the gapped pattern (♩ ♩ 𝄽) in triple meter. This is when the *bininj* dancers stamp the ground with their feet, and pause with the gap in the clapstick beat.

Generally, Nangamu begins his performance with songs in 'moderate even' or 'fast even' rhythmic mode, and gradually increases the tempo through the performance, performing a spell of fast-doubled rhythmic mode songs in the middle section for the *bininj* dancers. As he did later that evening, Nangamu then returns to moderate and slow tempo songs toward the end of the performance, finishing with the 'mother' song (these songs were not recorded and are therefore not represented in Figure 6). Similarly, songmen 'follow the

---

72 Marett, *Songs, Dreamings, and Ghosts*, 204. Marett outlines a number of rhythmic modes used for *wangga* repertories, on which I base my own tempo bands for western Arnhem Land song repertories. A number of other factors such as the vocal and didjeridu rhythm also determine the rhythmic mode, but for reasons of scope, I concern my analysis here mainly with the tempo of the songs.

73 See Gregory D. Anderson, 'Striking a Balance: Limited variability in performances of a clan song series from Arnhem Land', in *The Essence of Singing and the Substance of Song: Recent responses to the Aboriginal performing arts and other essays in honour of Catherine Ellis*, eds Linda Barwick, Allan Marett and Guy Tunstill (Sydney: University of Sydney, 1995), 14–16.

74 Songs in all rhythmic modes can also be performed without dancing.

track' of their ancestors by performing particular song items first in slow or moderate rhythmic modes before re-stating them in fast rhythmic mode (for example, song item MP06 in Figure 6).

So important is the consideration of tempo (along with the correct rhythm, and singing of the song text), that the songmen frequently repeat a song item and will not move on to the next one until they have performed it the 'right way'—adjusting the tempo down slightly by two or three beats per minute until they feel they have got it right (see tempo for song items marked 'R' for 'repeat' in Figure 6). Even after a long pause between songs, when Nangamu began to sing a new song item, the tempo frequently stayed the same—faster or slower within one or two beats per minute (see song numbers 20–24 and 28–30, Figure 6). Such accurate sense of tempo has been observed elsewhere among singers of Northern Australian Aboriginal song traditions.[75]

A further consideration for Nangamu is the way in which the performance environment calls for certain song items that he has assigned to particular categories or given particular associations. For example, a number of the songs he performed were what he calls *bobo* (or 'farewell') songs, which he 'brings out' for funeral ceremonies in particular (see songs 2–5, Figure 6). Song item MP11, for example, is a *bobo* song Nangamu performed at the funeral of his older brother in 2007; he explained to me that 'if one of my family passes away, I sing that song'.[76] Other associations given to song items included *warramumpik* (M: 'love songs', a reference to another sub-category of *kun-borrk* song-sets), songs that he associates with a spiritual return to his Country, expressed in English as 'going down' songs, and songs associated with all of the kinds of *man-me* (K: food or 'tucker') found at particular sites in his Country of north Goulburn Island. At times the choice to perform a song from one of these categories related what was going on around the singer, such as when Nangamu noticed people cooking their dinner on the fire, and returned to song item MP04, a *man-me* song (song number 13, Figure 6). Tellingly, the song Nangamu calls *kiwken* (M: boss)—MP01—features frequently here and in other recordings I have made of Mirrijpu songs, and is usually one that he opens his performance with and returns to throughout (here, he comes back to it midway through the performance and returns to it at the end). Finally, there is the *ngaya* (M: daughter)[77] song, which usually precedes the final *nigi* (M: mother) song. Later, in the early hours of the morning, Nangamu and Agalara sang the *ngaya/nigi* (daughter/mother) sequence to finish their performance.

---

75 For further discussion, see Freya Bailes and Linda Barwick, 'Absolute Tempo in Multiple Performances of Aboriginal Songs: Analyzing recordings of *Djanba 12* and *Djanba 14*', *Music Perception* 28:5 (2011): 473–90.
76 Solomon Nangamu, personal communication, 25 November 2012.
77 Nangamu translated this term as 'daughter', however it can be used by a woman to refer to her sons or daughters.

Further discussion with the singers revealed the extent to which the spirit world is understood as affecting the outcome of the performance. On one occasion (song number 16) Nangamu began singing one song item (MP08) and then unintentionally switched mid-song to another song item from *korroko* (MP09), before returning again to the first song item. At the completion of the song, all of the performers laughed at Nangamu's apparent disorientation, and in the discussion that followed, Nangamu remarked 'that spirit bin grab me by the throat and he changed my voice!' In another example of spirit intervention, Agalara attributed his musical ability to sing songs with Solomon from *korroko* that he had heard but not previously performed in ceremony, to the assistance of the spirit of his grandfather—Nangamu's brother—through whom he first learned to sing Mirrijpu:'[78]

> He connects me onto that group [of] songs [from *korroko*] what my granddad [sings] … he connects to me, when he sings it's sort of like a computer goes in my brain and I twist my tongue and start singing with him.'[79]

Agalara's comments recall once more Marett's observation about the possibility of song to open up a space between the spirit and living worlds. Through song, ancestral and deceased spirits can not only influence song order, but also intervene in the middle of songs and lead the songman in the direction of another song, or take control of the functions of his voice, the same way that a computer gamer might control an avatar.

---

78 Agalara's mother's father (deceased) was Nangamu's older brother. Nangamu and his brothers learned the Mirrijpu songs from their father. Agalara and Nangamu refer to each other by the reciprocal kinship term *mammam*, which is used for one's mother's (classificatory) father or mother's father's sister and conversely, one's daughter's daughter or daughter's son. (In the kinship system of western Arnhem Land one's father's brothers are all considered 'father', and one's mother's sisters considered 'mother'.)

79 Agalara, Brown, and Nangamu, 'That Spirit Changed My Voice'.

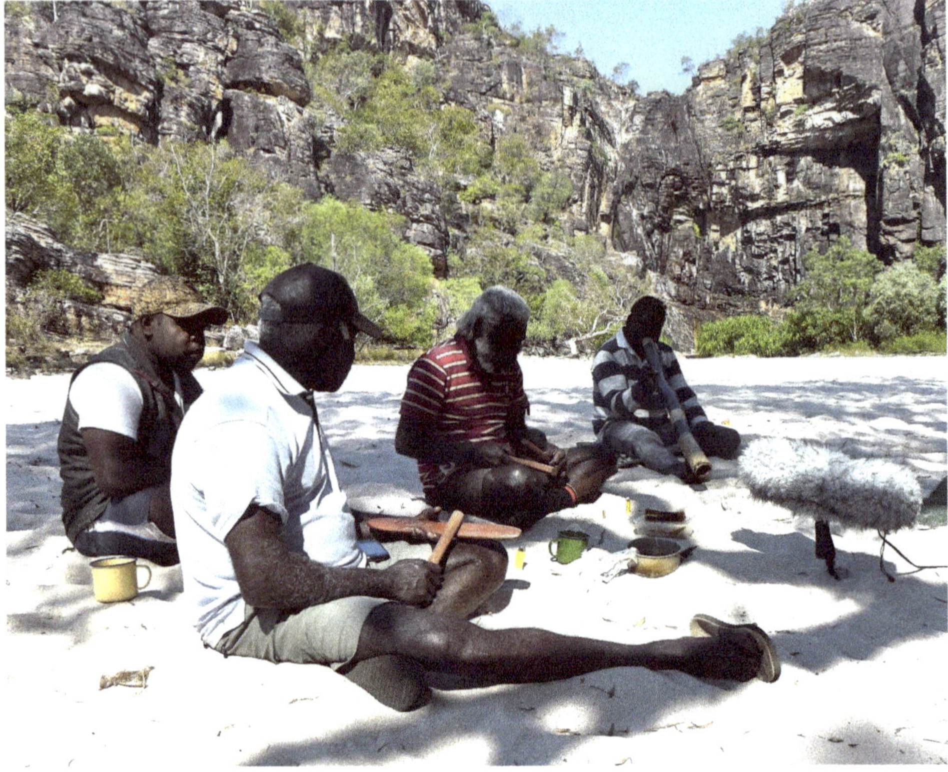

Figure 7: Singer Tommy Madjalkaidj (centre) performs Inyjalarrku songs near Gunbalanya. Russell Agalara (far left) and Alfred Gawaraidji (centre left) back up the singing, while Solomon Nangamu (right) accompanies on didjeridu.

Source: Photo by author.

Conclusion

Funeral ceremonies in western Arnhem Land continue to serve as the primary occasions in which relationships between different clan and cultural groups are acknowledged through ritual performance. The funeral ceremony for Nakodjok brought people from all over the region, who came to pay their respects and express their particular relationship with the deceased by performing their own song traditions. The diversity of music represented at this event points to the way songs express different linguistic, cultural and geographic identities and relationships.[80] It also showed the importance of funerals in providing an event in which these connections and differences can be played out, and the region's rich song traditions can be maintained.

In many ways, Nakodjok's was a very contemporary funeral ceremony, with the incorporation of Christian rituals and non-Aboriginal music genres alongside Bininj mortuary rites and song traditions, and with the charter plane playing an essential role in transporting the body to and from regional and local morgues, as well as facilitating the participation of distant kin in the ceremony. At the same time, the focus of the ceremonial action was centred on the transition of the deceased spirit between the living and ancestral worlds (eventually carried home to its traditional Country through the performance of the 'mother' song). *Kun-borrk* song repertories and dances, with their access to the ancestral world and its language, are key to ensuring such transitions are managed, and are therefore vital to Bininj spirituality and the life cycle of the spirit.

Kun-borrk singers show their respect for their ongoing relationship with the ancestors, and for the songs they have inherited, in different ways. Firstly, by reserving the performance of these new songs for the occasion of the funeral ceremony, when spirits familiar to them (Agalara's grandfather, for example) and the spirit of the deceased (in this case, Nakodjok) are likely to hear their performance. And secondly, by endeavouring to perform the songs and dances handed down to them in a way that would have made previous songmen happy—setting the songs to particular rhythmic modes and matching the songs to the mood of the mourners around them in order to balance their emotions.

Importantly, these songs help Bininj not only to deal with death and say goodbye to their deceased relatives, but also to maintain some kind of relationship with them. For Agalara, the Mirrijpu songs he sings are his connection to his grandfather, and as long as he feels that his grandfather's spirit is with him, he will continue to perform the Mirrijpu songs at funeral ceremonies, and pass them on to the next generation: 'That relates to the family … it doesn't matter where we go, the song is always there.'[81]

Acknowledgements

Thanks to the Mawng and Kunwinjku songmen, in particular Solomon Nangamu, Russell Agalara, Alfred Gawaraidji, Tommy Madjalkaidj and Eric Mardday, and to the family of Nakodjok, including Connie and Alfred Nayinggul, for their contribution to this chapter. Thanks also to Bill Ivory and Donna Nadjamerrek

---

80   See Treloyn, this volume.
81   Agalara, Brown, and Nangamu, 'That Spirit Changed My Voice'.

who assisted me during my stay in Gunbalanya and helped me to carry out my fieldwork. I am grateful to Ruth Singer for her help providing Mawng translations, as well as Linda Barwick, Amanda Harris and the two anonymous reviewers, for their generous feedback on this chapter.

References

Agalara, Russell, Reuben Brown, and Solomon Nangamu. 'That Spirit Changed My Voice: The performance of *kun-borrk* at a funeral ceremony in Mikkinj Valley, western Arnhem Land', Paper presented at the *Musicological Society of Australia Annual Conference*, The Australian National University, Canberra, 3–5 December 2012.

Anderson, Gregory D. 'Striking a Balance: Limited variability in performances of a clan song series from Arnhem Land', in *The Essence of Singing and the Substance of Song: Recent responses to the Aboriginal performing arts and other essays in honour of Catherine Ellis*, eds Linda Barwick, Allan Marett and Guy Tunstill (Sydney: University of Sydney, 1995), 13–25.

Apted, Meiki Elizabeth. 'Songs from the Inyjalarrku: The use of a non-translatable spirit language in a song set from north-west Arnhem Land, Australia', *Australian Journal of Linguistics* 30:1 (2010): 93–103.

Barwick, Linda. 'Tempo Bands, Metre and Rhythmic Mode in Marri Ngarr "Church *Lirrga*" Songs', *Australasian Music Research* 7 (2002): 67–83.

Barwick, Linda. 'Marri Ngarr *Lirrga* Songs: A Musicological Analysis of Song Pairs in Performance', *Musicology Australia* 28 (2005): 1–25.

Barwick, Linda. 'Musical Form and Style in Murriny Patha Djanba Songs at Wadeye (Northern Territory, Australia)', in *Analytical and Cross-Cultural Studies in World Music*, eds Michael Tenzer and John Roeder (Oxford Scholarship Online: Oxford University Press, 2011), 317–51.

Bailes, Freya, and Linda Barwick. 'Absolute Tempo in Multiple Performances of Aboriginal Songs: Analyzing recordings of *Djanba 12* and *Djanba 14*', *Music Perception* 28:5 (2011): 473–90.

Barwick, Linda, Bruce Birch, and Nicholas Evans. 'Iwaidja Jurtbirrk Songs: Bringing language and music together', *Australian Aboriginal Studies* 2 (2007): 6–34.

Barwick, Linda, and Allan Marett. 'Snapshots of Musical Life: The 1948 recordings', in *Exploring the Legacy of the 1948 Arnhem Land Expedition*, eds Martin Thomas and Margo Neale (Canberra: ANU E Press, 2011), 355–77.

Berndt, Ronald M. 'Ceremonial Exchange in Western Arnhem Land', *Southwestern Journal of Anthropology* 7:2 (1951): 156–76.

Berndt, Ronald M. *Australian Aboriginal Religion* (Leiden: E. J. Brill, 1974).

Berndt, Ronald M. *Love Songs of Arnhem Land* (Melbourne: T. Nelson, 1976).

Brown, Reuben. *Performance as Exchange: The role of western Arnhem Land song traditions in contemporary society* (PhD, Conservatorium of Music, The University of Sydney, 2014 forthcoming).

Deger, Jennifer. 'Imprinting on the Heart: Photography and contemporary Yolngu mournings', *Visual Anthropology* 21 (2008): 292–309.

Evans, Nicholas. *Bininj Gun-wok: A pan-dialectal grammar of Mayali, Kunwinjku and Kune*. 2 volumes (Canberra: Pacific Linguistics, 2003).

Fitzgerald, Jon, and Philip Hayward. 'At the Confluence: Slim Dusty and Australian country music', in *Outback and Urban: Australian country music*, ed. Philip Hayward (Gympie: AICM Press, 2003), 29–54.

Garde, Murray. 'The Language of *Kun-borrk* in Western Arnhem Land', *Musicology Australia* 28 (2006): 59–89.

Garde, Murray. 'Nakodjok Namanilakarr', *Bininj Gunwok* (blog), 27 June 2012, http://bininjgunwok.org.au/blog/page/3/.

Glaskin, Katie, Myrna Tonkinson, Yasmine Musharbash, and Victoria Burbank, eds. *Mortality, Mourning and Mortuary Practices in Indigenous Australia* (Surrey: Ashgate, 2008).

Keen, Ian. *Aboriginal Economy and Society: Australia at the threshold of colonisation* (South Melbourne: Oxford University Press, 2004).

Knopoff, Steven. 'Yuta Manikay: Juxtaposition of ancestral and contemporary elements in the performance of Yolngu clan songs', *Yearbook for Traditional Music* 24 (1992): 138–53

Magowan, Fiona. *Melodies of Mourning: Music and emotion in Northern Australia* (Crawley: University of Western Australia Press, 2007).

Marrala, Khaki et al. *Kindi Ngamin Nuwung? What Do I Call You? 'Ma!'* Vol. 1, (Jabiru: Iwaidja Inyman, 2008).

Marett, Allan. 'Ghostly Voices: Some observations on song-creation, ceremony and being in north western Australia', *Oceania* 71:1 (2000): 18–29.

Marett, Allan. *Songs, Dreamings, and Ghosts: The wangga of north Australia* (Middletown: Wesleyan University Press, 2005).

Marett, Allan, Linda Barwick, and Lysbeth Ford. *For the Sake of a Song: Wangga songmen and their repertories: The Indigenous music of Australia*, Book 2 (Sydney: Sydney University Press, 2013).

McKenzie, Kim. *Waiting for Harry* (Canberra: Australian Institute of Aboriginal Studies, 1980).

Morphy, Howard. *Journey to the Crocodile's Nest: An accompanying monograph to the film* Madarrpa funeral at Gurka'wuy (Canberra: Australian Institute of Aboriginal Studies, 1984).

Morphy, Howard, and Frances Morphy. 'Afterword: Demography and destiny', in *Mortality, Mourning and Mortuary Practices in Indigenous Australia*, eds Katie Glaskin, Myrna Tonkinson, Yasmine Musharbash and Victoria Burbank (Surrey: Ashgate, 2008), 209–15.

O'Keeffe, Isabel. 'Sung and Spoken: An analysis of two different versions of a Kun-Barlang love song', *Australian Aboriginal Studies* 2 (2007): 46–62.

O'Keeffe, Isabel. '*Kaddikkaddik Ka-Wokdjanganj "Kaddikkaddik* Spoke"': Language and music of the Kun-barlang *Kaddikkaddik* songs from western Arnhem Land', *Australian Journal of Linguistics* 30:1 (2010): 35–51.

Poignant, Roslyn, and Axel Poignant. *Encounter at Nagalarramba* (Canberra: National Library of Australia, 1996).

Reid, Janice. 'A Time to Live, a Time to Grieve: Patterns and processes of mourning among the Yolngu of Australia', *Culture, Medicine and Psychiatry* 3:4 (1979): 319–46.

Rose, Deborah B. *Dingo Makes Us Human: Life and land in an Australian Aboriginal culture* (Cambridge: Cambridge University Press, 2009).

Ross, Margaret Clunies, and Stephen A. Wild. 'Formal Performance: The relations of music, text and dance in Arnhem Land clan songs', *Ethnomusicology* 28:2 (1984): 209–35.

Spencer, Baldwin, Sir. *Native Tribes of the Northern Territory of Australia* (London: Macmillan, 1914).

Singer, Ruth. *Agreement in Mawng: Productive and lexicalised uses of agreement in an Australian language* (PhD, Department of Linguistics and Applied Linguistics, University of Melbourne, 2006).

Toner, P. G. 'Tropes of Longing and Belonging: Nostalgia and musical instruments in northeast Arnhem Land', *Yearbook for Traditional Music* 37 (2005): 1–24.

Tonkinson, Myrna. 'Solidarity in Shared Loss: Death-related observances among the Martu of the Western Desert', in *Mortality, Mourning and Mortuary Practices in Indigenous Australia*, eds Katie Glaskin et al. (Surrey: Ashgate, 2008).

Treloyn, Sally. 'Scotty Martin's *Jadmi Junba*: A song series from the Kimberley region of northwest Australia', *Oceania* 73:3 (2003): 208–20.

Treloyn, Sally. '"When Everybody There Together … Then I Call That One": Song order in the Kimberley', *Context* 32 (2007): 105–21.

Walker, Clinton. *Buried Country: The story of Aboriginal country music* (Sydney: Pluto Press, 2000).

Warner, Lloyd W. *A Black Civilization: A social study of an Australian tribe* (Gloucester: P. Smith, 1969).

8. Cross and Square: Variegation in the Transmission of Songs and Musical Styles Between the Kimberley and Daly Regions of Northern Australia

Sally Treloyn

Early in 2010 I heard for the first time a recording of a performance of *balga* songs made in 1974 in Port Keats (Wadeye). Intrigued to hear this performance of *balga*—a dance-song genre championed by language groups of the Kimberley region, but here being sung by people some hundreds of kilometres away in the Daly region—I was immediately struck by two songs that were very similar to two songs in the *balga* repertory of the Ngarinyin/Wunambal composer Scotty Martin.[1] Some months later I had the opportunity to listen to the recording in the company of Martin and other elder performers of Kimberley *balga* and *junba*.[2] Martin immediately recognised the two songs as very much like his own. How the songs came to be performed in Port Keats in 1974, less than five years after Martin composed them, however, was a mystery, and there was much discussion about who the singers, particularly the lead singer, could possibly be. Martin, himself an expert composer and singer of song styles of the Kimberley (including all types of *balga/junba* and *wolungarri*)[3] and the didjeridu-accompanied genres of the Daly (*wangga* and *lirrga*) provided an authoritative analysis of the songs: while the songs were indeed his and the entire repertory sounded Ngarinyin/ Wunambal, they were 'cross and square' and 'mixed up at the beginning'.

The chapters in this volume are concerned with the exchange and movement of records of culture through time, communities, and place. In the Kimberley and Daly regions of northern Australia, circulation via the sharing and adoption of songs, dance-songs and musical styles between neighbouring and distant groups permeates the social, ceremonial, linguistic and musical landscape. Ngarinyin elders have reported the movement of primarily vocal *balga/junba* repertories

---

1   A selection of these songs is presented in Linda Barwick and Scotty Martin, *Jadmi Junba by Nyalgodi Scotty Martin, Traditional Songman of the Dreamtime* (Sydney: Rouseabout Records, 2003), tracks 27–31.

2   There is substantial published research on the public Kimberley genre *junba*. The term *balga* is used in the east Kimberley to refer to *junba*, and elsewhere to delineate a subgenre of *junba* that uses string crosses and painted boards, also known as *jorrogorl* or *galinda*. It is distinguished from other subgenres of *junba*, including *jadmi* and *gulowada*.

3   *Wolungarri* is a ceremonial genre, performed annually in private settings.

beyond the Kimberley into the Daly since at least the 1950s, and genres such as *wangga* and *lirrga* have moved from the Daly into the Kimberley. *Djanba*, created in the early 1960s by composers in Port Keats (Wadeye) as a sister genre to *wangga* and *lirrga*,[4] presents a particularly interesting case: *djanba* composers drew on the musical style of the Kimberley *balga/junba* genre to create a new sounding genre;[5] the *djanba* genre was then traded back into the Kimberley.

Drawing on Nicholas Evans' description of the way in which small societies distinguish themselves from neighbouring and distant groups by a 'constructive fostering of variegation' in their languages,[6] Linda Barwick has considered the elements of *balga/junba* (from the Kimberley) and *wangga/lirrga* (from the Daly) in *djanba*. Through this analysis, Barwick shows how the new variegated Kimberley/Daly *djanba* song form supported the Port Keats tripartite ceremonial complex and enhanced social cohesion in the new social world of the mission community in the 1960s. Barwick found that, while the creators of *djanba* drew on the musical style of *balga/junba,* they did so within the musical framework of the *lirrga* (and *wangga*) traditions with which they and their Port Keats ceremonial partners were familiar. In doing so, Barwick showed that the *djanba*-holding clans and composer/performers 'consciously differentiated' their music, as well as their linguistic, cultural and geographical identities, from those of *lirrga*- and *wangga*-performing clans within or around Port Keats.[7] Akin to the 'intentional hybridizations' described by Sarah Weiss,[8] the conscious variegation of *balga/junba* and *wangga/lirrga* within *djanba* involves a selection and deliberate uptake of aspects of a musical style or song of an 'other' and juxtaposition or overlaying of these with aspects of one's own musical style. In the case of *djanba*, the creators consciously designed a uniquely variegated *wangga/lirrga:balga/junba* dance-song genre in order to articulate something of their own identity in relation to but also distinct from those of their *wangga*-holding and *lirrga*-holding neighbours.[9]

Barwick's analysis describes the role of conscious and intentional variegation in the development of the new *djanba* musical style in Port Keats based on a pre-existing one from the Kimberley. This chapter will investigate the occurrence

---

4   Linda Barwick, 'Musical Form and Style in Murriny Patha *Djanba* Songs at Wadeye (Northern Territory, Australia)', in *Analytical and Cross-Cultural Studies in World Music*, eds Michael Tenzer and John Roeder (New York: Oxford University Press, 2011), 316–54.

5   See also Allan Marett, *Songs, Dreamings, and Ghosts: The wangga of north Australia* (Middletown: Wesleyan University Press, 2005), 25.

6   Nicholas Evans, *Dying Words: Endangered languages and what they have to tell us* (Chichester: Wiley-Blackwell, 2010), 14.

7   Barwick, 'Musical Form and Style in Murriny Patha *Djanba* Songs at Wadeye (Northern Territory, Australia)', 348.

8   Sarah Weiss, 'Permeable Boundaries: Hybridity, music, and the reception of Robert Wilson's "I La Galigo"', *Ethnomusicology* 52:2 (2008): 203–38.

9   Barwick, *Musical Form and Style in Murriny Patha Djanba Songs at Wadeye* (Northern Territory, Australia)', 48.

and role of variegation in the aforementioned *balga* performance in Port Keats recorded by Michael Walsh in 1974.[10] I also consider the reactions of Kimberley *balga/junba* experts to the sound of *djanba* and to the Port Keats *balga*. Taking Martin's analysis of the *balga* performance as 'cross and square' as an entry point, I consider evidence that a kind of 'conscious variegation', grounded in an enduring *Larlan* (Dreaming) practice of articulating 'difference against a background of similarity' in social relationships,[11] is invoked when listening to and discussing the musical styles of linguistically, culturally and geographically distant, but connected groups. The chapter investigates the role of variegation in both the uptake of songs and styles transmitted from a neighbouring region, and in the reception of variegated songs and styles back in their source communities. The chapter considers what 'cross and square' means in relation to the transmission of songs from person to person in the Kimberley and in Port Keats (Wadeye) as well as to the geographies, cosmologies, and histories through which the songs have travelled; and how this 'cross and square' explanation of song transmission might also apply to the reception of songs heard across these boundaries, either via person-to-person sharing and innovation, or via legacy recordings.

The chapter is in three parts, beginning in Part One with an overview of the sharing and transmission of *balga/junba* repertories within and beyond the Kimberley, the trade of *wangga* and *lirrga* songs from Port Keats into the Kimberley, and an account of the characterisation (by expert Kimberley *balga*, *wangga* and *lirrga* singers) of traded *djanba* and *balga* musical styles and songs as variegated, same but different and, in the case of *balga*, 'cross and square'. Parts Two and Three consider how this located variegation is manifested in the 1974 Port Keats *balga* performance, through an analysis of its musical features in relation to those of Kimberley *balga*, and specifically those displayed in Martin's *balga* repertory. Using the analysis of this recording by Scotty Martin as like Kimberley *balga* but 'cross and square', the chapter will examine the role of variegation in the transmission of songs and styles, and their reception across cultures, time, languages, and geographical space.

---

10   A4357A and A4357B, AIATSIS, Canberra.

11   Anthony Redmond, *Rulug Wayirri: Moving kin and country in the northern Kimberley* (PhD, University of Sydney, 2001), 136.

Part One—Transmission of Songs and Styles in and between the Kimberley and Daly Region

Kimberley and to the Daly

In the Kimberley, the *balga/junba* genre originates with the Wurnan, a network of trade paths and an ethos of sharing between independent but complementary individual and community partners. Wurnan transactions reaffirm identities in relation to family, Country, ancestors, and changing social and economic landscapes.[12] Redmond has explained how Wurnan transactions and journeys, such as these, are founded in the 'collectivising' and 'differentiating' actions of the ancestral moiety heroes, Wodoi (the Spotted Nightjar) and Jun.gun (the Owlet Nightjar). As Redmond argues, continual, mutually provoked fights between Wodoi and Jun.gun laid the foundation for relationships between individuals, mother and child, and clans. When Wodoi and Jun.gun articulated shared and collective but differentiated identities, they set a foundational pattern of establishing relationships through assertion of 'difference against a background of similarity'. Redmond explains that this 'is something which requires continuous human interaction and effort' and must be 'socially created to elicit relationships'.[13] The pattern set down by Wodoi and Jun.gun continues to this day in exogamous marriage, indirect matrilineality, and the sharing of resources, including *balga/junba* repertories, between clans of opposite moieties according to Wurnan.[14] In these transactions, identities and relationships between individuals, generations, and clans, are established, negotiated and reaffirmed.

Balga/junba repertories, including songs, dances, and associated paraphernalia, have been transmitted between clan groups and communities, and across cultural and linguistic boundaries guided by Wurnan since its formation in the *Larlan*.[15] According to elder Ngarinyin people, this movement of Wurnan items, including *balga/junba*, to Port Keats (Wadeye) to the north-east was

---

12   Redmond, *Rulug Wayirri*; Anthony Redmond, 'Places That Move', in *Emplaced Myth: Space, narrative, and knowledge in Aboriginal Australasia and Papua New Guinea*, eds Alan Rumsey and J. F. Weiner (USA: University of Hawai'i Press, 2001), 120–38; Sally Treloyn, *Songs That Pull: Jadmi Junba from the Kimberley region of northwest Australia* (PhD, University of Sydney, 2006); Anthony Redmond, 'Tracking Wurnan: Transformations in the trade and exchange of resources in the northern Kimberley', in *Indigenous Participation in Australian Economies II: Historical engagements and current enterprises,* eds Natasha Fijn, Ian Keen, Christopher Lloyd and Michael Pickering (Canberra: ANU E Press, 2012), 57–72; Anthony Redmond and Fiona Skyring, 'Exchange and Appropriation: The Wurnan economy and Aboriginal land and labour at Karunjie Station, north-western Australia', in *Indigenous Participation in Australian Economies: Historical and anthropological perspectives*, ed. Ian Keen (Canberra: ANU E Press, 2010), 73–90.

13   Redmond, *Rulug Wayirri,* 136–8.

14   Redmond, *Rulug Wayirri*; Redmond, 'Places That Move'; Treloyn, *Songs That Pull.*

15   A *balga* repertory composed by the Worrorra man Alan Balbangu on the western coast of the Kimberley in the 1930s, for example, was traded to Ngarinyin people and then on to the far east and north-east Kimberley, as far as Legune Station (home of a large expatriate Garamau (Murrinhpatha) population from the Daly region) and possibly even further to Port Keats (Wadeye). Treloyn, *Songs That Pull*, 48–50.

not uncommon. A handful of recordings provide a record of the emergence of Kimberley *balga/junba* as a popular style through the late-1940s to 1970s amongst singers from Port Keats, who performed the genre both there and further afield. In 1948, Colin Simpson recorded *balga* performed by a group of people from Port Keats at Delissaville (now Belyuen); in 1957, W. E. H. Stanner recorded several different groups singing *balga* at Daly River; in 1962, Alice Moyle recorded *balga* at the Darwin Eisteddfod.[16] By far the most substantial recording of the performance of *balga* in Port Keats is that recorded by Michael Walsh in 1974. Walsh's recording comprises some twenty-one distinct songs, many of which are performed multiple times, led (most likely)[17] by Jaminjung speaker Frank Jinjair, a resident of Port Keats. While the song items contained in the earlier recordings clearly exhibit some distinctive elements of *balga/junba* musical style,[18] the Walsh recordings provide the first evidence that suggests that particular, identifiable songs that were composed in the Kimberley, by Kimberley composers, were incorporated into repertories in Port Keats. By the time Barwick and Marett were conducting research in Port Keats (Wadeye) in the 1980s there was no *balga* being performed.[19]

Daly to the Kimberley

The trade and sharing of songs and song styles has also occurred in the other direction, from Port Keats (Wadeye) into the Kimberley. The movement of *wangga* and *lirrga* songs into the east Kimberley and across into the west Kimberley has been documented in a range of sources. These include numerous references to the movement of *wangga* into the east Kimberley by Jack Sullivan (Miriwung), Grant Ngabidj (Gadgerong) and Peter Ngunung (Garamau);[20] Allan Marett's description of the trade of *wangga* into the Kimberley over 'many decades'[21] and his detailed analysis of the textual and melodic features of *wangga* and *lirrga* songs performed by Button Jones in the north-east Kimberley, Scotty Martin in the north-central Kimberley, and Jack Dann in the west Kimberley; as well as descriptions of *wangga* and *lirrga* spreading into the Kimberley via Wurnan

---

16   Linda Barwick and Allan Marett, 'Aural Snapshots of Musical Life: Simpson's 1948 Recordings', in *Exploring the Legacy of the 1948 Arnhem Land Expedition*, eds Martin Thomas and Margo Neale (Canberra: ANU E Press, 2011), 355–75. Barwick, 'Musical Form and Style in Murriny Patha *Djanba* Songs at Wadeye (Northern Territory, Australia)'.

17   Michael Walsh, personal communication, 2 March 2010.

18   Barwick and Marett, 'Aural Snapshots of Musical Life'.

19   Linda Barwick, personal communication, 5 February 2013.

20   Bruce Shaw, *Countrymen: The life histories of four Aboriginal men* (Canberra: Australian Institute of Aboriginal Studies, 1986); Bruce Shaw, *My Country of the Pelican Dreaming: The life of an Australian Aborigine of the Gadjerong, Grant Ngabidj, 1904–1977* (Canberra: Australian Institute of Aboriginal Studies, 1981); Bruce Shaw, *When the Dust Come in Between: Aboriginal viewpoints in the east Kimberley prior to 1982* (Canberra: Aboriginal Studies Press, 1992); *Banggaiyerri: The story of Jack Sullivan* (Canberra: Australian Institute of Aboriginal Studies, 1983).

21   Marett, *Songs, Dreamings, and Ghosts*, 26.

and stock routes provided by elder men and women in the course of my own research. It is also likely that *wangga/lirrga* moved to the Kimberley via the Murrinhpatha diaspora living in Kununurra and the east Kimberley, as well as via sea routes linking Port Keats to the east Kimberley, possibly via ports at Victoria River and Wyndham.[22] Substantial recordings of *wangga* and *lirrga* in the Kimberley have been made by me between 2000 and 2002, and earlier in 1963 by Peter Lucich, Alice Moyle in 1968 and Lesley Reilly between 1973 and 1981. To this day, *wangga/lirrga* is a common and popular form of dance-song across the Kimberley, performed at almost all public festivals and other informal events, as well as in ceremonial contexts.[23]

Djanba: The Kimberley to Port Keats to the Kimberley

One of the most intriguing cases of the transmission of songs between the Kimberley and the Daly region is presented by the genre of *djanba*. Invented in Port Keats in around 1960 by Murrinhpatha man Robert Dungoi Kolumboort[24] as the third genre in a tripartite ceremonial complex to enhance social cohesion in the new community,[25] the musical style of *djanba* was based on that of Kimberley *balga/junba*.[26]

Indeed, the *balga/junba*-like sound of *djanba* has been observed by scholars and singers alike.[27] Many aspects of *djanba* sound like *balga/junba*: there is substantial repetition of text phrases; song texts are performed isorhythmically and are accompanied by a regular percussion accompaniment of clapsticks and handclapping; and melodic settings consist of a series of descents followed by a period of level tonic movement.[28] Together, the combination of melody, text and rhythm give the overall impression of a cyclical musical style that places *djanba* and *balga/junba*, along with another genre from Wadeye called *malgarrin*,[29]

---

22   Michael Walsh, personal communication, 30 March 2011.

23   While elder performers differentiate *wangga* from *lirrga*, in the west Kimberley generally both are mixed in performances, collectively referred to as 'wangga'. A distinction between *wangga* and *lirrga* appears to be retained in the east.

24   Barwick, 'Musical Form and Style in Murriny Patha *Djanba* Songs at Wadeye (Northern Territory, Australia)'.

25   See also Marett, *Songs, Dreamings, and Ghosts*.

26   The archetypical Centralian stylistic elements of *balga/junba* (such as the absence of didjeridu, substantial repetition of text, the cyclical treatment of melody and isorhythmic texts, and the use of a regular percussion accompaniment), provided a distinct contrast to the northern musical conventions of the other two genres in the complex, *wangga* and *lirrga* (use of the didjeridu, clearly strophic treatment of melody and text, and non-isorhythmic setting of texts).

27   Alberto Furlan, *Songs of Continuity and Change: The reproduction of Aboriginal culture through traditional and popular music* (PhD, University of Sydney, 2005); Marett, *Songs, Dreamings, and Ghosts*; Barwick, 'Musical Form and Style in Murriny Patha *Djanba* Songs at Wadeye (Northern Territory, Australia)'.

28   See also Barwick, 'Musical Form and Style in Murriny Patha *Djanba* Songs at Wadeye (Northern Territory, Australia)'.

29   Murriny Patha Song Project, 'Malgarrin: Australian Research Discovery Project', accessed 3 February 2013, http://azoulay.arts.usyd.edu.au/mpsong/songs/songs/malgarrin.html.

at one end of a continuum of musical style reaching to the south into central Australia.[30] In 2002, when discussing the various references to *djanba* that appear in Bruce Shaw's east Kimberley oral histories with three senior Ngarinyin *balga/junba* experts, one of the most senior knowledgeable *balga/junba* singers in the Kimberley commented to me: 'He like a *jorrogorl* too that *djanba*.'[31] 'Yo', replied another.

Clearly *balga/junba*, both its style and particular songs, has played a significant role in the development of *djanba* in Port Keats (Wadeye).[32] At the same time, *djanba* is also clearly marked as a northern genre, with much in common with its ceremonial partners *wangga* and *lirrga*: its texts and melodies, while containing cyclical material, are variable and strophic; and the rhythmic setting of texts is variable rather than isorhythmic.[33] In the continuation of my 2002 discussion with the Kimberley *balga/junba* experts, the singers linked *balga/junba* and *wangga/lirrga* explicitly:

Singer 1: But he pretty fast longa *garn.bag* [clapsticks], *manamana-ngarri* [quick tempo].

Singer 2: Yuwe [Yes].

ST [Sally Treloyn]: *Manamana-ngarri gan.barg* [quick clapsticks]?

Singer 1: Mm [Yes], pretty fast. [demonstrates the quick, interlocked rhythmic pattern performed by two pairs of clapsticks in *wangga/lirrga*, and ends with a vocalisation common at the end of *wangga*].

ST: How do those *gan.barg* go? Like in *wangga*?

Singer 2: Yah.

Singer 1: [Demonstrates the distinctive *wangga* pattern again] Like a horse galloping.

---

30 Sally Treloyn, 'Songs That Pull: Composition/performance through musical analysis', *Context: Journal of music research* 31 (2006): 151–64.

31 As noted above, *jorrogorl* is an alternative name for *balga* used by some Ngarinyin people.

32 In addition to adopting elements of the musical style of *balga/junba*, there is explicit reference to particular Kimberley *balga/junba* songs in the Port Keats *djanba* corpus and in the glosses provided by the respective performers of these songs, suggesting that particular Kimberley repertories may have been key to the development of the new genre. For example, Flora Walkerbier's Ngarinyin *balga/junba* songs 'Iliji' (s05) and 'Wunbarowa' (s12), Aeroplane Nungulngunda's *balga* song 'mulala/Iliji' (s01), and Scotty Martin's *balga* song 'Wunbara' (s07), inform a *djanba* song composed by Robert Kolumboort 'Yilidji'. See PARADISEC, 'Wadeye Song Database', http://sydney.edu.au/arts/indigenous_song/wadeye/songtexts/169, Djanba000. Full texts of the Kimberley *balga/junba* songs can be found in Treloyn, *Songs That Pull*.

33 Barwick, 'Musical Form and Style in Murriny Patha *Djanba* Songs at Wadeye (Northern Territory, Australia)'.

A third expert singer then quietly sang a *djanba* song.[34] 'That the *djanba* now', explained Singer 1. 'That's it. Yo', confirmed Singer 2.[35]

Interested to elicit more detailed perspectives of expert Kimberley *balga/junba* singers on the sound of *djanba*, in 2010 I played a recording of Philip Pannikin Manbi and Button Jones singing *djanba*—recorded by Allan Marett in Kununurra[36] in 1998—to two Ngarinyin *balga/junba* experts and a Miriwung elder who was also an expert *wangga* singer and a countryman of the singers heard in the recording. Following a revealing question by one Ngarinyin expert, '*wangga?*', the second Ngarinyin expert and his Miriwung colleague explain that *djanba* is like *wangga* but different, marked by the absence of didjeridu. They go on to explain that *djanba* is also like *balga/junba* but different, marked by a quick *wangga/lirrga* stick pattern, and distinctive *wangga* dance style:

Ngarinyin singer [NS] 1: *Wangga?*

Ngarinyin singer [NS] 2: *Djanba.*

Miriwung singer [MS]: *Djanba.*

NS1: Ah.

NS2: He like a *wangga* too.

MS: He like a *wangga*. He different.

NS1: Ah.

Sally Treloyn [ST]: Like *wangga* with no didjeridu eh?

NS2: Hm. But this one he got nothing. He don't have didjeridu.

MS: That's the Pannikin now, they bin call him 'Djanba' then. Djanba himself, yeah, two bala [Button Jones and Pannikin Manbi] here singing.

ST: Do you think this sounds like *junba* at all? Does this sound more like *junba* or more like *wangga?*

NS2: Yeah, like a, he like a *junba.*

MS: He like a *junba.*

---

34 Barwick later identified this song as one composed by Philip Pannikin Manbi, appearing as Djanba066 in the Murriny Patha Song Database (personal communication, March 2010). See PARADISEC, 'Wadeye Song Database', http://sydney.edu.au/arts/indigenous_song/wadeye/songtexts/204.
35 Names have been omitted due to cultural sensitivities.
36 Kununurra *thanpa* (*djanba*) songs performed by Pannikin Manbi and Button Jones, recorded by Allan Marett, 3 September 1998 at Kununurra, WA (A16946-A16981, AIATSIS, Canberra).

NS2: [But] they never put it that way. Some *djanba* proper fast, people got to dance real fast too. [MS laughs]. [Listening to the recording] They gonna start soon, I think, that quick one.

[We listen, until sticks change from a slow pattern found in both *balga/junba* and *wangga*, to a quick pattern found in *wangga*]

NS2: There now. Quick one now. … They dance like a *wangga* too.

MS: Hm.

…

NS2: Ke! [NS2 joins in the singing at the end of the song] [MS laughs]

Djanba is an intriguing variegated form marked by both Kimberley *balga/junba* style and songs brought to the Daly via the Wurnan, and the pre-existing Daly styles, *wangga* and *lirrga*, that partner *djanba* in ceremony.

In her detailed discussion of the relationship between *djanba* and *lirrga*, Barwick explains the musical influences in *djanba* style as an example of what Nicholas Evans has described in relation to languages of small, isolated societies as a 'constructive fostering of variegation'.[37] Musical style is one of a number of ways in which *djanba* and *lirrga* are 'consciously differentiated by their creators', the others being dance and body paint designs, and use of language and references to place, ancestors and so on, in song texts.[38] Barwick makes the point that the *djanba* genre 'needs to be different enough from its sister repertories *wangga* and *lirrga* to allow it to be instantly recognisable from a distance, as the group approaches the ceremonial ground'. At the same time, Barwick continues, *djanba* music and dance needs to be similar in structure to *wangga* and *lirrga* so that ceremonial actions common to all three genres can be conducted.[39]

The responses of Kimberley *balga/junba* experts to the sound of *djanba* suggest that a similar 'conscious' and 'constructive fostering of variegation' is at work in the act of listening to and recalling the sound of *djanba* in the Kimberley. *Djanba* is heard as 'like a *jorrogorl* [*balga*]' but different, and 'like a *wangga*' but different. There is a recognition of variegation, similarity and difference in musical style that is part of a broader social and ceremonial complex, previously dominated by *balga/junba* and *wolungarri*, and into which *wangga/lirrga* then

---

37 Evans, *Dying Words*; Barwick, 'Musical Form and Style in Murriny Patha *Djanba* Songs at Wadeye (Northern Territory, Australia)', 349.
38 Barwick, 'Musical Form and Style in Murriny Patha *Djanba* Songs at Wadeye (Northern Territory, Australia)', 348.
39 Barwick, 'Musical Form and Style in Murriny Patha *Djanba* Songs at Wadeye (Northern Territory, Australia)', 349.

djanba entered. A great deal more is yet to be understood about the movement and role of *djanba* and *wangga/lirrga* in the Kimberley. Little is known about the cultural and ceremonial role that *djanba* took on in the Kimberley, other than that it arrived with the Wurnan into the east Kimberley and that it was performed by people from Kununurra in the north-east, including by Pannikin Manbi and Button Jones, and at Auvergne Station[40] and Karunjie station in the east.[41] Whether it was used as an alternative to *wolungarri* and *wangga* in initiation ceremonies, as it is to *wangga* and *lirrga* in Port Keats, or whether it was simply used as Wurnan trade item and in informal contexts is not known at present.

We do know that *djanba* was introduced into the Kimberley via the Wurnan,[42] possibly via both sea and overland routes. We can also imagine that it was likely a part of an 'efflorescence' of Wurnan ceremonial activity in the Kimberley, particularly Karunjie Station, in the 1960s and 1970s as Aboriginal station workers drew on both increased ritual exchanges and a new cash economy to negotiate the new relationships, economic and social structures imposed by the pastoral industry.[43] Insofar as the sharing of *balga/junba* and *djanba* on the Wurnan was partly done to forge and maintain relationships with the Daly region Murrinhpatha peoples, increasingly residing and working in the north-east Kimberley, the descriptions by *balga/junba* singers of *djanba* in the Kimberley as 'like a *jorrogorl*' but different, and 'like *wangga*, but different', likely spring from the mode of social reproduction of asserting 'difference against a background of similarity', founded in the ancestral actions of Wodoi and Jun.gun, the Wurnan and guiding relational and social interaction with closely and more distantly related groups. There is a bedrock identification of shared musical style and organisation when the Kimberley experts observe the *djanba* style: 'He like a *jorrogorl*', 'He like a *wangga*'. But in each case there is also recognition of difference. The case of *djanba* therefore reveals much about composers' uses of variegation to adopt and adapt a musical style to a pre-existing social and ceremonial context, as well as about listeners' attention to variegation to foreground what is familiar and what is unfamiliar, what is the same but different, in the musical styles of distant language groups with which they have ceremonial, and increasing social and economic contact.

A performance of songs in Port Keats (Wadeye) that are identified by the performers as *balga* provides us with further insight into the role of variegation in the transmission and reception of musical styles and songs across cultures, languages, time and space.

---

40   Alice Moyle recorded people from Auvergne Station (led by Barney Munggin, a resident at Daly River) at the Darwin Eisteddfod in 1963 performing *djanba* and *balga* together.

41   Nugget Gudurr Tataya (dec.), personal communication, date unknown 2010.

42   Shaw, *When the Dust Come in Between*, 51.

43   Redmond and Skyring, 'Exchange and Appropriation', 87.

'Cross and Square': Kimberley Responses to Port Keats *Balga*

It is clear that two songs in Walsh's 1974 Port Keats *balga* recording are based on two songs in Scotty Martin's *balga* repertory, the texts of which are set out here along with glosses provided by the composer.[44] Sketches of the Port Keats versions are also provided.

Scotty Martin's Bulgumirri (36SM-s06)		
Text	*Bulgumirri wona*	*Borangala gamarangerri*
Gloss	From Bulgumirri* *House Roof Hill	'Oh, that bloke he got to that place Borangala* already', one agula said * Marshland area near Wyndham
Port Keats version PKBalga-s09	*Pulkumirri jana/jalya*	*Darrarru ?* ...
Scotty Martin's Jilinya (36SM-s08)		
Text	*Jilinya mangalaluma*	*winjawurru badi bindi gala lemburr badi bindi*
Gloss	[Someone is saying] 'She [the Jilinya] came out here already'	She came out when that sun [lemburr] went down
Port Keats version PKBalga-s06	*Jilinya mangalaluma*	*winjawurru badi bindi gala lemburr badi bindi*

Figure 1: Two *balga* songs composed by Scotty Nyalgodi Martin c. 1972–1974 and Port Keats versions.[45]

During a session of listening by Martin and other *balga* singers and dancers in the Dodnun community in the north-central Kimberley, Martin immediately recognised both songs—PKBalga-s09 (Bulgumirri (36SM-s06)) and PKBalga-s06 (Jilinya (36SM-s08))—as very much like his own. A number of other songs were also identified as containing text and musical material from other Ngarinyin or Wunambal *balga* repertories. As described in the introduction to the chapter, Martin, who is an expert composer and singer of song styles of both the Kimberley (including *balga-type junba*, *jadmi-type junba*, and *wolungarri*) and

---

44   The glosses are drawn from a number of 'barra-barra' or talking sessions with Martin, Maisie Jodba, and other senior performers of the songs, conducted by Linda Barwick in 1999, and the author in 2001, 2002, and 2010. These sessions, structured around the transcription and elicitation of song texts (which do not change from performance to performance), their meaning, and any associated information about the song or its context that the participants wished to share, were recorded and then transcribed.

45   Each repertory in the *balga/junba* corpus has been assigned a unique identifier, consisting of a number and the composer's initials. See Treloyn, *Songs That Pull*. Martin's *jorrogorl balga* repertory is assigned the prefix 36SM. Songs in the Port Keats performance (recorded by Michael Walsh, 1974, AIATSIS archive number A4357A and A4357B) are given the prefix 'PKBalga'. Each unique song in a repertory is numbered s01, s02, and so on.

Port Keats (*wangga* and *lirrga*), provided an authoritative analysis of the songs: while the songs were indeed his and the entire repertory sounded Ngarinyin, they were 'cross and square' and 'mixed up at the beginning'.

I began by introducing Barwick's analysis that *djanba* presents a uniquely variegated *wangga/lirrga:balga/junba* dance-song genre, consciously designed in the 1960s to mark a distinctive identity within the ceremonial and cultural context of Port Keats. The testimony of Kimberley singers has also demonstrated that variegation of *balga/junba* and *wangga/lirrga* in *djanba* is heard and noted by singers, and that this variegation fits within a broader social framework of managing and fostering new and changing relationships across the geographical, cultural, social, economic, and linguistic reach of Wurnan. In the second and third parts of the chapter I take a closer look at the musical form of Kimberley *balga* and the Port Keats *balga*, and consider what Martin's analysis of the latter as 'cross and square' tells us about musical variegation in more direct transmissions of songs and a musical style.

Part Two—Kimberley *Balga* in the Daly: Variegated Musical Style

In the Kimberley, the terms '*balga*' and '*junba*' denote a tradition of dance-song that enacts relationships between living people, the spirits of their deceased relatives, their hereditary Country, and their stories and ancestral foundational events.[46] By articulating these relationships in song and dance, and in Wurnan trade, *balga/junba* conception stories, songs and dances inscribe and are inscribed with the physical, spiritual, personal, social and economic landscape. Since 1999, approximately 340 Kimberley *balga/junba* songs, encompassing thirty-one repertories, have been recorded or documented.[47] At present Scotty Martin, pictured in Figure 2, is one of only two living composers of *balga/junba*. Martin has received in dream and composed two repertories (comprising at least forty-six songs), one a *jorrogorl balga* and the other a *jadmi junba* (repertories 36SM and 11SM, respectively).

While the *jadmi* style of *junba* has been described and analysed at length, little attention has been paid to the *balga/junba* style. As a master singer and composer, still active in leading and teaching today, Martin's performances and explanations of his repertory provide an exemplary record of this style to use as

---

46   See Brown, this volume, for a discussion of a repertory that has a similar function in western Arnhem Land.

47   These recordings (made by the author, Barwick and others), and a handful of archival recordings dating from the 1960s–1990s provide the sample for the account of *balga* musical style upon which the description and analysis in this chapter is based.

a basis for such a description. The analysis presented here is therefore based on a sample of thirty-one song performances, consisting of multiple performances of twelve distinct songs that make up the current recorded corpus of Martin's *balga*, supported by the larger corpus of *balga/junba* songs, including those referred to as *galinda* and *jorrogorl*.[48]

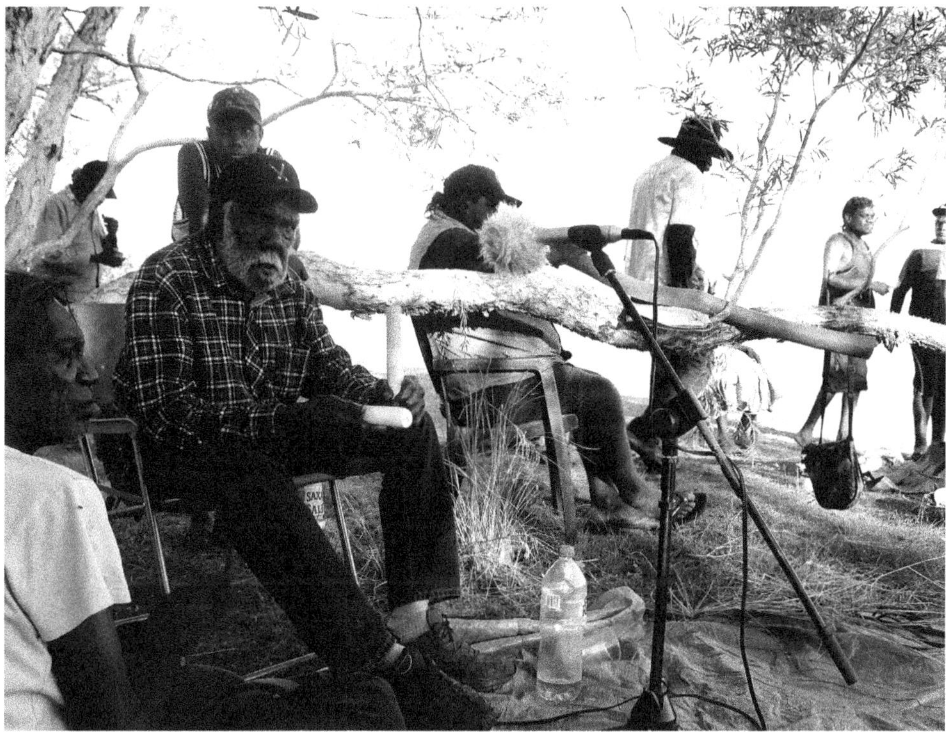

Figure 2: Scotty Nyalgodi Martin: master *junba* (*balga* and *jadmi*) and *wangga/lirrga* composer and singer.

Source: Photograph by Sally Treloyn, 7 July 2014.

Martin composed his *balga* in two sets. The first of these, consisting of seven songs (referred to here as 36SM-s06–36SM-s12), was composed by Martin between 1972 and 1974 when he was shown them by the spirit of his mother's deceased father in dreams. I recorded this early set of songs in March 2002. A later, second set, consisting of a further five songs (36SM-s01–36SM-s05), was composed in the early-to-mid-1990s and was recorded by Linda Barwick at Bijili near Dodnun in May 1999.[49]

---

48   The terms *'galinda'* and *'jorrogorl'* are used to refer to *balga/junba* in Worrorra and Ungarinyin languages, respectively.

49   These were later released by Martin on CD. Barwick and Martin, *Jadmi Junba*, tracks 27–31.

Walsh's 1974 Port Keats *balga* recording includes thirty-three distinct song items. Twenty-one distinct songs—here labelled PKBalga-s01, PKBalga-s02, and so on—are included in the performance. Many are audibly accompanied by dance. From my first hearing of this recording in 2010, it was very clear that the songs shared the basic characteristics of the Kimberley *balga/junba* style:

1. the melodic contour is reminiscent of the Kimberley *balga/junba* melodic contour;

2. texts are performed cyclically and isorhythmically;

3. the cycling of the text is interrupted and recommenced at melodic cycle boundaries;

4. the singing is accompanied by a regular percussion accompaniment consisting of clapsticks and clapping that is paused and restarted at regular intervals throughout each song performance.

Indeed, as described above, when Kimberley *balga/junba* experts, including Martin, listened to the Port Keats recording, the consensus was that the songs by and large sounded like Ngarinyin *balga*. Furthermore, Martin made a clear analytical statement that the songs that were most like his—Bulgumirri (PKBalga-s09/36SM-s06) and Jilinya (PKBalga-s06/36SM-s08)—were 'cross and square' and 'mixed up at the beginning'.

A closer look at the performances reveals evidence of variegation of musical style, distinguishing the musical style of the Port Keats songs from that of Kimberley *balga/junba*, and aligning it with other Daly genres such as *wangga/lirrga* and *djanba*. This variegation occurs on multiple levels of the organisation of the repertory, from song order to melody, text and rhythm, and how these are combined.

Song Order

As is common throughout the Kimberley *balga/junba* corpus, each song in the Port Keats *balga* performance is repeated once or twice, before moving on to the next. Marking a distinct contrast to danced Kimberley performances, there is very little repetition of songs otherwise. The deployment of songs in Kimberley *balga/junba* performances features the repeated reiteration of one or sometimes two songs known as *galanba* (also known as *guroguro* or *warami*), 'warm up' songs. These songs have the purpose of drawing the singers, dancers and audience to the performance space in the lead up to the danced performance. Throughout the performance these songs, which are not accompanied by dance, are returned to and repeated, giving the dancers the opportunity to prepare for the next dance and drawing the dancers onto the dance ground.[50] By contrast, in the Port Keats *balga* performance almost all songs are introduced one after the other. In the sample of twenty-one songs, only one song is returned to following its introduction. While this contrasts the Kimberley style, it clearly flows on from the conventional series-based, juxtaposition-orientated format of other Daly genres, such as *lirrga*.[51]

Melody

Melodic Cycles

Both Martin's *balga* and the Port Keats *balga* songs are performed with a basic melodic contour that consists of a series of two or more melodic cycles. Each melodic cycle features a long descent section led by the song leader sometimes with other men singers.[52] This is often followed by an extended period of level movement on a tonic pitch (the lowest pitch of the melody contour) carried by women singers, referred to here as the tonic section.[53] The descent section incorporates in both cases small reiterative ascents and descents to a third or second above the tonic pitch.

As set out in Figure 3, in both repertories, melodic cycles take one of two forms, depending on the use or non-use of the tonic section:

1. a 'Short' form that consists primarily of the descent section with either no or just a very short section of level tonic movement;

2. a 'Long' form that consists of the descent section, followed by the tonic section that may be as long or longer than the descent section.[54]

In both repertories, 'Short' and 'Long' melodic cycles are deployed in the performance of each song in one of two ways. Songs are performed with either a series of 'Long' cycles only (||: Long :||); or alternating 'Short' and 'Long' cycles, beginning with a 'Short' cycle (||: Short + Long :||).

---

50   Sally Treloyn, '"When Everybody There Together … Then I Call That One": Song order in the Kimberley', *Context: Journal of music research* 32 (2007): 105–21

51   Linda Barwick, `Marri Ngarr Lirrga Songs: A musicological analysis of song pairs in performance', *Musicology Australia* 28:1 (2005): 1 -25.

52   This moves through three registers or *langgan* 'throats', referred to in Ungarinyin as *arrungun* (high), *belaga* (middle) and *alya* (low) registers. See Treloyn, *Songs That Pull*.

53   This tonic section corresponds to the *biyobiyo* 'pulling' section previously described for *jadmi junba*. See Treloyn, *Songs That Pull,* and Treloyn, 'Songs That Pull'.

54   Note that these are not to be confused with 'Short' (Type II) and 'Long' (Type I) descents in *jadmi* style *junba* which are differentiated from each other on the basis of the starting pitch (short descents commencing a third lower than long descents). See Sally Treloyn, 'Scotty Martin's *Jadmi Junba*: A song series from the Kimberley region of northwest Australia', *Oceania* 73:3 (2003): 208–20; Treloyn, *Songs That Pull.*

In the sample of Martin's *balga* and the Port Keat's *balga*, every time a song is performed it is performed with the same pattern of deployment, as set out in Figure 4.

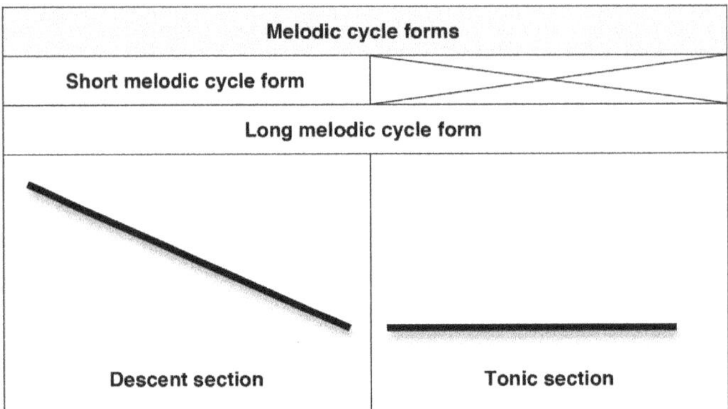

Figure 3: Melodic cycle forms in Martin's *balga* and the Port Keats *balga*.

Melodic cycle contour	Song	Proportion of repertory
Scotty Martin's balga		
||: Short + Long :||	s01, s02, s03, s04, s05, s06, s09, s10	8/12 (66%)
||: Long :||	s07, s08, s11, s12	4/12 (33%)
Port Keats balga		
||: Short + Long :||	s06, s08, s09, s10, s11, s12, s13, s14, s15, s16, s17, s18, s19, s20, s21	15/20*(75%)
||: Long :||	s02, s03, s04, s05, s07	5/20 (25%)

Figure 4: Song item melodic contour: deployment of Short and Long melodic cycles in Martin's *balga* and the Port Keats *balga*.

* Only twenty of the twenty-one songs are included as only a short excerpt of one song (s01) is included in the Walsh recording and melodic contour cannot be determined.

While \|\|: Short + Long :\|\| and \|\|: Long :\|\| melodic cycle contours are deployed in relatively similar proportions across both repertoires (66%:33% in Martin's *balga*, and 75%:25% in the Port Keats sample) the melodic contours of repertories diverge significantly when it comes to the number of melodic cycles that are used in each song performance. In Martin's *balga* a high proportion of song performances comprise an even number of melodic cycles (two, four, six, and so on). This is the case in all but two of the thirty-one items in the sample of Martin's songs and marks a striking contrast to *jadmi*-type *junba* repertories, which show a preference for odd numbered descents (three, five, seven, and so on). However, in the Port Keats sample, while all of the | |: Short + Long :| | form songs are (logically) performed with an even number of descents, all but one of the five songs with the | |: Long :| | form are performed with just three cycles.[55]

Melodic Sections

Looking more closely at the internal contour of the melodic cycles, for the purposes of analysis the descent can be divided into four 'melodic sections', labelled melodic section (MS) 1, MS 2, MS 3 and MS 4. While both repertories share basic melodic cycle contours, the range of the descent in the Port Keats *balga* is cropped. In Martin's *balga* songs, the descent section covers an octave (transcribed as c – C), however the majority of the Port Keats *balga* songs (including the versions of Martin's songs, PKBalga-s09 and PKBalga-s06) cover a range of only a fifth or sixth (transcribed as G/A – C). As set out in Figure 5, these cycles comprise only Melodic Sections 2–4, followed (in the Long form) by the tonic section.

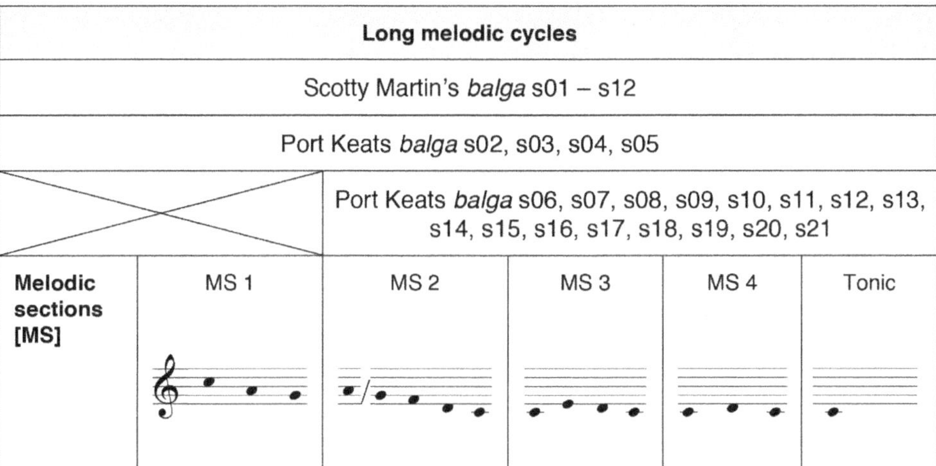

Figure 5: Melodic sections in Long melodic cycles in Martin's *balga* and the Port Keats *balga*.

Text

Balga/junba songs comprise relatively short texts that are repeated in a cyclical fashion through the course of a song performance. The text of a song is unique

---

55 Intriguingly, each of these three-cycle performances is followed by a performance with two cycles. These songs therefore appear to be performed as a pair of song items, the first time with three cycles and the second time with two cycles. While it is common for songs in the Kimberley sample to be performed twice, no such pairing based on the number of melodic cycles in the contour occurs to my knowledge.

and is the key factor that distinguishes one from another. The glosses provided by Martin, and patterns of repetition within the text cycle, delineate 'text lines', as set out in Figure 6. These text lines are labelled 'Text line A' and 'Text line B'.

Scotty Martin's Bulgumirri (36SM-s06)	
Text line A	**Text line B**
Bulgumirri wona	*Borangala gamarangerri*
From Bulgumirri* * House Roof Hill	"Oh, that bloke he got to that place Borangala* already", one agula said * Marshland area near Wyndham
Scotty Martin's Jilinya (36SM-s08)	
Text line A	**Text line B**
Jilinya mangalaluma	*winjawurru badi bindi gala lemburr badi bindi*
[Someone is saying] "She [the Jilinya] came out here already"	She came out when that sun [lemburr] went down

Figure 6: Text lines in Bulgumirri (36SM-s06) and Jilinya (36SM-s08).

As set out in Figure 7, in a large number of songs from both Martin's and the Port Keats repertory A and B text lines are deployed in a 'doubled' form, in which each is repeated once before moving on to the next (AABBAABB, and so on). Each repertory also displays a significant number of 'undoubled' forms. In Martin's repertory, six text cycles have the 'undoubled' structure in which each text line is performed only once before moving on to the next (in the form AB or ABC). The Port Keats *balga* repertory demonstrates a greater range of structures, as well the multiple text cycle forms (A repeated for several melodic cycles, followed by B repeated for several melodic cycles (A/B), for example).[56] These structures are common in wider Kimberley *balga/junba* corpus.[57]

---

56   While the 'doubled' AABB form is the predominant and usual structure in the *jadmi* corpus of Kimberley *junba*, previously described by Treloyn, *Songs That Pull,* and Barwick, 'Musical Form and Style in Murriny Patha *Djanba* Songs at Wadeye (Northern Territory, Australia)', these forms occur frequently in the wider Kimberley *balga/junba* corpus.

57   While these structures maintain an essence of cyclic patterning, they also point towards the traditions of the Daly region. Evidence of variegation in Kimberley *balga*, however, is beyond the scope of the current chapter.

Text cycle structure	Repertory and Song	Occurrence
Scotty Martin's *balga*		
Doubled AABB	s03, s07, s08, s09, s11, s12	6/12 (50%)
Undoubled AB or ABC	s01, s02, s04, s05, s06, s10	6/12 (50%)
Port Keats *balga*		
Doubled AABB	s01, s02, s03, s04, s05, s08, s09, s11, s12, s14, s16, s17, s19, s21	14/21 (66%)
Undoubled AAB, A, A/B, or A/B/C	s06, s07, s10, s13, s15, s18, s20	7/21 (33%)

Figure 7: Deployment of text cycle structures in Martin's *balga* and the Port Keats *balga.*

Rhythm

As is common in Kimberley *balga/junba* of all types, songs in both repertories are accompanied by a regular percussion accompaniment, of clapsticks (played by the song leader) and clapping performed by the rest of the singing ensemble at half the rate of the clapsticks. Throughout this repertory the clapsticks (transcribed as x) and clapping (transcribed as O) exhibit a 2/4 pattern.

Also, as is common in Kimberley *balga/junba* of all types, songs in both repertories are performed isorhythmically, and each time a text is repeated it has an identical rhythmic setting, as set out in Figure 8.

36SM-s06 Bulgumirri and PKBalga-s09 Pulkumirri		
Repertory, Song and tempo	**Text line A**	**Text line B**
	Rhythmic segment	**Rhythmic segment**
36SM-s06 ♩ = c.82 bpm	[rhythmic notation] Bulgumirri wona ⊗ x ⊗ x	[rhythmic notation] Borangala gamarangerri ⊗ x ⊗ x ⊗ x
PKBalga-s09 ♩ = c.78 bpm	[rhythmic notation] Pulkumirri jana/jalya ⊗ x ⊗ x	[rhythmic notation] Darrarru ? ⊗ x ⊗ x ⊗ x

36SM-s08 Jilinya and PKBalga-s06 Jilinya			
Repertory, song and tempo	**Text line A**	**Text line B**	
	Rhythmic segment	**Rhythmic segment**	**Rhythmic segment**
36SM-s08 ♩. = c.112 bpm	[rhythmic notation] Jilinya mangalaluma ⊗ x ⊗ x ⊗ x	[rhythmic notation] winjawurru badi bindi ⊗ x ⊗ x ⊗ x	[rhythmic notation] gala lemburr badi bindi ⊗ x ⊗ x ⊗ x
PKBalga-s06 ♩. = c.104 bpm	[rhythmic notation] Jilinya mangalaluma ⊗ x ⊗ x ⊗ x	[rhythmic notation] winjawurru badi bindi ⊗ x ⊗ x ⊗ x	[rhythmic notation] gala lemburr badi bindi ⊗ x ⊗ x ⊗ x

Figure 8: Rhythmic settings of Bulgumirri/Pulkumirri and Jilinya.

Moreover, as set out in Figure 8, in both repertories, the rhythmic setting of text lines comprises one or two rhythmic segments, defined by patterns of repetition and the occurrence of one or a series of two (in the case of Bulgumirri) relatively long durations.[58] As is common throughout the entire *balga/junba* corpus, most rhythmic segments consist of two, three or four clap (♩ or ♩.) beats. 36SM-s06 comprises a two-beat rhythmic segment (²₄ ♪ ♫ ♩ ♪♩, *Bulgumirri wona*) followed by a three-beat rhythmic segment (²₄ ♪♫ ♩ ♫ ♫♪♩, *Borangala gamarangerri*). 36SM-s08 comprises one three-beat rhythmic segment (♪♫♫♩♩, *Jilinya mangalaluma*) in Text line A, and two three-beat rhythmic segments (3+3) in Text line B (♪♫♫♩♩, *winjawurru badi bindi*; ♪♫♫♩♩, *gala lemburr badi bindi*).

These characteristics closely align the Port Keats performance with Kimberley *balga/junba*. However there are also a number of differences. Firstly, while the Port Keats *balga* percussion accompaniment displays the common Kimberley

---

58 As is common in northern genres such as *wangga* and *lirrga*, these units coincide with the end of meaningful text segments. While detailed linguistic analysis of the texts is yet to be done, it is clear from the glosses and explanation provided by Martin that the rhythmic segments that are demarcated by these long durations are coterminous with semantic and structural units within the text cycle, such as text lines and phrases.

balga/junba 2/4 metre, the clapsticks are also performed at half their usual rate. This marks a striking departure from Kimberley *balga/junba* style and, simultaneously, an affinity with Daly genres such as *wangga* and *lirrga* that exhibit a greater range of stick beating patterns.

Secondly, while the percussion accompaniment in Kimberley *balga/junba* is performed at two tempi—'slow' (80–86 bpm) and 'fast' (112–114 bpm) (referred to as *abalan* or *banngun-ngarri* and *manamana-ngarri*, respectively, in Ungarinyin)—three tempi occur in the Port Keats repertory: 'very slow' (72–74 bpm; 77–80 bpm); 'slow' (78–86 bpm); and 'fast' (96–104 bpm). Again, this marks a striking departure from Kimberley *balga/junba* style and, simultaneously, an affinity with Daly genres such as *wangga* and *lirrga* that exhibit a greater number of tempo bands.[59]

Thirdly, in both repertories the isorhythmic settings display just one of two different metres: a simple duple metre (such as in Bulgumirri 36SM-s06/PKBalga-s09) and a simple triple metre (such as in Jilinya 36SM-s08/PKBalga-s06). However, in Martin's repertory all simple duple texts are performed at the slow tempo (80–86 bpm) and all simple triple songs are performed at the fast tempo (112–114 bpm). Thus the repertory exhibits just two rhythmic modes: slow 2/4 (see 36SM-s06) and fast 3/8 (see 36SM-s08). In the Port Keats repertory, by contrast, while texts in the simple triple metre occur in the fast tempo (see, for example, PKBalga-s06), texts in the simple duple metre occur at three tempi: 'very slow' (72–74 bpm; 77–80 bpm); 'slow' (78–86 bpm) (see, for example, PKBalga-s09); and 'fast' (96–104 bpm). Consequently, this repertory displays no less than four distinct rhythmic modes: very slow 2/4; slow 2/4; fast 2/4; and, fast 3/8.

Finally, while song performances across Kimberley *balga/junba* corpus only ever use one rhythmic mode,[60] four of the twenty-one songs in the Port Keats *balga* (PKBalga-s02, PKBalga-s04, PKBalga-s11, and PKBalga-s16) use two rhythmic modes in the same song item. In each case they use the undoubled very slow 2/4 mode, followed by the doubled fast 2/4 mode.

Each of these points—the number of stick patterns, tempo bands, and rhythmic modes used in a repertory, as well as the number of rhythmic modes used in any one song performance—marks a striking departure from Kimberley *balga/junba* style and, simultaneously, an affinity with Daly genres such as *wangga*,[61] *lirrga*[62] and *djanba*.[63]

---

59 Treloyn, *Songs That Pull*.
60 ibid.
61 Marett, *Songs, Dreamings, and Ghosts*.
62 Linda Barwick, 'Tempo Bands, Metre and Rhythmic Mode in Marri Ngarr "Church Lirrga" Songs', *Australasian Music Research* 7 (2003): 67–83; Barwick, 'Marri Ngarr Lirrga Songs'.
63 Barwick, 'Musical Form and Style in Murriny Patha *Djanba* Songs at Wadeye (Northern Territory, Australia)'; Freya Bailes and Linda Barwick, 'Absolute Tempo in Multiple Performances of Aboriginal Songs:

Coterminous Versus Non-Coterminous Melodic Contour

A key factor that distinguishes *djanba* from *balga/junba* relates to the coincidence of boundaries between melodic cycles and text units. Barwick finds that *djanba* displays a 'coterminous' relationship between melody and text, wherein the boundaries of text stanzas coincide with those of melodic units.[64] In Kimberley *balga/junba*, however, the relationship between melody and text/rhythm is relatively non-coterminous with independently cycling text cycles and melodic cycles.[65] Evidence of non-coterminosity in the current sample requires some further consideration.

As noted earlier, the cycling of texts in both Martin's and the Port Keats repertories is interrupted and recommenced at the beginning of each melodic cycle. It is not uncommon for the structure of text cycles to be broken between one melodic cycle and another as in 36SM-s07 and PKBalga-s17 (marked in bold in Figure 9).

Scotty Martin's *balga* (36SM-s07), MD200218				
Melodic cycle in song item	1st	2nd	3rd	4th
Text lines	AABBA	AABBA	AABBA	AABBAA
Port Keat's *balga* (PKbalga-s17), A4357B				
Melodic cycle in song item	1st	2nd	3rd	4th
Text lines	AABB**AA**	AABB**AABBAA**	AABB**AA**	AABB**AABBAA**

Figure 9: Breaking of text cycles at the commencement of new melodic cycles in Martin's *balga* and the Port Keats *balga*.

This has previously led to the conclusion that text is somewhat strophic in relation to melodic cycles (i.e. there is a degree of coterminosity): the boundaries in the text are determined by melodic cycles.[66] If we take a closer look at the

---

Analyzing recordings of Djanba 12 and Djanba 14', *Music Perception: An interdisciplinary journal* 28:5 (2011): 473–90.

64   See Barwick, 'Musical Form and Style in Murriny Patha *Djanba* Songs at Wadeye (Northern Territory, Australia)'.

65   Relativity is cited here because, as argued elsewhere—Treloyn, *Songs That Pull*—compared to Centralian style isorhythmic cyclical songs, *junba* exhibits a relatively strophic relationship, suggesting a degree of coterminosity between melody and text.

66   Treloyn, *Songs That Pull*.

melodic cycles, however, namely how a regular cessation and recommencement of the clapsticks cues melodic contour in each of the repertories, it is clear that text and melody also remain independent. It has been well established that the cessation of clapsticks in *jadmi* type *junba* cues melodic structure. In *jadmi* type *junba*, where melodic cycles commence from one of two different pitches, the cessation and recommencement of the sticks correspond to two different melodic descent types, suggesting that the stick pattern provides a melodic cue to the singers.[67] Such a device is not needed in *balga*-type *junba,* however, where all melodic cycles in a song performance commence from the same pitch. In *balga*-type *junba,* the lead-singer appears to stop and restart the sticks instead to indicate that the melodic cycle currently being sung will be a 'short' melodic cycle (with no tonic section), rather than a 'long' melodic cycle (with a tonic section). In both Martin's and the Port Keats repertories, in songs that use the ||:Short + Long:|| melodic contour, the percussion accompaniment ceases at the commencement of each 'short' cycle, restarting shortly after. In these songs the accompaniment stops at the beginning of the first, third, fifth descents and so on (shaded in Figure 10).

Scotty Martin's *balga*				
Melodic cycle form	**Short**	**Long**	**Short**	**Long**
Melodic cycle in song item	1st	2nd	3rd	4th
Port Keats *balga*				
Melodic cycle form	**Short**	**Long**	**Short**	**Long**
Melodic cycle in song item	1st	2nd	3rd	4th

	Cessation of clapsticks

Figure 10: Cessation of clapsticks in ||: Short + Long :|| song performances in Martin's *balga* and the Port Keats *balga*.

Likewise, in Martin's *balga* songs that use the ||: Long :|| melodic contour, the cessation also occurs, usually at the beginning of first, third, fifth melodic

---

67   Treloyn, 'Scotty Martin's *Jadmi Junba*'; Treloyn, *Songs That Pull.*

cycles and so on, as in all Kimberley *balga*.[68] This cessation of sticks on the first, third and fifth melodic cycles throughout the Kimberley repertory has a major implication. It has the effect of pairing cycles together, regardless of their ||: Short + Long :|| or ||: Long :|| format; each pair is marked by a cessation of the sticks. The even length of all performances in the repertory (i.e., two, four, six cycles) further supports this grouping. Viewed in relation to the text, which, irrespective of this pairing, is organised around the commencement of each new melodic cycle, a 2:1 non-coterminous relationship between melodic and text units emerges, as set out in Figure 11.

By contrast, in the Port Keats *balga* repertory the accompaniment ceases and restarts at the commencement of *every* cycle in song performances that have the ||: Long :|| form (rather than just the first, third, fifth, and so on) (see Figure 11). The use of an uneven number of melodic cycles in ||: Long :|| songs and the marking of every cycle with a cessation of the sticks), suggests that melodic cycles in the Port Keats contour are conceived of as individual (unpaired) cycles that are coterminous with the text units: each new iteration of the text coincides with a new melodic unit.

Scotty Martin's *balga*	Paired melodic cycles, non-coterminous with text				
	II: Short + Long :II	Melodic cycle pair		Melodic cycle pair	
		Short	Long	Short	Long
	II: Long :II	Melodic cycle pair		Melodic cycle pair	
		Long	Long	Long	Long
Port Keats *balga*	II: Short + Long :II	Melodic cycle pair		Melodic cycle pair	
		Short	Long	Short	Long
	Unpaired melodic cycles, coterminous with text				
	II: Long :II	Single melodic cycle	Single melodic cycle	Single melodic cycle	
		Long	Long	Long	

	Cessation of clapsticks

Figure 11: Coterminous (Port Keats) versus non-coterminous (Martin's) treatments of melody and text.

---

68 While additional analysis is needed, it appears that this marks an historical melodic form, wherein the descent section comprised two descents (one an octave lower that the other) before moving onto the tonic section. In the present day ||: Long :|| forms, it appears that the sticks remain as a trace of this earlier form that was, assuming octave equivalence, in effect also a ||: Short + Long :|| form.

Again, this element of the Port Keats setting clearly distinguishes Port Keats *balga/junba* from the Kimberley practice and appears to mark it as a Daly musical tradition.

The Port Keats *balga* repertory is clearly based on Kimberley *balga* musical style. However, as shown, song order, elements of rhythm and rhythmic mode, and the coterminous relationship between melody and text clearly mark it as a Daly performance. The Port Keats *balga*, like *djanba*, is variegated, marked both with new musical traditions of the Kimberley and the familiar ones from the Daly.

A question that emerges is: how do performers who are familiar with the musical styles in question perceive this variegation? Is this variegation conscious and intentional as observed by Barwick in *djanba*[69] and elsewhere by Weiss[70] and Evans[71] or is it 'implicit' musical knowledge[72] arrived at simply through complex comparative musical analysis? To begin to answer these questions, I now turn to Martin's observation that the Port Keats *balga* is 'cross and square'.

Part Three — Cross and Square

Cross and Square Text/Rhythm and Melody

As noted, two Port Keats songs are clearly based on Martin's *balga* repertory. The texts and rhythmic settings of these songs are set out in Figure 12 for reference throughout the following discussion. PKbalga-s06 has an identical text and rhythmic setting to Jilinya 36SM-s08; PKBalga-s09 begins by naming Bulgumirri (House Roof Hill) that occurs in 36SM-s06 and, while the remainder of the text varies from Martin's song, the two versions have an identical rhythmic setting.

---

69   Barwick, 'Musical Form and Style in Murriny Patha *Djanba* Songs at Wadeye (Northern Territory, Australia)'.
70   Weiss, 'Permeable Boundaries'.
71   Evans, *Dying Words*.
72   Richard Widdess, 'Implicit Rāga Knowledge in the Kathmandu Valley', *Analytical Approaches to World Music* 1:1 (2011): 73–92.

36SM-s06 Bulgumirri and PKBalga-s09 Pulkumirri		
Repertory, Song and tempo	**Text line A**	**Text line B**
	Rhythmic segment	**Rhythmic segment**
36SM-s06 ♩ = c.82 bpm	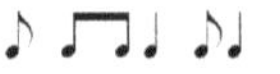 [rhythmic notation] Bulgumirri wona ⊗ x ⊗ x	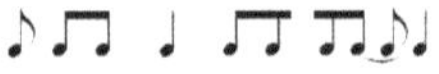 [rhythmic notation] Borangala gamarangerri ⊗ x ⊗ x ⊗ x
PKBalga-s09 ♩ = c.78 bpm	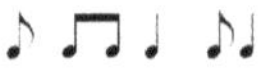 [rhythmic notation] Pulkumirri jana/jalya ⊗ x ⊗ x	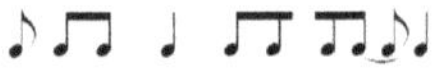 [rhythmic notation] Darrarru ? ⊗ x ⊗ x ⊗ x

36SM-s08 Jilinya and PKBalga-s06 Jilinya			
Repertory, Song and tempo	**Text line A**	**Text line B**	
	Rhythmic segment	**Rhythmic segment**	**Rhythmic segment**
36SM-s08 ♩. = c.112 bpm	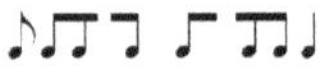 [rhythmic notation] Jilinya mangalaluma ⊗ x ⊗ x ⊗ x	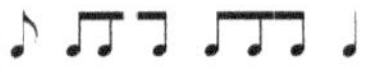 [rhythmic notation] winjawurru badi bindi ⊗ x ⊗ x ⊗ x	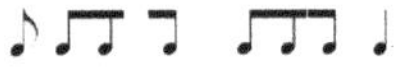 [rhythmic notation] gala lemburr badi bindi ⊗ x ⊗ x ⊗ x
PKBalga-s06 ♩. = c.104 bpm	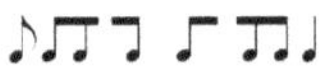 [rhythmic notation] Jilinya mangalaluma ⊗ x ⊗ x ⊗ x	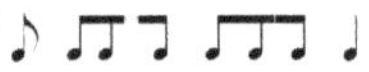 [rhythmic notation] winjawurru badi bindi ⊗ x ⊗ x ⊗ x	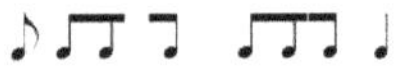 [rhythmic notation] gala lemburr badi bindi ⊗ x ⊗ x ⊗ x

Figure 12: Songs that occur in Martin's and the Port Keats *balga*.

While similarities between the songs and style were noted by Martin, he was also strongly of the view that the singing was 'all a bit cross and square', and that they were 'mixed up at the beginning'. On first listening to the songs, two differences immediately stand out. Firstly, whereas Martin presents the song-text of Jilinya (36SM-s08) with a doubled AABB form, the Port Keats group presents the same text (PKBalga-s06) with an undoubled AAB form; and, whereas Martin presents the Bulgumirri (36SM-s06) song-text with an undoubled AB structure, the Port Keats group presents it with a doubled AABB structure.[73]

---

73   Also, in the Jilinya song, whereas Martin sets the text to the ||: Long :|| melodic cycle contour, the Port Keats group set it to the ||: Short + Long :|| form.

Jilinya		
Repertory, Song	**Text structure**	
Scotty Martin's 36SM-s08	Doubled	AABB
Port Keats PKBalga-s06	Undoubled	AAB
Bulgumirri/Pulkumirri		
Repertory, song	**Text structure**	
Scotty Martin's 36SM-s06	Undoubled	AB
Port Keats PKBalga-s09	Doubled	AABB

Figure 13: Changes to text structure between Martin's *balga* and the Port Keats *balga*.

Secondly, as described in Part Two, while Martin's songs cover a range of an octave (MS 1–MS 4), the Port Keats versions cover a range of only a fifth/sixth (MS 2–MS 4).

Previous analysis of Martin's *jadmi junba* repertory has shown that these two factors—the cropping of the melodic range and whether a text is doubled or undoubled—have a profound effect on the melodic contour of a song.[74] It is here that we see the clearest illustration of Martin's point that the performances are 'cross and square' and that they are 'mixed up at the beginning'. In short, because the basic melodic contour in the Port Keats *balga* repertory melodic cycle has a compressed range of a fifth/sixth and the structure of the texts is altered, there is a necessary realignment—a 'cross'—of some melodic sections, text lines and rhythmic segments, in order that others can be aligned—'square'. Before showing this it is necessary to briefly describe the alignment of melodic sections, text lines and rhythmic segments in Martin's *balga* repertory.

Detailed analyses of the expansion and contraction of a basic melodic contour within melodic cycles to accommodate text lines and rhythmic segments of different lengths has been conducted for various Kimberley repertories.[75] The key observation to note in these analyses is that there is a regular relationship between melodic sections, text lines and rhythmic segments each time a

---

74 Treloyn, 'Scotty Martin's *Jadmi Junba*'; Treloyn, *Songs That Pull*.
75 Ray Keogh 'Process Models for the Analysis of Nurlu Songs from the Western Kimberleys', in *The Essence of Singing and the Substance of Song: Recent responses to the Aboriginal performing arts and other essays in honour of Catherine Ellis*, eds Linda Barwick, Allan Marett and Guy Tunstill (Sydney: Oceania, University of Sydney, 1995), 39–51; Treloyn, 'Scotty Martin's *Jadmi Junba*'; Treloyn, *Songs That Pull*.

particular song is performed: while the number of melodic cycles, and the number of text lines in those melodic cycles may change from performance to performance in relation to dance or other accompanying action, the alignment between the first, second, third, fourth rhythmic segments, and so on, and MS 1, 2, 3, 4 does not alter. The primary factor that guides this is that the cycling of the text in the course of a song performance is, as described above, interrupted and recommenced from the beginning of the text cycle at each new melodic cycle: each melodic cycle begins with a new text cycle.

In the sample of twelve songs from Martin's repertory, four songs, including Bulgumirri (36SM-s06) have an undoubled AB structure with one rhythmic segment in each line. These display a straightforward alignment wherein the first text line (A) coincides with MS1, the second text line (B) coincides with MS2, and the third and fourth text lines (A and B) coincide with MS3. The fifth text line (A) coincides with MS 4, and the tonic section commences from the sixth text line (B).

Melodic sections	MS 1	MS 2	MS 3	MS 4	Tonic
Text-line, rhythmic segment length	A 3 beats	B 3 beats	A 2 beats B 3 beats	A 2 beats	B beats …

Figure 14: Alignment of melodic sections and undoubled, one rhythmic segment, text lines in Bulgumirri (36SM-s06).

When text lines have a duration that is longer than three beats and/or consist of more than one rhythmic segment, such as in Jilinya (36SM-s08), the alignment becomes more complex. Jilinya (36SM-s08) has one three-beat segment in its A text line, and two three-beat segments in its B text line. In this case melodic sections, text lines and rhythmic segments are deployed as set out in Figure 15.

Melodic sections	MS 1	MS 2	MS 3	MS 4	Tonic
Text-line, rhythmic segment length	A 3 beats	A 3 beats B 3+3 beats	B 3+3 beats	A 3 beats	…

Figure 15: Alignment of melodic sections and rhythmic segments in Jilinya (36SM-s08).

The modifications of text and melody that are made to Bulgumirri (36SM-s06) and Jilinya (36SM-s08) in the Port Keats *balga* repertory have dramatic ramifications for these melodic settings. In Figure 16 the alignment between melodic sections, text lines and rhythmic segments in 36SM-s06 (Bulgumirri) and PKBalga-s09 are compared. In order to accommodate the cropped cycle range and the use of a doubled, rather than an undoubled structure (described above), a number of modifications are made: the first A text line in PKBalga-s09 is set to MS 2 (rather than MS 1); the second articulation of the A text line is set to MS 2 (rather than MS 3); and the first B text line is set to MS 3 (rather than MS 2). The settings of the first B and second A text lines literally 'cross' over between Martin's version and the Port Keats version: the setting is literally 'mixed up at the beginning' as Martin observed. By the time the second rhythmic segment of MS 3 is reached, the settings become 'square', and both are set to the second articulation of the B text line. Likewise, MS 4 is set 'square' to the third articulation of the A text line.

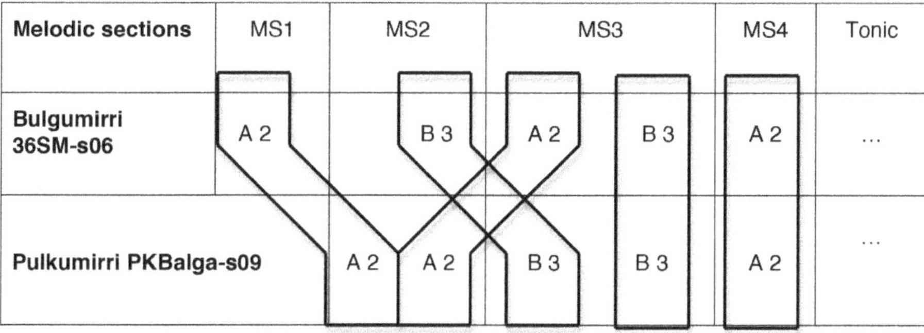

Figure 16: Cross and square alignment of melodic sections, text lines and rhythmic segments (Bulgumirri/Pulkumirri).

Similarly, though less dramatically, in Jilinya (36SM-s08 and PKBalga-s06), in order to accommodate the cropped cycle range and the use of an undoubled, rather than a doubled structure, the first three text lines of PKBalga-s06 are shifted from MS 1 and MS 2 (in Martin's version) into MS 2 and MS 3; the B text lines compress or condense into one melodic section. The settings 'square' themselves again by MS 4.

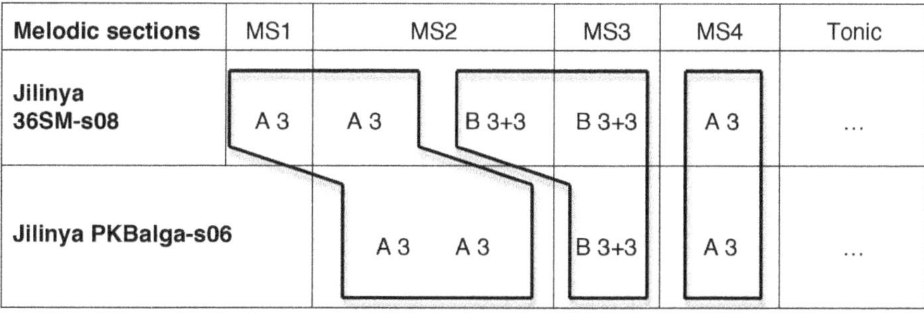

Figure 17: Cross and square alignment of melodic sections, text lines and rhythmic segments (Jilinya).

As Martin is an expert singer and composer, with acute aural comprehension, knowledge and expertise that is considered to be at the peak of the *balga* tradition, it seems possible that his analysis was indeed speaking of this 'cross and square', 'mixed up at the beginning' realignment of pitch and text in the Port Keats versions of his songs.

Cross and Square Perspectives of Country

Finally, it is important that we consider the semantic content of these songs, specifically the geography and stories to which they refer. The songs, as in other *junba* repertories, relate the composer's experiences in dreams in which he travelled with spirits of deceased family members. Bulgumirri (36SM-s06) cites the speech of a spirit, standing at Bulgumirri (House Roof Hill) in the north-east Kimberley between the towns of Kununurra and Wyndham, observing another spirit arriving in Borangala, marshland near the town of Wyndham (see Figure 18). Jilinya (36SM-s08) describes a Jilinya spirit travelling to Borangala, and cites another spirit who observes that the Jilinya already had arrived when the sun went down. Other songs in the repertory refer similarly to spirits, ancestral and contemporary events, and name and describe places in the north-central Kimberley, and in the north-east Kimberley, moving beyond as far as Darwin. They describe contemporary events such as the wake of Cyclone Tracy, ancestral events and beings, conversations, animals, and natural phenomena such as water and fog.[76]

While we cannot know without further research in Wadeye what the Bulgumirri and Jilinya songs meant to performers in Port Keats in 1974, or what they mean to them today, it does appear that both repertories name places in the north-east corner of the Kimberley. Preceding one song (PKBalga-s05) it sounds as though a male voice amongst the singers exclaims 'Bulgumirri! Jigumirri!', referring to Bulgumirri and the nearby Jigumirri (False House Roof Hill). Bulgumirri is itself named in PKBalga-s09 as 'Pulkumirri'. However, while Martin's song pairs Bulgumirri (House Roof Hill) with Borangala (Wyndham Marshland), the Port Keats version appears to pair Bulgumirri with (what sounds like) Darrarru (Cockburn Range), to the south-west of Borangala. In short excerpts of spoken commentary on the Port Keats songs that are included in Walsh's recording, Harry Luke Palada Kolumboort can be heard explaining that one song (PKBalga-s11) is about places on Legune Station: Kulamangguwa (the site that the station is on) and Parrindarr (a place about 11 kilometres away from Kulamangguwa).

---

76 Text transcriptions, glosses and explanations were prepared by Barwick with Martin for s01–s05 following the 1999 recording session, and by Treloyn with Martin for s01–s12 in 2001, 2002 and 2010.

What is interesting here is the perspective that the respective performance groups bring to these places. Whereas Martin's Bulgumirri song speaks of a spirit travelling from Bulgumirri north-west to Borangala (near the port of Wyndham), the Port Keats song appears to refer to travel from Bulgumirri across to Darrurru in the south-west. Any conclusions from this are tentative at best, and further research into both repertories is needed, but it does appear that the paths travelled in these songs 'cross' between the versions, as represented in Figure 18. When we take into account the origins of the performances and the fact that these songs may relate to contemporary or historical Wurnan trade, it is apparent that Martin's songs outline a northbound route from the central Kimberley where he resided (Mt Elizabeth Station), north-east to Bulgumirri, further north to Borangala. Other songs refer to Wunbara, a place west of Adolphus Island, even further to the north, in the passage where boats come through, and ultimately, as is described in one song, Darwin. Given that the Wurnan moves outbound from the Kimberley (presumably via Kununurra, Wyndham and stock routes towards the Northern Territory) it is possible that the songs outline an outbound Wurnan route connecting the Kimberley with the Daly.

The Port Keats (Wadeye) versions of the songs, on the other hand, appear to point towards a different perspective on this and follow a westbound route from the Daly to the Kimberley: from Port Keats (Wadeye), through Kulamangguwa and Parrindarr (Legune Station), to Bulgumirri and then further to the west to Darrarru, following the Wurnan trade into rather than out of the Kimberley.

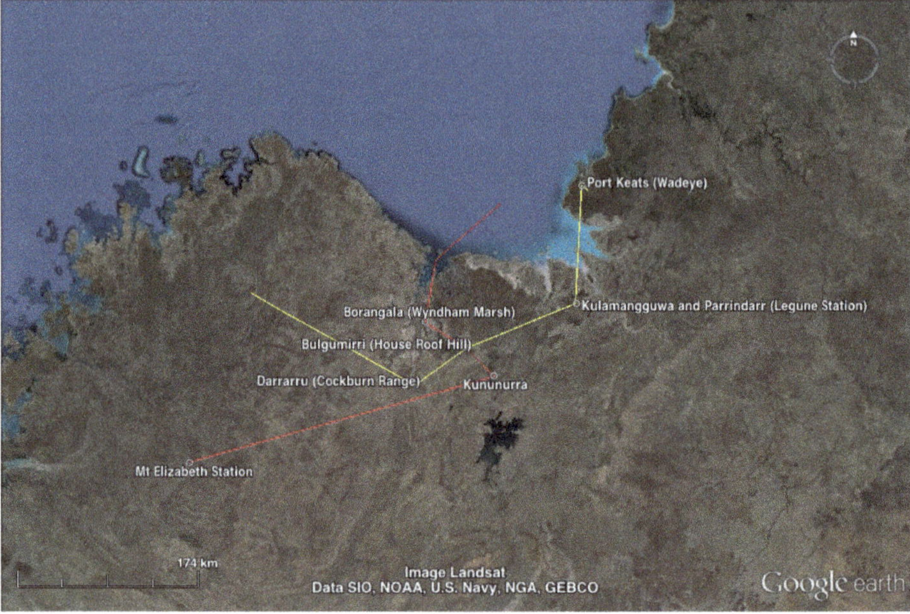

Figure 18: Cross and square perspectives on Country.

Source: Google Earth 7.0.3.8542, private data set by author, accessed 30 July 2014, www.google.com/earth/index.html.

In this way the paths 'cross' different perspectives on the Wurnan system (one viewed from Port Keats into the Kimberley, and the other viewed from the Kimberley towards Port Keats). However, insofar as they share a Wurnan trajectory and ethos they are, indeed, 'square'. Thus, in true Wurnan style, when Martin points towards the alignment of melody, text and rhythm in the Port Keats *balga*, and possibly the alignment of places, he gestures not only to musical features but also an underlying relationship founded on Wurnan connections and continued in the contemporary economy of the pastoral industry: the Port Keats performers, like their music, are same but different, 'cross and square'.

Conclusion

The Port Keats *balga* performance, like *djanba*, exhibits variegation in its musical style evident on multiple layers, ranging from song order, to melodic, rhythmic and textual components, to the way in which these are combined. Barwick explains the emergence of *djanba* in Port Keats as an example of a 'constructive fostering of variegation' wherein aspects of a new musical style are drawn upon to differentiate its bearers from those of partner genres *wangga* and *lirrga*.

Djanba is consciously and intentionally variegated, drawing on the distant *balga* tradition and the local *wangga/lirrga* tradition, in order that ceremony shared by the clans that hold all three genres can be conducted and so that new social structures can be negotiated.

Like *djanba* in the Kimberley, we know relatively little of the social and ceremonial role of *balga* in Port Keats. Also like *djanba* in the Kimberley, *balga* in Port Keats has fallen out of use. Therefore we can say little about the issue of whether and how the variegation identified in the Port Keats *balga* is intentional.[77] It is clear, however, that this variegation is noted and foregrounded by Kimberley singers, namely the composer Scotty Martin, who when listening to the recording declared that they were Kimberley *balga/junba* but 'cross and square'. It is also clear that the songs likely ended up in Port Keats via the Wurnan system of exchange. Port Keats is said to have been a frequent destination for repertories travelling from the west to the east-north-east in Wurnan exchanges, and the songs emerged in Port Keats in the 1970s, a time when travel by singers/stockmen between Port Keats and the east Kimberley cattle stations increased, hand in hand with a flourishing or 'efflorescence'[78] of Wurnan ceremonial exchange.

Like the use of conscious musical variegation in *djanba* to adapt to changing ceremonial and social circumstances, Wurnan transactions are underpinned by a productive, relational assertion of 'difference against a background of similarity'[79] that has enabled people to reinforce and foster new relationships with other people, places, and histories as social structures and economies have changed in the region. Relationships are fostered and maintained by noting what one shares with an 'other', and what sets them apart.

On first hearing, it seemed to me that Martin's reaction to the Port Keats performance pointed towards inadequacies or inaccuracies, as if the Port Keats performers simply got his songs wrong in some way. However, I have considered strong evidence that Martin, as a highly-skilled expert in the musical organisation of genres from across the Kimberley and Daly regions, was referring to a located variegation of style and a realignment of melody, text and rhythm, when he

---

77 Adding further to the questions that arise from the analysis presented in the chapter, and as something of a postscript, in June 2014 (some eighteen months after the initial composition of this chapter) I played an excerpt of the Walsh 1974 *balga* recording to a senior Miriwung singer of *balga*, *wangga*, *lirrga* and *djanba* in Kununurra. In his opinion the singers were Gija (from the east Kimberley) indicating that the recording may in fact be of an east Kimberley group visiting Port Keats. I was unable to enquire further at the time or to clarify whether he was aware that the recording was made in Port Keats. Clearly if the singers were Gija, the interpretation of the analysis presented in this chapter may indeed be revised. Irrespective of whether the singers were Gija from the Kimberley or from Port Keats, however, Martin's response to the performance as if they were from somewhere distant but connected to his own group holds.

78 See Redmond, *Rulug Wayirri*, citing Kim Akerman, 'The Renascence of Aboriginal Law in the Kimberleys', in *Aborigines of the West: Their past and their present*, eds Ronald Berndt and Catherine Berndt (Nedlands: University of Western Australia Press, 1979), 234–42.

79 Redmond, *Rulug Wayirri*.

observed that the Port Keats *balga* songs were like his, and like Kimberley *balga*, but 'cross and square'. I have also considered how this 'cross and square'-ness outlines distinctive respective geographical perspectives of Port Keats (Wadeye) and Martin in the north-central Kimberley on Wurnan trade routes, potentially represented by the recombination and selective naming of places in song texts. If we consider Martin's analysis of the Port Keats *balga* as 'cross and square' in the context of the Wurnan ceremonial network we can see that, as well as an astute analysis of musical organisation, it also gestures towards a relationship with Port Keats (Wadeye) people. Variegation in song styles across the Kimberley and Daly is musical, social and relational, citing and eliciting relationships between distinctive groups of people across time, cultures and place.

Acknowledgements

I would like to thank Linda Barwick for comments on early drafts of this chapter as well as Scotty Martin and other elders quoted for sharing their insights into various performance traditions of northern Australia. This article is based on research funded by AIATSIS (G2001/G6569 and G2009/7458) and the Australian Research Council (LP0990650, investigators Sally Treloyn and Allan Marett).

References

Akerman, Kim. 'The Renascence of Aboriginal Law in the Kimberleys', in *Aborigines of the West: Their past and their present*, eds Ronald Berndt and Catherine Berndt (Nedlands: University of Western Australia Press, 1979), 234–42.

Bailes, Freya, and Linda Barwick. 'Absolute Tempo in Multiple Performances of Aboriginal Songs: Analyzing recordings of Djanba 12 and Djanba 14', *Music Perception: An interdisciplinary journal* 28:5 (2011): 473–90.

Barwick, Linda. 'Tempo Bands, Metre and Rhythmic Mode in Marri Ngarr "Church Lirrga" Songs', *Australasian Music Research* 7 (2003): 67–83.

Barwick, Linda. 'Marri Ngarr Lirrga Songs: A musicological analysis of song pairs in performance', *Musicology Australia* 28:1 (2005): 1–25.

Barwick, Linda. 'Musical Form and Style in Murriny Patha *Djanba* Songs at Wadeye (Northern Territory, Australia)', in *Analytical and Cross-Cultural Studies in World Music*, eds Michael Tenzer and John Roeder (New York: Oxford University Press, 2011), 316–54.

Barwick, Linda, and Allan Marett. 'Aural Snapshots of Musical Life: Simpson's 1948 Recordings', in *Exploring the Legacy of the 1948 Arnhem Land Expedition*, eds Martin Thomas and Margo Neale (Canberra: ANU E Press, 2011), 355–75.

Barwick, Linda, and Scotty Martin. *Jadmi Junba by Nyalgodi Scotty Martin, Traditional Songman of the Dreamtime* (Sydney: Rouseabout Records, 2003).

Evans, Nicholas. *Dying Words: Endangered languages and what they have to tell us* (Chichester: Wiley-Blackwell, 2010).

Furlan, Alberto. *Songs of Continuity and Change: The reproduction of Aboriginal culture through traditional and popular music* (PhD, University of Sydney, 2005).

Keogh, Ray. 'Process Models for the Analysis of Nurlu Songs from the Western Kimberleys', in *The Essence of Singing and the Substance of Song: Recent responses to the Aboriginal performing arts and other essays in honour of Catherine Ellis*, eds Linda Barwick, Allan Marett and Guy Tunstill (Sydney: Oceania, University of Sydney, 1995), 39–51.

Marett, Allan. *Songs, Dreamings, and Ghosts: The wangga of north Australia* (Middletown: Wesleyan University Press, 2005).

Redmond, Anthony. *Rulug Wayirri: Moving kin and country in the northern Kimberley* (PhD, University of Sydney, 2001).

Redmond, Anthony. 'Places That Move', in *Emplaced Myth: Space, narrative, and knowledge in Aboriginal Australasia and Papua New Guinea*, eds Alan Rumsey and J. F. Weiner (USA: University of Hawai'i Press, 2001), 120-38.

Redmond, Anthony. 'Tracking Wurnan: Transformations in the trade and exchange of resources in the northern Kimberley', in *Indigenous Participation in Australian Economies II: Historical engagements and current enterprises*, eds Natasha Fijn, Ian Keen, Christopher Lloyd and Michael Pickering (Canberra: ANU E Press, 2012), 57–72.

Redmond, Anthony, and Fiona Skyring. 'Exchange and Appropriation: The Wurnan economy and Aboriginal land and labour at Karunjie Station, north-western Australia', in *Indigenous Participation in Australian Economies: Historical and anthropological perspectives*, ed. Ian Keen (Canberra: ANU E Press, 2010), 73–90.

Shaw, Bruce. *My Country of the Pelican Dreaming: The life of an Australian Aborigine of the Gadjerong, Grant Ngabidj, 1904–1977* (Canberra: Australian Institute of Aboriginal Studies, 1981).

Shaw, Bruce. *Countrymen: The life histories of four Aboriginal men* (Canberra: Australian Institute of Aboriginal Studies, 1986).

Shaw, Bruce. *When the Dust Come in Between: Aboriginal viewpoints in the east Kimberley prior to 1982* (Canberra: Aboriginal Studies Press, 1992).

Sullivan, Jack, and Bruce Shaw. *Banggaiyerri: The story of Jack Sullivan* (Canberra: Australian Institute of Aboriginal Studies, 1983).

Treloyn, Sally. 'Scotty Martin's *Jadmi Junba*: A song series from the Kimberley region of northwest Australia', *Oceania* 73:3 (2003): 208–20.

Treloyn, Sally. *Songs That Pull: Jadmi Junba from the Kimberley region of northwest Australia* (PhD, University of Sydney, 2006).

Treloyn, Sally. 'Songs That Pull: Composition/performance through musical analysis', *Context: Journal of music research* 31 (2006): 151–64.

Treloyn, Sally. 'Flesh with Country: Juxtaposition and minimal contrast in the construction and melodic treatment of Jadmi song texts', *Australian Aboriginal Studies* 2 (2007): 90–99.

Treloyn, Sally. '"When Everybody There Together … Then I Call That One": Song order in the Kimberley', *Context: Journal of music research* 32 (2007): 105–21.

Treloyn, Sally. 'Half Way: Appreciating the poetics of northern Kimberley song', *Musicology Australia* 31:1 (2009): 41–62.

Weiss, Sarah. 'Permeable Boundaries: Hybridity, music, and the reception of Robert Wilson's "I La Galigo"', *Ethnomusicology* 52:2 (2008): 203–38.

Widdess, Richard. 'Implicit Rāga Knowledge in the Kathmandu Valley', *Analytical Approaches to World Music* 1:1 (2011): 73–92.

9. Listening to Heavy Metal in Wadeye

John Mansfield

Introduction

Most of the chapters in this volume examine how Aboriginal cultural artefacts have travelled outwards from their places of origin, being distributed, deployed or displaced in distant social contexts. This chapter treats the inverse situation: how a cultural product that has its origins in Europe and North America has been received and re-used in an Aboriginal town of tropical northern Australia. The cultural product in question is heavy metal—primarily a musical genre, which first emerged in Britain and the US in the 1980s, but also an associated array of images, texts and fashion statements.[1] The site of reception is Wadeye, Australia's largest remote Aboriginal town, with a population of some 2,500 people, whose antecedents moved in to settle the Port Keats Mission in the mid-twentieth century. In 1975 the Mission was dissolved, and the newly secular town renamed as Wadeye.[2] Since the late-1980s the youth have become avid fans of heavy metal, though the extensive equipment required for producing heavy metal music has prevented any metal bands from forming in Wadeye. The music has come to be associated with public disorder and what the media describe as 'heavy metal gangs'.[3] The popularity of metal in Wadeye tends to arouse great curiosity among visitors, presumably because metal is reflexively associated with urban or suburban settings, while Wadeye is an isolated town some 400 kilometres from the larger urban centres of Darwin and Katherine.

My analysis of heavy metal in Wadeye focuses on social practices and the material objects that facilitate them. My primary aim is to examine the social contexts in which Wadeye youth listen to heavy metal, share and distribute metal, talk about metal, wear, dance, draw and graffiti metal, based on some fifteen months of fieldwork I conducted during 2011–2013. Secondarily, I use these empirical observations to analyse what metal might *mean* to those who listen to it in Wadeye. I aim to provide a brief but holistic account of how

---

1   Ian Christie, *Sound of the Beast: The complete headbanging history of heavy metal* (New York: Harper Collins, 2003).

2   Br John MSC Pye, *The Port Keats Story* (Darwin: Colemans, 1972); 'The Port Keats Story: Part Two.' unpublished ms; accessed at Wadeye community archive, n.d.

3   Lindsay Murdoch, 'Hate Stalks a Community Where Gangs Rule Roost', *The Age*, 23 May 2006; Hannah Brooks and Jonathan West, *Heavy Metal Gangs of Wadeye* (VBS, 2009); Paul Toohey, 'Gangsters' Paradise', *Bulletin*, 10 February 2004.

metal culture has been adopted at Wadeye, and in doing so I hope to expose a productive intersection between media studies and the anthropology of cultural diffusion. The first section of the chapter reviews previous scholarship that I consider most relevant to such an intersection.

The transmission of heavy metal to Wadeye first occurred by means of music video programming, which began appearing in television broadcasts from about 1987. Cassettes and later CDs allowed favourite recordings to be played repeatedly, and fandom became established, with band allegiances giving rise to the social groupings that have been previously labelled heavy metal 'gangs', though I prefer the term 'mobs'.[4] More recently, mobile phones have become at least as important in listening to and distributing heavy metal music at Wadeye, while graphic elements of heavy metal culture also circulate as graffiti and fashion. The second section of this chapter describes the main ways in which heavy metal cultural artefacts circulate in Wadeye, as material technologies distributed through social interactions. The section summarises as much as can be reconstructed about the early period of metal in Wadeye, while giving more detail on recent practices that I have observed in my fieldwork during 2011.

The third section of this chapter draws on the observations of the previous section to develop an analysis of what heavy metal means to the young men of Wadeye. This is by necessity a more interpretive task, and does not purport to be exhaustive or exclusive of contrasting interpretations. However, by situating meaning within social observable practices, this analysis does aim to have a somewhat objective basis. The section is structured around two particular social interactions, which are used as spring-boards for discussing the meaning of heavy metal in Wadeye more widely. The first of these interactions is a series of group dances held at a 'heavy metal disco' that I did not observe directly but rather saw in a documentary filmed in 2008.[5] The dance event reflects a series of related concepts: brotherhood, consubstantiality, spirit beings, power, subversion and evil, and these concepts are evidently developed in other social practices at Wadeye. The second interaction was one I observed directly, a fleeting moment in which one local made an unselfconscious comment about heavy metal to another. But the comment references a conceptual opposition between 'blackfella' and 'whitefella', which can be seen as an unresolved tension in the meaning of heavy metal at Wadeye.

Though this chapter deals with Aboriginal reception of whitefella culture, rather than whitefella reception of Aboriginal culture, it is like other chapters in the book an instance of 'transformation of the meanings with which cultural

---

4   John Mansfield, 'The Social Organisation of Wadeye's Heavy Metal Mobs', *The Australian Journal of Anthropology* 24:2 (2013):156.
5   Brooks and West, *Heavy Metal Gangs of Wadeye*.

objects are imbued'.[6] The moral, spiritual and symbolic dimensions that metal takes on in Wadeye are only obliquely related to the meanings it bears in its sites of origin.

Aboriginal Adoption of Foreign Cultural Materials

There is a considerable body of work discussing how foreign cultural influences have been absorbed and modified by Aboriginal people, and a rather smaller range of studies that examine Aboriginal reception of mass media. Probably the most researched topic in the former category is the introduction of Christianity among Aboriginal people,[7] although Sutton has also examined the adoption of New Age spirituality.[8] Most other studies of cultural adoption deal with material culture such as mass-produced alcohol, cash, vehicles, houses, playing cards, and digital information devices.[9]

With regards to the reception of mass media there are a few notable studies, though the area has not been widely researched, and there is rather more work on Aboriginal people as media producers.[10] Michaels' work on television

---

6   Harris, Chapter 1, this volume.

7   Fiona Magowan, 'Faith and Fear in Aboriginal Christianity', in *Aboriginal Religions in Australia: An anthropology of recent writings,* eds M. Charlesworth, Francoise Dussart, and Howard Morphy (Aldershot: Ashgate, 2005), 279–96; R. Tonkinson, 'Reflections on a Failed Crusade', in *Aboriginal Australians and Christian Missions,* eds T. Swain and Deborah Bird Rose (Bedford Park: Australian Association for the Study of Religions, 1988), 60–73; 'Christianity in Aboriginal Australia Revisited', *The Australian Journal of Anthropology* 21 (2010): 1–13.

8   Peter Sutton, 'Aboriginal Spirituality in a New Age', *The Australian Journal of Anthropology* 21 (2010): 71–89.

9   Alcohol: M. Brady, *Heavy Metal: The social meaning of petrol sniffing in Australia* (Canberra: Aboriginal Studies Press, 1992); Basil Sansom, *The Camp at Wallaby Cross: Aboriginal fringe dwellers in Darwin* (Canberra: Australian Institute of Aboriginal Studies, 1980); David McKnight, *From Hunting to Drinking: The devastating effects of alcohol on an Australian Aboriginal community* (London: Routledge, 2002). Cash: Basil Sansom, 'A Grammar of Exchange', in *Being Black: Aboriginal cultures in 'settled' Australia,* ed. Ian Keen (Canberra: Australian Institute of Aboriginal Studies, 1988), 159–78; Nicolas Peterson, 'Cash, Commoditisation and Authenticity: When do Aboriginal people stop being hunter-gatherers? In *Cash, Commoditisation and Changing Foragers,* eds Nicolas Peterson and Toshio Matsuyama (Osaka: National Museum of Ethnology, 1991), 67–90. Vehicles: John Altman and Melinda Hinkson, 'Mobility and Modernity in Arnhem Land: The social use of Kuninjku trucks', *Journal of Material Culture* 12:2 (2007): 181–203; Glenn Dawes, 'Figure Eights, Spin Outs and Power Slides: Aboriginal and Torres Strait Islander youth and the culture of joyriding', *Journal of Youth Studies* 5:2 (2002): 195–208. Houses: Yasmine Musharbash, *Yuendumu Everyday: Contemporary life in a remote Aboriginal settlement* (Canberra: Aboriginal Studies Press, 2008). Playing cards: John Altman, *Hunter-Gatherers Today: An Aboriginal economy in northern Australia* (Canberra: Aboriginal Studies Press, 1987); David Fernandes Martin, *Autonomy and Relatedness: An ethnography of Wik people of Aurukun, Western Cape York Penninsula* (PhD, The Australian National University, 1993), 115–35. Digital devices: Inge Kral, *Plugged in: Remote Australian Indigenous youth and digital culture* (Canberra: CAEPR, 2010).

10   Eric Michaels, *The Aboriginal Invention of Television in Central Australia, 1982–1986* (Canberra: Australian Institute of Aboriginal Studies, 1986); Wendy Bell, *A Remote Possibility: The battle for Imparja television* (Alice Springs: IAD Press, 2008); Jennifer Deger, *Shimmering Screens: Making media in an Aboriginal community* (University of Minnesota Press, 2006); Heather Molnar and Michael Meadows, *Songlines to Satellites: Indigenous communication in Australia, the South Pacific and Canada* (Sydney and Wellington: Pluto Press and Huia Publishers, 2001).

production among the Warlpiri is deservedly celebrated, though he also makes some valuable observations on Warlpiri viewing practices of Hollywood videos in the days before television broadcasts began. According to Michaels, Warlpiri viewers pay less attention than Western audiences to the matter of fictional characters' motivations, but instead take a great interest in the kin relationships at work in the film—which they find to be much under-specified.

> When Hollywood videos fail to say where Rocky's grandmother is, or who's taking care of his sister-in-law, Warlpiri viewers discuss the matter and need to fill in the missing content.[11]

From the 1950s until the 1980s, Hollywood films were watched by the Warlpiri at film nights in the community dining room. These gatherings were somewhat problematic in that they created inappropriate conjunctions of taboo kin relations in the shared space. This was resolved in the 1980s when film viewing switched to VCR videos, which could be viewed by smaller groups in private homes— though the upkeep of video equipment in the dusty desert environment proved very expensive.[12] There were evidently communal film nights in many remote Aboriginal communities—Wadeye had them from the 1960s—which in general gave way to video in the 1980s. Scattered references attest to a preference for action and kung-fu movies,[13] which might be related to the fact that these can be easily followed without needing to comprehend English dialogue.

In the realm of mass-mediated popular music, the Aboriginal reception of two particular genres has been described: country music and hip-hop. Country music is much loved by older Aboriginal men across central and northern Australia, especially those who have worked in the cattle industry. Brown describes how the country music of Slim Dusty and Charley Pride was played alongside local ceremonial music as part of a burial rite at Gunbalanya.[14] Ottosson gives particular attention to the social events at which Aboriginal people play and listen to country music, how they evaluate musicianship and determine band membership.[15] She argues that Aboriginal understanding of country music is linked to concepts of legitimate masculinity, and emotive relations with the land.

---

11   Eric Michaels, 'Hollywood Iconography: A Warlpiri reading', in *Second International Television Studies Conference, 1986*, eds Phillip Drummond and Richard Patterson (London : BFI Publishing, 1988), 119.
12   Michaels, *The Aboriginal Invention of Television in Central Australia, 1982–1986*, 37–45.
13   Brady, *Heavy Metal*, 89; McKnight, *From Hunting to Drinking*, 101, 222.
14   Brown, this volume.
15   Ase Ottosson, 'The Intercultural Crafting of Real Aboriginal Country and Manhood in Central Australia', *The Australian Journal of Anthropology* 23 (2012): 179–96; Alberto Furlan, *Songs of Continuity and Change: The reproduction of Aboriginal culture through traditional and popular music* (PhD, University of Sydney, 2005), 217–22.

The reception and production of hip-hop has been described with respect to urban Aboriginal people,[16] and though anecdotal evidence suggests that it is also very popular in some remote areas, it has not been studied in the latter context. The works on urban Aboriginal hip-hop all argue that hip-hop is an authentic and local Aboriginal cultural form, not just a copy of something 'foreign'. Indeed Pennycook and Mitchell maintain that hip-hop is 'a continuation of Indigenous traditions', arguing that it is authentically Aboriginal because it renews a timeless tradition of transmitting culture by song and dance.[17]

In the description that follows I do not attempt to define heavy metal at Wadeye as authentically local, though neither do I consider it to be a corruption of local culture by foreign influence. Culture is always diffuse and always in the process of diffusion; particular forms adhere to social and geographic localities, but are always sliding down a spectrum from the foreign to the autochthonous to the forgotten. Trying to place things on this spectrum seems far less productive than identifying the social practices and interactions through which a cultural import is integrated, and examining how it might contribute to 'the structures of meaning through which [people] give shape to their experience'.[18]

Heavy Metal in Wadeye: Material Technologies and Social Exchange

Heavy metal is essentially an extreme version of rock music, which emerged in the 1980s when its precursors, 'hard rock' and 'glam rock', tried to outdo each other in rock'n'roll extravagance.[19] Metal is characterised by loud, insistent, distorted guitars and vocals that tend towards wailing or growling. It is a music of strident machismo, in contrast to disco and punk, two late-70s genres against which metal rebelled.[20] Metal also contrasts with punk in being highly concerned with complex musicianship. In the course of the 1980s metal was transformed from a commercially insignificant genre limited to certain cities

---

16   George Morgan and Andrew Warren, 'Aboriginal Youth, Hip Hop and the Politics of Identification', *Ethnic and Racial Studies* 34:6 (2011): 925–47; Alastair Pennycook and Tony Mitchell, 'Hip Hop as Dusty Foot Philosophy: Engaging locality', in *Global Linguistic Flows: Hip hop cultures, youth identities and the politics of language*, ed. H. Samy Alim, Awad Ibrahim, and Alistair Pennycook (New York: Routledge, 2009), 25–42; Tony Mitchell, 'Blackfellas Rapping, Breaking and Writing: A short history of Aboriginal hip-hop', *Aboriginal History* 30 (2006): 124–37.

17   Pennycook and Mitchell 'Hip Hop as Dusty Foot Philosophy': 35.

18   Clifford Geertz, *The Interpretation of Cultures* (New York: Basic Books, 1973), 312.

19   Christie, *Sound of the Beast*.

20   Steve Waksman, *This Ain't the Summer of Love: Conflict and crossover in heavy metal and punk* (Berkeley: University of California Press, 2009); Leigh Krenske and Jim McKay, '"Hard and Heavy": Gender and power in a heavy metal music subculture', *Gender, Place and Culture* 7:3 (2000): 287–304.

in Britain and the US, to a globally successful cultural commodity. Bands that led this global conquest included Iron Maiden, Judas Priest, Def Leppard, and above all Metallica.

There is at least one exemplary study of how heavy metal culture has reached social contexts far from its origins, in Baulch's study of the Bali death metal scene.[21] Baulch describes how death metal music was largely introduced to Bali via a single individual who imported cassette tapes, and was more generally a trendsetter in the scene.[22] Much of what she reports of the Bali scene might apply to any death metal scene anywhere—for example the formation of local bands that initially imitate what they hear on recordings, or the sense of subcultural opposition to 'the mainstream'.[23] However, after some years the Bali death metal bands have begun to incorporate local melodies and mythology into the music.[24]

The use of heavy metal at Wadeye is rather different to what Baulch reports from Bali. For one thing, metal in Wadeye is not a 'scene' among the diverse musical subcultures of an urban environment; rather, it is a cultural form that has been taken on by the whole of the young male population, through forms of interaction and exchange quite distinct to those that might characterise urban metal culture. A more typical urban metal scene, focused on specific nightclubs and record shops, is described by Krenske and McKay,[25] while the 'underground' scenes of death metal and black metal are described in Purcell[26] and Murphy[27] respectively. The young men of Wadeye are often blamed as a group for social unrest in the town, but there is no special disapproval or marginalisation associated with heavy metal. There are no distinctions involving different social groups following different sub-genres of metal, but rather a highly conventionalised metal fandom that is shared to some extent by all the young men. By contrast, older people in Wadeye dislike heavy metal music, while the young women, with whom I have not been able to do any ethnographic research due to local taboos against mixed-gender sociality, express affiliation to the metal social groupings of their brothers, but show less interest in the music itself.

---

21 Emma Baulch, *Making Scenes: Reggae, punk, and death metal in 1990s Bali* (Durham: Duke University Press, 2007).

22 ibid., 53–7.

23 ibid., 23, 61.

24 ibid., 161–70.

25 Krenske and McKay, '"Hard and Heavy"'.

26 Natalie J. Purcell, *Death Metal Music: The passion and politics of a subculture* (Jefferson: McFarland & Company, 2003).

27 David Jo Murphy, *Hate Couture: Subcultural fundamentalism and the Serbian black metal scene* (PhD, NUI Maynooth, 2011).

The Arrival of Metal in Wadeye

At a distance of some twenty-five years, it is difficult to trace with certainty how heavy metal first arrived in Wadeye, but much of the evidence points to *Rage*, the music video program that commenced broadcasting in 1987. It was at about the same time that the Broadcasting for Remote Aboriginal Communities Scheme—stimulated in large part by Michaels' collaborative work with Francis Jupurrurla at Yuendumu—commenced television broadcasts in dozens of remote Aboriginal towns, including Wadeye.[28]

In the late 1980s, heavy metal was one of the most commercially successful popular music genres, and its tendency towards extravagant visual spectacle was particularly well suited to the new medium of music videos. Indeed, the rise of heavy metal and rise of the music video format were substantially interdependent,[29] and it seems that heavy metal music videos were among the most influential forms of content when television started broadcasting at Wadeye. Various Wadeye men have related to me how they first discovered their favourite metal bands on *Rage*, and how they would remember the band names so that they could buy cassettes, and later CDs, from Kmart on their next trip to Darwin. For example:

> *First hear television ngarra* Rage. *"Ah, I wanna be like that man! Ngamanu mangi kardu nimi-ka kanarntel, ini-ka. Nukunu-ka marda manganart kardu geng ini-ka, ngay-ka kanyi le nganam. Kardu pelpitj wiye, pemarr pangkuy." Yuwu, first-time ngay binyepup, ngay-ka mam "Nangkul pup? Ku bamam. Tjung patha kanyi," mam ne. Good songs. And I understand ngamam what it's about. Tjung ini ngarra war, war story kama mam. Tju murrinh story pumam.*

> I first heard [White Lion] on the television program *Rage*. "Ah, I wanna be like that man! I will be like that man singing, like that. I want to make my gang like him, this is something I like. A crazy man, with long hair." Yes, the first time I heard them, I said, "Who is this? A whitefella. This is a good song," I said. And I understood what it was about. That song was about war, maybe a war story. It was a fighting story.[30]

It is noticeable that the heavy metal bands most popular in Wadeye are in all cases commercially successful ones of the type that might be expected to be included in *Rage* programming (for example, Iron Maiden, Judas Priest, Metallica, Bullet for My Valentine), while bands of the more extreme, 'underground' metal subgenres such as death metal and black metal seem to be unknown at

---

28   Molnar and Meadows, *Songlines to Satellites*, 34.
29   Christie, *Sound of the Beast*, 77–83.
30   SL, aged 49; author's recording, 13 October 2011.

Wadeye, presumably because they are too offensive to ever be included on *Rage*. Extreme metal subgenres first spread through fanzines and mail-order cassette networks,[31] and more recently have been distributed predominantly through online networks. Neither of these types of media networks have much presence in Wadeye, where young men usually lack both literacy and computer access.

Perhaps the most noticeable impact of heavy metal in Wadeye was the fact that, soon after its introduction, *kardu kigay* (young men from teenage years through till their 30s) began to name their peer groups after metal bands. In news reports these groups have been labelled 'heavy metal gangs', though they are in fact kin groupings, generally connected by classificatory 'brother' (Br, MoZiSo, FaBrSo) or 'cousin' (MoBrSo, FaZiSo) relationships, and are in many ways dissimilar from urban gangs. Elsewhere I describe in detail how these 'metal mobs' are constituted by collateral kinship, and how this differs from the patrilineal kinship organisation of traditional clans.[32] For the purposes of this chapter, it should suffice to note that heavy metal music in Wadeye is not just a matter of individual musical taste, but has taken on a major role in symbolising groups of kigay in the social arena. Every kigay can be identified by affiliation with one or more metal mobs, and the metal bands to which one affiliates are known as one's *ku spidi* (from English 'speed metal'). Actual enjoyment of the music is not necessary for mob affiliation, which is in essence a form of social classification. However, many kigay do enjoy metal music, and often listen to it, though there are no local metal bands in Wadeye. The lack of any local metal music production is probably due to the lack of musical equipment (guitars, amplifiers, drum kits, etc.), of which heavy metal is quite demanding.

Listening to Metal

When a heavy metal band has been 'discovered' and a cassette or CD obtained, the next step is to play the music in Wadeye. The long-standing method for this is the home stereo system, which facilitates playing the music at high volume. Kigay of the same mob, or related mobs, gather in groups at any house that has a stereo system, and listen to metal together, often accompanied by the smoking of marijuana. Kigay say that the effect of marijuana goes well with heavy metal, and when a strong effect is obtained, they describe the experience as *frikinet* (from 'freaking out').

Houses in Wadeye are built quite close together, so that when heavy metal is played loudly in one house (or often, on the veranda of a house), it is audible to a large number of people in surrounding houses. This sort of metal 'broadcasting' occurs to a degree that would be considered socially unacceptable in most

---

31   Christie, *Sound of the Beast*, 49–55; Baulch, *Making Scenes*, 52–3.

32   Mansfield, 'The Social Organisation of Wadeye's Heavy Metal Mobs'.

Australian towns, but although some older people at Wadeye have mentioned to me that they find it unpleasant, I have not observed anybody trying to intervene in another's music playing. This is quite consistent with a widely observed reluctance among Aboriginal people to constrain the behaviour of others.[33] Late afternoon and evening—sometimes late into the night—are the main times for these metal broadcasts. No doubt this is because many kigay sleep for much of the day.

Playing metal music at high volume makes an aggressive demarcation of social space—by playing the music of one's ku spidi, one announces the presence of the associated metal mob. For example, kigay staying at the house adjacent to mine in Wadeye in 2012 were Tera mob, and they often played Pantera music loudly on their back porch. Other kigay visiting my house readily recognised this as Pantera music, and knew that this was the *spidi* of the kigay living in that house. Depending on context, the area around the house could be described as 'Tera area'. The association of ku spidi with particular parts of town is further demarcated by graffiti, as described below.

The playing of heavy metal music at Wadeye was undoubtedly first established as a loud public statement using home stereo equipment. This practice is still current, though there is now a second mode of audio reproduction. The use of mobile phones at Wadeye is now very widespread, though the manner in which this technology is used by kigay has some key differences with respect to urban Australian norms. The main difference between Wadeye phone usage and that of urban Australia is that phones in Wadeye are not as strongly attached to individual owners. Among close kin, phones regularly change hands, which radically affects their function as a communication technology. Kigay sometimes know which phone number should be used to reach a person; but much of the time there is no such reliable association, so kigay make phone calls by scrolling through the phone's recent call records and trying various numbers, connecting somewhat unpredictably to a range of kin, and with luck, heuristically approaching a connection with the target person—or at least gaining knowledge of their whereabouts. Text messages are not much used by kigay, due to limited literacy, though some formulaic messages are sent, such as 'CALL ME KREATOR', where the last part is the sender's ku spidi.

All phone models now have the capacity to store, exchange, and play back digital media in image, sound and video formats, and at Wadeye this aspect of the phone as a 'media device' is used to create a social network of digital exchange. The wandering of phones (not just 'mobile phones', but 'socially mobile phones') from person to person means that each phone accretes a collection of image, audio and video files that have been added by its various

---

33   McKnight, *From Hunting to Drinking*; Martin, *Autonomy and Relatedness*.

users. Since phones move between close kin, this collection tends to be a fairly coherent set of media with respect to socially symbolic ku spidi represented in songs and band images. Many other media genres are included in social phone networks, including Australian Football League team images, photographs of oneself and one's kin (sometimes with mob identifiers superimposed using image editing software on the phone, see Figure 1), pornography, and locally made videos that most often portray dancing or fighting. But the discussion here will be restricted to the heavy metal content.

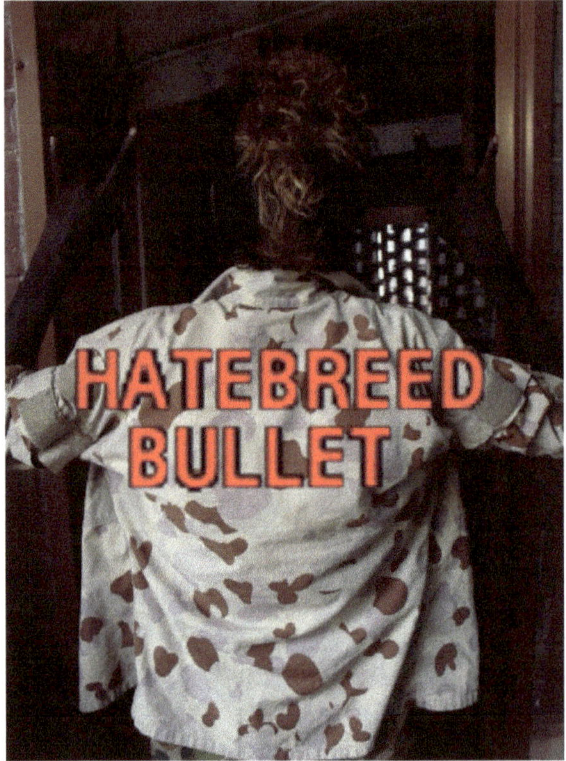

Figure 1: Mobile phone background image, created using image editing software on the phone.

Source: Used with permission of image creator, KM.

Phones have small, rather tinny speakers that allow songs to be played back. When I ask kigay about their mob affiliations, they will often not just tell me their affiliation, but demonstrate it by playing a sample of the ku spidi on their phone. This practice includes kigay who do not particularly like heavy metal music, but nonetheless carry it with them as a sort of digital badge representing social identity when required. Other kigay, who are more enthusiastic about the music, habitually play tracks on their phones as they walk around town.

Phones move from person to person, while media files can be copied from phone to phone when in close physical proximity, using the Bluetooth file transfer protocol that operates wirelessly over short distances.[34] Kigay are highly proficient in performing Bluetooth transfers, and just about any other of the myriad functions available on contemporary phones. This clearly requires some functionally specific literacy in being able to read menu options and file names, which contrasts with an extremely limited ability to write, either by pen or keyboard, in either English or Murrinhpatha. Many kigay struggle to write their names, though they may be more proficient writing the names of their ku spidi.[35] The combination of Bluetooth file reproduction and the physical circulation of devices together creates a digital, social media network among kardu kigay. This is now the primary means by which heavy metal is circulated and 'performed' in Wadeye, and it is also a key technological basis for the expression of social relatedness.

It is evident that heavy metal music circulates very freely among related kigay via mobile phones, but there is something of a mystery as to how the mp3 files first enter this dense local network. The internet is the obvious suspect—but kigay generally have very limited access to computers. Home computers are non-existent among Aboriginal households in Wadeye, and though computers are available at the Wadeye library, most kigay seem uncomfortable entering this supposedly 'community' space. Occasionally some kigay do use the library, and when they do so, watching heavy metal videos via YouTube is one of their main goals. It may be that these kigay also download some metal music— though I have never witnessed this, and it is not clear how many kigay have the computer proficiency to do so. Another possibility is that heavy metal sound files originally enter the Wadeye network via links with Aboriginal kin in larger urban centres, such as Katherine and Darwin, where perhaps there is greater internet access and proficiency. In any case, the key to the mystery of how such an internet-disconnected social group should have so much digital media circulating within it probably has to do with the minimal inputs required. With such dense social connectedness, and the infinite reproducibility of digital media, a particular heavy metal song or album only needs to be received once to be shared and reproduced widely within the local network.

Drawing, Writing and Wearing Heavy Metal

Heavy metal is not just a musical style, but also an associated graphic style, a particular vocabulary used in band names, song and album titles, and a fashion palette. The circulation of heavy metal at Wadeye includes not just the music

---

34 Jay Wyant, 'What Is Bluetooth?', *Volta Voices* 13:1 (2006): 54–5.
35 Kral, *Plugged In*.

but also the graphic elements in the reproduction of written names, symbols and other imagery. Heavy metal band t-shirts are one mode in which such names and images circulate, being physically attached to kigay. In general, t-shirts worn by individuals correspond to ku spidi affiliations, but like mobile phones, clothing items circulate quite freely among kin, and occasionally this may result in kigay wearing t-shirts that do not reflect their own affiliations. The Judas Priest mob augment their metal fashion by wearing matching denim jackets emblazoned with 'JP' badges. They are also visually distinguished as a mob by their preference for the 'mullet' hairstyle, though it is not clear whether this is directly inspired by metal bands.

Social signification is more intensive in the names and images that kigay reproduce themselves as graffiti. The walls of Wadeye are richly adorned with graffiti that is always focused on social identity, and never of the political or philosophical variety (for a while I thought that the graffito 'METAL UP YOUR ASS' was a possible exception, but I later learnt that this is a Metallica album title). Graffiti is painted or drawn onto both public buildings and private houses, where it appears mostly on outside walls but also to some extent inside. Graffiti is often painted on road surfaces, benches, road-signs and any other markable public surfaces, including occasionally trees. Kigay sometimes use pen to draw names or insignia of their ku spidi on the skin of their arms, creating pseudo-tattoos—though I do not know of any kigay who has a real tattoo. Kigay's graffiti messages are almost exclusively declarations of social identity, either individual, or jointly declared by two or more kin. Here are some examples of individual declarations:

(1) GSW FEAR ON ME[36]

(2) EVIL TERA THATS ME GCYD ONLY TERA IN 2005

(3) EVIL DAVE LJMPMK

(4) SJKYDK G卐P FOREVER IN 2008

(5) BLACK LABEL SOCIETY 4 EVER ZAKK WYLDE 2007 4LIFE

Example (1) is a simple statement of Fear Factory affiliation by an individual represented as GSW. The next three examples include more elaborate individual initialisms: GCYD, LJMPMK and SJKYDK. These represent highly specified social identity, with initials representing both the European and Aboriginal names of the individual, as well as totem, initiation name, clan estate and other personally significant place names. Such matrices of individual identity are deliberately difficult to decode, and are recognisable only to fairly close kin.

---

36 All graffiti here is documented in the author's photographic collection, image numbers 4896, 4998, 5781, 5403, 5452, 5429.

Examples (2) and (3) include compound mob affiliations: Evil + Tera; Evil + Megadeth (represented obliquely by reference to Megadeth's lead guitarist, Dave Mustaine). Example (4) is probably a reference to German Punks (partially represented by the swastika, which is a graphic code for the German mob), or perhaps a compound reference to German + Priest. These mob encodings may be difficult to decipher for outsiders, but are universally understood by kigay.

Example (5) references a heavy metal band, Black Metal Society, which as far as I am aware does not have a mob associated with it. It also mentions the name of the band's lead guitarist, Zakk Wylde. I interpret this graffito to be a statement of personal musical taste, rather than a mob identifier; such a personal metal affiliation is sometimes described by the individual kigay as *praibat ngay*, 'my own (private) band metal'.

Here are some examples of jointly inscribed graffiti:

(6) MAD BOYS FF BFLN MTBD DBLM ANLP

(7) LICA BIG T MRKTD STDWM OU2F

Example (6) declares the relatedness of four kigay, and affiliates them as a group to the Mad Boys and Fear Factory (FF) mobs—though it leaves some ambiguity as to whether all four affiliate to both these mobs, or if some affiliate to one but not the other. Example (7) declares a joint affiliation to Lica (Metallica) and Big T (Testament), with the added code OU2F standing for 'only us two forever'. Such statements of apparent exclusivity (also present in example (2) above) are rather curious because they are clearly not statements of fact: GCYD is certainly not the 'only' affiliate of Tera, and in fact what his graffito affirms is relatedness to others. There is also plenty of Wadeye graffiti written by young women, which tends to focus more on romantic connections and other forms of social relatedness that are not expressed in terms of metal mobs—but the study of women's lifeworlds is beyond the scope of my research.

Finally, Wadeye metal graffiti is not limited to alphabetic names, but also includes various graphic devices, of which we have already seen one—the swastika. There are various other graphic symbols associated with various mobs, as shown in Figure 2. Most of these are copied from heavy metal album covers, though there is some innovation and experimentation in how these are reproduced.

The Meaning of Heavy Metal in Wadeye

In the previous section I described how heavy metal is circulated through social interactions and material technologies. In this section I will look more closely at two particular instances of social interaction to examine what these might tell us about the *meaning* of metal at Wadeye. This is by necessity rather more interpretive than the previous section, since meanings, concepts and ideas cannot be observed directly. However it is clear that cultural circulation is not just a matter of travelling artefacts, but also, perhaps more interestingly, the meanings that travel with them.[37] Therefore it seems in order to make some comments here about what heavy metal might mean to kardu kigay.

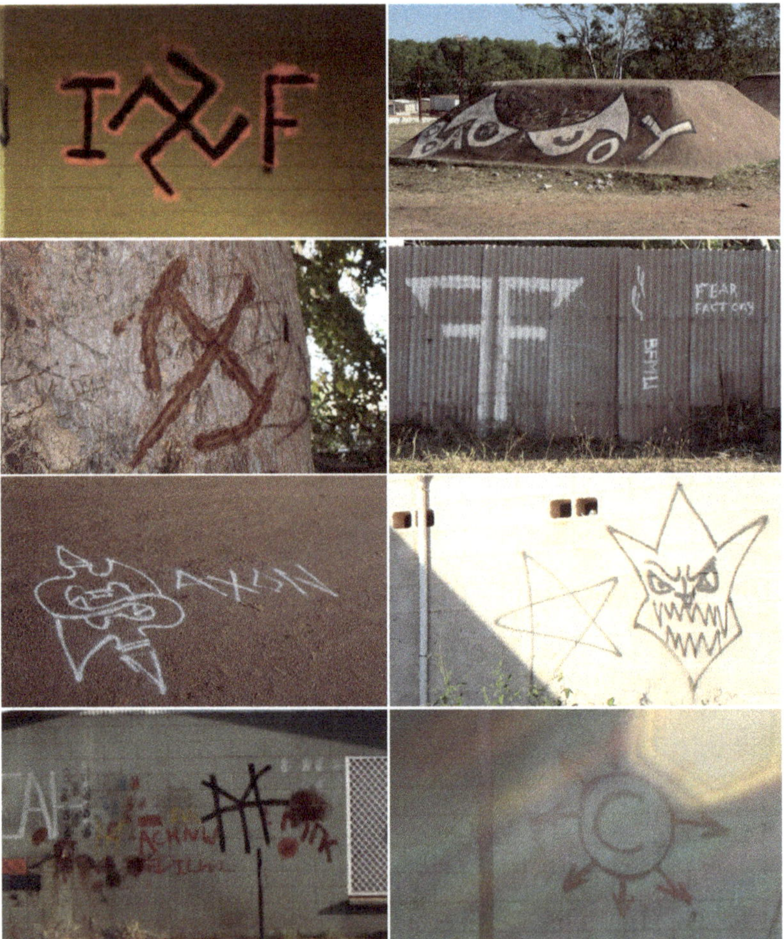

Figure 2: Graphic symbols of metal mobs, clockwise from top-left: German (swastika) + In Flames; Bad Boys (copied from a popular car sticker); Fear Factory (logo featured on album covers); Evil Warriors (devil image); Chimaria (logo featured on album covers); Machine Head (logo invented in Wadeye?); Saxon (logo featured on album covers); Judas Priest (device featured on album covers).

Source: All photos taken by the author during Wadeye fieldwork 2011–13.

---

37 Ulf Hannerz, *Transnational Connections: Culture, people, places* (London: Routledge, 1996); Arjun Appadurai, *Modernity at Large: Cultural dimensions of globalization* (Minneapolis: University of Minnesota Press, 1996).

Dancing With the Devil

I take as my starting point a scene—in fact the climactic scene—from the documentary *Heavy Metal Gangs of Wadeye*.[38] Much of the film is not particularly informative—two young documentary makers from Melbourne visit Wadeye armed with a video camera, and spend a few days asking kigay a lot of direct questions, to which they predictably receive a lot of short answers like 'yes' and 'I don't know', and from which the film-makers reach their own conclusions.[39] But the footage recorded in the climactic scene is quite fascinating: it shows kigay dancing as groups to their respective ku spidi at a nocturnal party.[40] A stereo has been set up at a house, and floodlights create an illuminated dancefloor on the sand out the front. A series of heavy metal songs are played, each from a different metal band—Megadeth, Slayer, Exodus, etc.—and as each plays, affiliates of the relevant mob take to the dancefloor. The dance is a sort of whirlpool: a dozen kigay form a loose conglomerate that revolves counter-clockwise, each kigay marching around, headbanging, occasionally raising a fist or playing air guitar.

This dance gathering is linked to two other dance practices at Wadeye. One involves a lighter style of rock music that is locally produced and sung in Murrinhpatha, with lyrics celebrating clan estates, and the totems and ancestors that reside there.[41] The male dance practice for this also involves moving around in whirlpool formation, with the raised fists of the heavy metal dance replaced by a pointing action that signals the direction of the relevant clan estate. Men join such a dance for Country with which they have a kin-based relationship, much as the metal dance is joined by those who have a kin-based affiliation to the ku spidi.

An older form of dance is the ceremonial gathering in which traditional song genres *djanba*, *wangga* and *lirrga* are performed, accompanied by didjeridu and/or clapsticks.[42] This style of dance is also dedicated to clan estates, totems and ancestors, though the references are rather more elaborate and loaded with long traditions of sacred knowledge.[43] The styles of dancing in these genres are often

---

38   Brooks and West, *Heavy Metal Gangs of Wadeye*.

39   I also find the methodology of the film to be ethically dubious, as many scenes appear to have been filmed without seeking permission, and kigay can be seen trying to hide their faces from the camera. Such practices promote the idea that whitefellas are intrusive and disrespectful.

40   Similar dances are reported in Furlan, *Songs of Continuity and Change*, 249; Bill Ivory, *Kunmanggurr, Legend and Leadership* (PhD, Charles Darwin University, 2009), 311.

41   Furlan, *Songs of Continuity and Change*.

42   See also Treloyn, this volume.

43   Linda Barwick 'Musical Form and Style in Murriny Patha Djanba Songs at Wadeye (Northern Territory, Australia)', in *Analytical and Cross-Cultural Studies in World Music*, eds Michael Tenzer and John Roeder (Oxford: Oxford University Press, 2011), 316–54; Linda Barwick, 'Marri Ngarr Lirrga Songs: A musicological analysis of song pairs in performance', *Musicology Australia* 28 (2006): 1–25; Allan Marett, *Songs, Dreamings, and Ghosts: The wangga of north Australia* (Middletown: Wesleyan University Press, 2005); Linda Barwick,

mimetic of totemic natural species, though the whirlpool formation may also be performed for ragburning (mortuary) ceremonies.[44] Again, the dance event is structured around various kin groups taking turns to dance according to the songs with which they have a relationship.

The 'heavy metal disco' of the documentary, then, is continuous with practices in which social groups use dance to invoke entities with which they have a symbolic relationship, and which empower the social groups through mystical consubstantiality with those entities. The social world is a highly structured network of related humans, with kinship operating throughout as a taxonomy of relationships, but the groups that are formed in this social world are also related to, or symbolised by, entities outside the social domain: natural species, sacred places, the spirits of the dead … and heavy metal bands. The question naturally occurs, do ku spidi abide in the same domain as totems and ancestors? In general the answer is no, though heavy metal does invoke one Wadeye clan totem. When asking about heavy metal, I have more than once been told simply that it is music about *ku karratj* ('the devil'), and the Evil Warriors, once the largest and most fearsome mob in Wadeye, are said to have taken their name from *ku karratj*, as some of their founding members belong to the clan for which this is a totem.[45]

The idea of the devil or some other dark power is a common motif in global heavy metal culture,[46] and one which has clearly been adopted in Wadeye, though it is refracted through local cosmology. The syncretic melding of concepts clearly works both ways, as *ku karratj* has in turn taken up some European characteristics. For example, he is said to be covered in flames, and he lives in 'hell'.[47]

While traditional ceremony genres invoke totemic ancestors that guarantee the maintenance of the social order, listening to heavy metal invokes a power that is violent, chaotic and antisocial. Kigay have grown up in a milieu of great instability, typically witnessing incidents of violence and public disorder from a young age: '*kardu mamay ngatha, ngardiwerrerrdha, bamkardu kardu kura, kardu murlak, tju-mini mebatj pirrini tju litjpurr*', 'when I was a child I was shaking (from fear), I saw drunken men, crazy men, when they fought they

---

Allan Marett, Joe Blythe and Michael Walsh, 'Arriving, Digging, Performing, Returning: An exercise in rich interpretation of a Djanba song text in the sound archive of the Wadeye knowledge centre, Northern Territory of Australia', in *Oceanic Encounters: Festschrift for Mervyn McLean*, ed. R.M. Moyle (Auckland: Research in Anthropology and Linguistics Monographs, 2007), 13–24.

44   Linda Barwick, personal communication.

45   There are alternative stories as to how the Evil Warriors got their name, but this is the one I find most convincing. The second part of the name is probably derived from *The Warriors* (1979), a dystopian film about gang wars in New York City.

46   Christie, *Sound of the Beast*, 240–75; Purcell, *Death Metal Music*.

47   Narrative recorded 1 September 2011. Video recording by Joe Blythe, transcription and translation by the author.

would bring axes'.[48] Listening to metal is not an escape from these threats, but their embrace: finding power in chaos, transmuting fear into strength. One story tells of how a man now deceased, who is the grandfather of many Evil Warriors affiliates, once engaged *ku karratj* in a fist fight, on the road out to Daly River. The man defeated *ku karratj*, and then *'pewa nukunu punirdirdi'*, 'his power went into them'—the man and his companions were miraculously transformed—*'aa nakurl patha'*, 'and afterwards they felt good'.[49] Although it was one individual who defeated *ku karratj*, his subversive power went into all of them: it was the whole group that was spiritually increased, or perhaps even the whole Evil Warriors mob. Similarly the dancing at the heavy metal disco is always a group activity.

The unity of brothers is another key concept among the metal mobs. This is often expressed using the word *run*, derived from English 'own', but used with a slightly different range of meaning that suggests both separation from others and strong internal unity. *'Runrun kem pigunu run Bullet, mu ngankunime run Kreator'*, 'they have their own Bullet mob, but we here have our own Kreator mob'.[50] Heavy metal provides a neat symbol for this concept of brotherhood, since it is always a music of bands, not solo artists. The band is typically pictured together as a macho tableau on album covers, usually dressed similarly and often in poses that suggest they are fighting some sort of battle together. Walser identifies this masculine peer solidarity as 'the hero team', a key figure of heavy metal lyrics and imagery.[51] It is through the unity of brothers (the metal mob, the hero team) that kigay find empowerment in chaos.

Kardu Tjipmam and *Ku Bamam*

The second incident I wish to explore involves a brief comment heard in passing, but one that points to some conceptual tensions. One day I was driving with three or four kigay from Wadeye to Ngarntimeli beach, DP in the front next to me, checking through the discs in the glove box, while others in the back asked about what sort of music was available. When somebody in the back asked if there was anything 'heavy', DP replied *'wurda, manangka music kardu tjipmam'*, 'no, there's no blackfella music'.

It was strange that DP referred to heavy metal as blackfella music, when all the band members of all the mobs' ku spidi are, without exception, *ku bamam* ('whitefellas'). But it is not inexplicable. I take it that DP sees metal as relating

---

48   CK, age 19, author's recording, 17 September 2011.
49   Conversation and narratives recorded 1 September 2011. Video recording by Joe Blythe, transcription and translation by John Mansfield.
50   Narrative recorded 1 September 2011. Video recording, transcription and translation by John Mansfield.
51   Robert Walser, *Running with the Devil: Power, gender, and madness in heavy metal music* (Middletown: Wesleyan University Press, 1993), 114.

to blackfellas since in Wadeye all Aboriginal youth have ku spidi, and many actively enjoy the music, while whitefellas who live in Wadeye as teachers, doctors and other service workers in general listen to other popular genres. Wadeye has quite firm black/white social segregation, with much contact during the workday, but very little social engagement in people's free time. Even linguistically, *kardu tjipmam* (blackfella) and *ku bamam* (whitefella) fit into separate categories of the ten-part Murrinhpatha noun classification system: *kardu* is the class of Aboriginal people, *ku* is a class that includes whitefellas, animals, totems and various other spirit beings. Kigay often contrast themselves to whitefellas, pointing out differences such as shoe-wearing (whitefella) versus barefoot (blackfella), keeping one's tobacco to oneself (whitefella) versus sharing it freely among relatives (blackfella). There is a firm conceptual divide between the two types of people, and heavy metal falls clearly on the blackfella side.

But this doesn't explain away the fact that the metal bands, such an intense symbol of social identity among kigay, are all made up of whitefellas. Indeed, globally heavy metal is a very 'white' music genre. Non-white metal bands are remarkable by their absence,[52] and some metal bands either subtly allude to or explicitly propose a white supremacist philosophy.[53] Kigay seem either unaware of these connections or simply indifferent to them, and the same goes for use of the swastika as a symbol of the German mob, a very long-standing group which predates the arrival of heavy metal, and was named after Nazi villains seen in war movies—presumably not because of what they represented philosophically, but because they were identifiable as the 'bad guys'.[54]

In concrete social interactions kigay have fairly superficial contact with whitefellas. Their school attendance and participation in formal work are both at very low levels,[55] which leaves their interaction with whitefellas mostly limited to brief transactions at the shop or takeaway (notwithstanding the occasional linguist or ethnographer). But in their world of ideas, whitefellas figure prominently. The fact that the metal bands are all made up of whitefellas is not dismissed, but on the contrary is often referenced, as can be seen for example in the narrative fragment above—'A crazy man, with long hair … Who is this? A whitefella. This is a good song.' It is widely known that some of the bands, such as Kreator and Sodom, are more specifically *ku german*, 'Germans', which links them conceptually to the German mob, though Kreator at least is recognised as a separate mob. The kigay who make up the metal mobs are sometimes imaginatively figured in this vein, as gangs of *ku*. For example, in one story about

---

52   Christie, *Sound of the Beast*, 206.
53   Nicholas Goodrick-Clarke, *Black Sun: Aryan cults, esoteric Nazism, and the politics of identity* (New York: New York University Press, 2003).
54   Steve Bunk, 'Mixed Justice', *The Bulletin*, 6 September 1988.
55   John Taylor, *Demography as Destiny: Schooling, work and Aboriginal population change at Wadeye* (Canberra: CAEPR, 2010), 19, 34.

a fight between the Lica mob and the Evil Warriors, the narrator adds colour by describing the two groups as *'ku soldier'*—'two desperate armies', classified as *ku* rather than *kardu*, facing off for battle. In another passing comment that caught my attention, at football training one evening the kigay were struggling to keep up with the fitness regime, and one joked out loud that they were *'ku gengsta terert'*, 'all a bunch of gangsters'—the implication being that they spend their time smoking and fighting, rather than keeping fit. I found it curious that again, the kigay were classed as *ku* in this humorous, imaginative reference. *Ku* versus *kardu* is a major grammatical distinction in Murrinhpatha, and I would argue, a deep conceptual distinction among people at Wadeye. The local social domain is classed as *kardu*, while animate entities foreign to this are *ku*. Of course kigay are *kardu*, but they sometimes imagine themselves as *ku*.

Kigay perceive that whitefellas have a certain capacity for rebellion, freedom and licentiousness, and the appeal of these images goes back to well before heavy metal. Furlan records memories of 1970s Wadeye motorbike gangs, in which the kigay of the day wore 'proper whitefella boots, gloves and scarfs'.[56] Heavy metal is a more recent cultural resource that feeds into imaginative play with the *kardu/ku* dichotomy. This is somewhat reminiscent of an exchange Musharbash records with a seventeen-year-old Warlpiri girl: when asked what she would do with a million dollars, she says she would build herself a big house, with lots of rooms, each furnished, and with televisions, stereos, video players and Playstations. But no-one else would be allowed to live there, she would live in the house alone.[57] The girl's wish is clearly for an autonomy that is hard to find in the densely related world of an Aboriginal community. But further, I wonder if this is how she imagines that whitefellas live? For Wadeye kigay, the consumer goods and luxurious houses of whitefellas seem to hold only a limited appeal, but what really captures their imagination is the wildness and freedom of whitefella rebel figures, young men like themselves who spurn all authority and make their own rules.

Conclusion

Listening to heavy metal at Wadeye is paradoxical in that it affirms and reproduces highly localised forms of social interaction, while connecting people both materially and imaginatively with a globalised genre of cultural production. The artefacts of this global circulation trickle in to Wadeye via fairly narrow channels of cultural contact—cassettes, CDs, mp3 tracks and t-shirts—but little

---

56 Furlan, *Songs of Continuity and Change*, 221.
57 Musharbash, *Yuendumu Everyday*, 1.

or no direct social connections with any external heavy metal 'scene'. However, once heavy metal artefacts reach Wadeye, they are intensively circulated through kin networks.

Being such an important cultural resource for kardu kigay, the meanings of heavy metal at Wadeye are complex, manifold, and undoubtedly vary greatly from one individual to another. However, I have tried to identify some major threads of meaning, describing how social practices relate metal to concepts of evil, chaos, subversion, power, brotherhood, solidarity, whitefellas and blackfellas.

In this chapter I have aimed to contribute to our understanding of the Aboriginal reception of mass media, and to show how an ethnographic approach can enrich such a study. There is great scope for further research in this field; for example, a study of Aboriginal film viewing, which has a history going right back to mission days, might prove fascinating. Television provides another more recent media stream for investigation, and in communities where English is not the main language, raises some interesting questions about cross-linguistic media reception. Further research might also be done on young Aboriginal people's use of popular music genres; and this should include hip-hop, for although it has already been investigated to some extent, there is not yet any ethnographic account of how Aboriginal people engage with hip-hop, nor how this engagement might differ between urban communities and those in the desert. Such research would not be constrained within the discipline of 'media studies', but rather would contribute to a broader project that analyses how culture circulates or diffuses from one place to another. The relatively recent contact of radically different cultures in central and northern Australian provides particularly rich material for such a project.

Acknowledgements

My field research for this chapter is heavily indebted to DP, LP and KM, as well as financial support from Thamarrurr Development Corporation, Wadeye. Invaluable comments were provided by Amanda Harris, and two anonymous reviewers.

References

Altman, John. *Hunter-Gatherers Today: An Aboriginal economy in northern Australia* (Canberra: Aboriginal Studies Press, 1987).

Altman, John, and Melinda Hinkson. 'Mobility and Modernity in Arnhem Land: The social use of Kuninjku trucks', *Journal of Material Culture* 12:2 (2007): 181–203.

Appadurai, Arjun. *Modernity at Large: Cultural dimensions of globalization* (Minneapolis: University of Minnesota Press, 1996).

Barwick, Linda. 'Musical Form and Style in Murriny Patha Djanba Songs at Wadeye (Northern Territory, Australia)', in *Analytical and Cross-Cultural Studies in World Music*, eds Michael Tenzer and John Roeder (Oxford: Oxford University Press, 2011), 316–54.

Barwick, Linda. 'Marri Ngarr Lirrga Songs: A musicological analysis of song pairs in performance', *Musicology Australia* 28 (2006): 1–25.

Barwick, Linda, Allan Marrett, Joe Blythe, and Michael Walsh. 'Arriving, Digging, Performing, Returning: An exercise in rich interpretation of a Djanba song text in the sound archive of the Wadeye knowledge centre, Northern Territory of Australia', in *Oceanic Encounters: Festschrift for Mervyn McLean*, ed. R.M. Moyle (Auckland: Research in Anthropology and Linguistics Monographs, 2007), 13–24.

Baulch, Emma. *Making Scenes: Reggae, punk, and death metal in 1990s Bali* (Durham: Duke University Press, 2007).

Bell, Wendy. *A Remote Possibility: The battle for Imparja television* (Alice Springs: IAD Press, 2008).

Brady, M. *Heavy Metal: The social meaning of petrol sniffing in Australia* (Canberra: Aboriginal Studies Press, 1992).

Brooks, Hannah, and Jonathan West. *Heavy Metal Gangs of Wadeye* (VBS, 2009).

Bunk, Steve. 'Mixed Justice', *The Bulletin*, 6 September 1988.

Christie, Ian. *Sound of the Beast: The complete headbanging history of heavy metal* (New York: Harper Collins, 2003).

Dawes, Glenn. 'Figure Eights, Spin Outs and Power Slides: Aboriginal and Torres Strait Islander youth and the culture of joyriding', *Journal of Youth Studies* 5:2 (2002): 195–208.

Deger, Jennifer. *Shimmering Screens: Making media in an Aboriginal community* (University of Minnesota Press, 2006).

Furlan, Alberto. *Songs of Continuity and Change: The reproduction of Aboriginal culture through traditional and popular music* (PhD, University of Sydney, 2005).

Geertz, Clifford. *The Interpretation of Cultures* (New York: Basic Books, 1973).

Goodrick-Clarke, Nicholas. *Black Sun: Aryan cults, esoteric Nazism, and the politics of identity* (New York: New York University Press, 2003).

Hannerz, Ulf. *Transnational Connections: Culture, people, places* (London: Routledge, 1996).

Ivory, Bill. *Kunmanggurr, Legend and Leadership* (PhD, Charles Darwin University, 2009).

Kral, Inge. *Plugged in: Remote Australian Indigenous youth and digital culture* (Canberra: CAEPR, 2010).

Krenske, Leigh, and Jim McKay. '"Hard and Heavy": Gender and power in a heavy metal music subculture', *Gender, Place and Culture* 7:3 (2000): 287–304.

Magowan, F. 'Faith and Fear in Aboriginal Christianity', in *Aboriginal Religions in Australia: An anthropology of recent writings,* eds M. Charlesworth, Francoise Dussart, and Howard Morphy (Aldershot: Ashgate, 2005), 279–96.

Mansfield, John. 'The Social Organisation of Wadeye's Heavy Metal Mobs', *The Australian Journal of Anthropology* 24:2 (2013): 148–65.

Marett, Allan. *Songs, Dreamings, and Ghosts: The wangga of north Australia* (Middletown: Wesleyan University Press, 2005).

Martin, David Fernandes. *Autonomy and Relatedness: An ethnography of Wik people of Aurukun, Western Cape York Penninsula* (PhD, The Australian National University, 1993).

McKnight, David. *From Hunting to Drinking: The devastating effects of alcohol on an Australian Aboriginal community* (London: Routledge, 2002).

Michaels, Eric. *The Aboriginal Invention of Television in Central Australia, 1982–1986* (Canberra: Australian Institute of Aboriginal Studies, 1986).

Michaels, Eric. 'Hollywood Iconography: A Warlpiri reading', in *Second International Television Studies Conference, 1986,* eds Phillip Drummond and Richard Patterson (London: BFI Publishing, 1988).

Mitchell, Tony. 'Blackfellas Rapping, Breaking and Writing: A short history of Aboriginal hip-hop', *Aboriginal History* 30 (2006): 124–37.

Molnar, Heather, and Michael Meadows. *Songlines to Satellites: Indigenous communication in Australia, the South Pacific and Canada* (Sydney and Wellington: Pluto Press and Huia Publishers, 2001).

Morgan, George, and Andrew Warren. 'Aboriginal Youth, Hip Hop and the Politics of Identification', *Ethnic and Racial Studies* 34:6 (2011): 925–47.

Murdoch, Lindsay. 'Hate Stalks a Community Where Gangs Rule Roost', *The Age*, 23 May 2006.

Murphy, David Jo. *Hate Couture: Subcultural fundamentalism and the Serbian black metal scene* (PhD, NUI Maynooth, 2011).

Musharbash, Yasmine. *Yuendumu Everyday: Contemporary life in a remote Aboriginal settlement* (Canberra: Aboriginal Studies Press, 2008).

Ottosson, Ase. 'The Intercultural Crafting of Real Aboriginal Country and Manhood in Central Australia', *The Australian Journal of Anthropology* 23 (2012): 179–96.

Pennycook, Alastair, and Tony Mitchell. 'Hip Hop as Dusty Foot Philosophy: Engaging locality', in *Global Linguistic Flows: Hip hop cultures, youth identities and the politics of language*, eds H. Samy Alim, Awad Ibrahim, and Alistair Pennycook (New York: Routledge, 2009), 25–42.

Peterson, Nicolas. 'Cash, Commoditisation and Authenticity: When do Aboriginal people stop being hunter-gatherers? In *Cash, Commoditisation and Changing Foragers*, eds Nicolas Peterson and Toshio Matsuyama (Osaka: National Museum of Ethnology, 1991), 67–90.

Purcell, Natalie J. *Death Metal Music: The passion and politics of a subculture* (Jefferson: McFarland & Company, 2003).

Pye, Br John MSC. *The Port Keats Story* (Darwin: Colemans, 1972).

Sansom, Basil. *The Camp at Wallaby Cross: Aboriginal fringe dwellers in Darwin* (Canberra: Australian Institute of Aboriginal Studies, 1980).

Sansom, Basil. 'A Grammar of Exchange', in *Being Black: Aboriginal cultures in 'settled' Australia*, ed. Ian Keen (Canberra: Australian Institute of Aboriginal Studies, 1988), 159–78.

Schwarz, Carolyn, and Francoise Dussart. 'Christianity in Aboriginal Australia Revisited', *The Australian Journal of Anthropology* 21 (2010): 1–13.

Sutton, Peter. 'Aboriginal Spirituality in a New Age.' *The Australian Journal of Anthropology* 21 (2010): 71–89.

Taylor, John. *Demography as Destiny: Schooling, work and Aboriginal population change at Wadeye* (Canberra: CAEPR, 2010).

Tonkinson, R. 'Reflections on a Failed Crusade', in *Aboriginal Australians and Christian Missions*, eds T. Swain and Deborah Bird Rose (Bedford Park: Australian Association for the Study of Religions, 1988), 60–73.

Toohey, Paul. 'Gangsters' Paradise', *Bulletin*, 10 February 2004.

Waksman, Steve. *This Ain't the Summer of Love: Conflict and crossover in heavy metal and punk* (Berkeley: University of California Press, 2009).

Walser, Robert. *Running with the Devil: Power, gender, and madness in heavy metal music* (Middletown: Wesleyan University Press, 1993).

Wyant, Jay. 'What Is Bluetooth?', *Volta Voices* 13:1 (2006): 54–5.

Index

Page numbers in **bold** refer to figures.